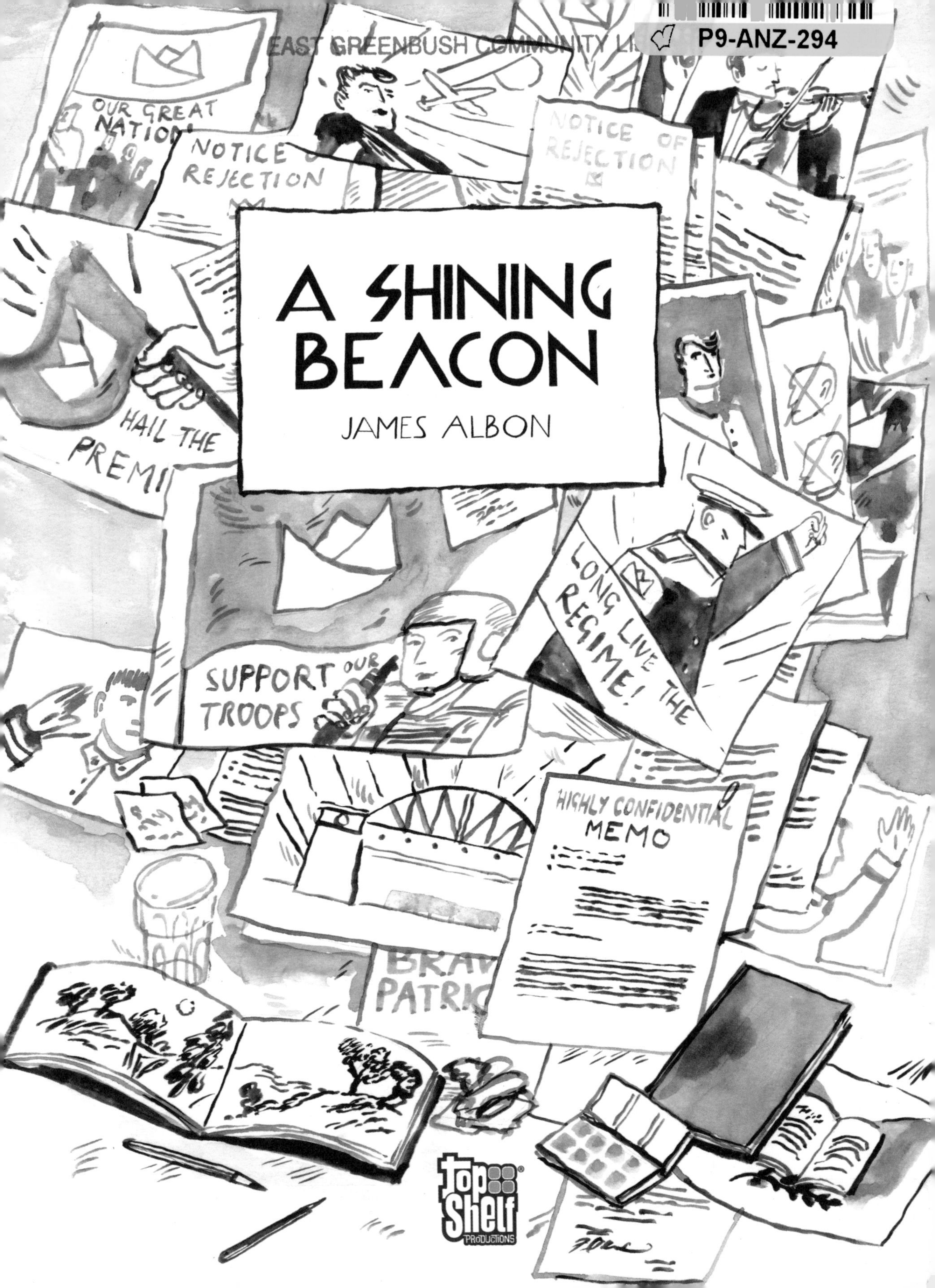
A SHINING BEACON
JAMES ALBON
OUR GREAT NATION
NOTICE OF REJECTION
NOTICE OF REJECTION
HAIL THE PREMI
SUPPORT OUR TROOPS
LONG LIVE THE REGIME!
HIGHLY CONFIDENTIAL MEMO
BRAV PATRIC
Top Shelf PRODUCTIONS

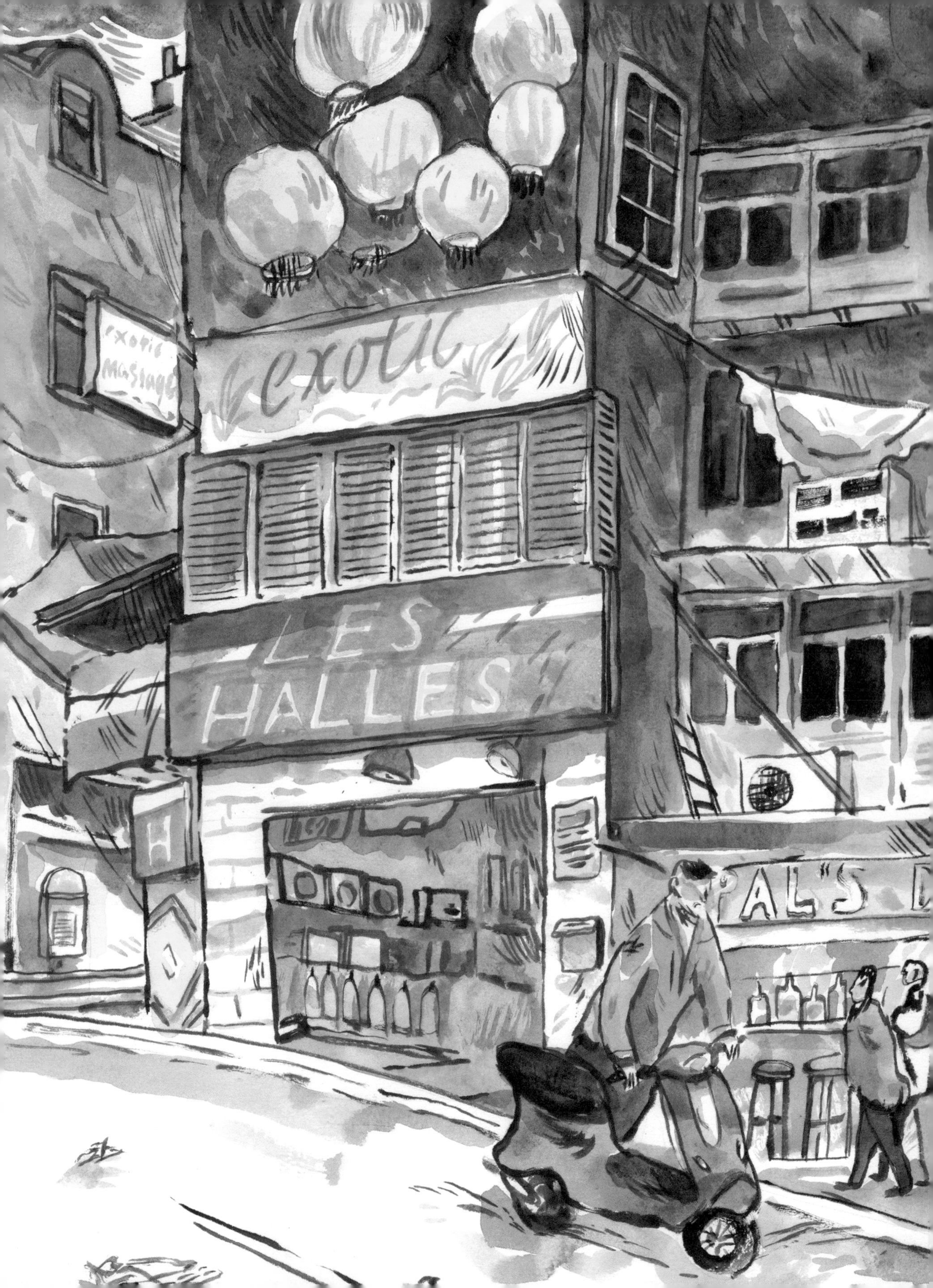
exotic
exotic
masiage
LES HALLES
H
PAL'S

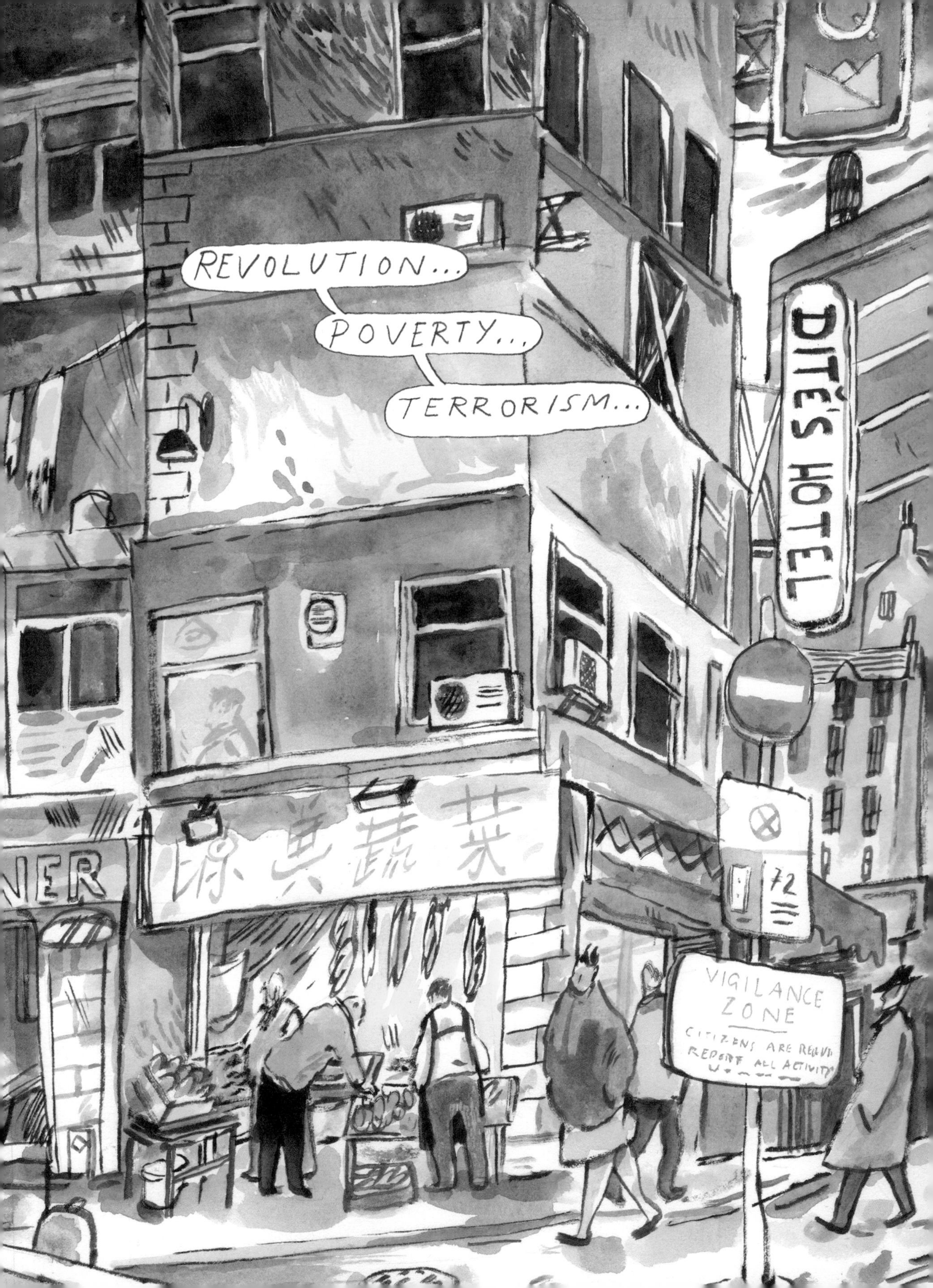
REVOLUTION...
POVERTY...
TERRORISM...
DITÉS HOTEL
VIGILANCE ZONE
72

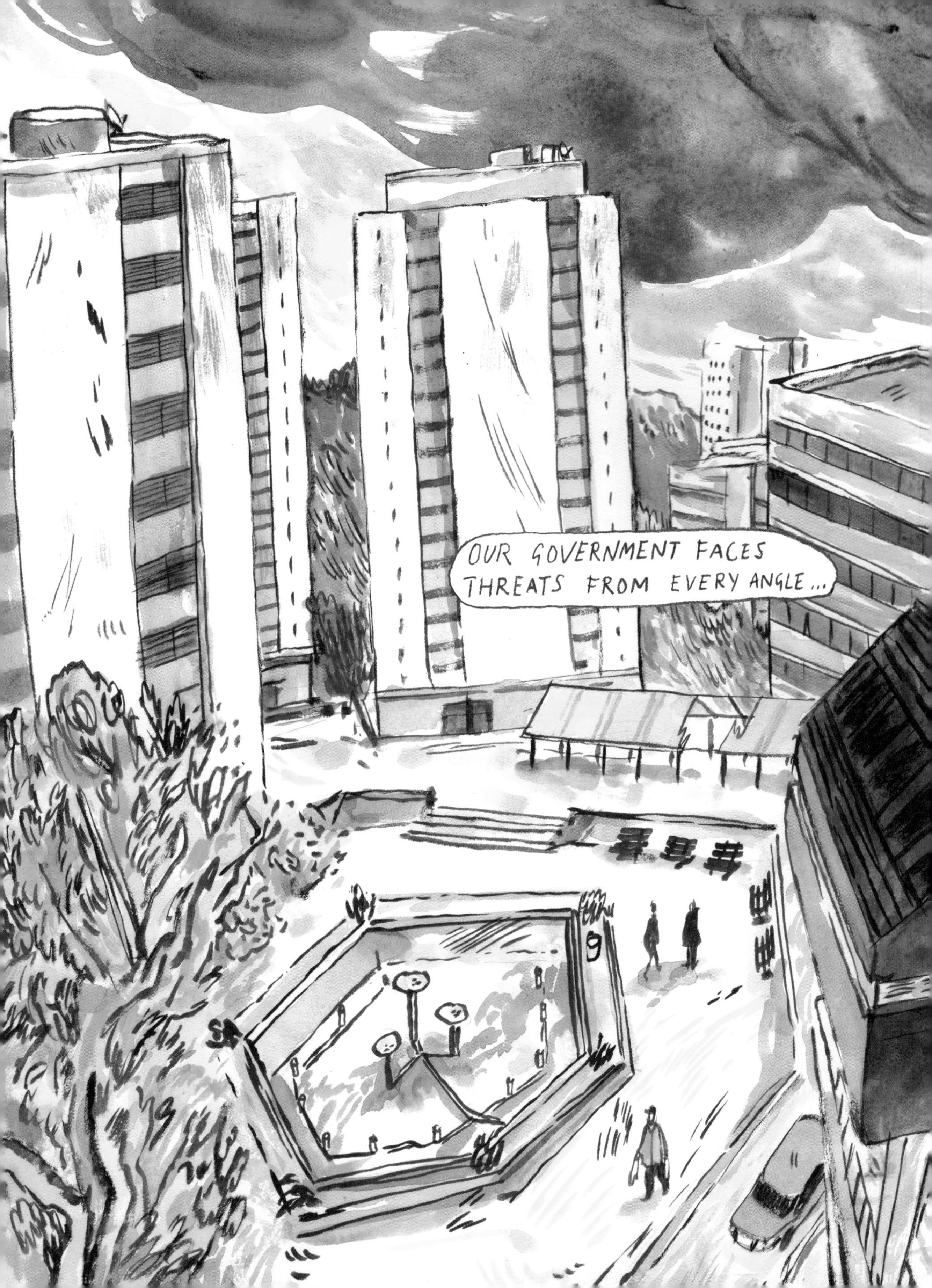
OUR GOVERNMENT FACES THREATS FROM EVERY ANGLE...

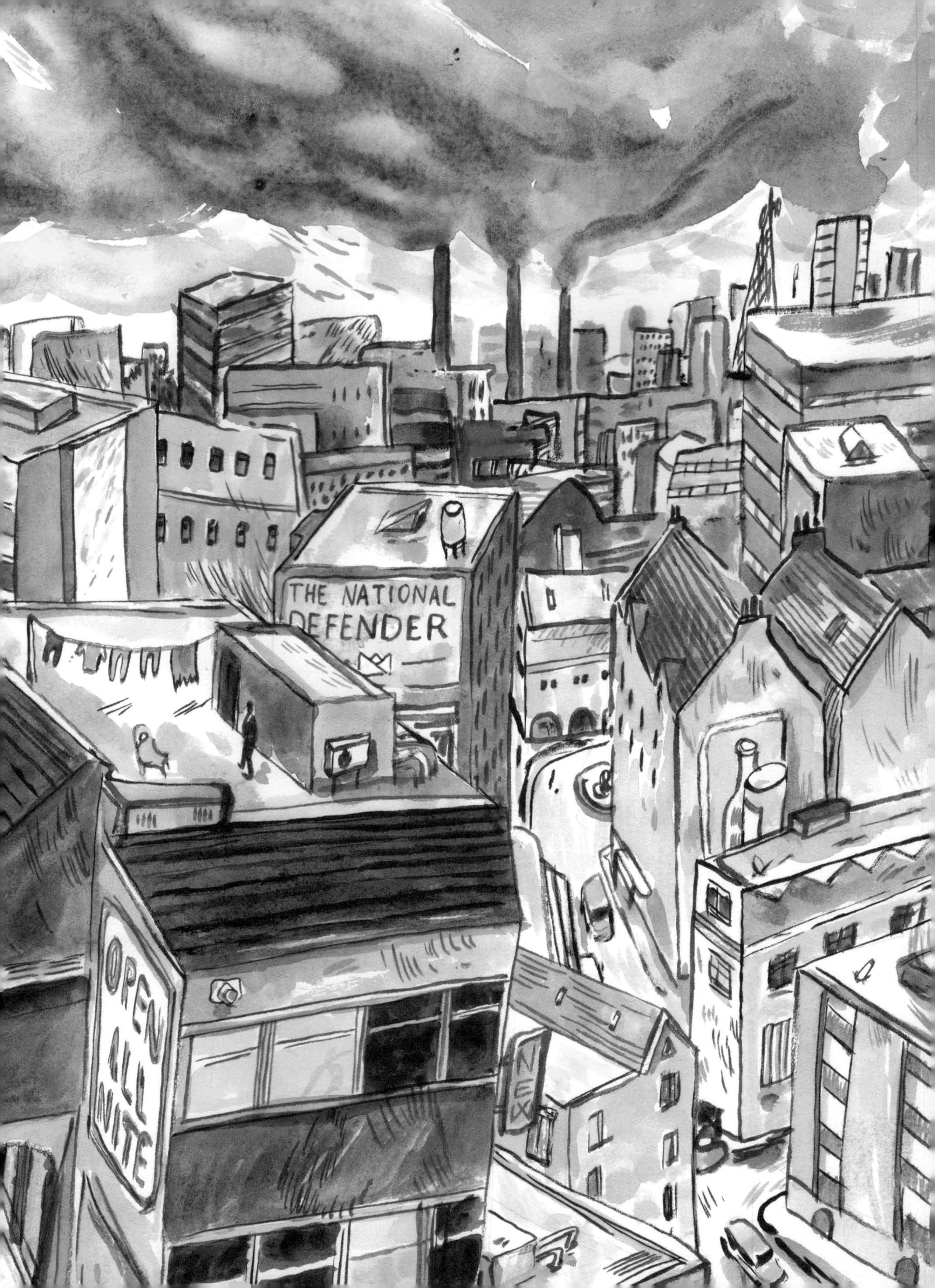
THE NATIONAL DEFENDER
OPEN ALL NITE

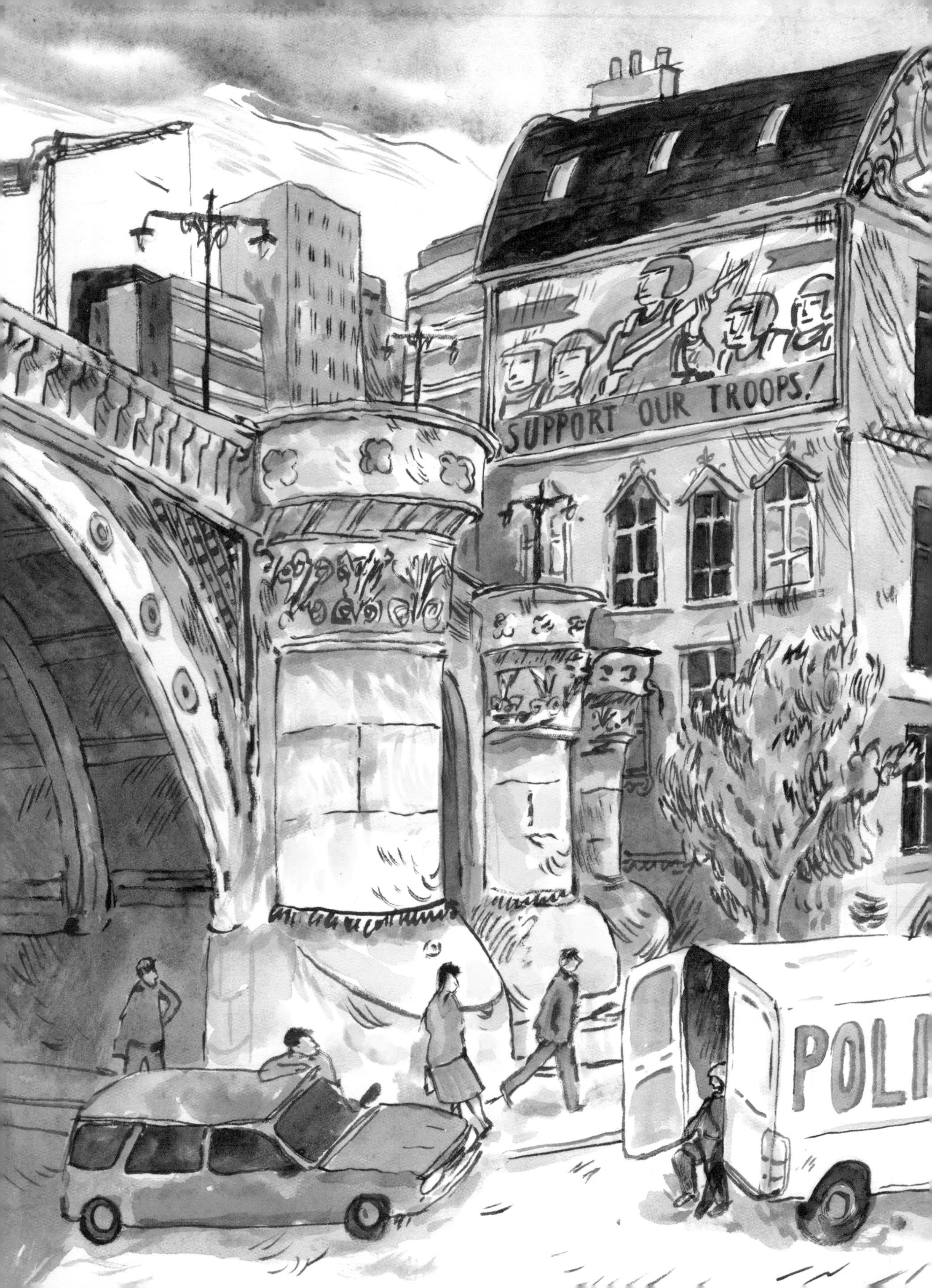
SUPPORT OUR TROOPS!
POLI

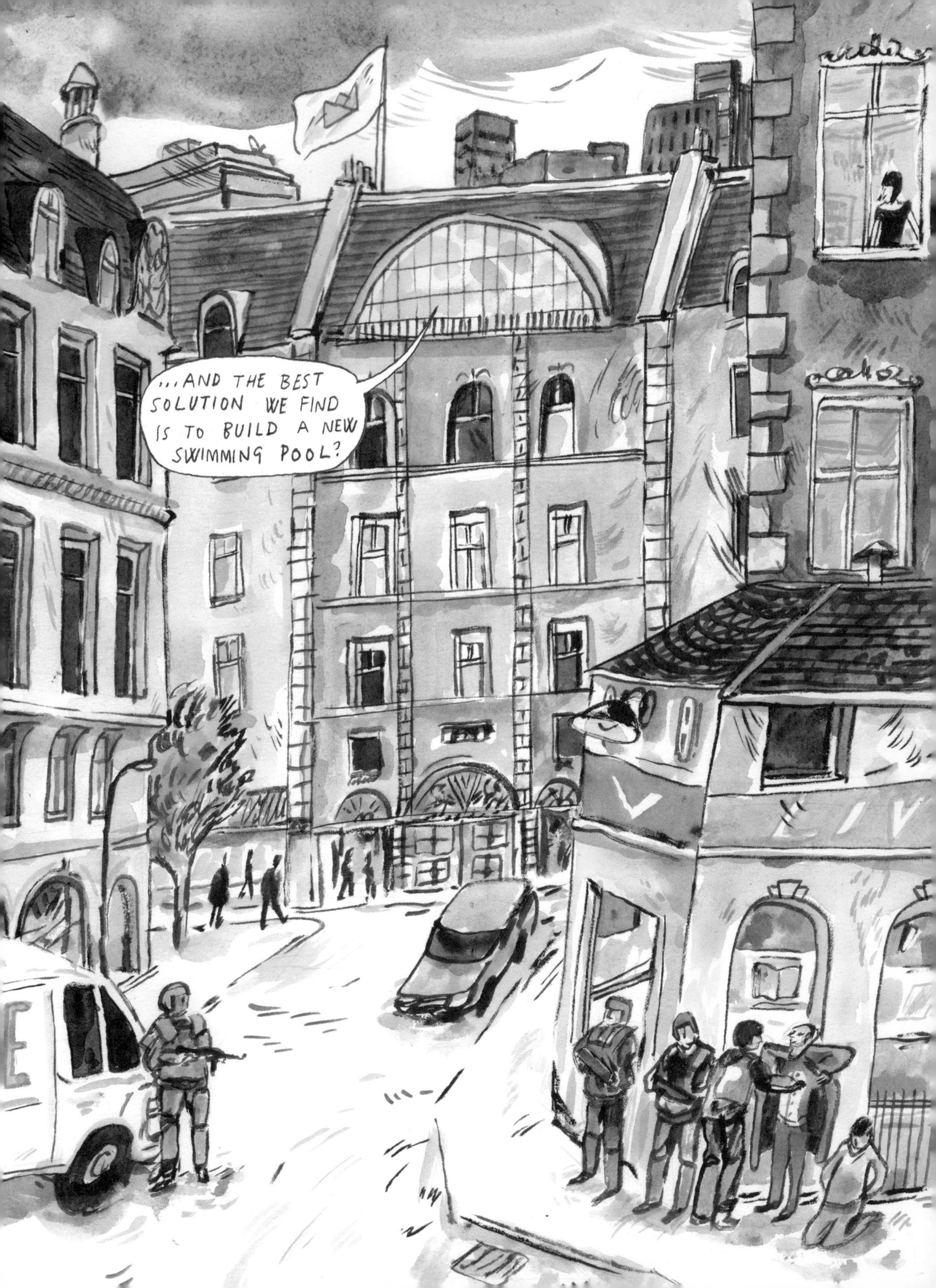
...AND THE BEST SOLUTION WE FIND IS TO BUILD A NEW SWIMMING POOL?

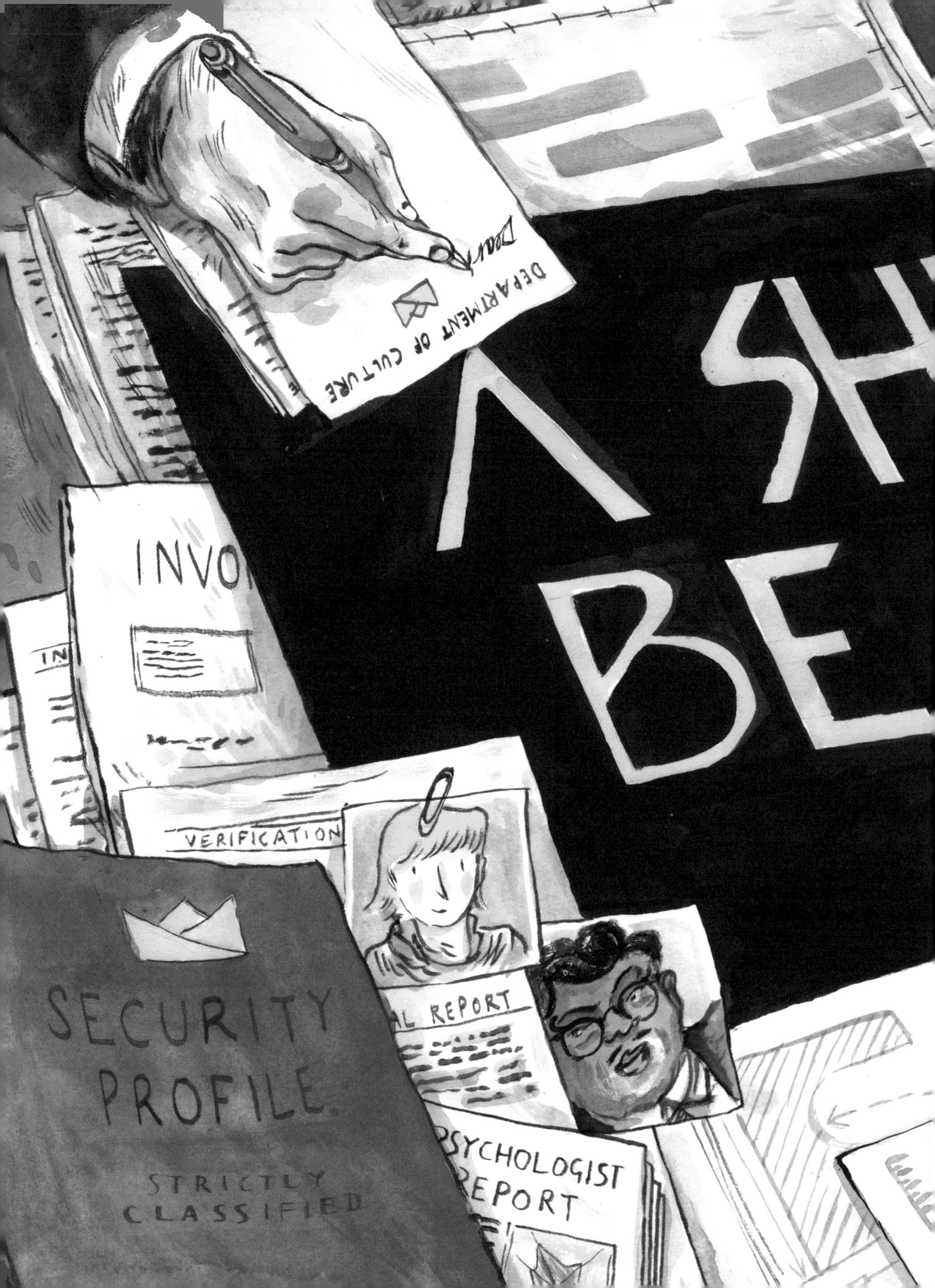

DEPARTMENT OF CULTURE
A SH
BE
INVO
IN
VERIFICATION
AL REPORT
SECURITY PROFILE
STRICTLY CLASSIFIED
PSYCHOLOGIST REPORT

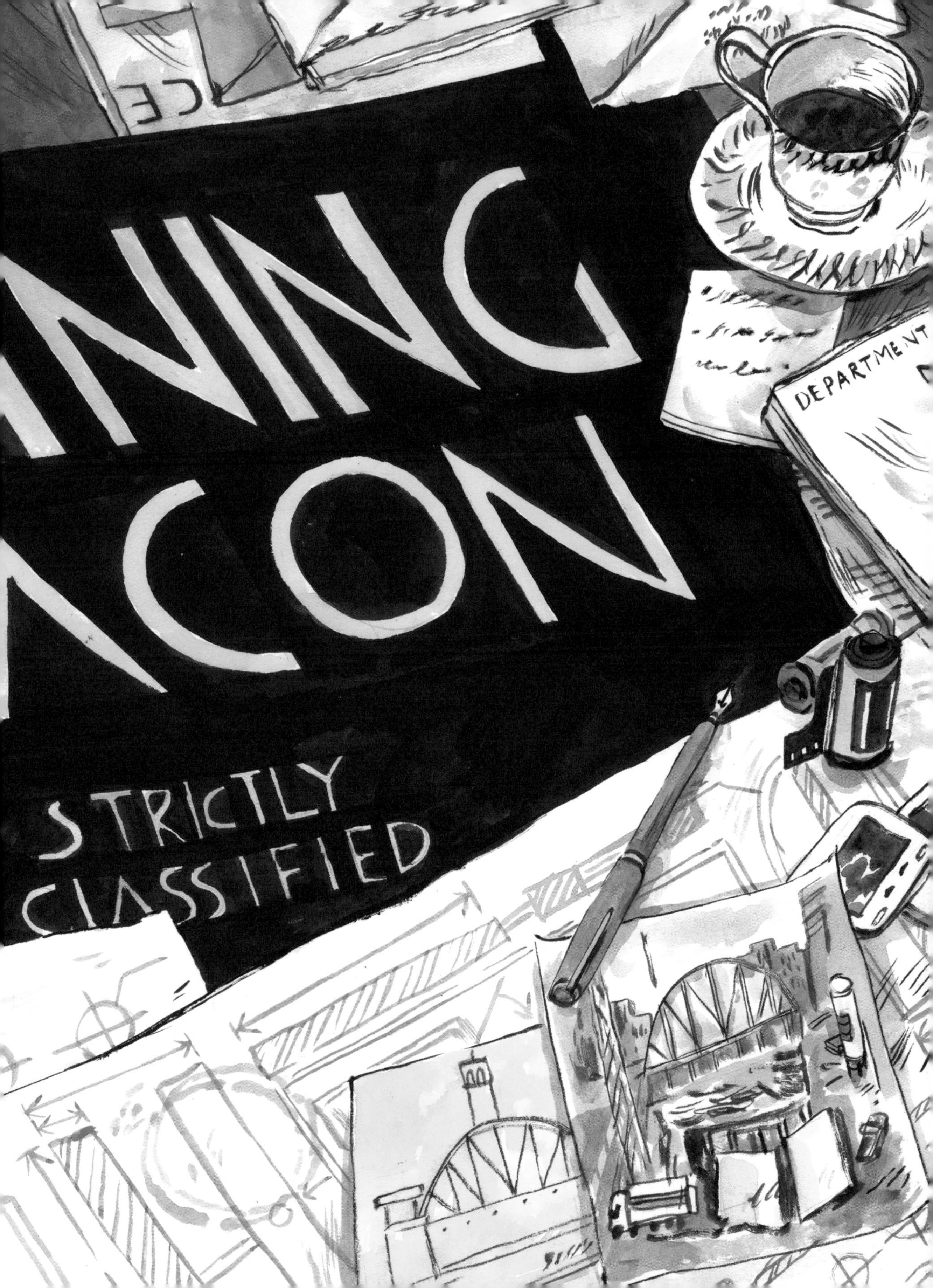

NING
ACON
STRICTLY
CLASSIFIED
DEPARTMENT

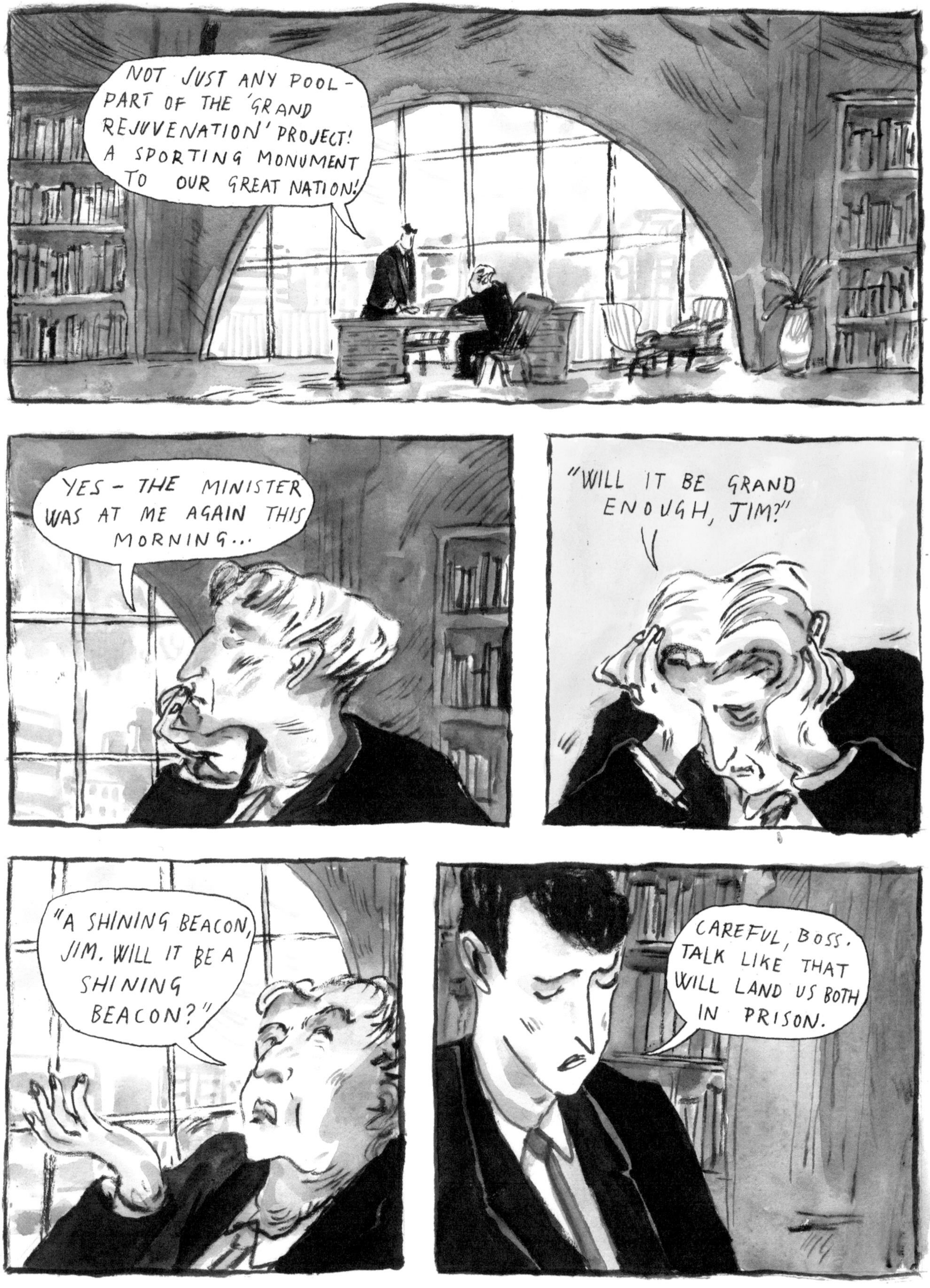
NOT JUST ANY POOL - PART OF THE 'GRAND REJUVENATION' PROJECT! A SPORTING MONUMENT TO OUR GREAT NATION!
YES - THE MINISTER WAS AT ME AGAIN THIS MORNING...
"WILL IT BE GRAND ENOUGH, JIM?"
"A SHINING BEACON, JIM. WILL IT BE A SHINING BEACON?"
CAREFUL, BOSS. TALK LIKE THAT WILL LAND US BOTH IN PRISON.

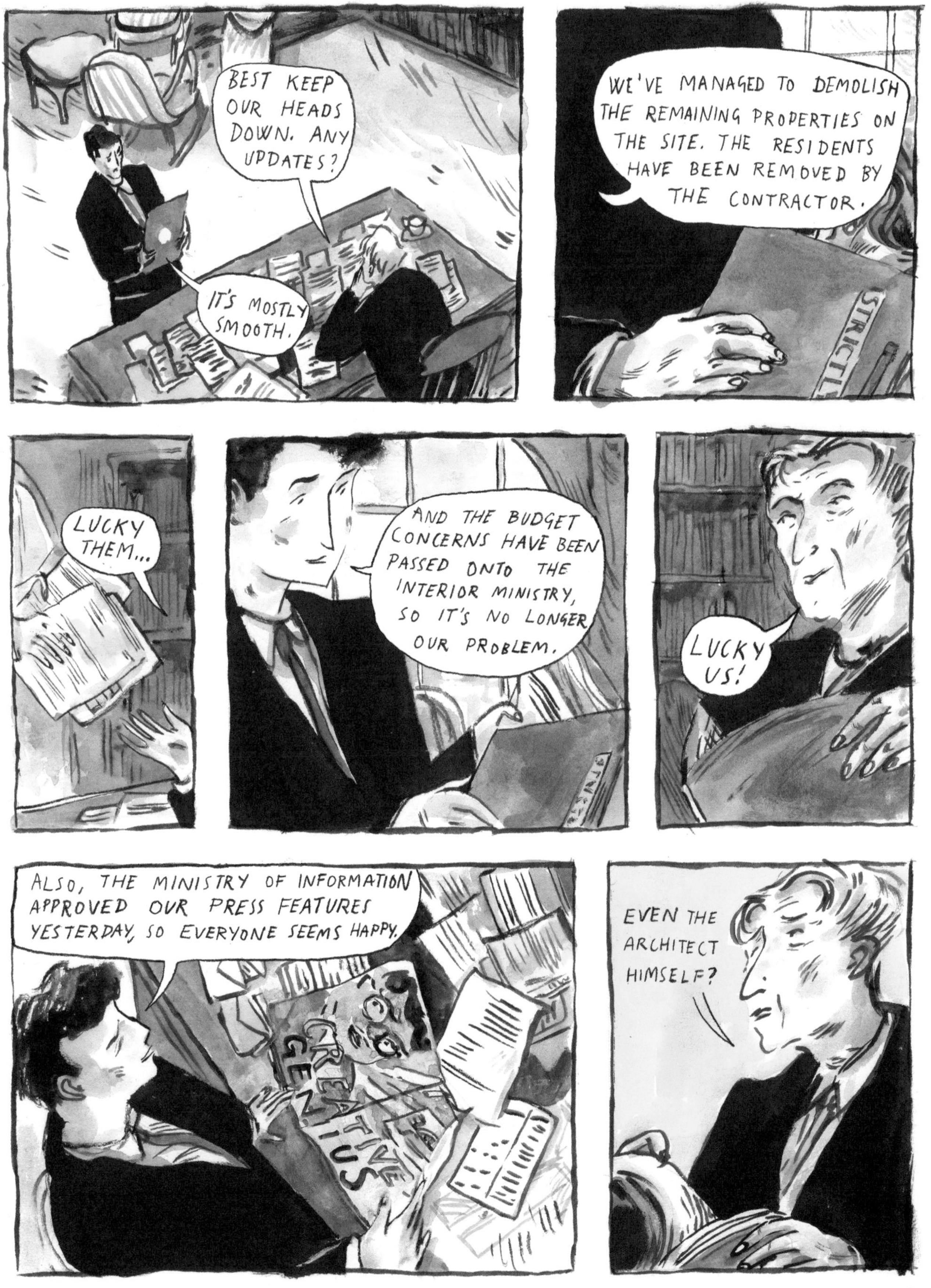
BEST KEEP OUR HEADS DOWN. ANY UPDATES?
IT'S MOSTLY SMOOTH.
WE'VE MANAGED TO DEMOLISH THE REMAINING PROPERTIES ON THE SITE. THE RESIDENTS HAVE BEEN REMOVED BY THE CONTRACTOR.
STRICTLY
LUCKY THEM...
AND THE BUDGET CONCERNS HAVE BEEN PASSED ONTO THE INTERIOR MINISTRY, SO IT'S NO LONGER OUR PROBLEM.
LUCKY US!
ALSO, THE MINISTRY OF INFORMATION APPROVED OUR PRESS FEATURES YESTERDAY, SO EVERYONE SEEMS HAPPY.
CREATIVE GENIUS
EVEN THE ARCHITECT HIMSELF?

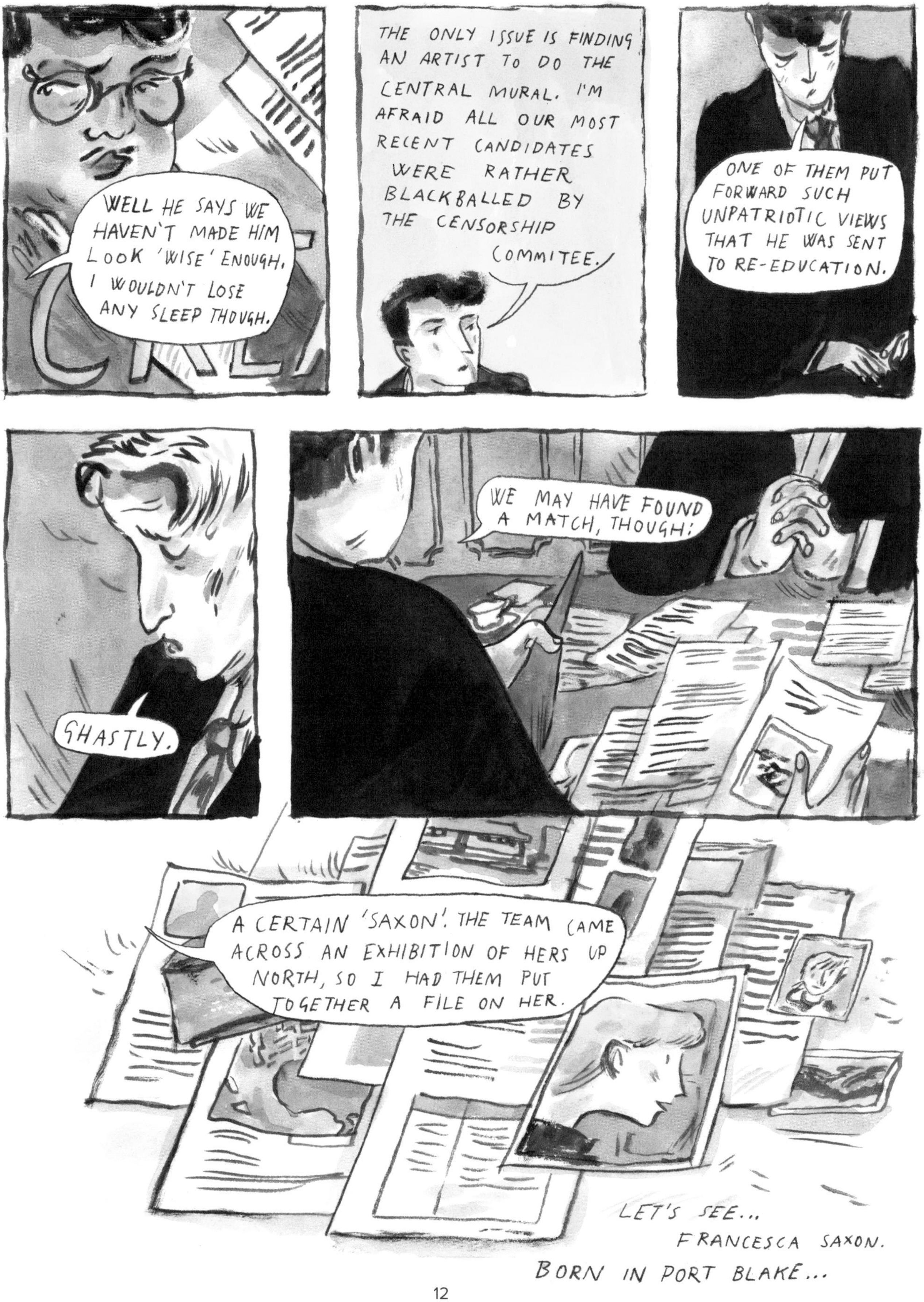

WELL HE SAYS WE HAVEN'T MADE HIM LOOK 'WISE' ENOUGH. I WOULDN'T LOSE ANY SLEEP THOUGH.
THE ONLY ISSUE IS FINDING AN ARTIST TO DO THE CENTRAL MURAL. I'M AFRAID ALL OUR MOST RECENT CANDIDATES WERE RATHER BLACKBALLED BY THE CENSORSHIP COMMITEE.
ONE OF THEM PUT FORWARD SUCH UNPATRIOTIC VIEWS THAT HE WAS SENT TO RE-EDUCATION.
GHASTLY.
WE MAY HAVE FOUND A MATCH, THOUGH!
A CERTAIN 'SAXON'. THE TEAM CAME ACROSS AN EXHIBITION OF HERS UP NORTH, SO I HAD THEM PUT TOGETHER A FILE ON HER.
LET'S SEE... FRANCESCA SAXON. BORN IN PORT BLAKE...

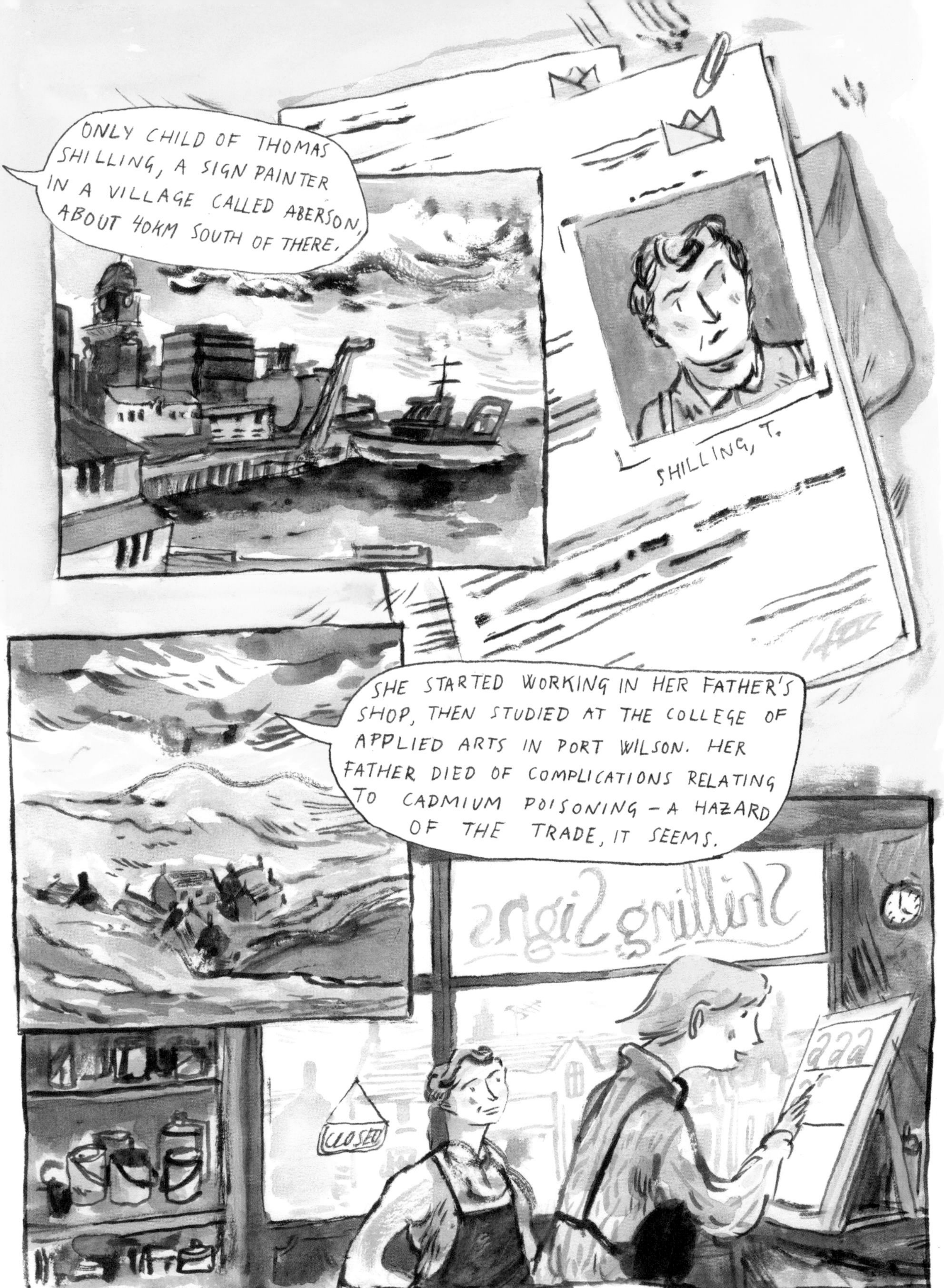
ONLY CHILD OF THOMAS SHILLING, A SIGN PAINTER IN A VILLAGE CALLED ABERSON, ABOUT 40KM SOUTH OF THERE.
SHILLING, T.
SHE STARTED WORKING IN HER FATHER'S SHOP, THEN STUDIED AT THE COLLEGE OF APPLIED ARTS IN PORT WILSON. HER FATHER DIED OF COMPLICATIONS RELATING TO CADMIUM POISONING – A HAZARD OF THE TRADE, IT SEEMS.
Shilling Signs
CLOSED

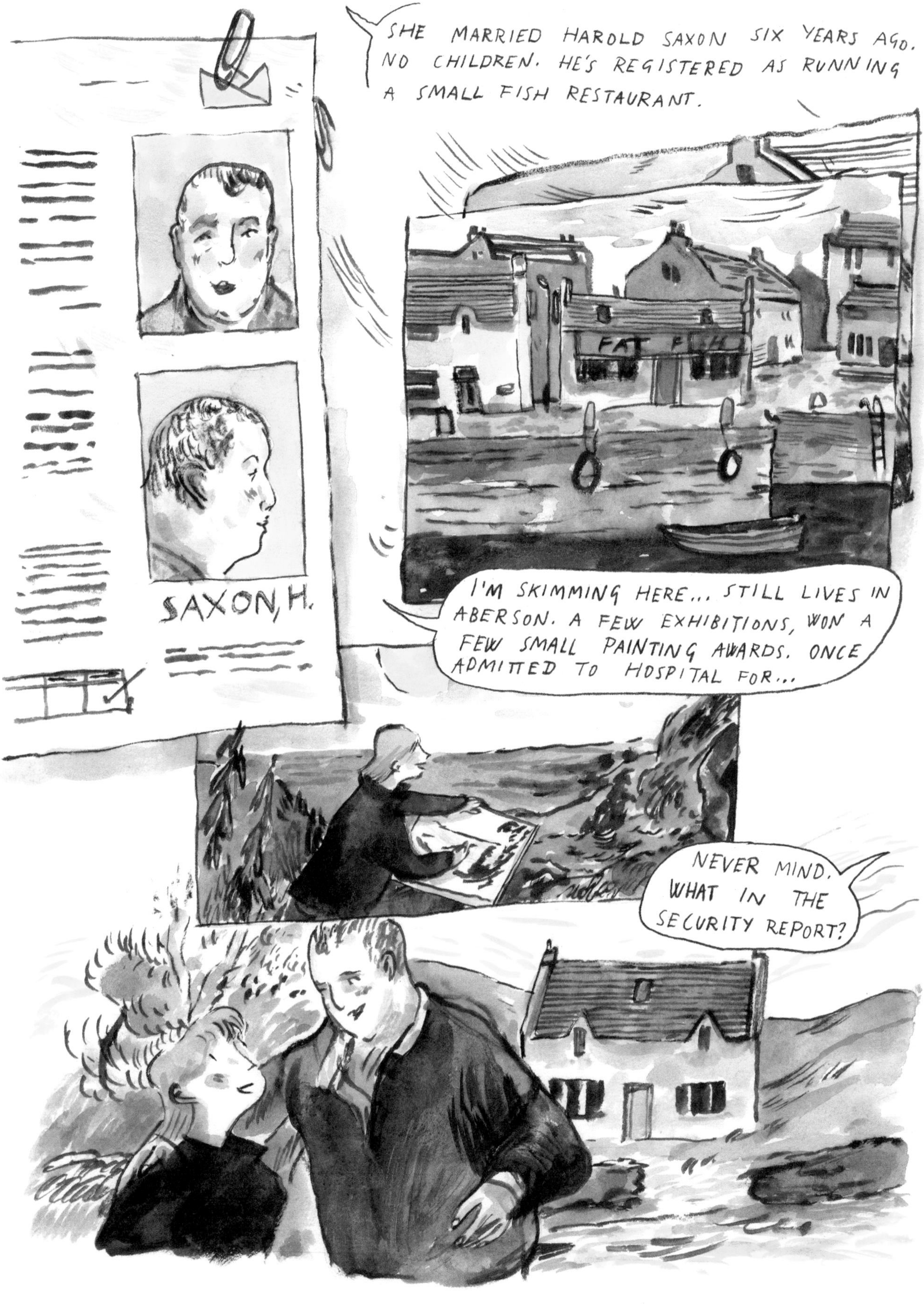
SHE MARRIED HAROLD SAXON SIX YEARS AGO. NO CHILDREN. HE'S REGISTERED AS RUNNING A SMALL FISH RESTAURANT.
SAXON, H.
FAT FISH
I'M SKIMMING HERE... STILL LIVES IN ABERSON. A FEW EXHIBITIONS, WON A FEW SMALL PAINTING AWARDS. ONCE ADMITTED TO HOSPITAL FOR...
NEVER MIND. WHAT IN THE SECURITY REPORT?

IT'S PRETTY CLEAR— NO CRIMINAL RECORD, NO 'MALIGN ASSOCIATES,' NO POLITICAL RECORD TO SPEAK OF. SHE HAS A DISTANT COUSIN WHO WAS IMPRISONED FOR AGITATION, BUT WE SEE NO SUGGESTION THAT THEY'RE CLOSE...

OH, AND HER HUSBAND ONCE PAID HIS TAXES LATE. DO YOU THINK SHE'LL TOE THE PARTY LINE?

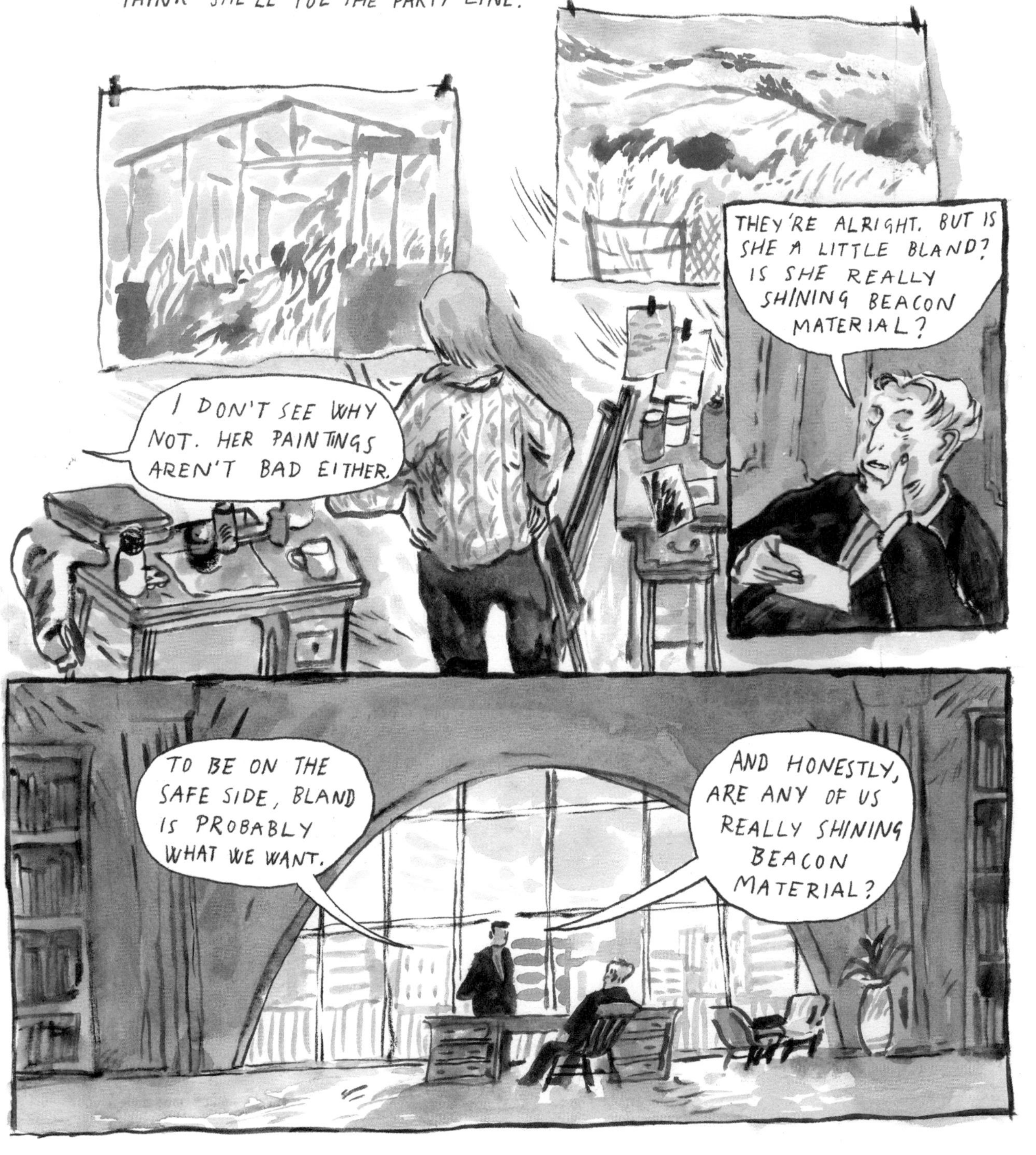
THEY'RE ALRIGHT. BUT IS SHE A LITTLE BLAND? IS SHE REALLY SHINING BEACON MATERIAL?
I DON'T SEE WHY NOT. HER PAINTINGS AREN'T BAD EITHER.
TO BE ON THE SAFE SIDE, BLAND IS PROBABLY WHAT WE WANT.
AND HONESTLY, ARE ANY OF US REALLY SHINING BEACON MATERIAL?

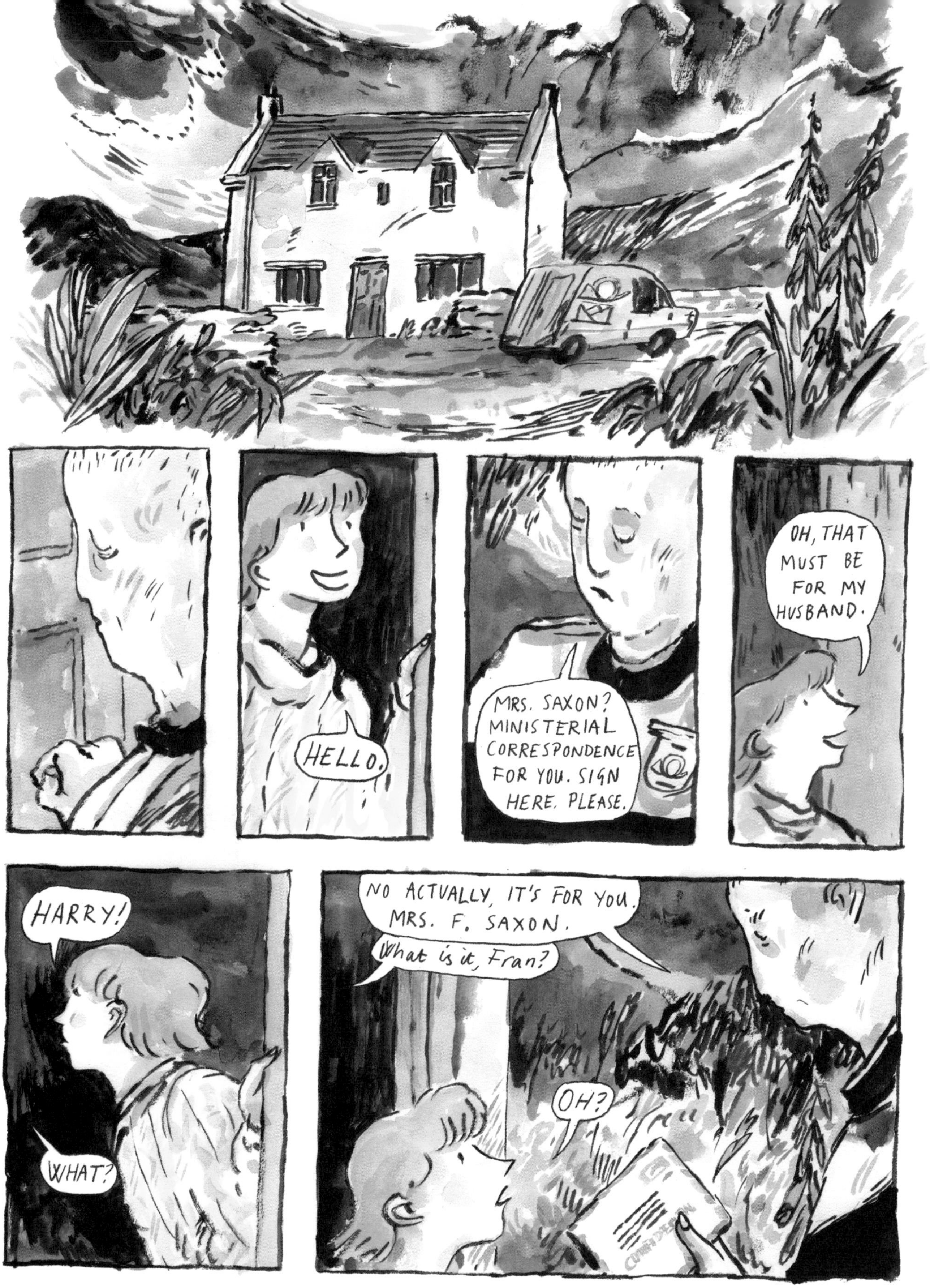
HELLO.
MRS. SAXON? MINISTERIAL CORRESPONDENCE FOR YOU. SIGN HERE, PLEASE.
OH, THAT MUST BE FOR MY HUSBAND.
HARRY!
WHAT?
NO ACTUALLY, IT'S FOR YOU. MRS. F. SAXON.
What is it, Fran?
OH?

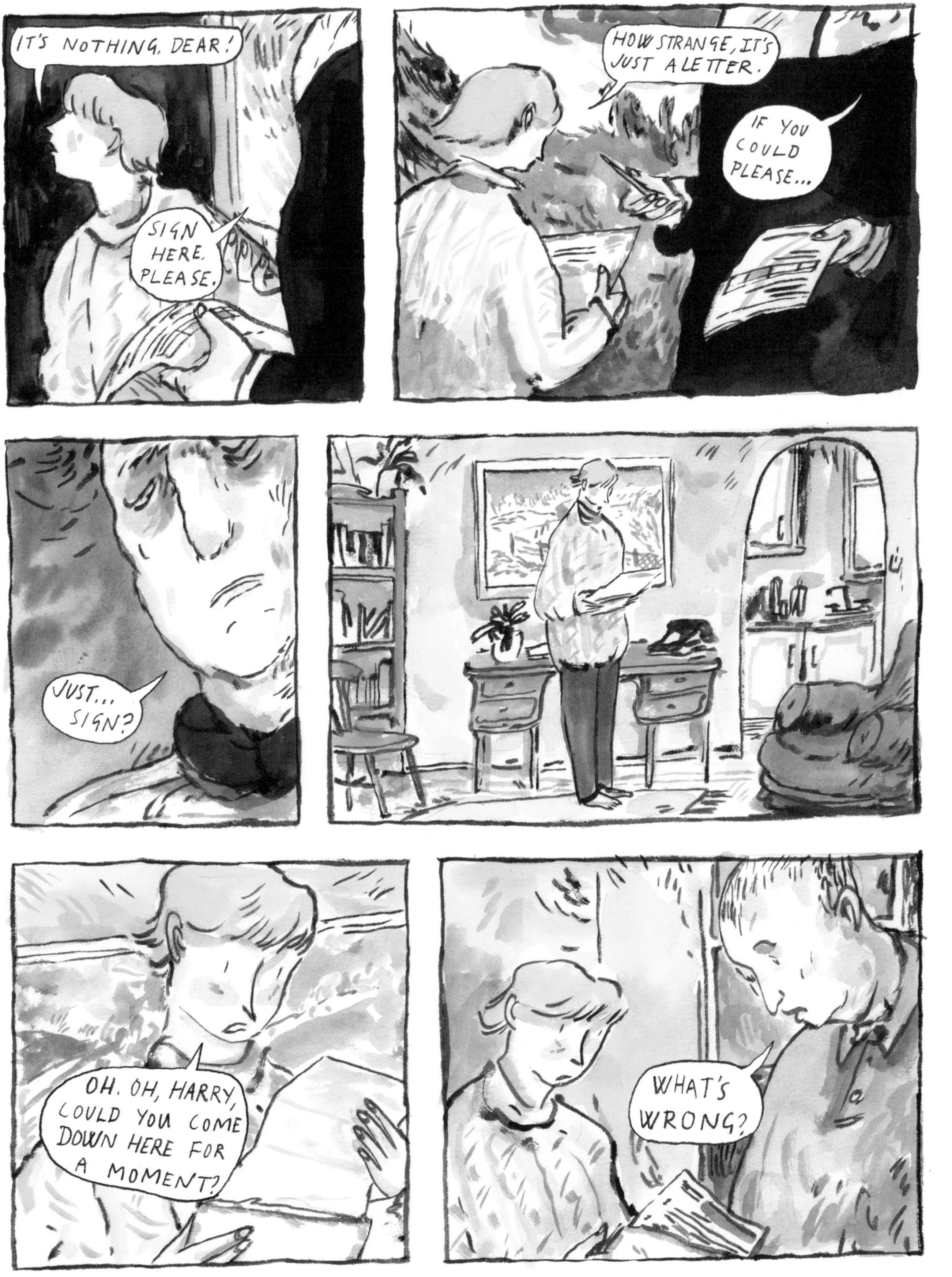
IT'S NOTHING, DEAR!
SIGN HERE, PLEASE.
HOW STRANGE, IT'S JUST A LETTER.
IF YOU COULD PLEASE...
JUST... SIGN?
OH. OH, HARRY, COULD YOU COME DOWN HERE FOR A MOMENT?
WHAT'S WRONG?

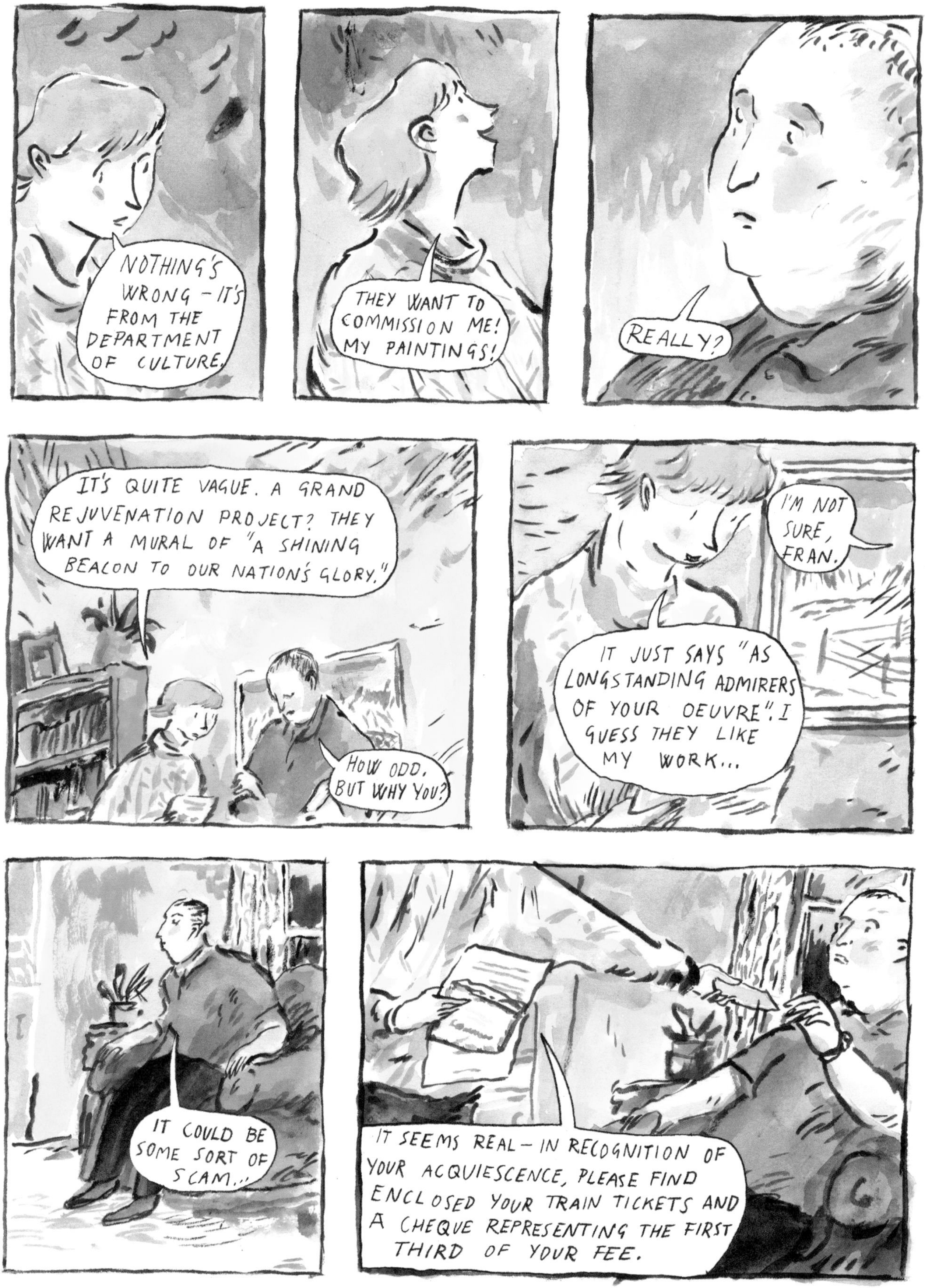
NOTHING'S WRONG - IT'S FROM THE DEPARTMENT OF CULTURE.
THEY WANT TO COMMISSION ME! MY PAINTINGS!
REALLY?
IT'S QUITE VAGUE. A GRAND REJUVENATION PROJECT? THEY WANT A MURAL OF "A SHINING BEACON TO OUR NATION'S GLORY."
HOW ODD. BUT WHY YOU?
I'M NOT SURE, FRAN.
IT JUST SAYS "AS LONGSTANDING ADMIRERS OF YOUR OEUVRE". I GUESS THEY LIKE MY WORK...
IT COULD BE SOME SORT OF SCAM...
IT SEEMS REAL - IN RECOGNITION OF YOUR ACQUIESCENCE, PLEASE FIND ENCLOSED YOUR TRAIN TICKETS AND A CHEQUE REPRESENTING THE FIRST THIRD OF YOUR FEE.

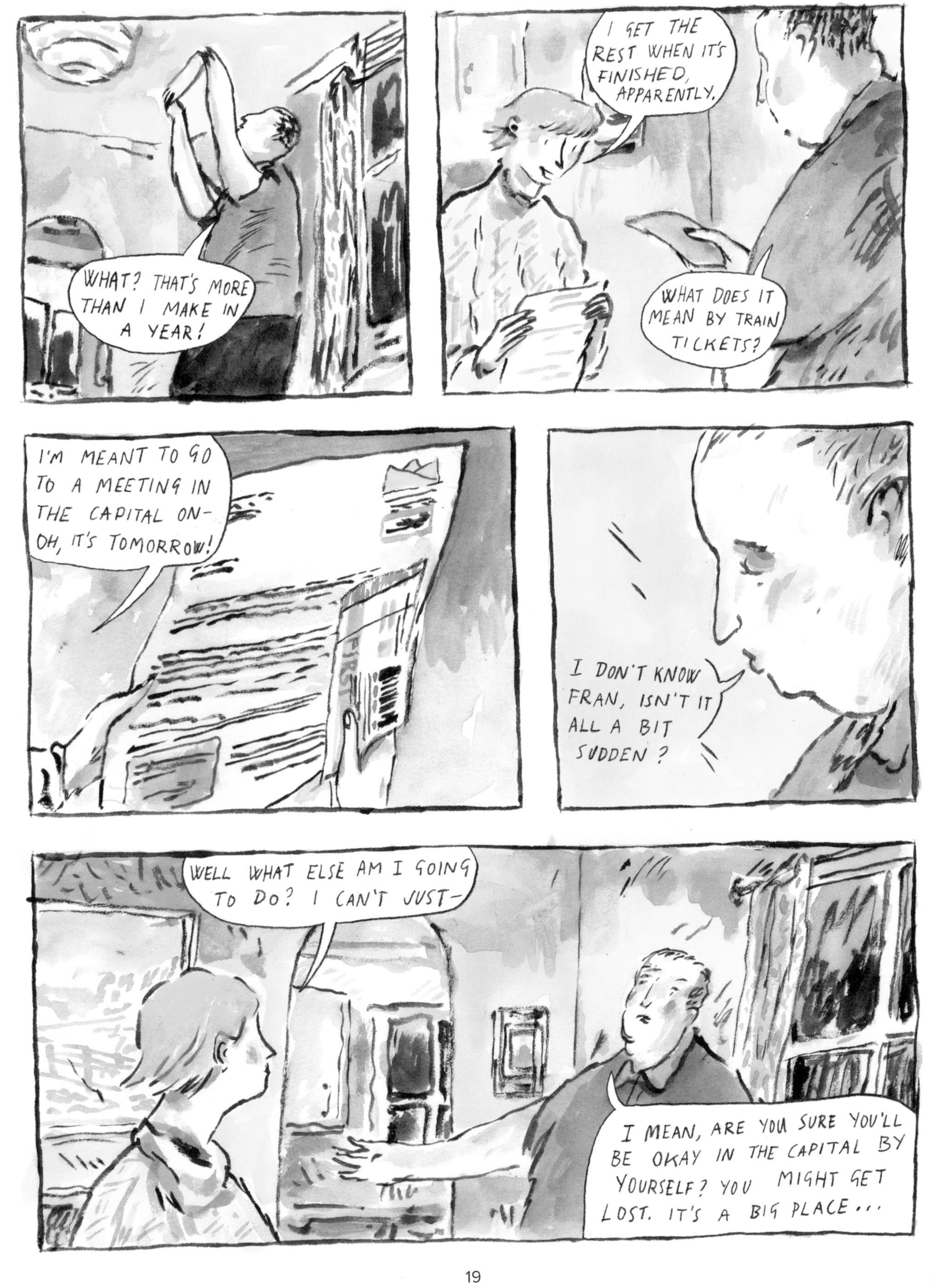
WHAT? THAT'S MORE THAN I MAKE IN A YEAR!
I GET THE REST WHEN IT'S FINISHED, APPARENTLY.
WHAT DOES IT MEAN BY TRAIN TICKETS?
I'M MEANT TO GO TO A MEETING IN THE CAPITAL ON- OH, IT'S TOMORROW!
I DON'T KNOW FRAN, ISN'T IT ALL A BIT SUDDEN?
WELL WHAT ELSE AM I GOING TO DO? I CAN'T JUST-
I MEAN, ARE YOU SURE YOU'LL BE OKAY IN THE CAPITAL BY YOURSELF? YOU MIGHT GET LOST. IT'S A BIG PLACE...

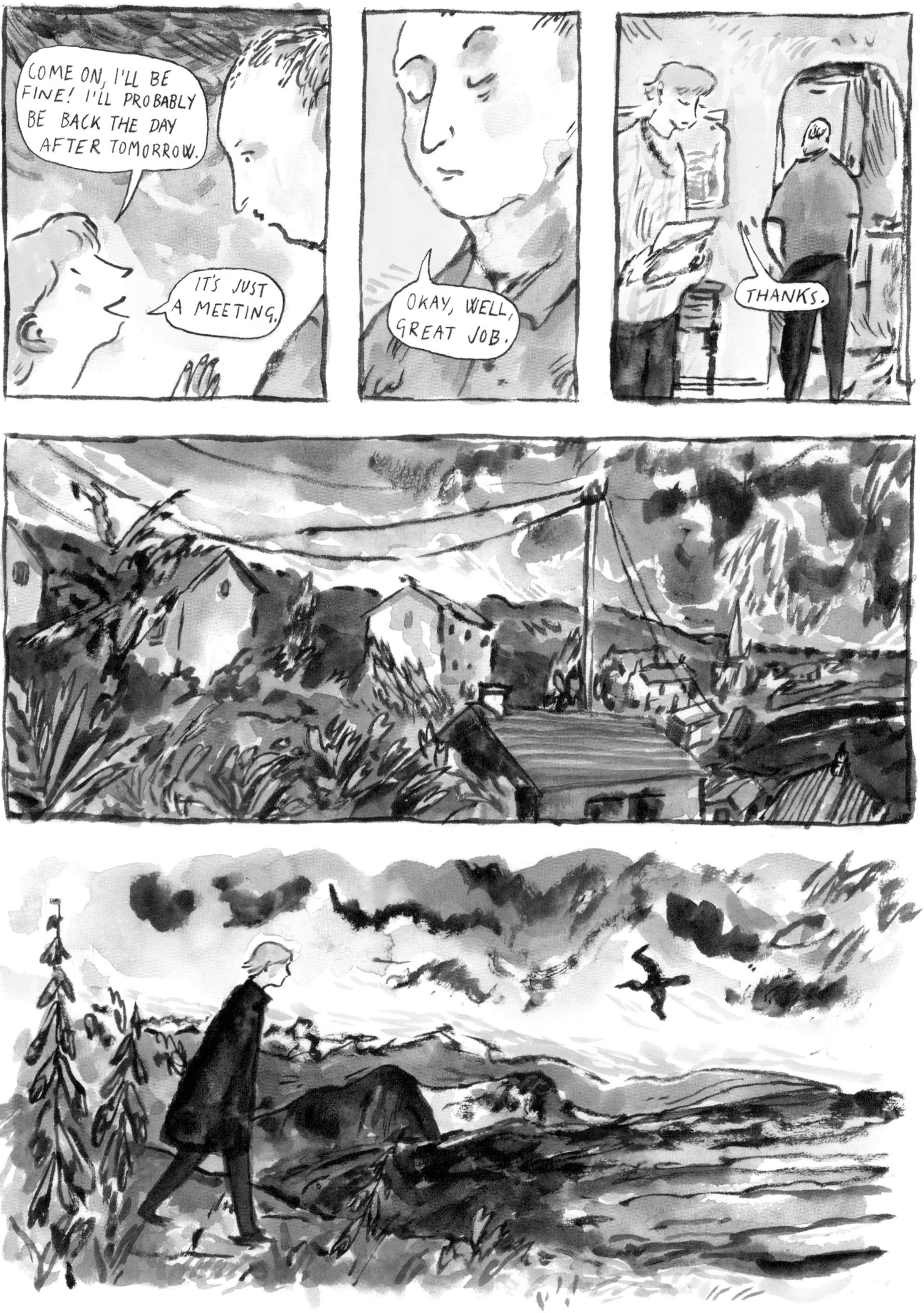
COME ON, I'LL BE FINE! I'LL PROBABLY BE BACK THE DAY AFTER TOMORROW.
IT'S JUST A MEETING.
OKAY, WELL, GREAT JOB.
THANKS.

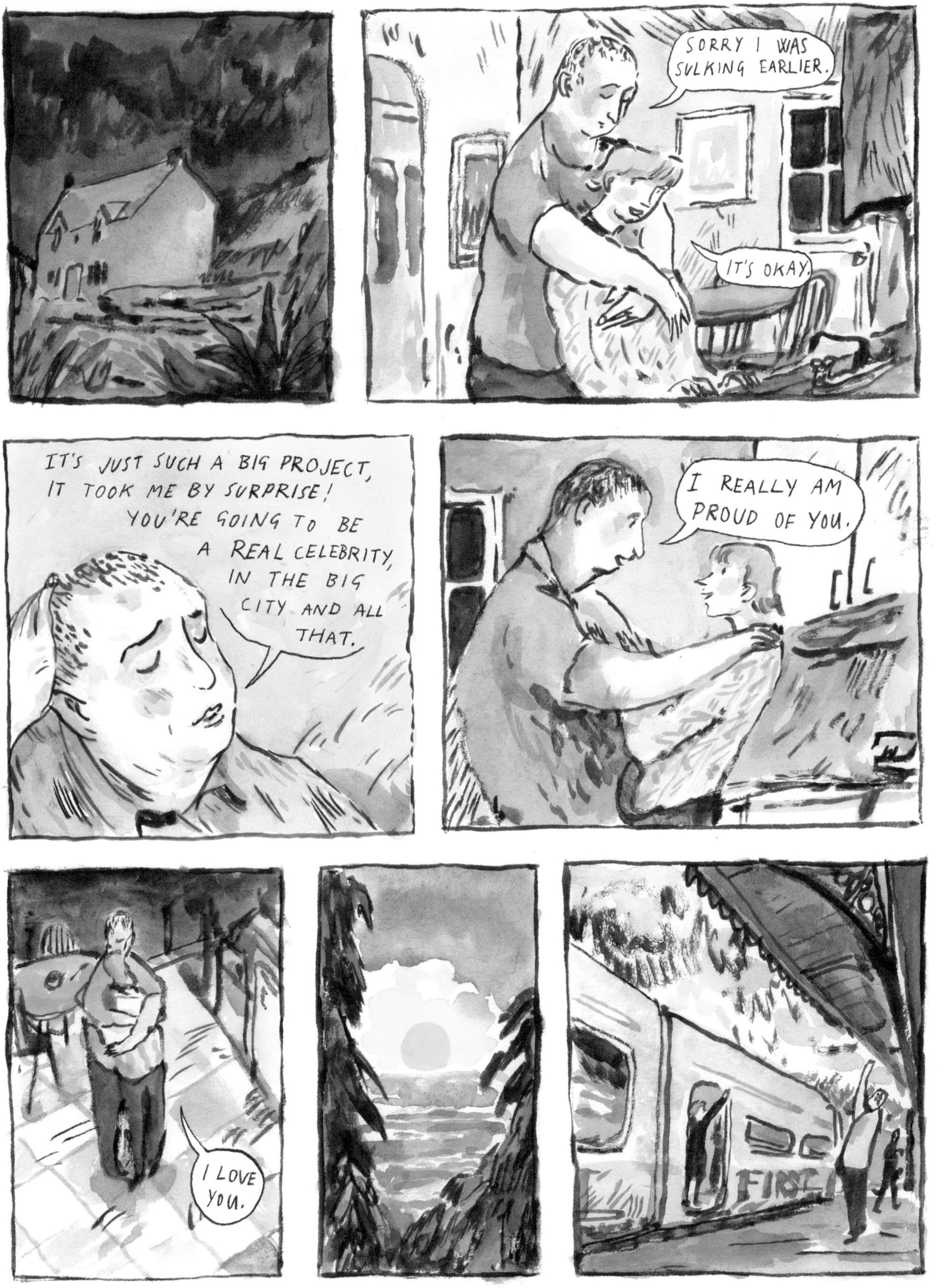
SORRY I WAS SULKING EARLIER.
IT'S OKAY.
IT'S JUST SUCH A BIG PROJECT, IT TOOK ME BY SURPRISE! YOU'RE GOING TO BE A REAL CELEBRITY, IN THE BIG CITY AND ALL THAT.
I REALLY AM PROUD OF YOU.
I LOVE YOU.
FIRST

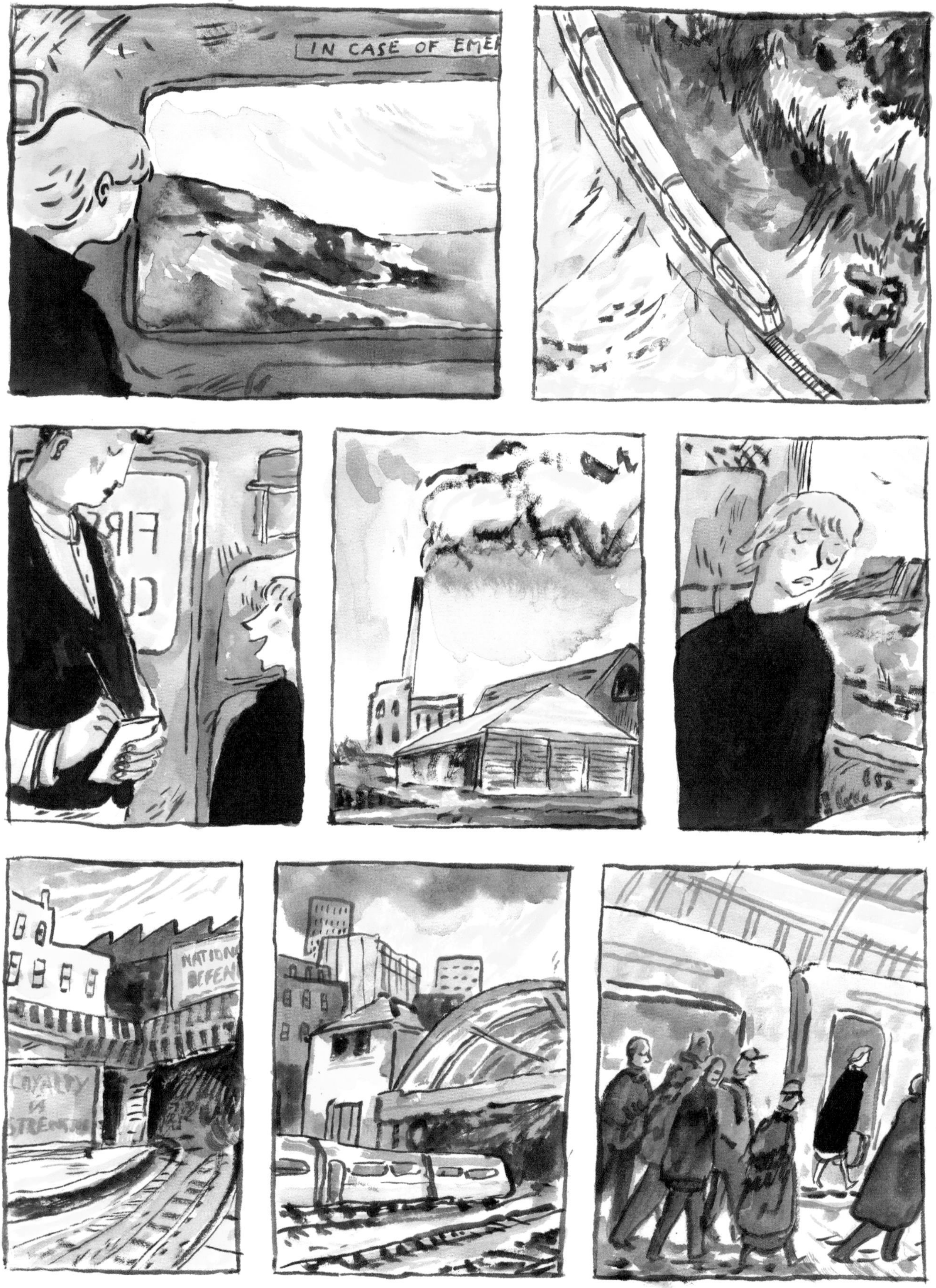
IN CASE OF EME

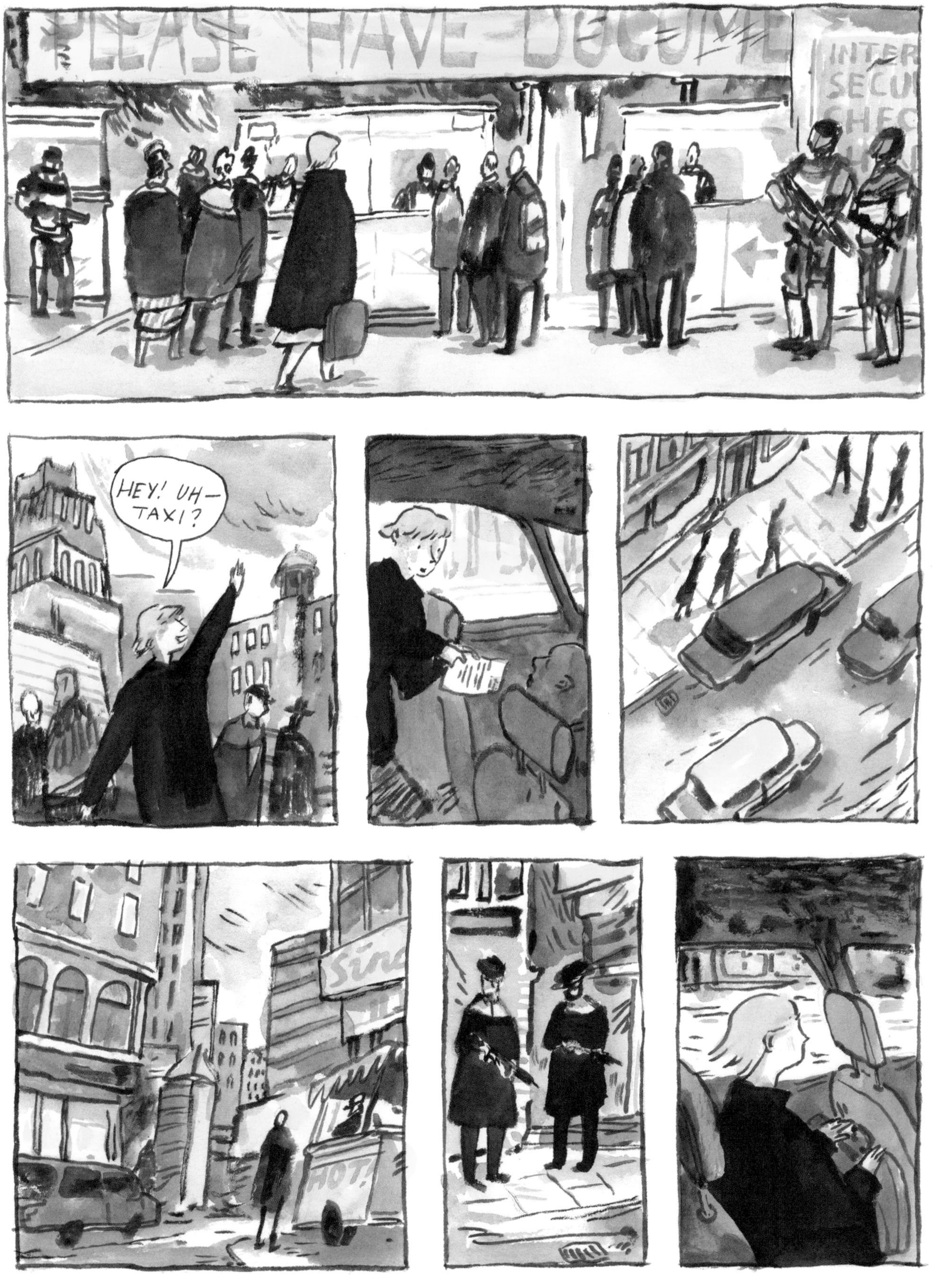
PLEASE HAVE DOCUME
INTER
SECU
CHEC
HEY! UH— TAXI?
HOT!

UMM... I'M HERE TO SEE—

AH, MADAME SAXON! WHAT AN HONOUR!

THANK YOU FOR INVITING ME.

I TRUST THE JOURNEY WAS ACCEPTABLE?

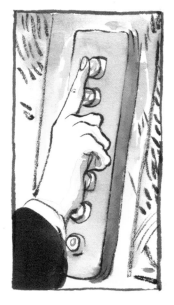

IT WAS! I'VE NEVER BEEN FIRST CLASS BEFORE. DID YOU SEE THE BUFFET?

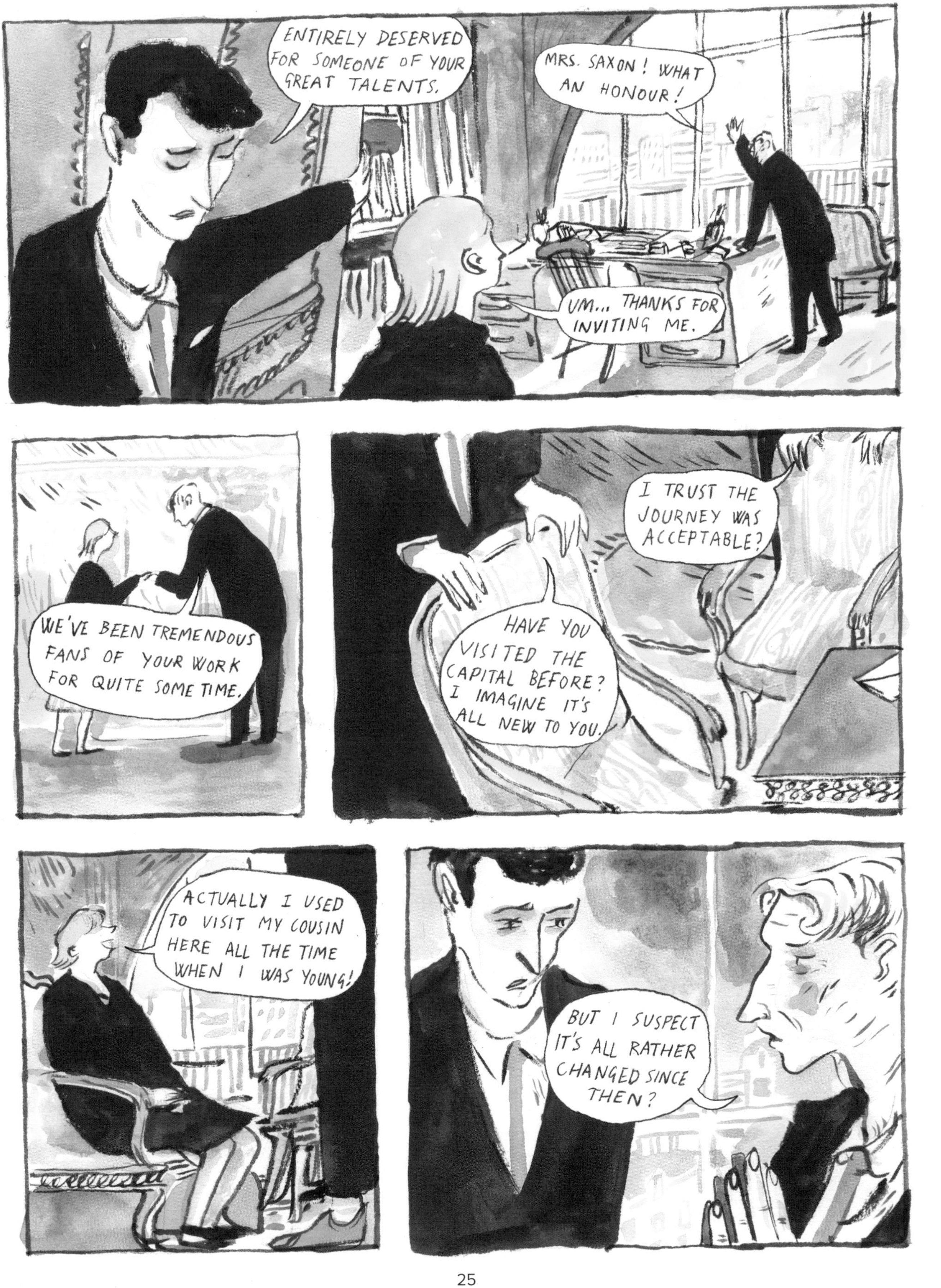
ENTIRELY DESERVED FOR SOMEONE OF YOUR GREAT TALENTS.
MRS. SAXON! WHAT AN HONOUR!
UM... THANKS FOR INVITING ME.
WE'VE BEEN TREMENDOUS FANS OF YOUR WORK FOR QUITE SOME TIME.
I TRUST THE JOURNEY WAS ACCEPTABLE?
HAVE YOU VISITED THE CAPITAL BEFORE? I IMAGINE IT'S ALL NEW TO YOU.
ACTUALLY I USED TO VISIT MY COUSIN HERE ALL THE TIME WHEN I WAS YOUNG!
BUT I SUSPECT IT'S ALL RATHER CHANGED SINCE THEN?

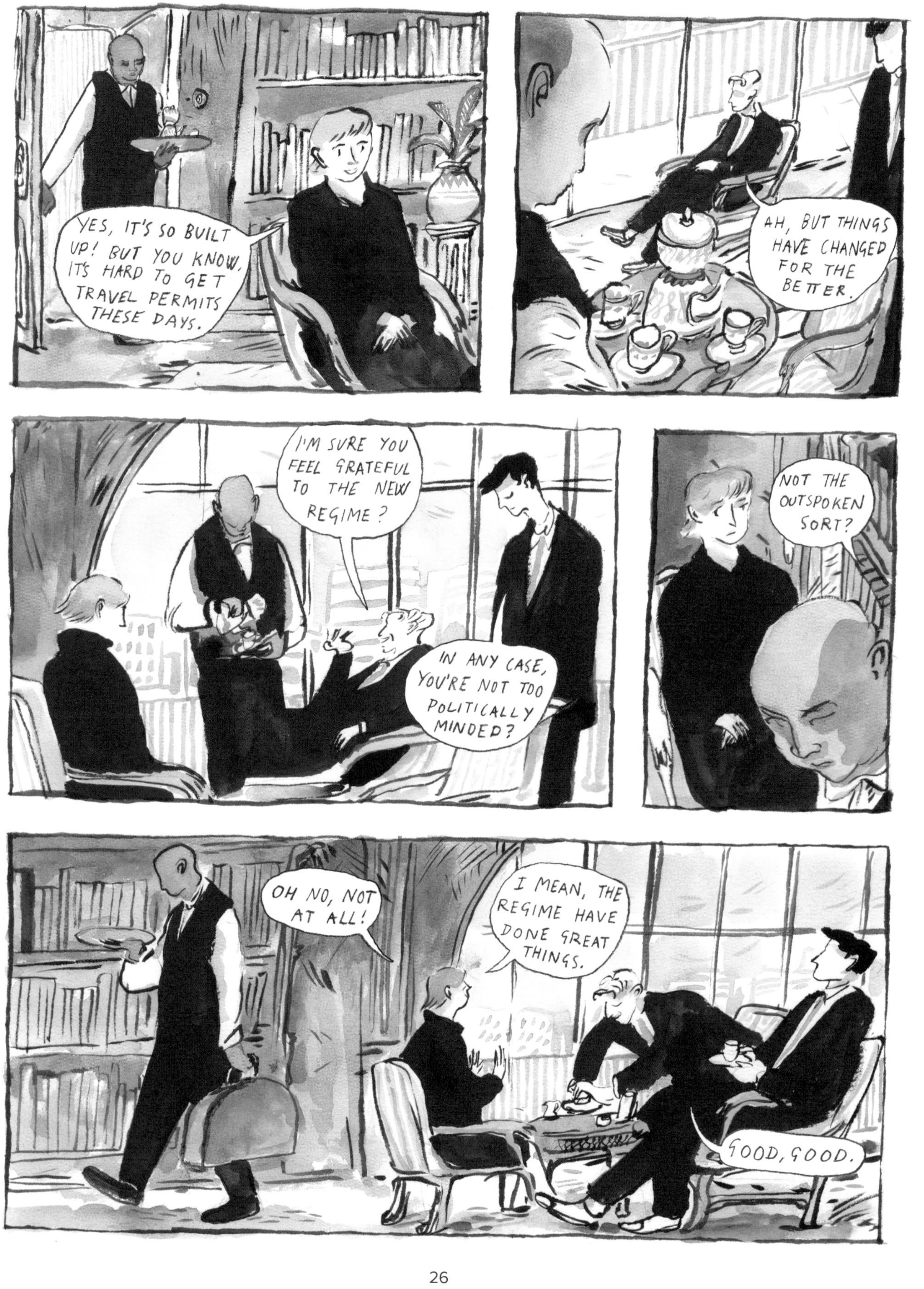
YES, IT'S SO BUILT UP! BUT YOU KNOW, IT'S HARD TO GET TRAVEL PERMITS THESE DAYS.
AH, BUT THINGS HAVE CHANGED FOR THE BETTER.
I'M SURE YOU FEEL GRATEFUL TO THE NEW REGIME?
IN ANY CASE, YOU'RE NOT TOO POLITICALLY MINDED?
NOT THE OUTSPOKEN SORT?
OH NO, NOT AT ALL!
I MEAN, THE REGIME HAVE DONE GREAT THINGS.
GOOD, GOOD.

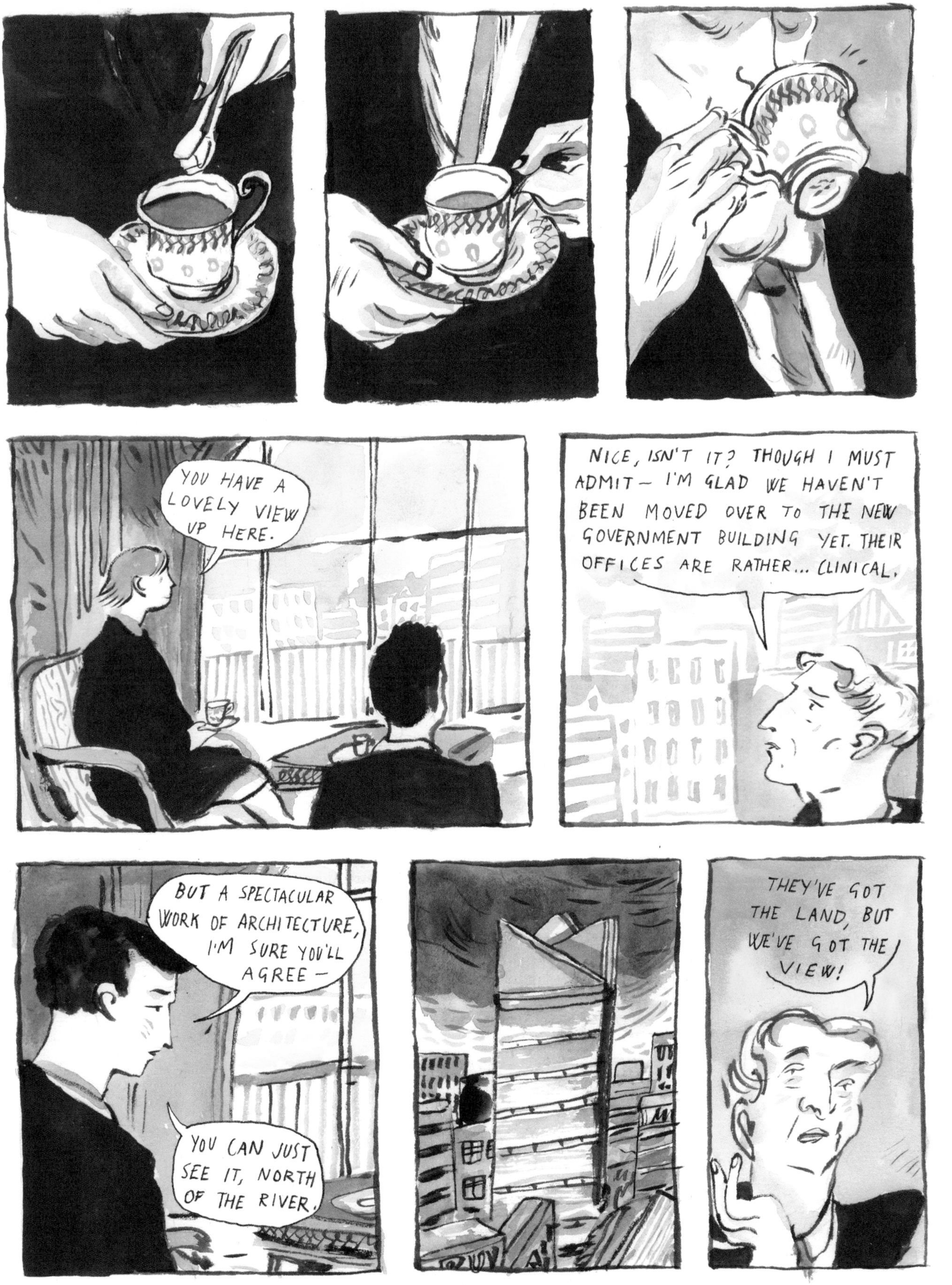
YOU HAVE A LOVELY VIEW UP HERE.
NICE, ISN'T IT? THOUGH I MUST ADMIT— I'M GLAD WE HAVEN'T BEEN MOVED OVER TO THE NEW GOVERNMENT BUILDING YET. THEIR OFFICES ARE RATHER... CLINICAL.
BUT A SPECTACULAR WORK OF ARCHITECTURE, I'M SURE YOU'LL AGREE—
YOU CAN JUST SEE IT, NORTH OF THE RIVER.
THEY'VE GOT THE LAND, BUT WE'VE GOT THE VIEW!

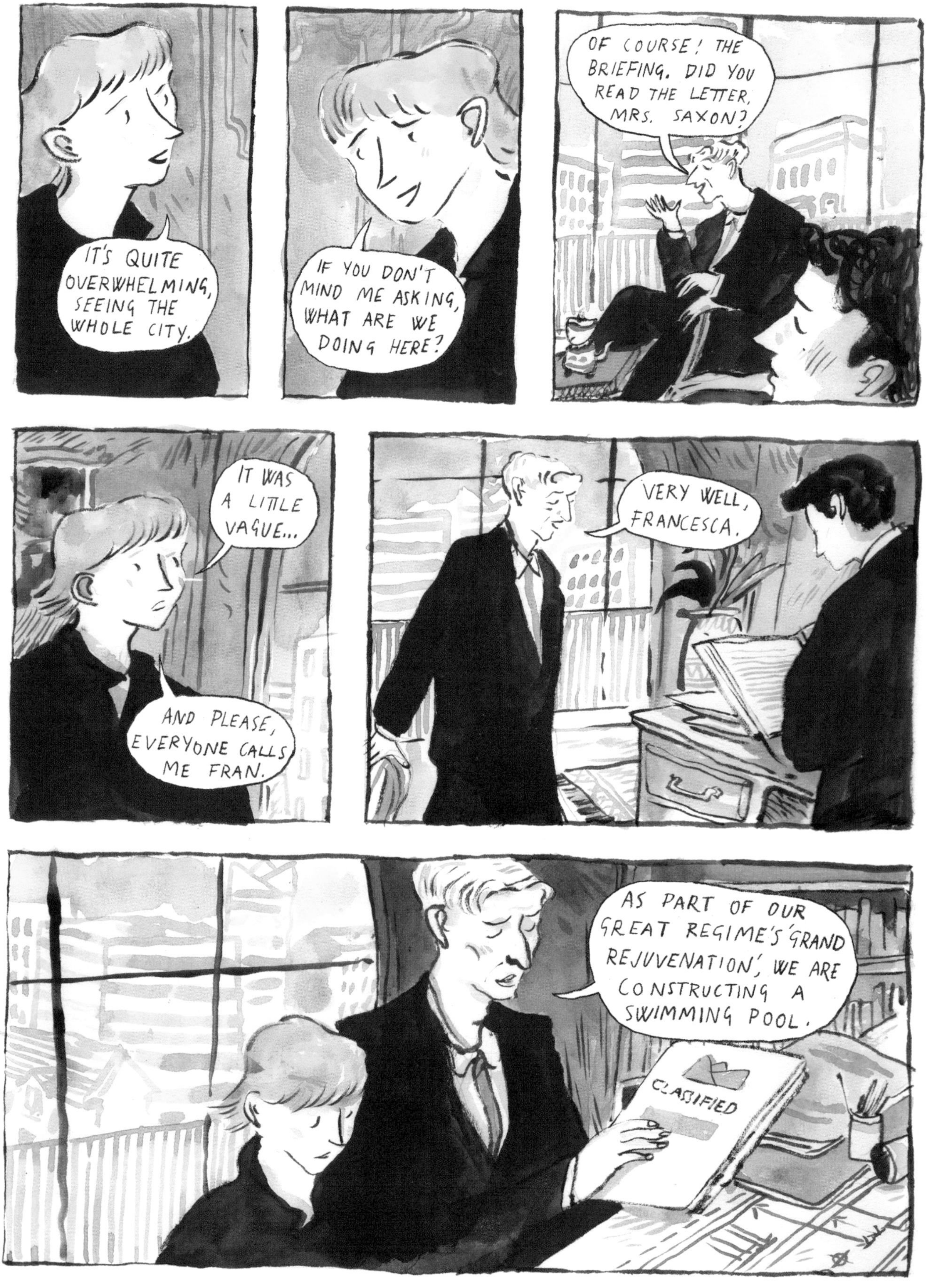
IT'S QUITE OVERWHELMING, SEEING THE WHOLE CITY.
IF YOU DON'T MIND ME ASKING, WHAT ARE WE DOING HERE?
OF COURSE! THE BRIEFING. DID YOU READ THE LETTER, MRS. SAXON?
IT WAS A LITTLE VAGUE...
AND PLEASE, EVERYONE CALLS ME FRAN.
VERY WELL, FRANCESCA.
AS PART OF OUR GREAT REGIME'S 'GRAND REJUVENATION', WE ARE CONSTRUCTING A SWIMMING POOL.
CLASSIFIED

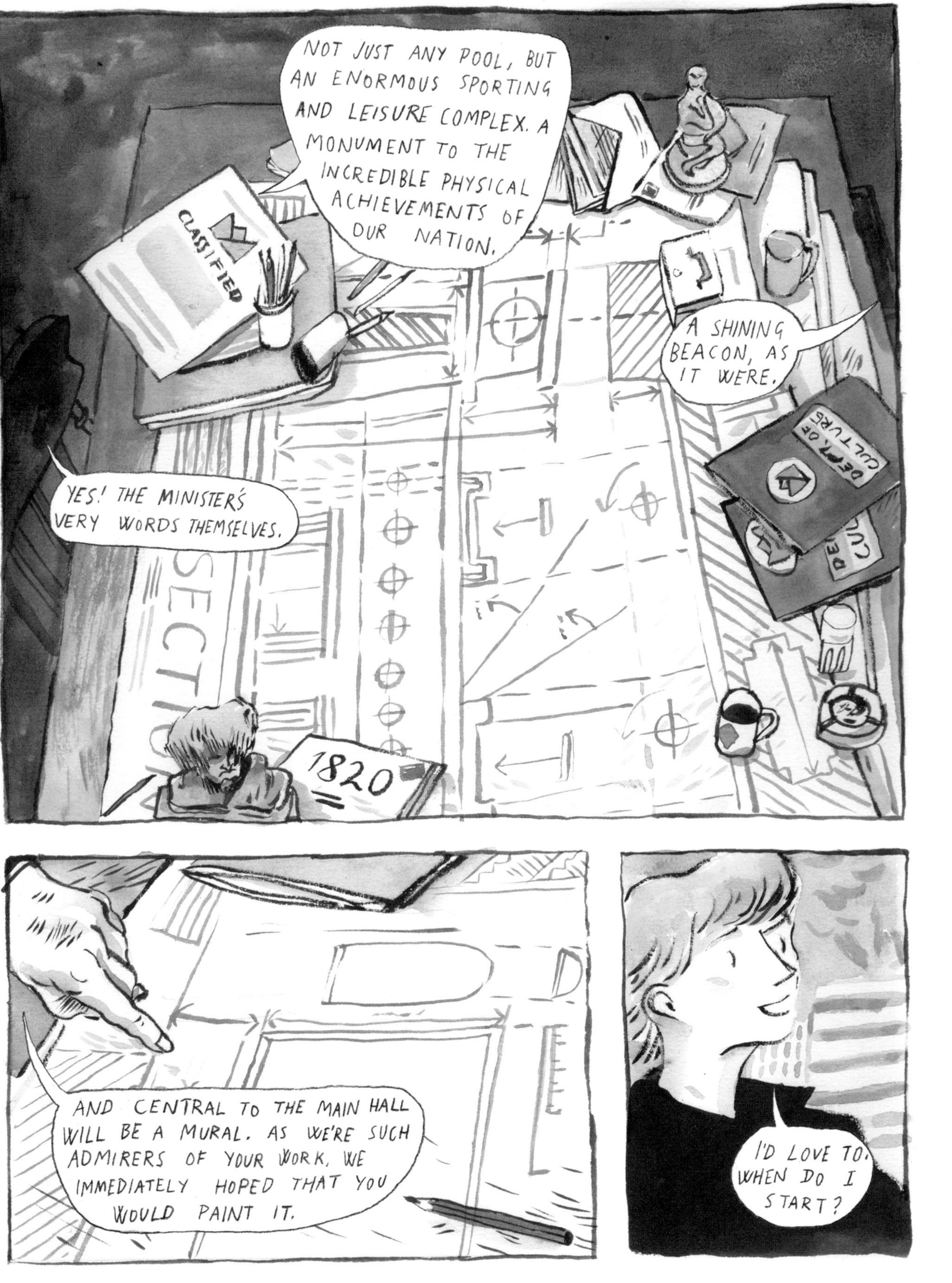
NOT JUST ANY POOL, BUT AN ENORMOUS SPORTING AND LEISURE COMPLEX. A MONUMENT TO THE INCREDIBLE PHYSICAL ACHIEVEMENTS OF OUR NATION.
CLASSIFIED
A SHINING BEACON, AS IT WERE.
DEPT. OF CULTURE
YES! THE MINISTER'S VERY WORDS THEMSELVES.
SECTI
1820
AND CENTRAL TO THE MAIN HALL WILL BE A MURAL. AS WE'RE SUCH ADMIRERS OF YOUR WORK, WE IMMEDIATELY HOPED THAT YOU WOULD PAINT IT.
I'D LOVE TO! WHEN DO I START?

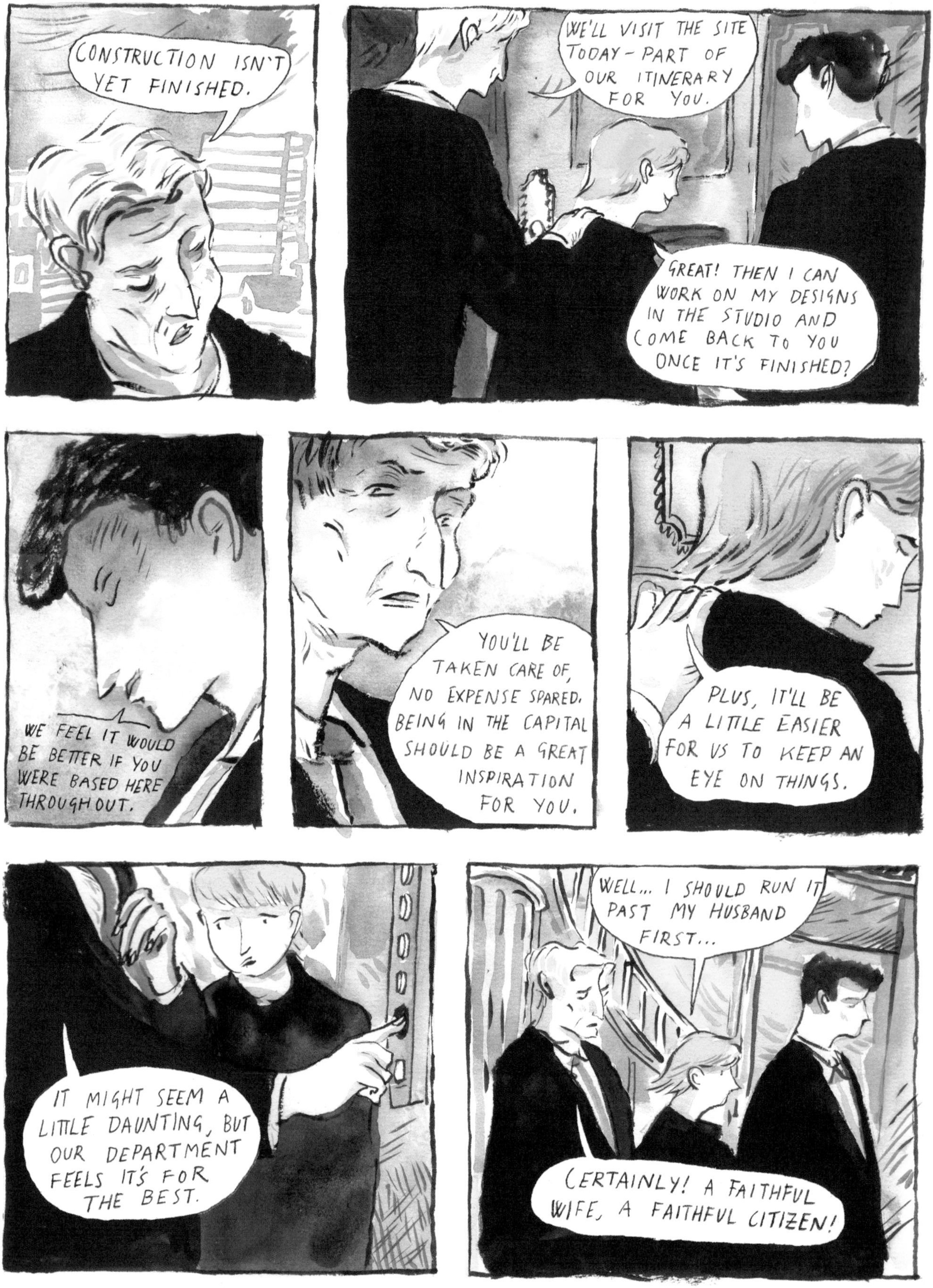
CONSTRUCTION ISN'T YET FINISHED.
WE'LL VISIT THE SITE TODAY - PART OF OUR ITINERARY FOR YOU.
GREAT! THEN I CAN WORK ON MY DESIGNS IN THE STUDIO AND COME BACK TO YOU ONCE IT'S FINISHED?
WE FEEL IT WOULD BE BETTER IF YOU WERE BASED HERE THROUGHOUT.
YOU'LL BE TAKEN CARE OF, NO EXPENSE SPARED. BEING IN THE CAPITAL SHOULD BE A GREAT INSPIRATION FOR YOU.
PLUS, IT'LL BE A LITTLE EASIER FOR US TO KEEP AN EYE ON THINGS.
IT MIGHT SEEM A LITTLE DAUNTING, BUT OUR DEPARTMENT FEELS IT'S FOR THE BEST.
WELL... I SHOULD RUN IT PAST MY HUSBAND FIRST...
CERTAINLY! A FAITHFUL WIFE, A FAITHFUL CITIZEN!

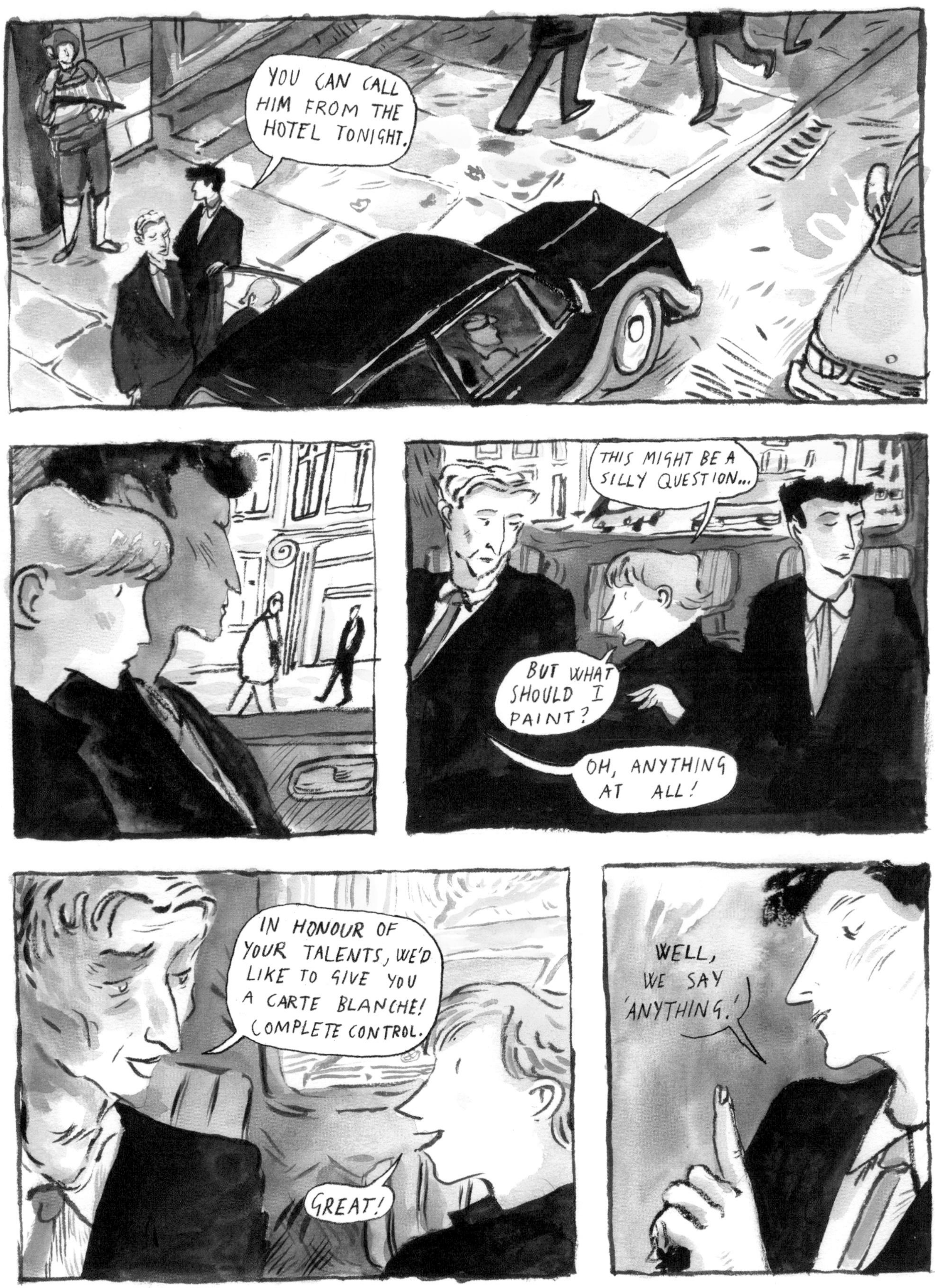
YOU CAN CALL HIM FROM THE HOTEL TONIGHT.
THIS MIGHT BE A SILLY QUESTION...
BUT WHAT SHOULD I PAINT?
OH, ANYTHING AT ALL!
IN HONOUR OF YOUR TALENTS, WE'D LIKE TO GIVE YOU A CARTE BLANCHE! COMPLETE CONTROL.
GREAT!
WELL, WE SAY 'ANYTHING.'

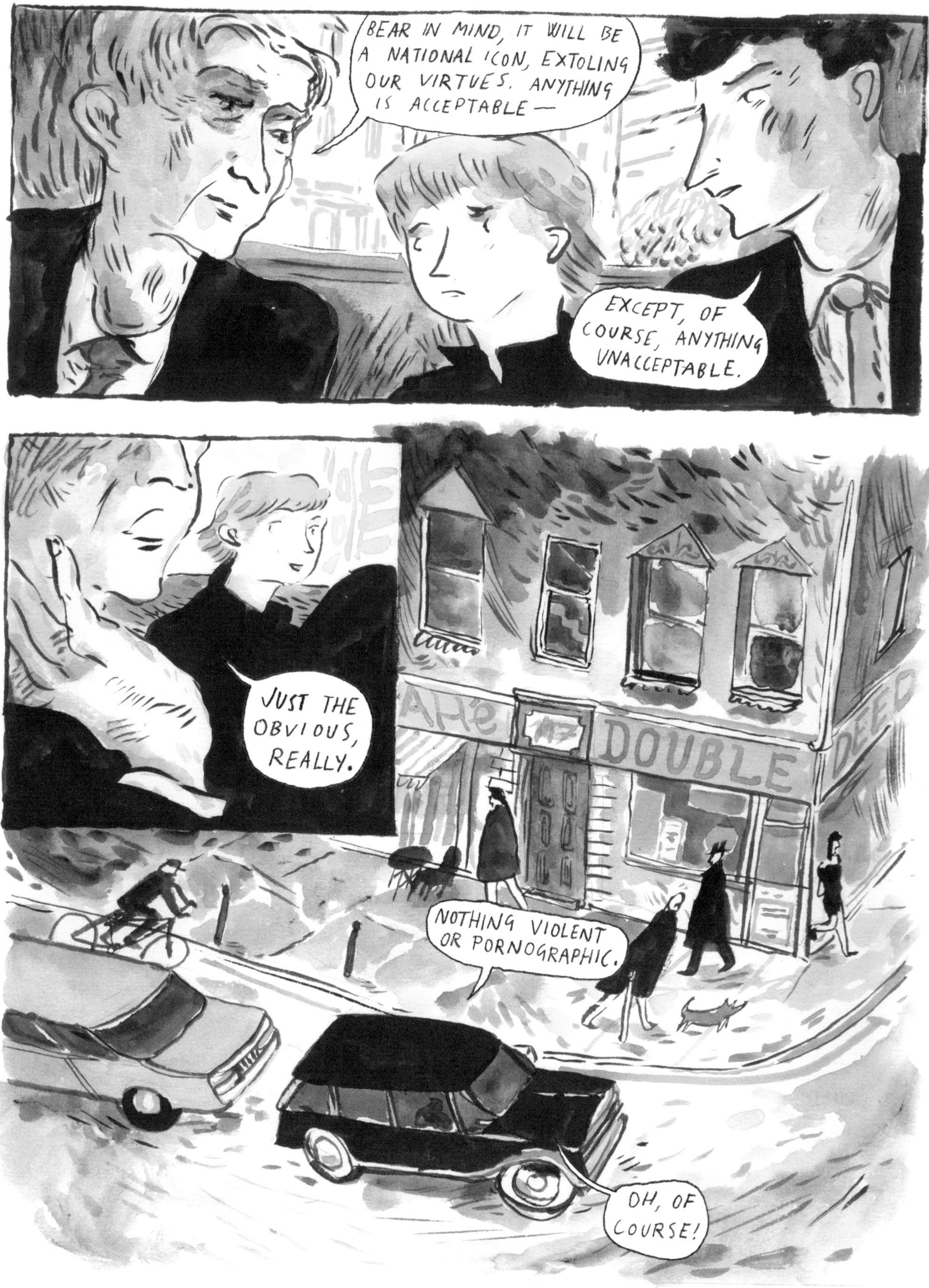
BEAR IN MIND, IT WILL BE A NATIONAL ICON, EXTOLING OUR VIRTUES. ANYTHING IS ACCEPTABLE—
EXCEPT, OF COURSE, ANYTHING UNACCEPTABLE.
JUST THE OBVIOUS, REALLY.
DOUBLE
NOTHING VIOLENT OR PORNOGRAPHIC.
OH, OF COURSE!

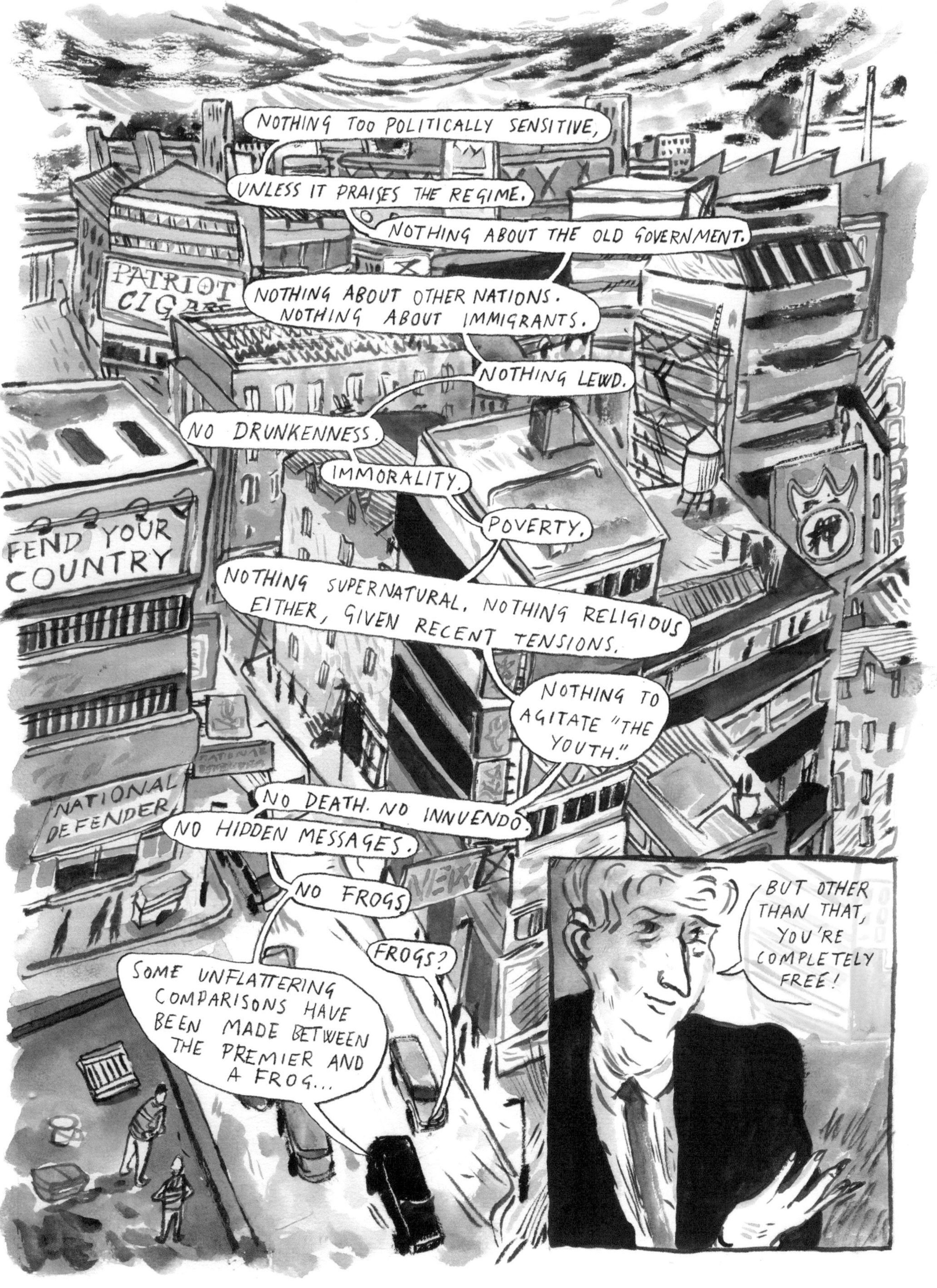
NOTHING TOO POLITICALLY SENSITIVE,
UNLESS IT PRAISES THE REGIME.
NOTHING ABOUT THE OLD GOVERNMENT.
NOTHING ABOUT OTHER NATIONS. NOTHING ABOUT IMMIGRANTS.
NOTHING LEWD.
NO DRUNKENNESS.
IMMORALITY.
POVERTY.
NOTHING SUPERNATURAL, NOTHING RELIGIOUS EITHER, GIVEN RECENT TENSIONS.
NOTHING TO AGITATE "THE YOUTH."
NO DEATH. NO INNUENDO.
NO HIDDEN MESSAGES.
NO FROGS.
FROGS?
SOME UNFLATTERING COMPARISONS HAVE BEEN MADE BETWEEN THE PREMIER AND A FROG...
BUT OTHER THAN THAT, YOU'RE COMPLETELY FREE!
PATRIOT CIG
FEND YOUR COUNTRY
NATIONAL DEFENDER

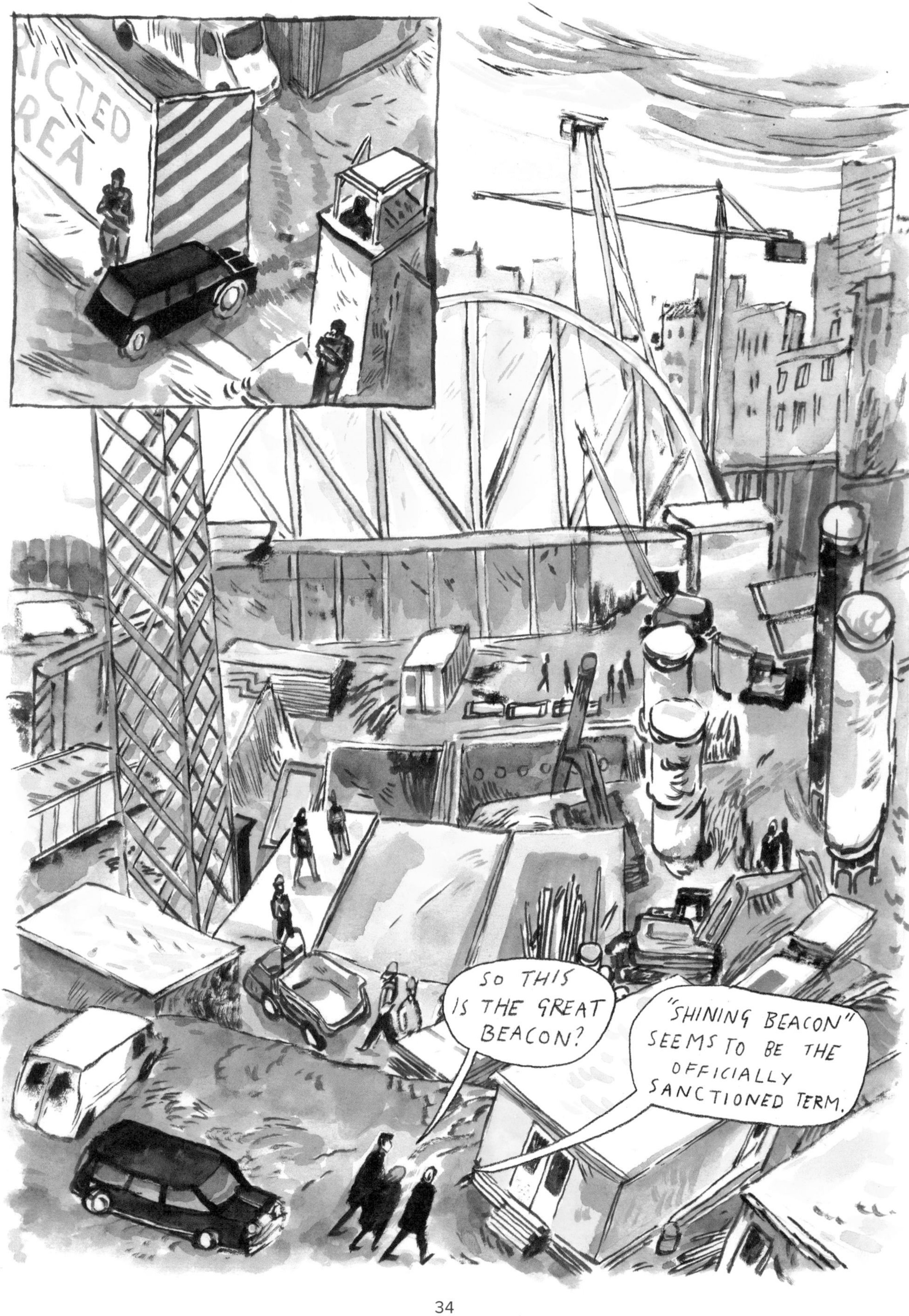
RICTED
REA
SO THIS IS THE GREAT BEACON?
"SHINING BEACON" SEEMS TO BE THE OFFICIALLY SANCTIONED TERM.

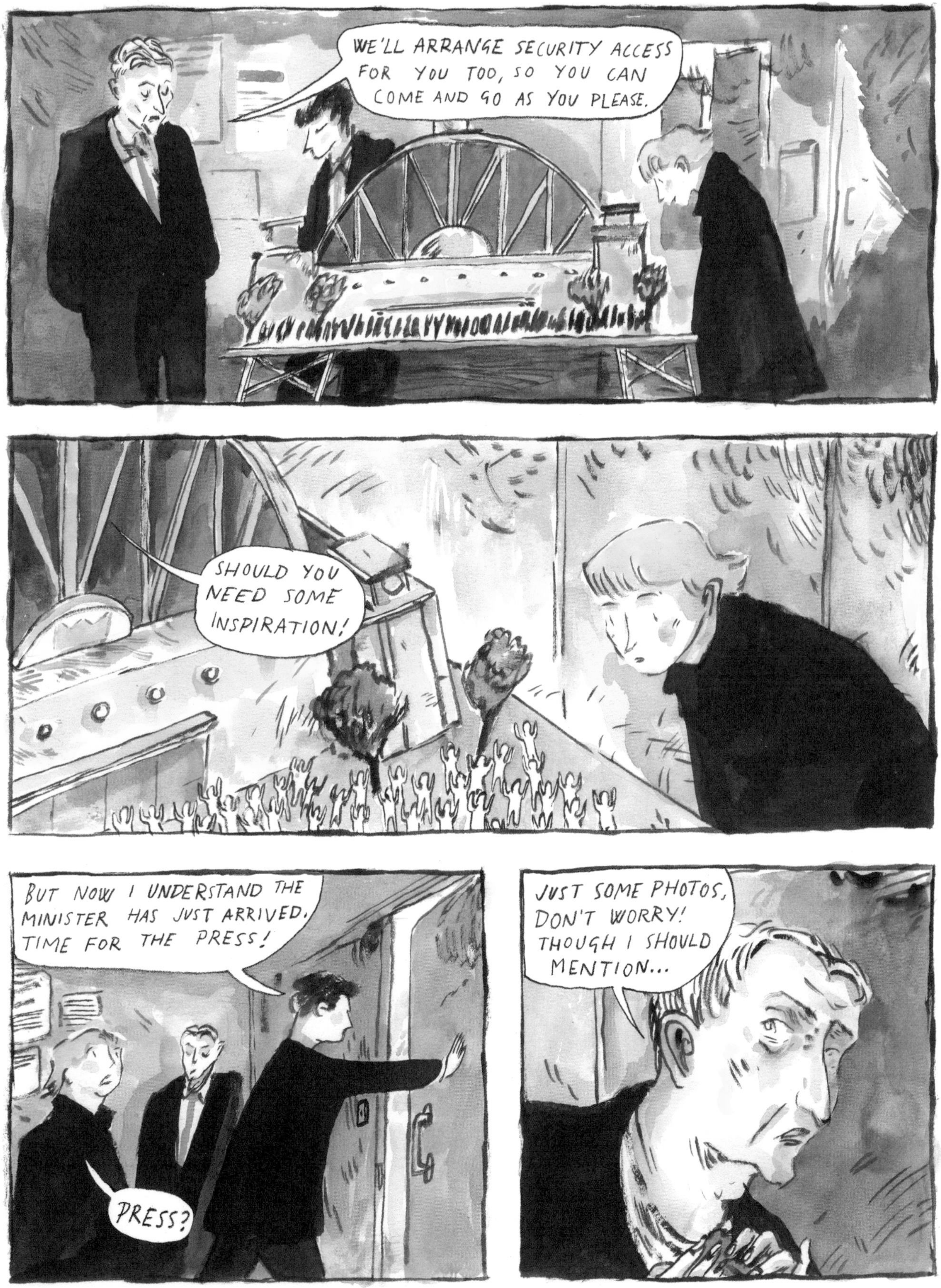
WE'LL ARRANGE SECURITY ACCESS FOR YOU TOO, SO YOU CAN COME AND GO AS YOU PLEASE.
SHOULD YOU NEED SOME INSPIRATION!
BUT NOW I UNDERSTAND THE MINISTER HAS JUST ARRIVED. TIME FOR THE PRESS!
PRESS?
JUST SOME PHOTOS, DON'T WORRY! THOUGH I SHOULD MENTION...

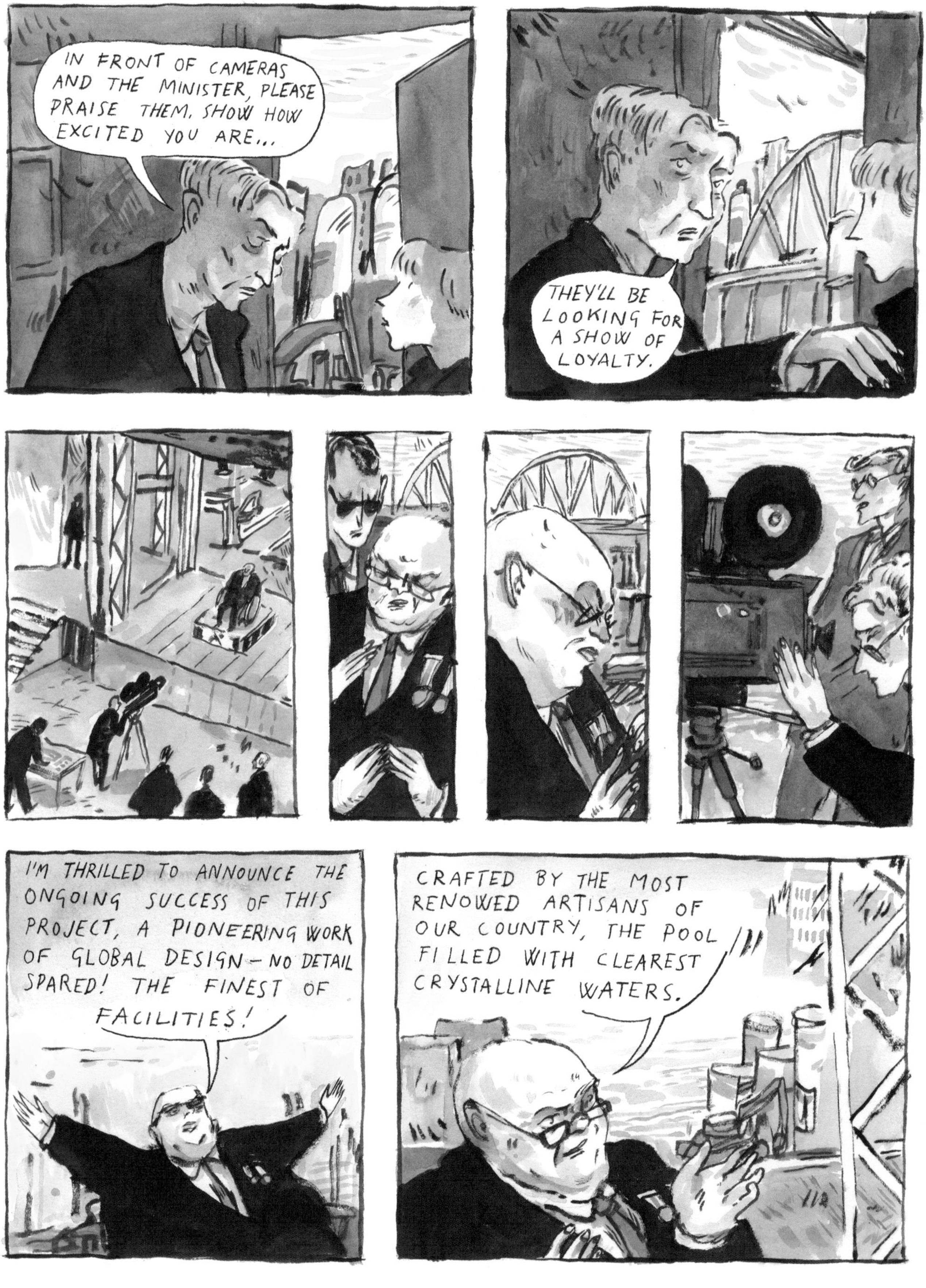

IN FRONT OF CAMERAS AND THE MINISTER, PLEASE PRAISE THEM. SHOW HOW EXCITED YOU ARE...
THEY'LL BE LOOKING FOR A SHOW OF LOYALTY.
I'M THRILLED TO ANNOUNCE THE ONGOING SUCCESS OF THIS PROJECT, A PIONEERING WORK OF GLOBAL DESIGN – NO DETAIL SPARED! THE FINEST OF FACILITIES!
CRAFTED BY THE MOST RENOWED ARTISANS OF OUR COUNTRY, THE POOL FILLED WITH CLEAREST CRYSTALLINE WATERS.

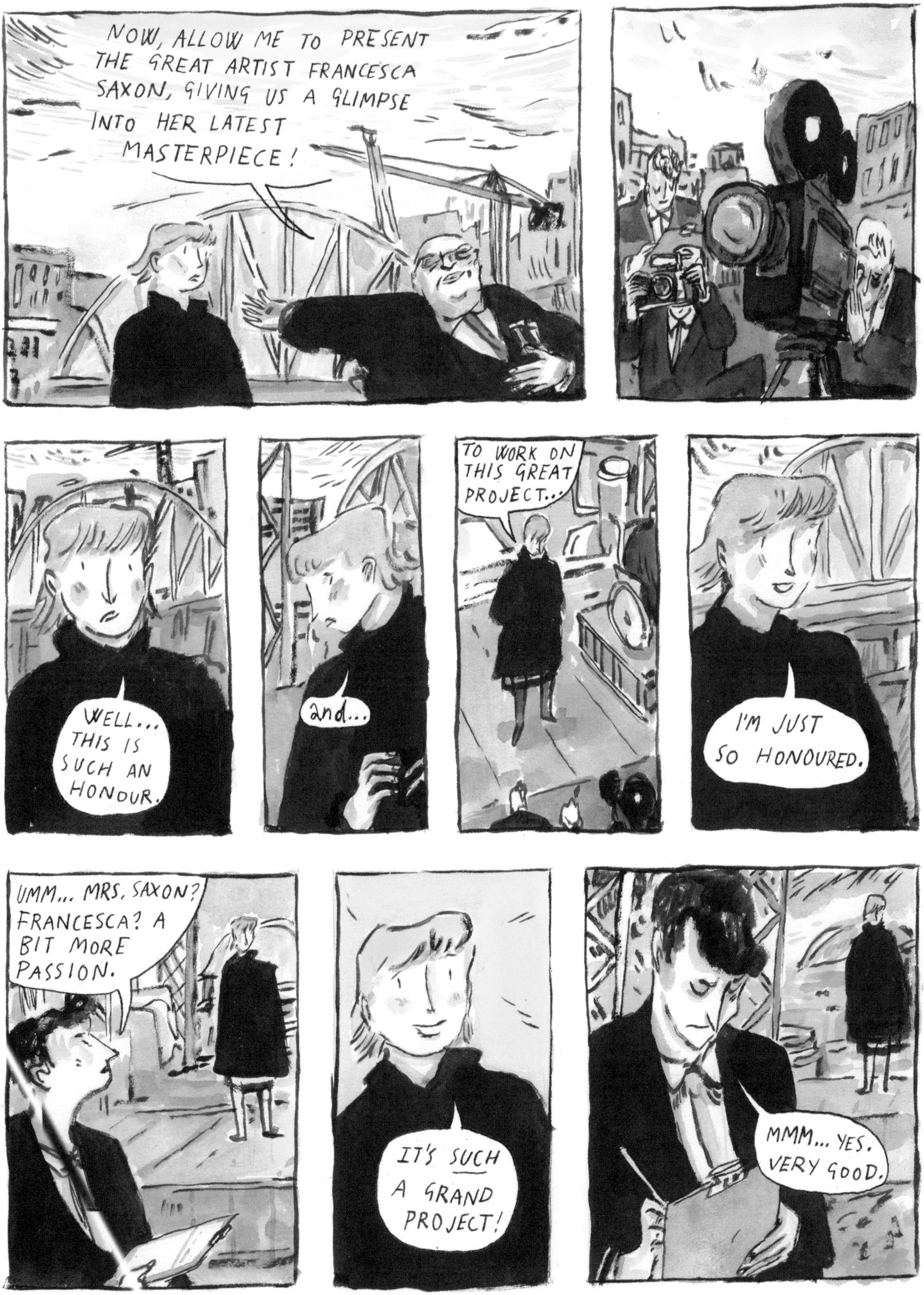
NOW, ALLOW ME TO PRESENT THE GREAT ARTIST FRANCESCA SAXON, GIVING US A GLIMPSE INTO HER LATEST MASTERPIECE!
WELL... THIS IS SUCH AN HONOUR.
and...
TO WORK ON THIS GREAT PROJECT...
I'M JUST SO HONOURED.
UMM... MRS. SAXON? FRANCESCA? A BIT MORE PASSION.
IT'S SUCH A GRAND PROJECT!
MMM... YES. VERY GOOD.

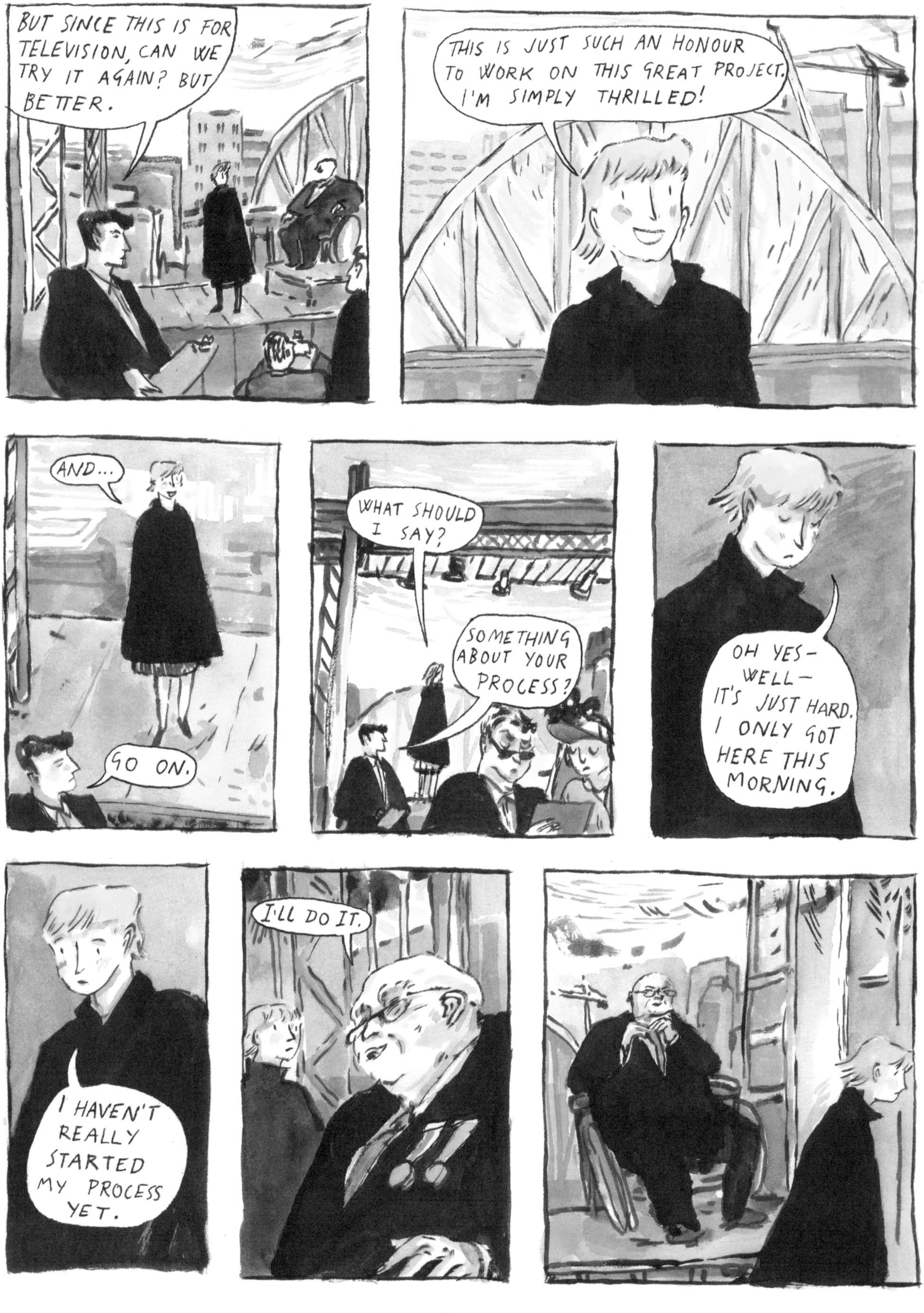
BUT SINCE THIS IS FOR TELEVISION, CAN WE TRY IT AGAIN? BUT BETTER.
THIS IS JUST SUCH AN HONOUR TO WORK ON THIS GREAT PROJECT. I'M SIMPLY THRILLED!
AND...
GO ON.
WHAT SHOULD I SAY?
SOMETHING ABOUT YOUR PROCESS?
OH YES- WELL- IT'S JUST HARD. I ONLY GOT HERE THIS MORNING.
I HAVEN'T REALLY STARTED MY PROCESS YET.
I'LL DO IT.

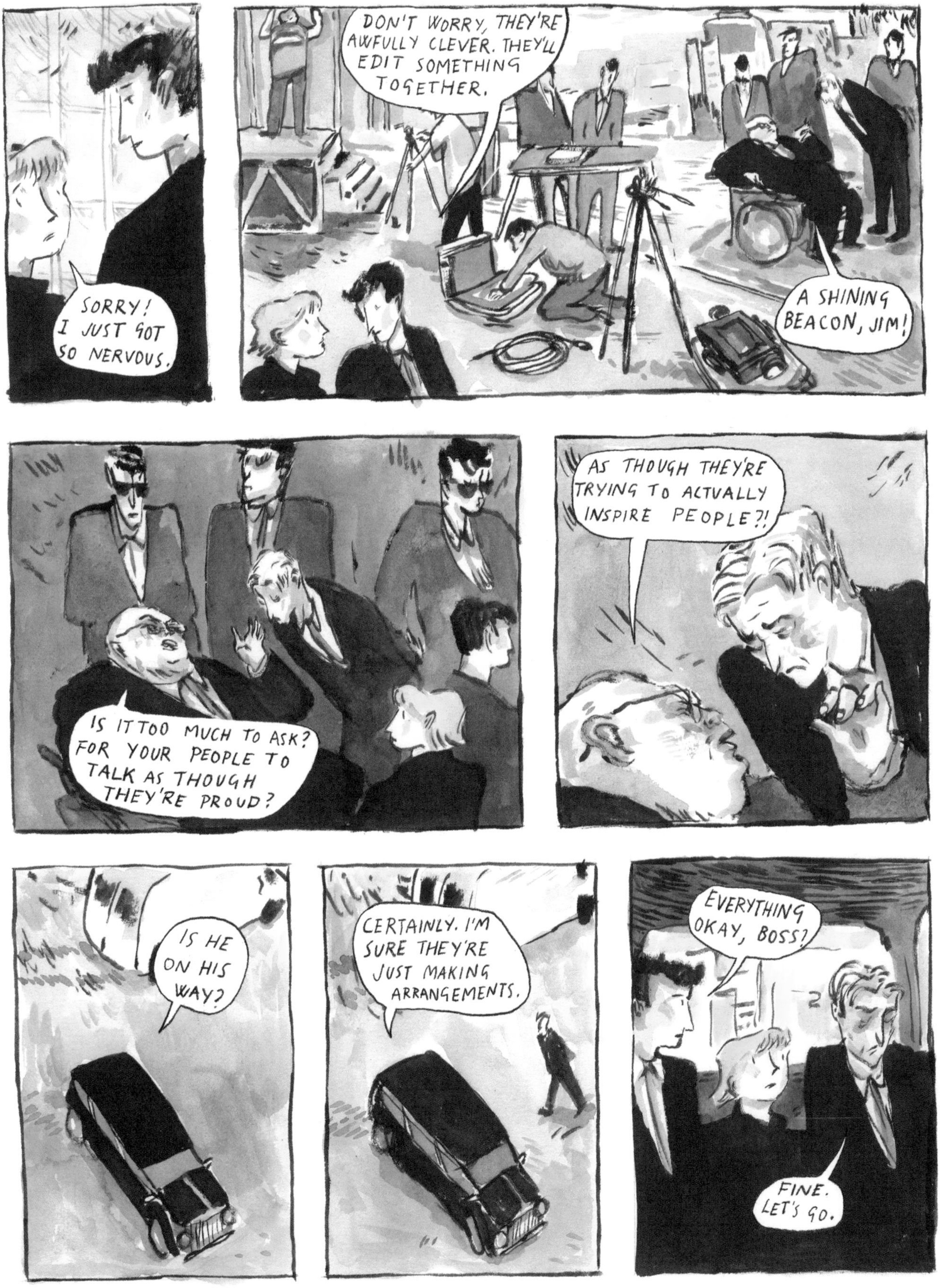
SORRY! I JUST GOT SO NERVOUS.
DON'T WORRY, THEY'RE AWFULLY CLEVER. THEY'LL EDIT SOMETHING TOGETHER.
A SHINING BEACON, JIM!
IS IT TOO MUCH TO ASK? FOR YOUR PEOPLE TO TALK AS THOUGH THEY'RE PROUD?
AS THOUGH THEY'RE TRYING TO ACTUALLY INSPIRE PEOPLE?!
IS HE ON HIS WAY?
CERTAINLY. I'M SURE THEY'RE JUST MAKING ARRANGEMENTS.
EVERYTHING OKAY, BOSS?
FINE. LET'S GO.

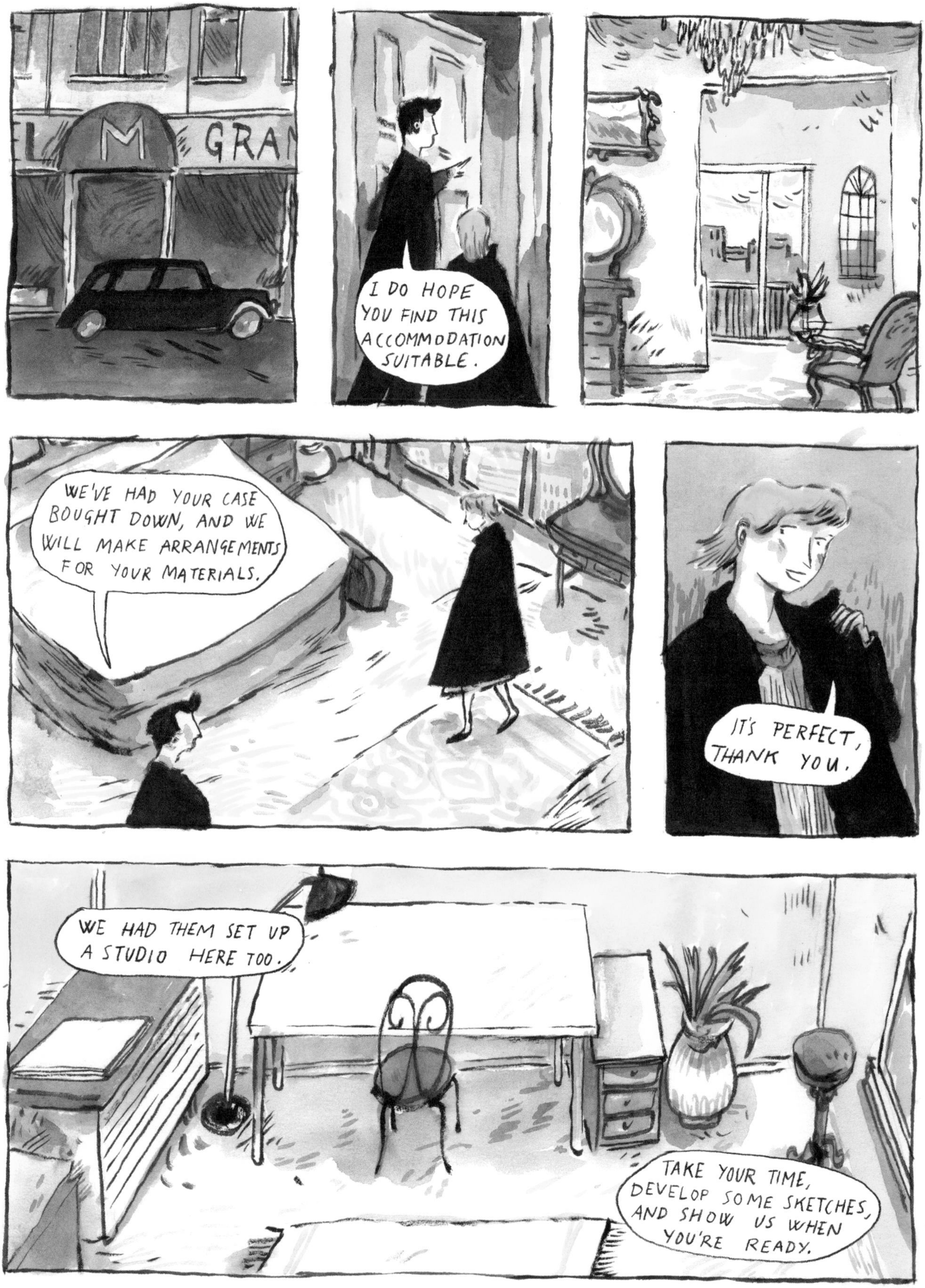
I DO HOPE YOU FIND THIS ACCOMMODATION SUITABLE.
WE'VE HAD YOUR CASE BOUGHT DOWN, AND WE WILL MAKE ARRANGEMENTS FOR YOUR MATERIALS.
IT'S PERFECT, THANK YOU.
WE HAD THEM SET UP A STUDIO HERE TOO.
TAKE YOUR TIME, DEVELOP SOME SKETCHES, AND SHOW US WHEN YOU'RE READY.

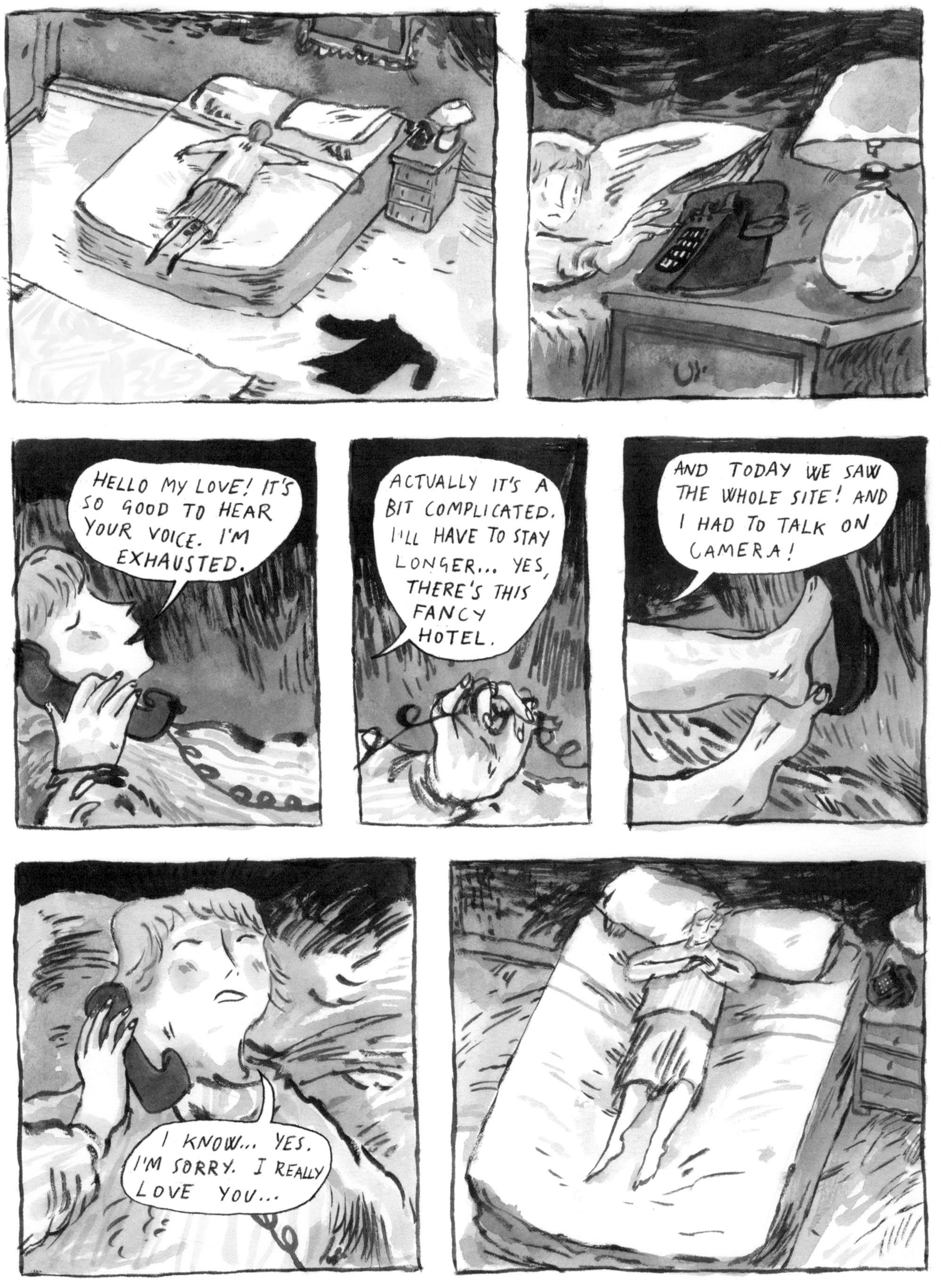
HELLO MY LOVE! IT'S SO GOOD TO HEAR YOUR VOICE. I'M EXHAUSTED.
ACTUALLY IT'S A BIT COMPLICATED. I'LL HAVE TO STAY LONGER... YES, THERE'S THIS FANCY HOTEL.
AND TODAY WE SAW THE WHOLE SITE! AND I HAD TO TALK ON CAMERA!
I KNOW... YES. I'M SORRY. I REALLY LOVE YOU...

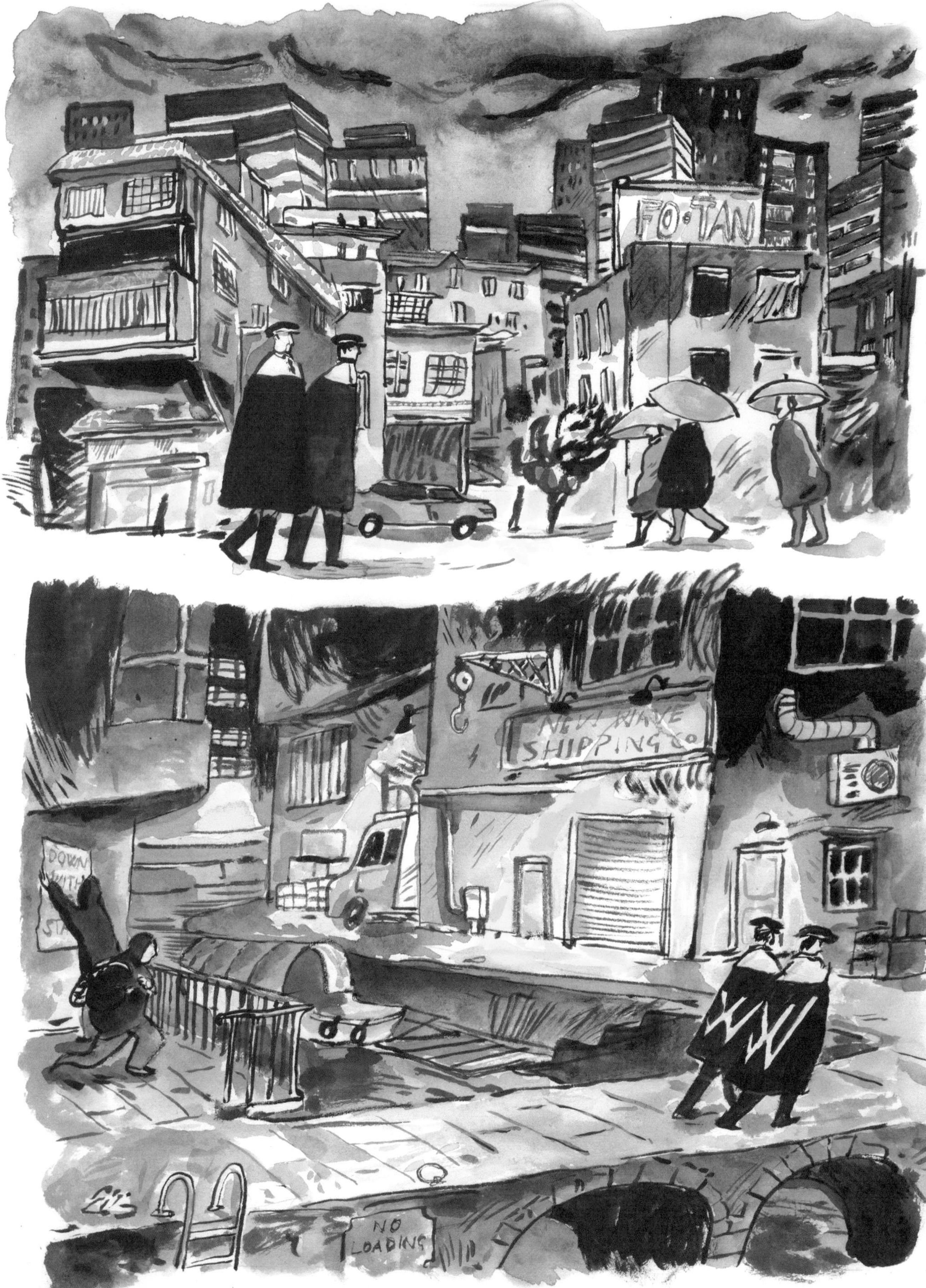
FO·TAN
NEW WAVE
SHIPPING Co
NO LOADING

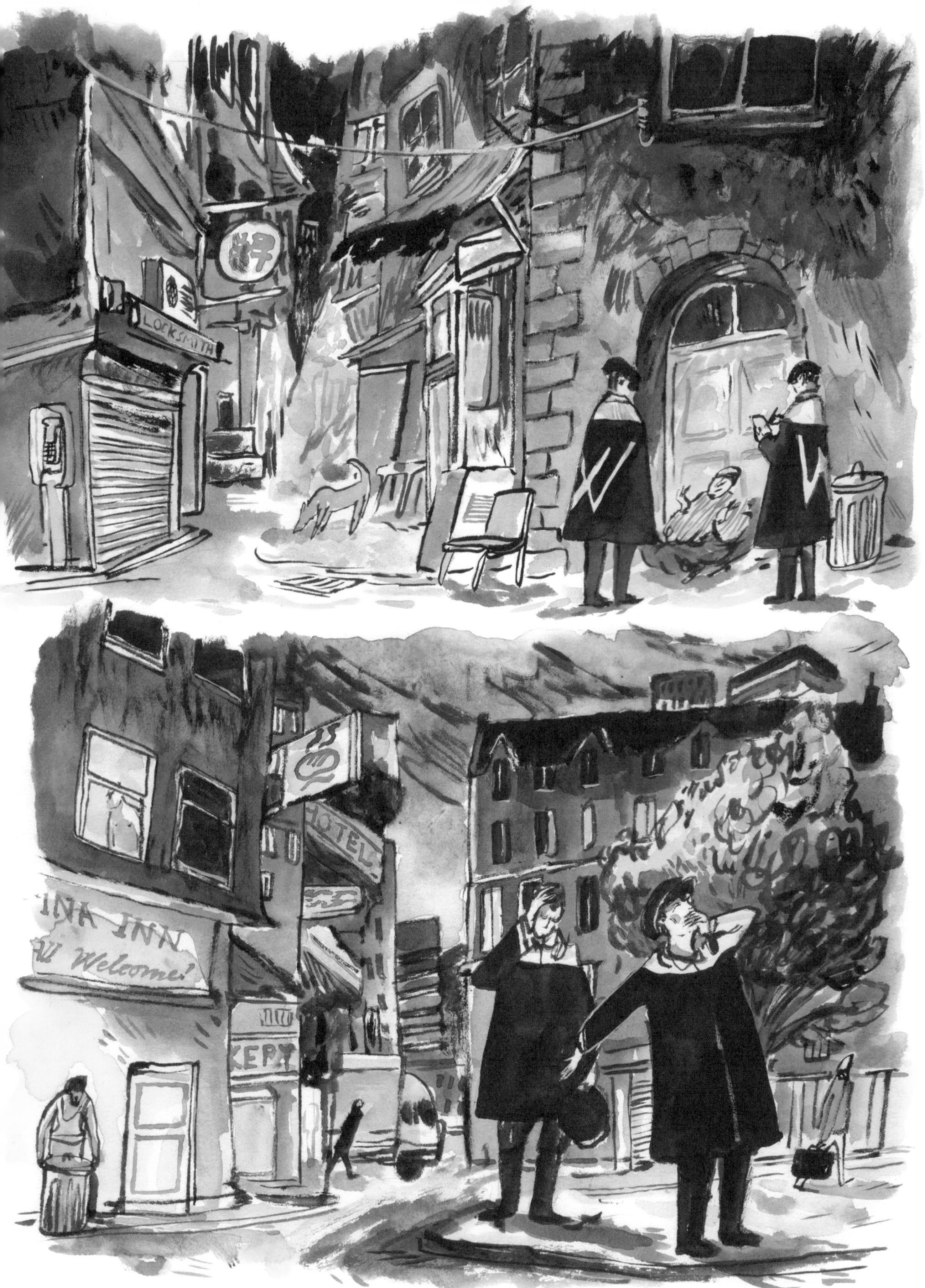
LOCKSMITH
INA INN
Welcome!
HOTEL
KERY

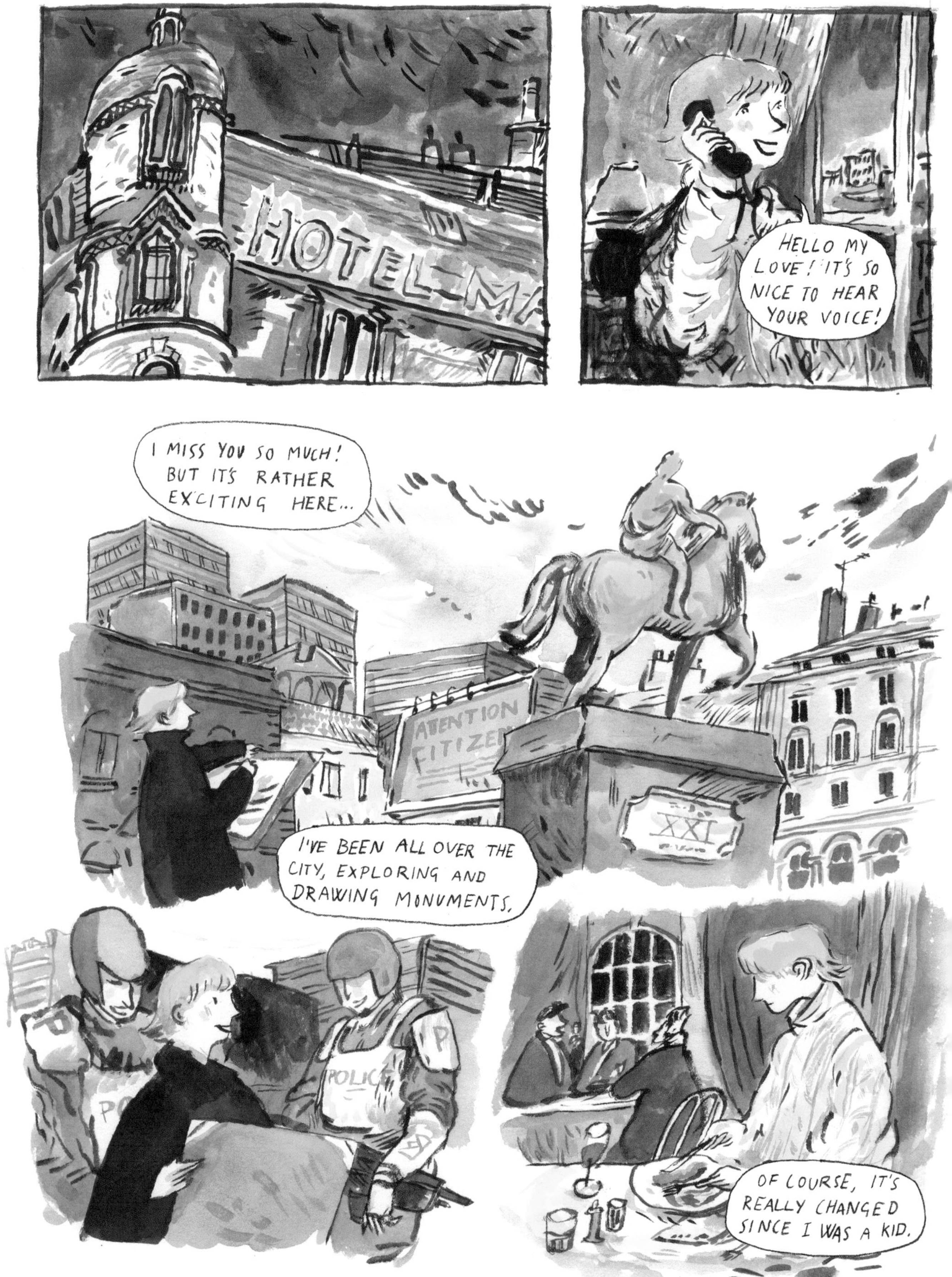
HOTEL M
HELLO MY LOVE! IT'S SO NICE TO HEAR YOUR VOICE!
I MISS YOU SO MUCH! BUT IT'S RATHER EXCITING HERE...
ATENTION FITIZEN
XXI
I'VE BEEN ALL OVER THE CITY, EXPLORING AND DRAWING MONUMENTS.
POLICE
OF COURSE, IT'S REALLY CHANGED SINCE I WAS A KID.

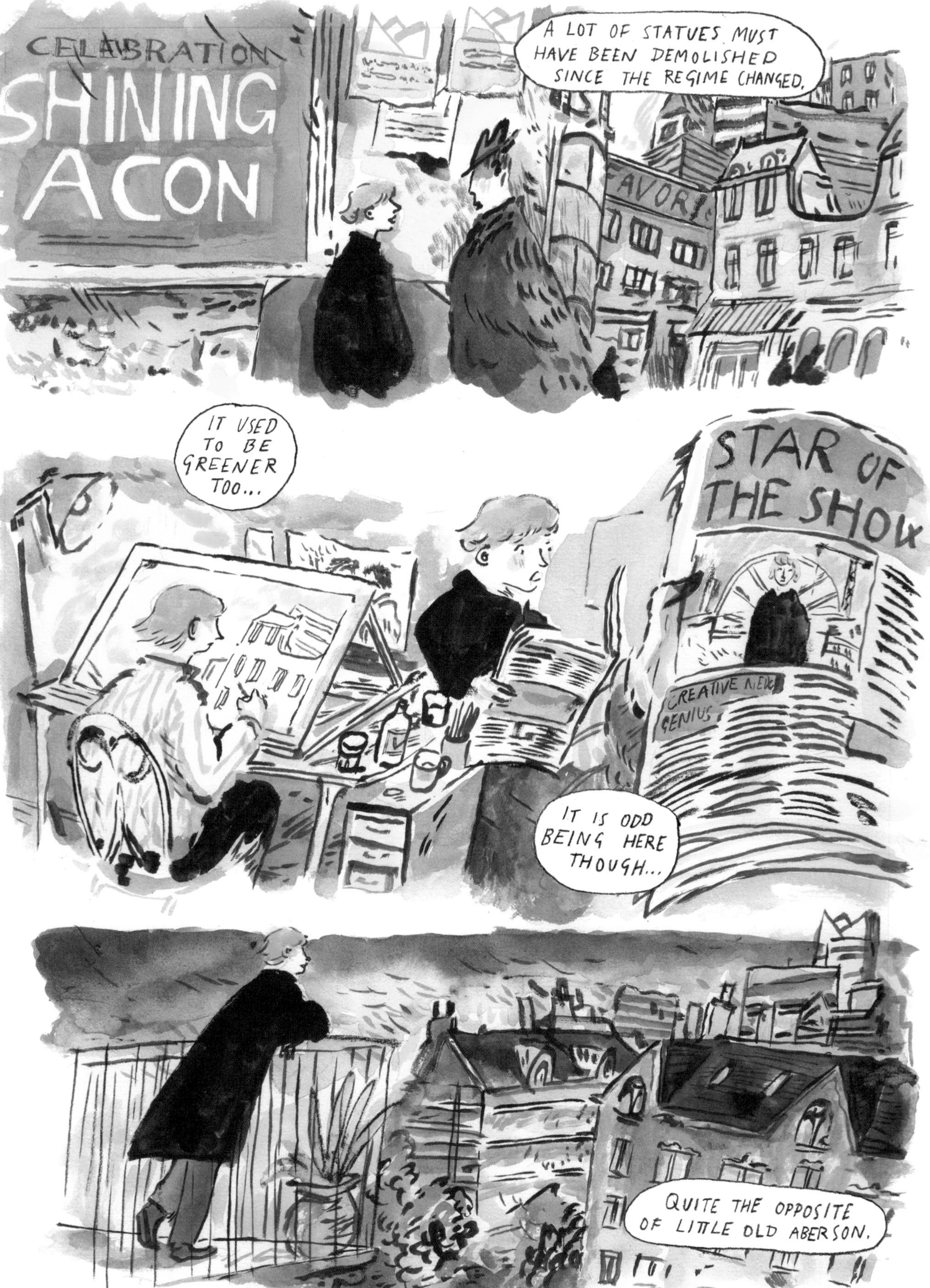
CELEBRATION
SHINING
ACON
A LOT OF STATUES MUST HAVE BEEN DEMOLISHED SINCE THE REGIME CHANGED.
FAVOR
IT USED TO BE GREENER TOO...
STAR OF THE SHOW
CREATIVE NEWS
GENIUS
IT IS ODD BEING HERE THOUGH...
QUITE THE OPPOSITE OF LITTLE OLD ABERSON.

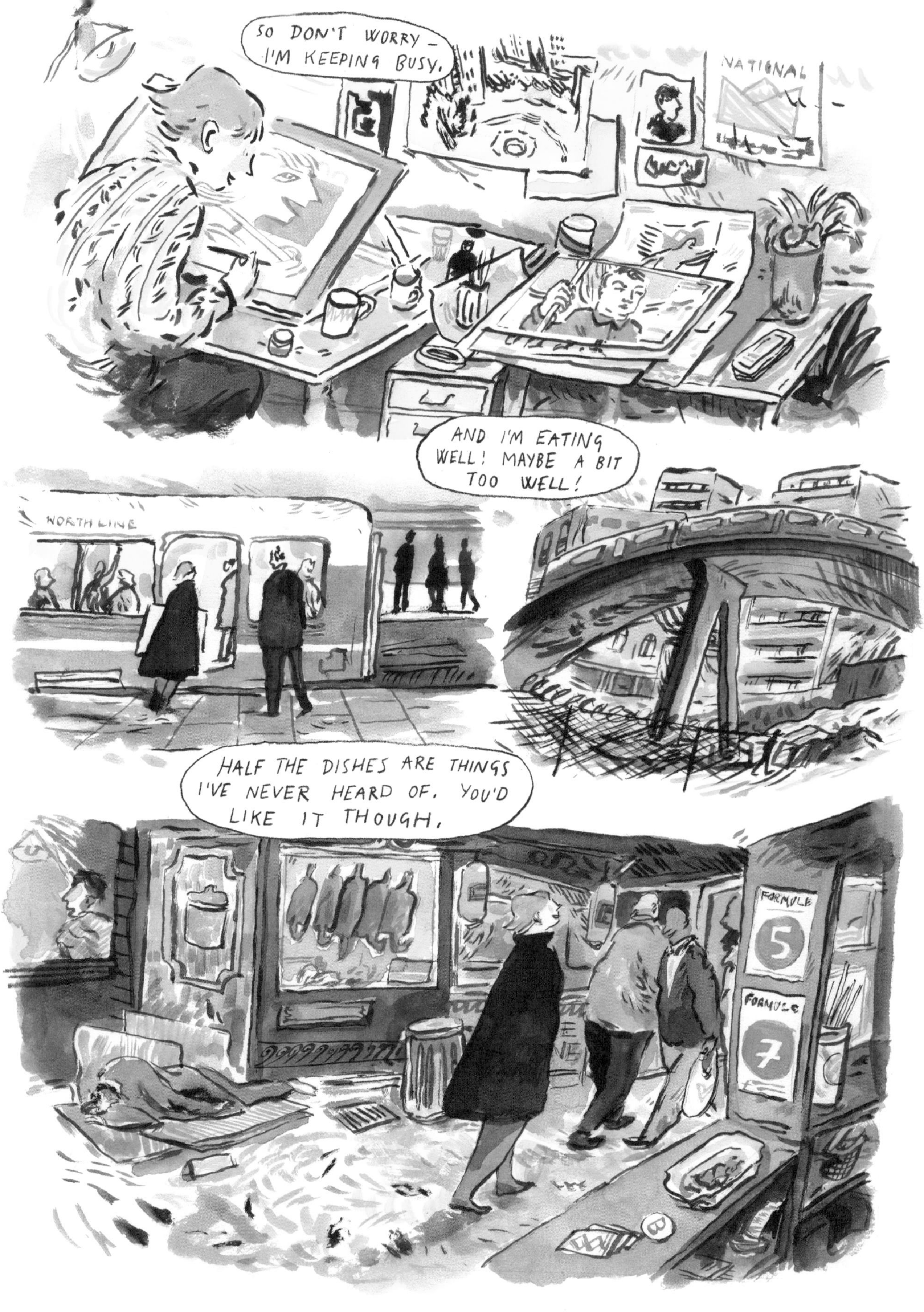
SO DON'T WORRY – I'M KEEPING BUSY.
NATIONAL
AND I'M EATING WELL! MAYBE A BIT TOO WELL!
NORTH LINE
HALF THE DISHES ARE THINGS I'VE NEVER HEARD OF. YOU'D LIKE IT THOUGH.
FORMULE 5
FORMULE 7

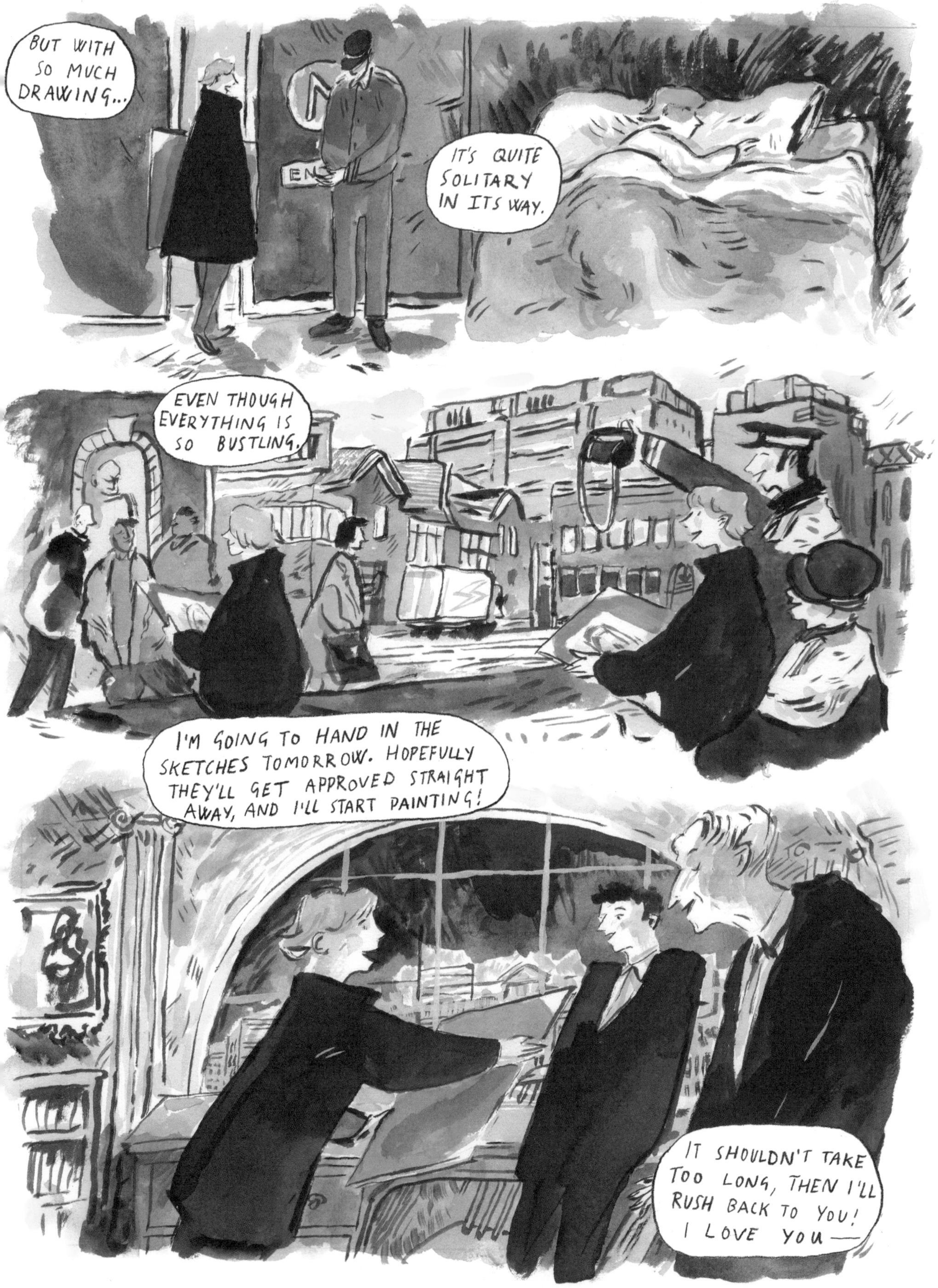
BUT WITH SO MUCH DRAWING...
EN
IT'S QUITE SOLITARY IN ITS WAY.
EVEN THOUGH EVERYTHING IS SO BUSTLING.
I'M GOING TO HAND IN THE SKETCHES TOMORROW. HOPEFULLY THEY'LL GET APPROVED STRAIGHT AWAY, AND I'LL START PAINTING!
IT SHOULDN'T TAKE TOO LONG, THEN I'LL RUSH BACK TO YOU! I LOVE YOU—

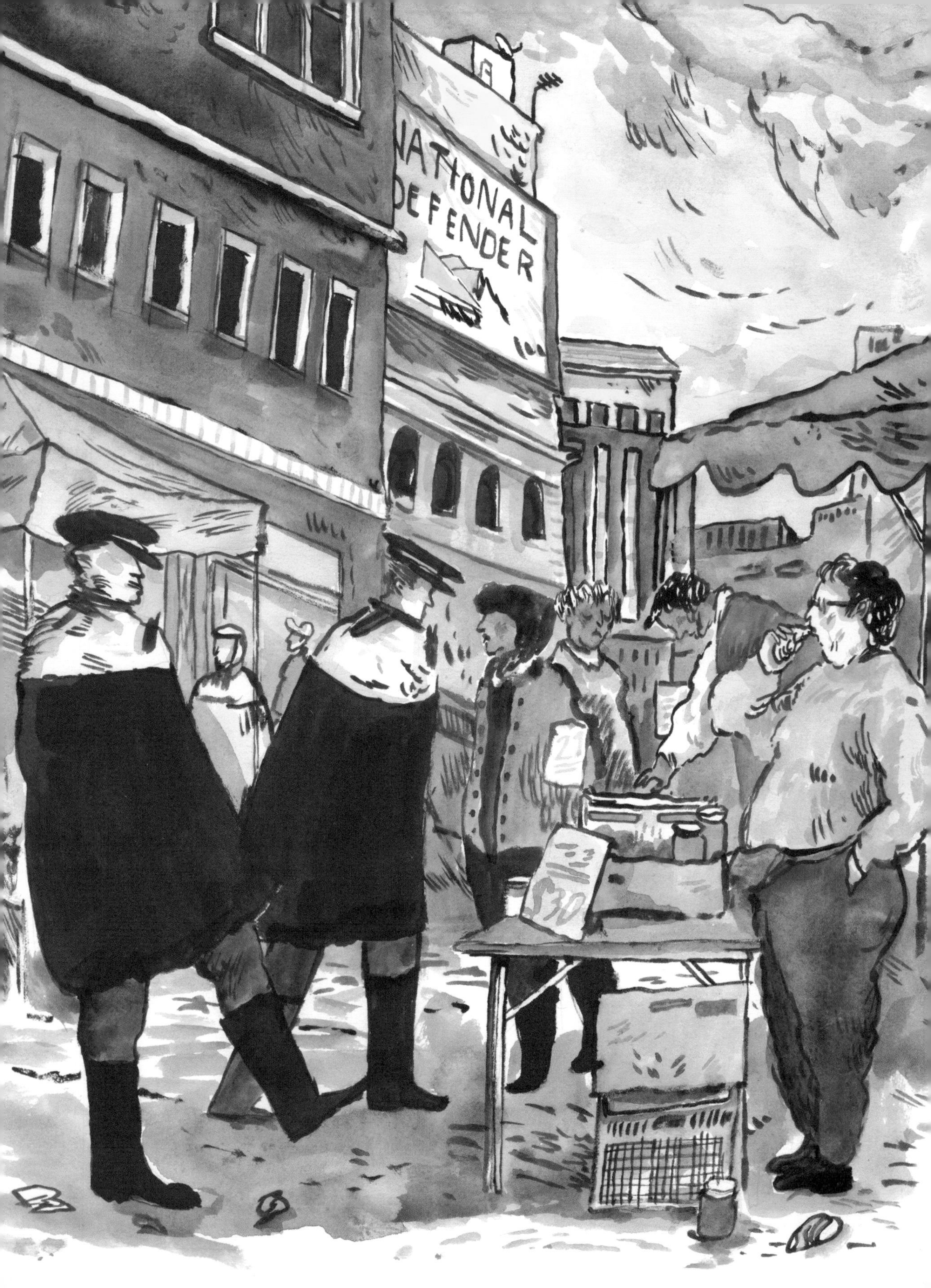
NATIONAL
DEFENDER
21
$30

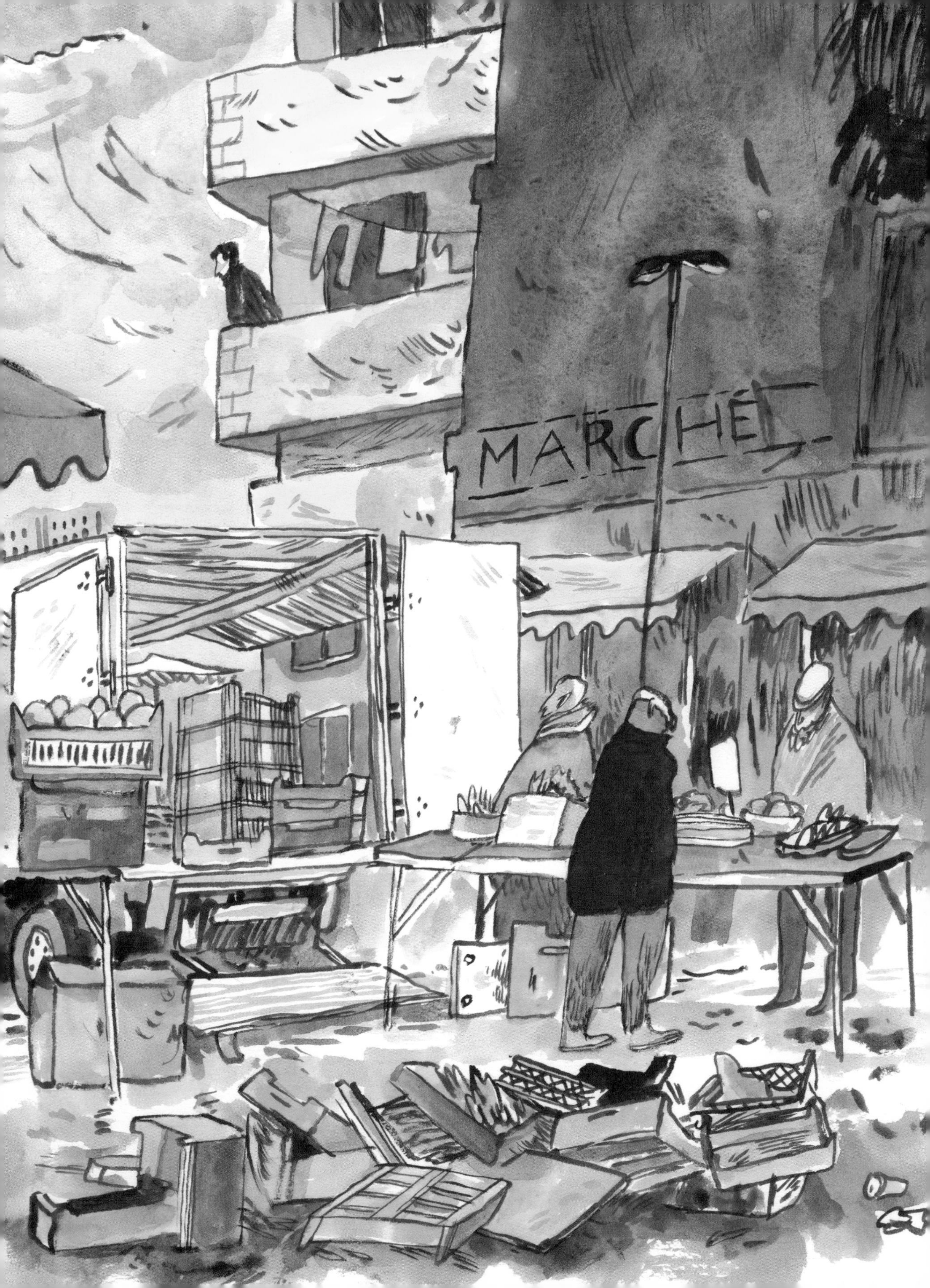
MARCHE

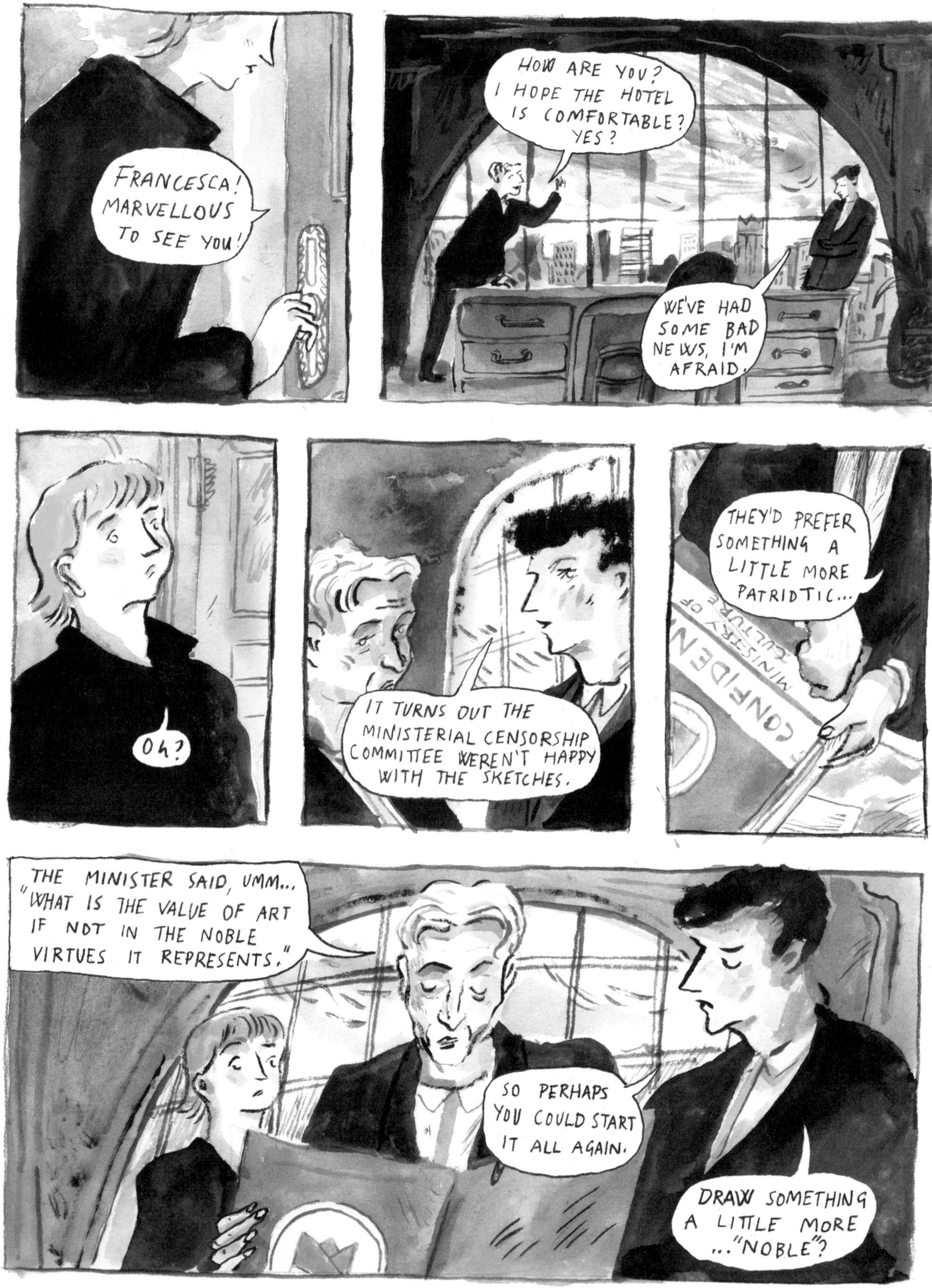
FRANCESCA! MARVELLOUS TO SEE YOU!
HOW ARE YOU? I HOPE THE HOTEL IS COMFORTABLE? YES?
WE'VE HAD SOME BAD NEWS, I'M AFRAID.
OH?
IT TURNS OUT THE MINISTERIAL CENSORSHIP COMMITTEE WEREN'T HAPPY WITH THE SKETCHES.
THEY'D PREFER SOMETHING A LITTLE MORE PATRIOTIC...
CONFIDEN
MINISTRY OF CULTURE
THE MINISTER SAID, UMM... "WHAT IS THE VALUE OF ART IF NOT IN THE NOBLE VIRTUES IT REPRESENTS."
SO PERHAPS YOU COULD START IT ALL AGAIN.
DRAW SOMETHING A LITTLE MORE ..."NOBLE"?

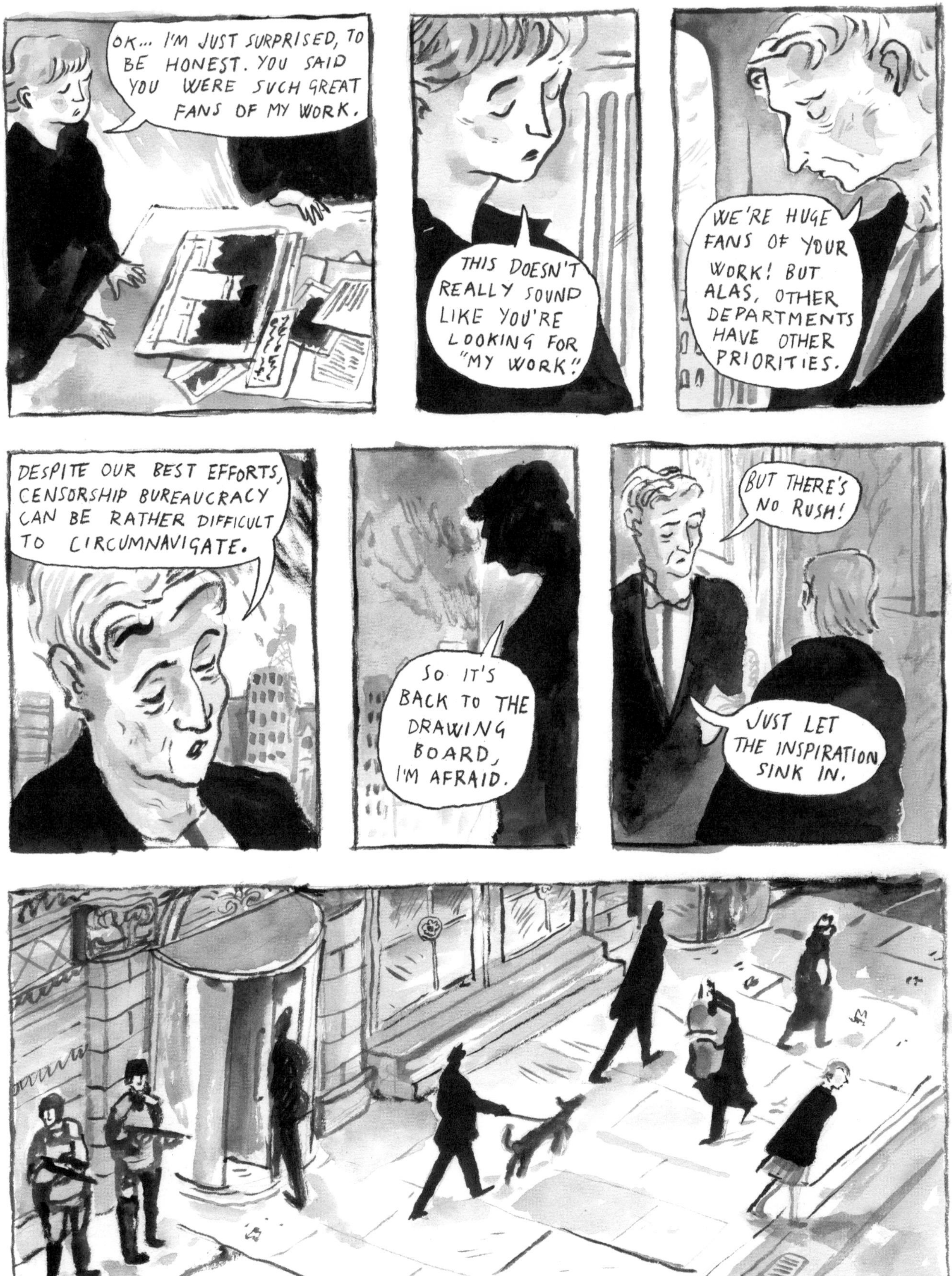
OK... I'M JUST SURPRISED, TO BE HONEST. YOU SAID YOU WERE SUCH GREAT FANS OF MY WORK.
THIS DOESN'T REALLY SOUND LIKE YOU'RE LOOKING FOR "MY WORK!"
WE'RE HUGE FANS OF YOUR WORK! BUT ALAS, OTHER DEPARTMENTS HAVE OTHER PRIORITIES.
DESPITE OUR BEST EFFORTS, CENSORSHIP BUREAUCRACY CAN BE RATHER DIFFICULT TO CIRCUMNAVIGATE.
SO IT'S BACK TO THE DRAWING BOARD, I'M AFRAID.
BUT THERE'S NO RUSH!
JUST LET THE INSPIRATION SINK IN.

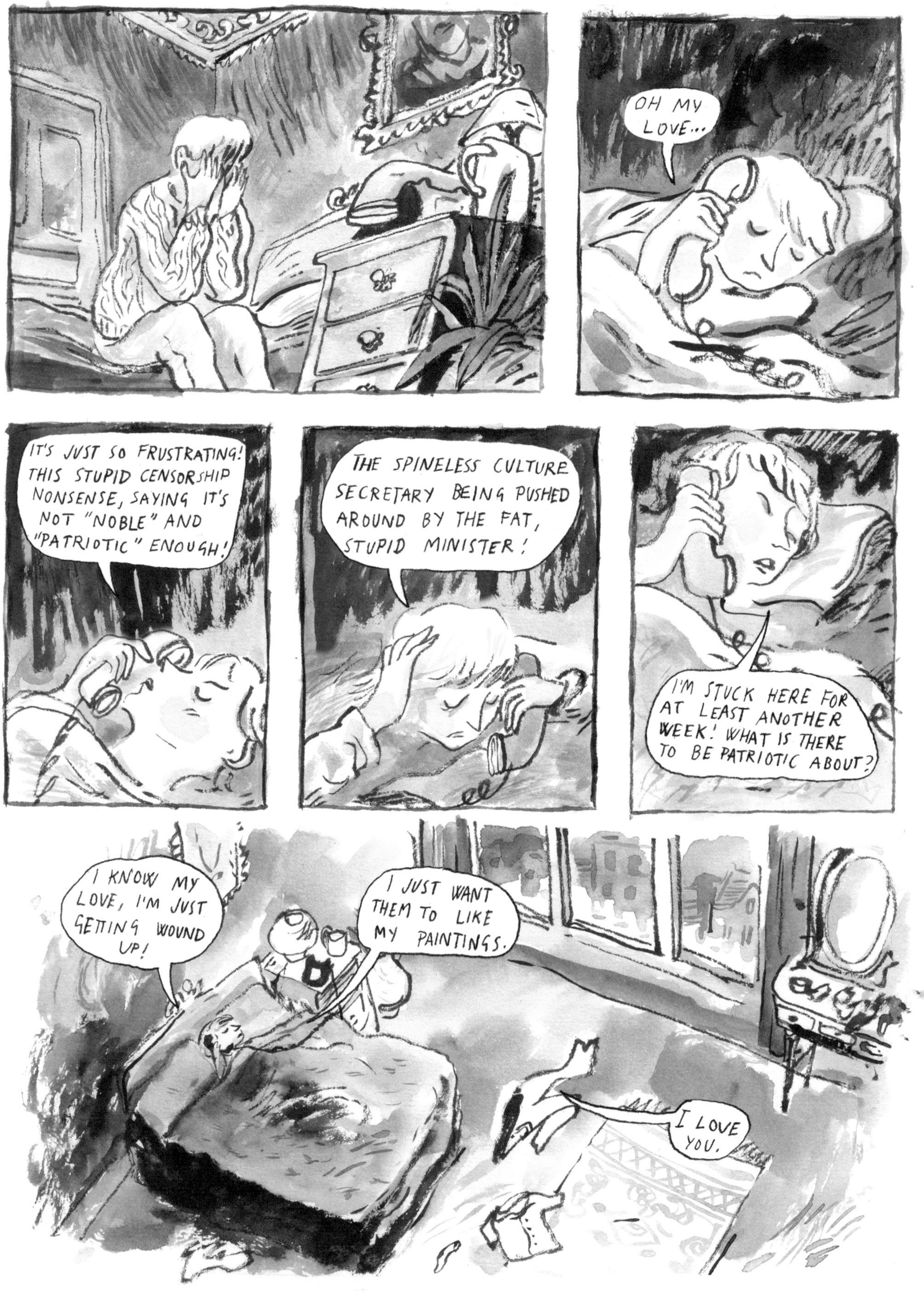
OH MY LOVE...
IT'S JUST SO FRUSTRATING! THIS STUPID CENSORSHIP NONSENSE, SAYING IT'S NOT "NOBLE" AND "PATRIOTIC" ENOUGH!
THE SPINELESS CULTURE SECRETARY BEING PUSHED AROUND BY THE FAT, STUPID MINISTER!
I'M STUCK HERE FOR AT LEAST ANOTHER WEEK! WHAT IS THERE TO BE PATRIOTIC ABOUT?
I KNOW MY LOVE, I'M JUST GETTING WOUND UP!
I JUST WANT THEM TO LIKE MY PAINTINGS.
I LOVE YOU.

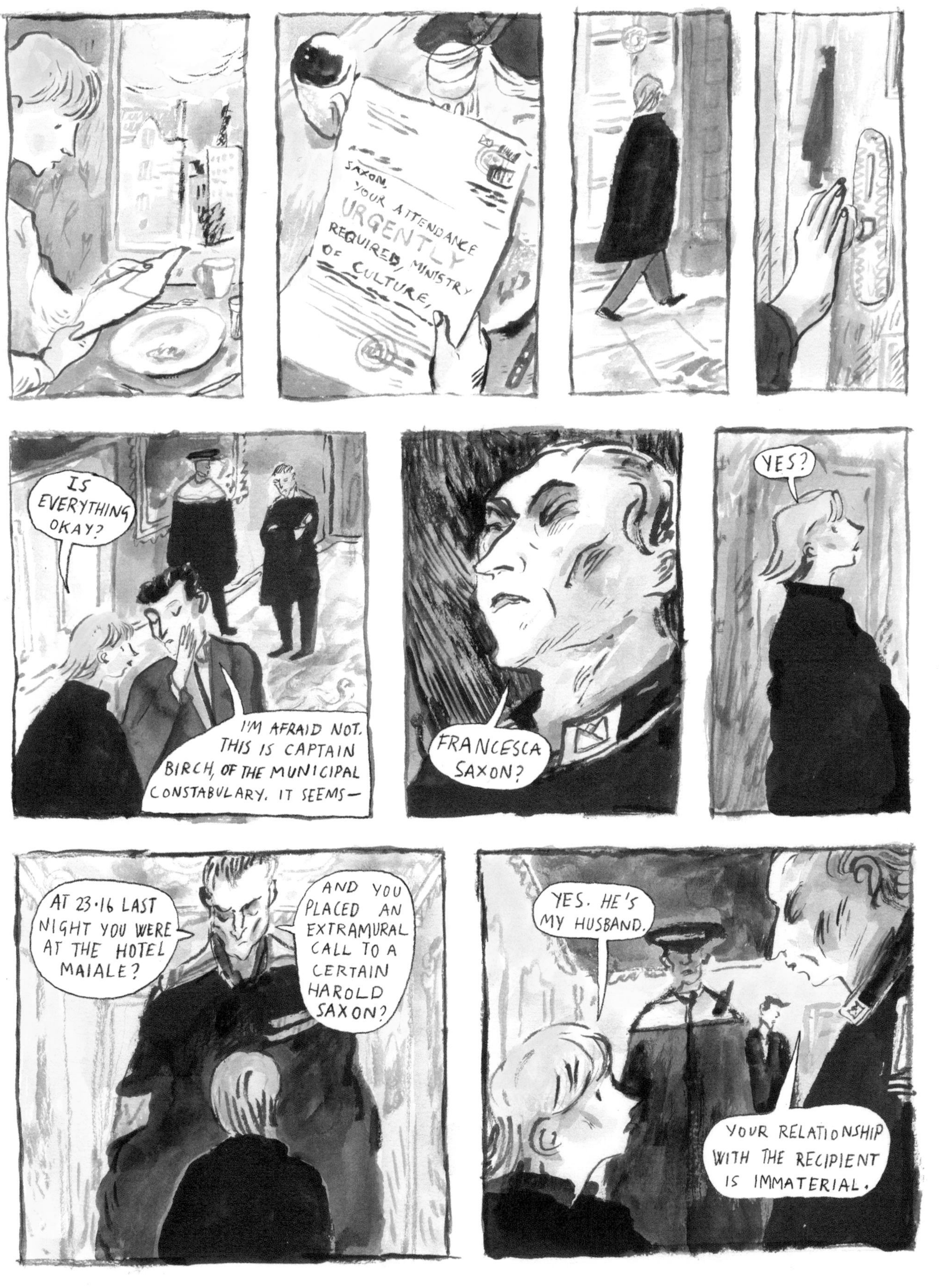
SAXON, YOUR ATTENDANCE URGENTLY REQUIRED, MINISTRY OF CULTURE.
IS EVERYTHING OKAY?
I'M AFRAID NOT. THIS IS CAPTAIN BIRCH, OF THE MUNICIPAL CONSTABULARY. IT SEEMS—
FRANCESCA SAXON?
YES?
AT 23·16 LAST NIGHT YOU WERE AT THE HOTEL MAIALE?
AND YOU PLACED AN EXTRAMURAL CALL TO A CERTAIN HAROLD SAXON?
YES. HE'S MY HUSBAND.
YOUR RELATIONSHIP WITH THE RECIPIENT IS IMMATERIAL.

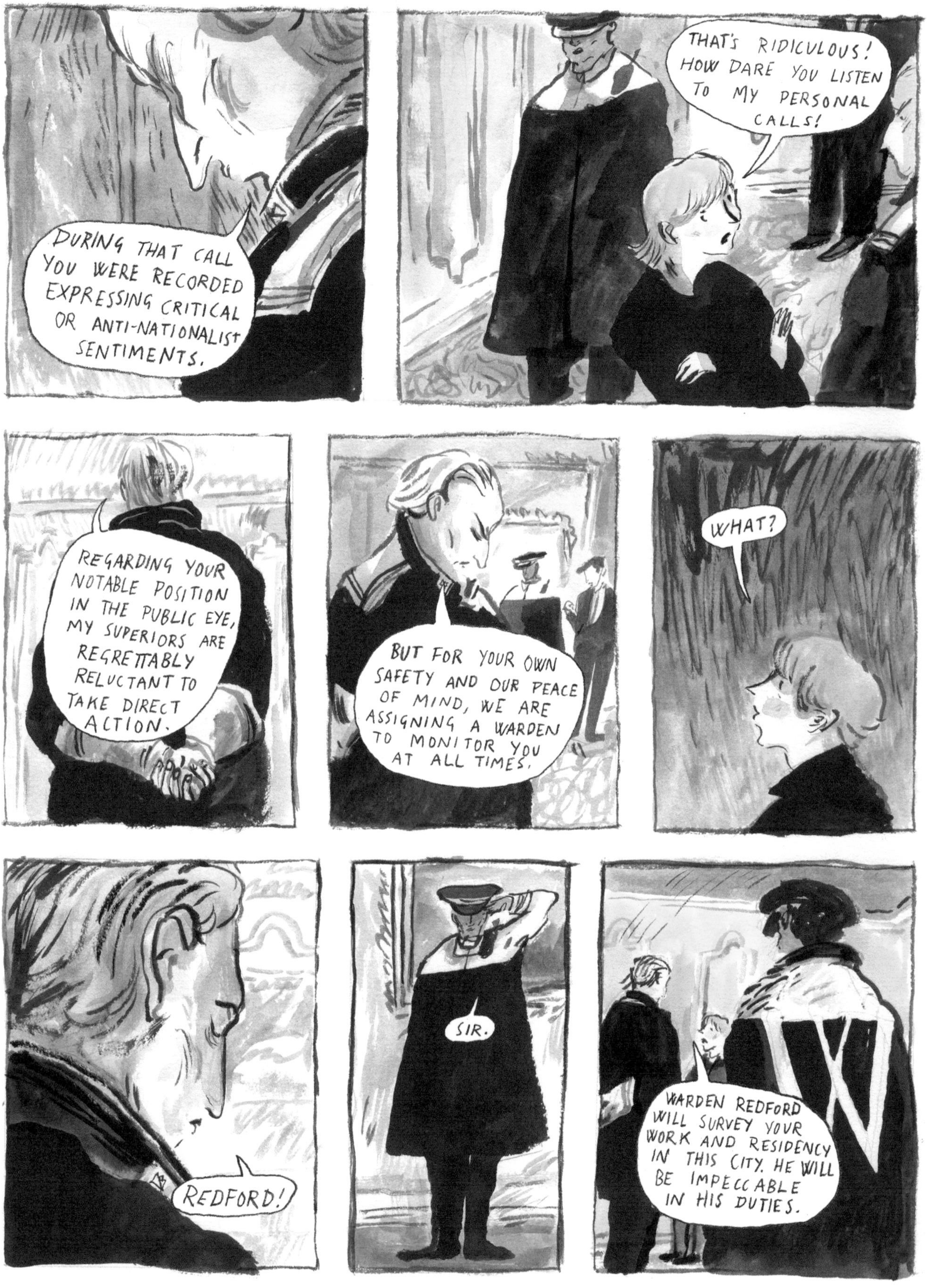
DURING THAT CALL YOU WERE RECORDED EXPRESSING CRITICAL OR ANTI-NATIONALIST SENTIMENTS.
THAT'S RIDICULOUS! HOW DARE YOU LISTEN TO MY PERSONAL CALLS!
REGARDING YOUR NOTABLE POSITION IN THE PUBLIC EYE, MY SUPERIORS ARE REGRETTABLY RELUCTANT TO TAKE DIRECT ACTION.
BUT FOR YOUR OWN SAFETY AND OUR PEACE OF MIND, WE ARE ASSIGNING A WARDEN TO MONITOR YOU AT ALL TIMES.
WHAT?
REDFORD!
SIR.
WARDEN REDFORD WILL SURVEY YOUR WORK AND RESIDENCY IN THIS CITY. HE WILL BE IMPECCABLE IN HIS DUTIES.

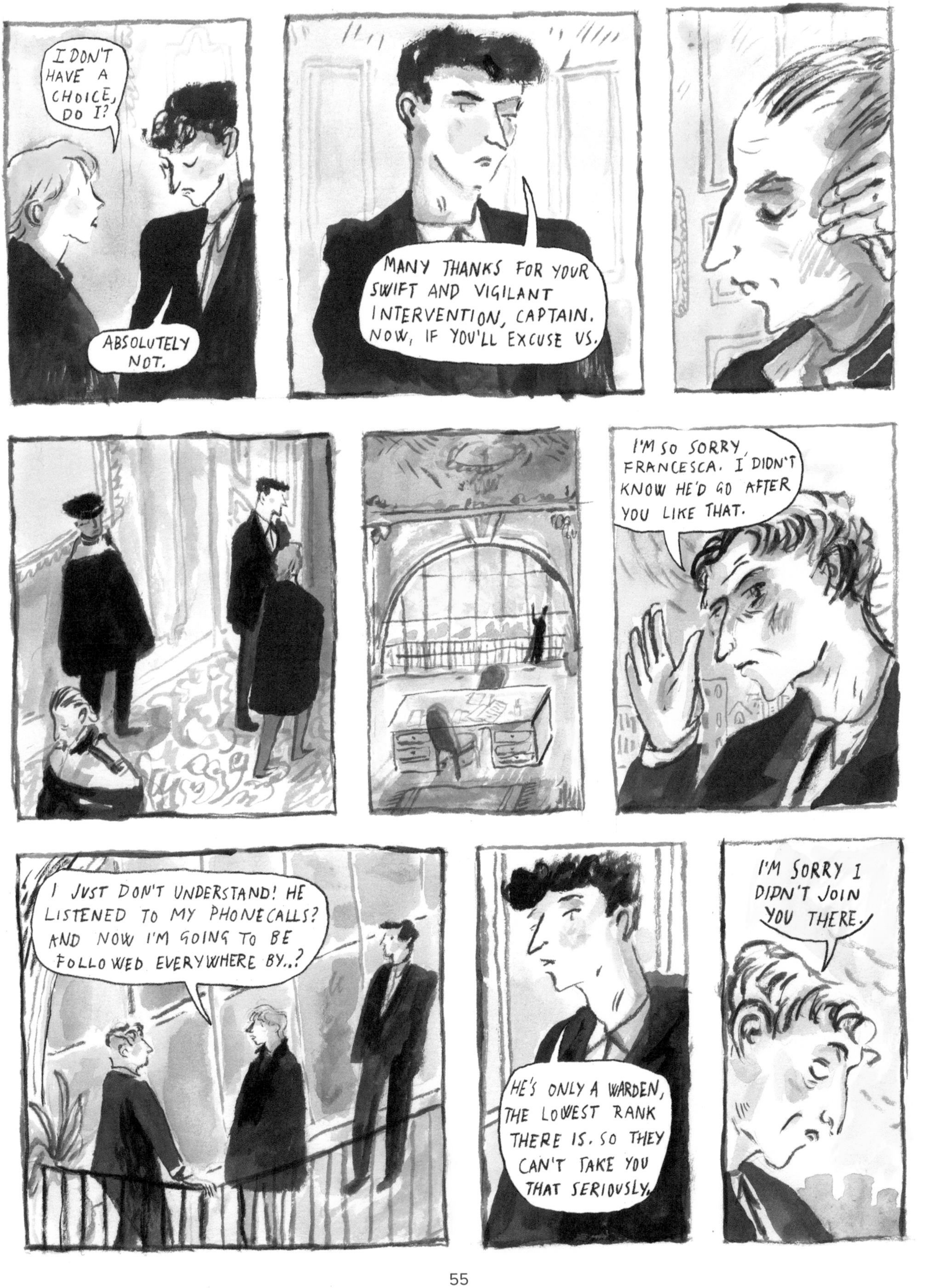
I DON'T HAVE A CHOICE, DO I?
ABSOLUTELY NOT.
MANY THANKS FOR YOUR SWIFT AND VIGILANT INTERVENTION, CAPTAIN. NOW, IF YOU'LL EXCUSE US.
I'M SO SORRY, FRANCESCA. I DIDN'T KNOW HE'D GO AFTER YOU LIKE THAT.
I JUST DON'T UNDERSTAND! HE LISTENED TO MY PHONECALLS? AND NOW I'M GOING TO BE FOLLOWED EVERYWHERE BY..?
HE'S ONLY A WARDEN, THE LOWEST RANK THERE IS. SO THEY CAN'T TAKE YOU THAT SERIOUSLY.
I'M SORRY I DIDN'T JOIN YOU THERE.

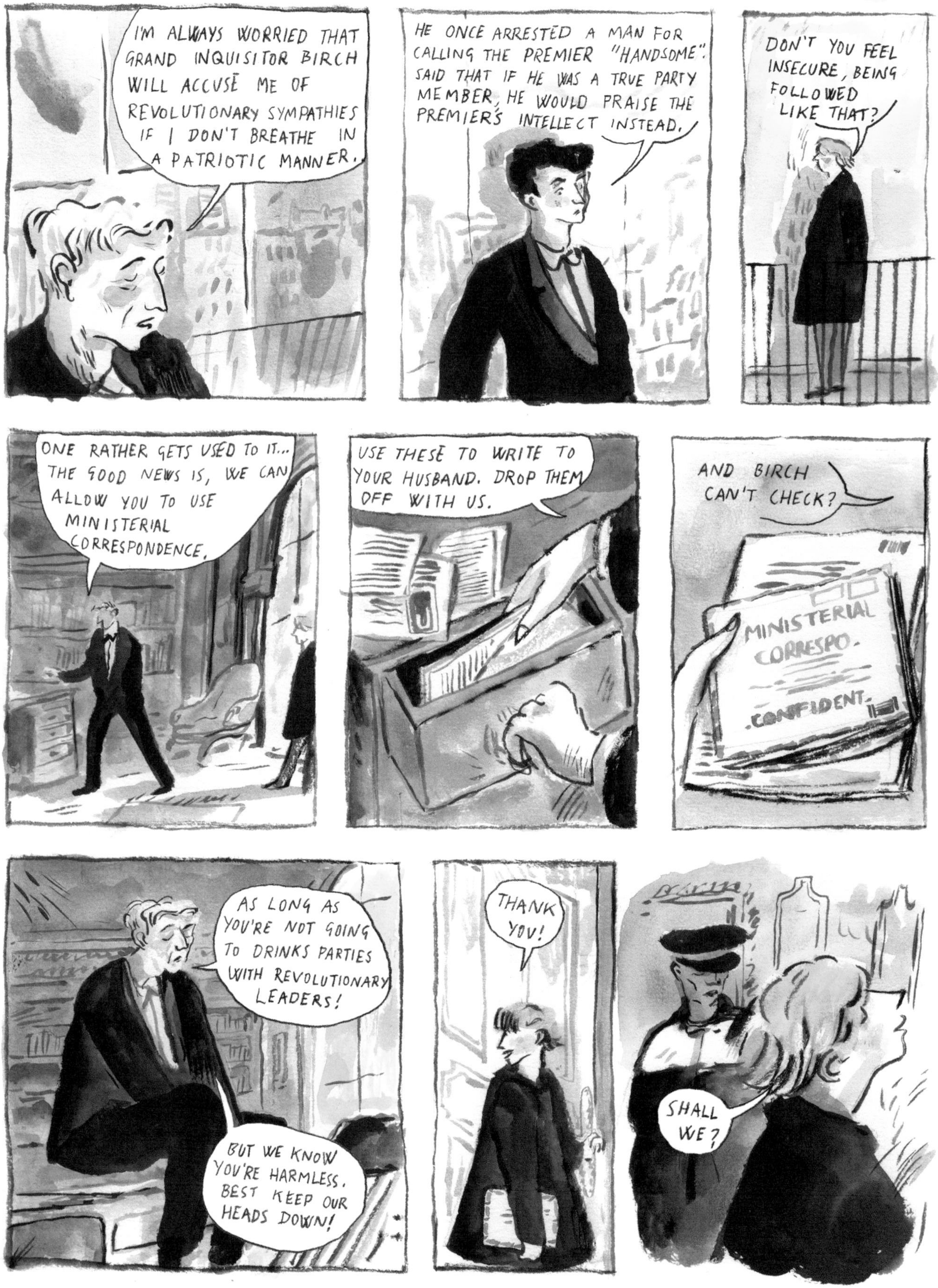
I'M ALWAYS WORRIED THAT GRAND INQUISITOR BIRCH WILL ACCUSE ME OF REVOLUTIONARY SYMPATHIES IF I DON'T BREATHE IN A PATRIOTIC MANNER.
HE ONCE ARRESTED A MAN FOR CALLING THE PREMIER "HANDSOME". SAID THAT IF HE WAS A TRUE PARTY MEMBER, HE WOULD PRAISE THE PREMIER'S INTELLECT INSTEAD.
DON'T YOU FEEL INSECURE, BEING FOLLOWED LIKE THAT?
ONE RATHER GETS USED TO IT... THE GOOD NEWS IS, WE CAN ALLOW YOU TO USE MINISTERIAL CORRESPONDENCE.
USE THESE TO WRITE TO YOUR HUSBAND. DROP THEM OFF WITH US.
AND BIRCH CAN'T CHECK?
MINISTERIAL CORRESPO
CONFIDENT
AS LONG AS YOU'RE NOT GOING TO DRINKS PARTIES WITH REVOLUTIONARY LEADERS!
BUT WE KNOW YOU'RE HARMLESS. BEST KEEP OUR HEADS DOWN!
THANK YOU!
SHALL WE?

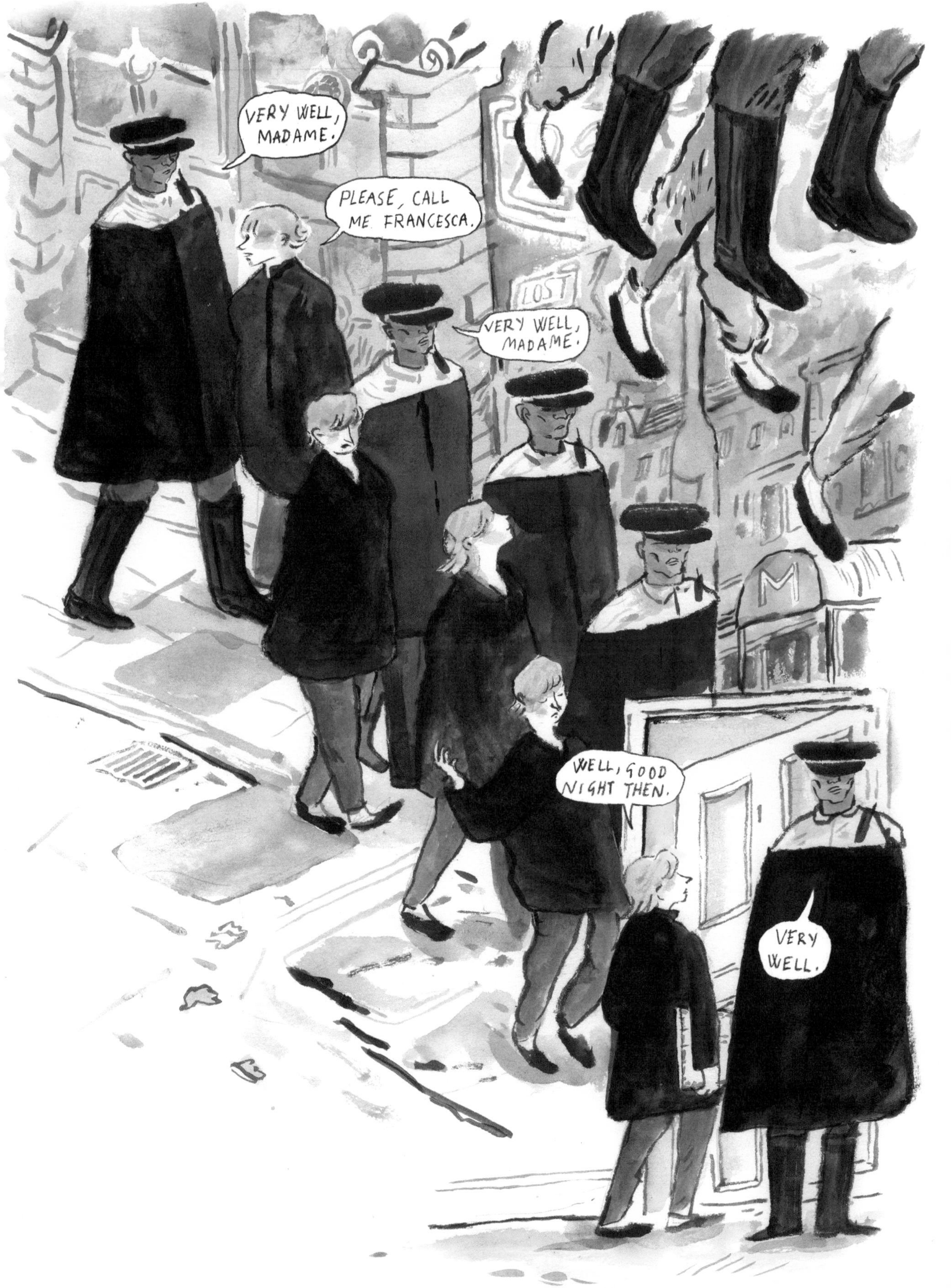
VERY WELL, MADAME.
PLEASE, CALL ME FRANCESCA.
LOST
VERY WELL, MADAME.
M
WELL, GOOD NIGHT THEN.
VERY WELL.

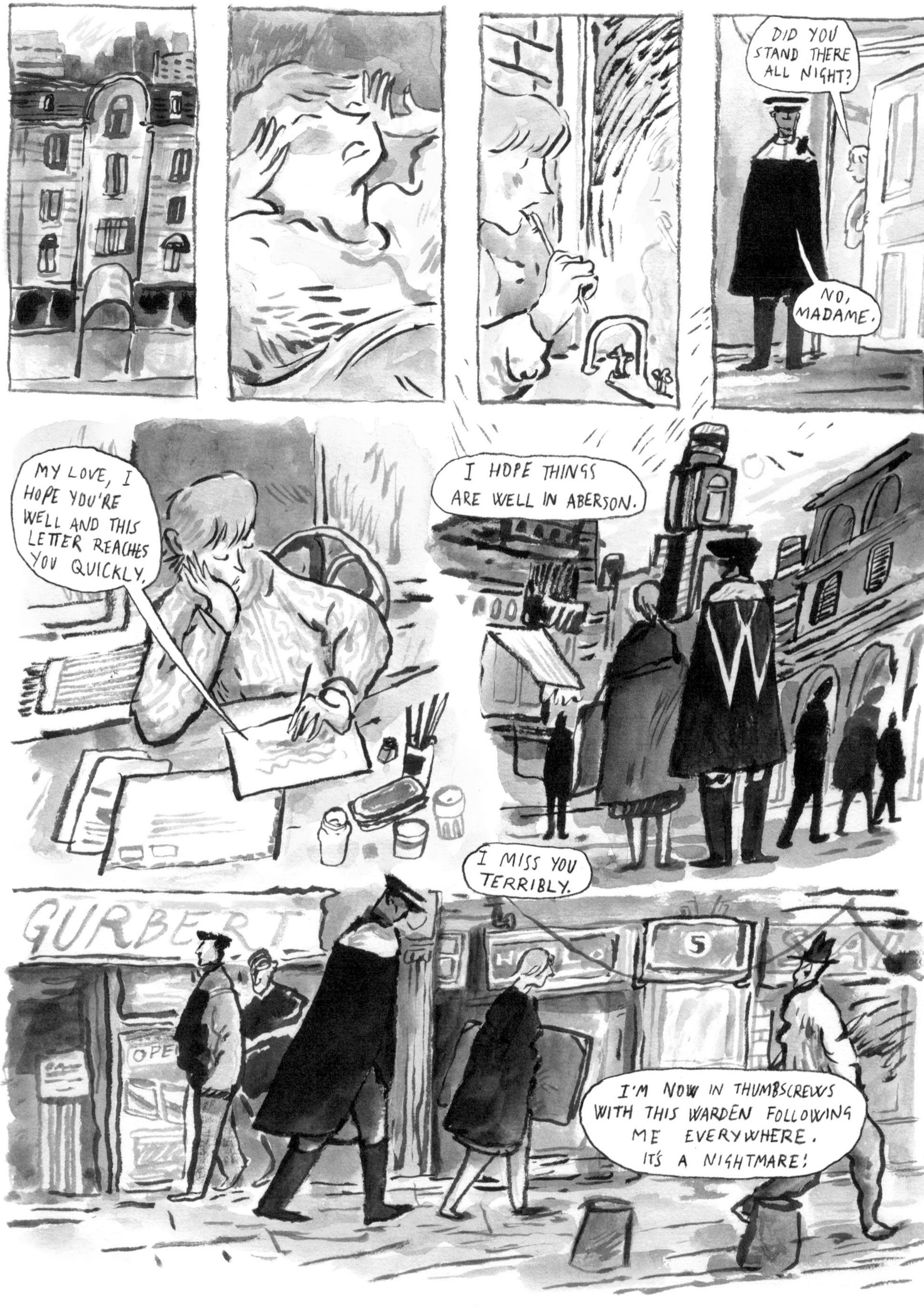
DID YOU STAND THERE ALL NIGHT?
NO, MADAME.
MY LOVE, I HOPE YOU'RE WELL AND THIS LETTER REACHES YOU QUICKLY.
I HOPE THINGS ARE WELL IN ABERSON.
I MISS YOU TERRIBLY.
GURBERT
OPE
5
I'M NOW IN THUMBSCREWS WITH THIS WARDEN FOLLOWING ME EVERYWHERE. IT'S A NIGHTMARE!

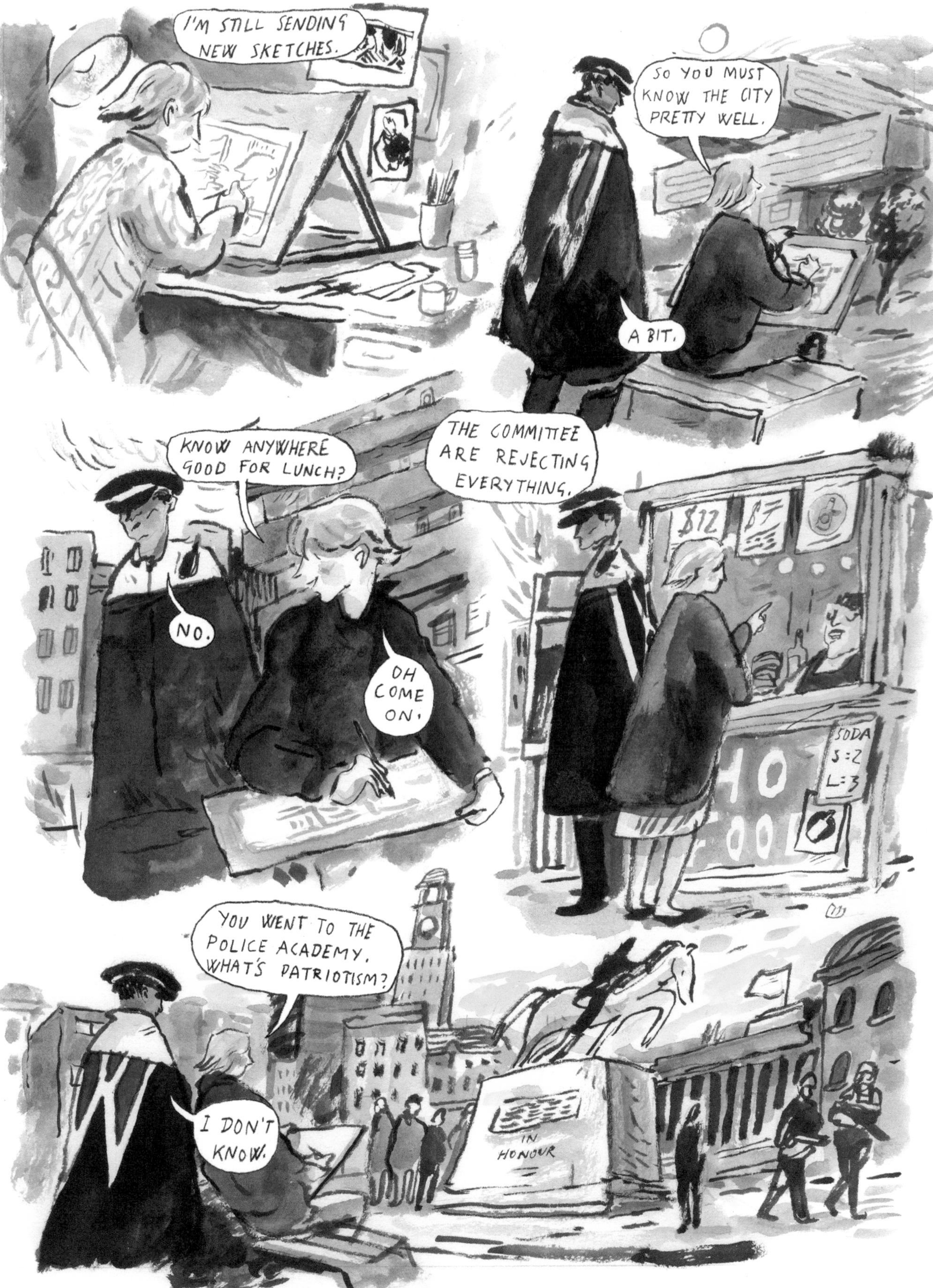
I'M STILL SENDING NEW SKETCHES.
SO YOU MUST KNOW THE CITY PRETTY WELL.
A BIT.
KNOW ANYWHERE GOOD FOR LUNCH?
NO.
OH COME ON.
THE COMMITTEE ARE REJECTING EVERYTHING.
$12
SODA
S=2
L=3
YOU WENT TO THE POLICE ACADEMY. WHAT'S PATRIOTISM?
I DON'T KNOW.
IN HONOUR

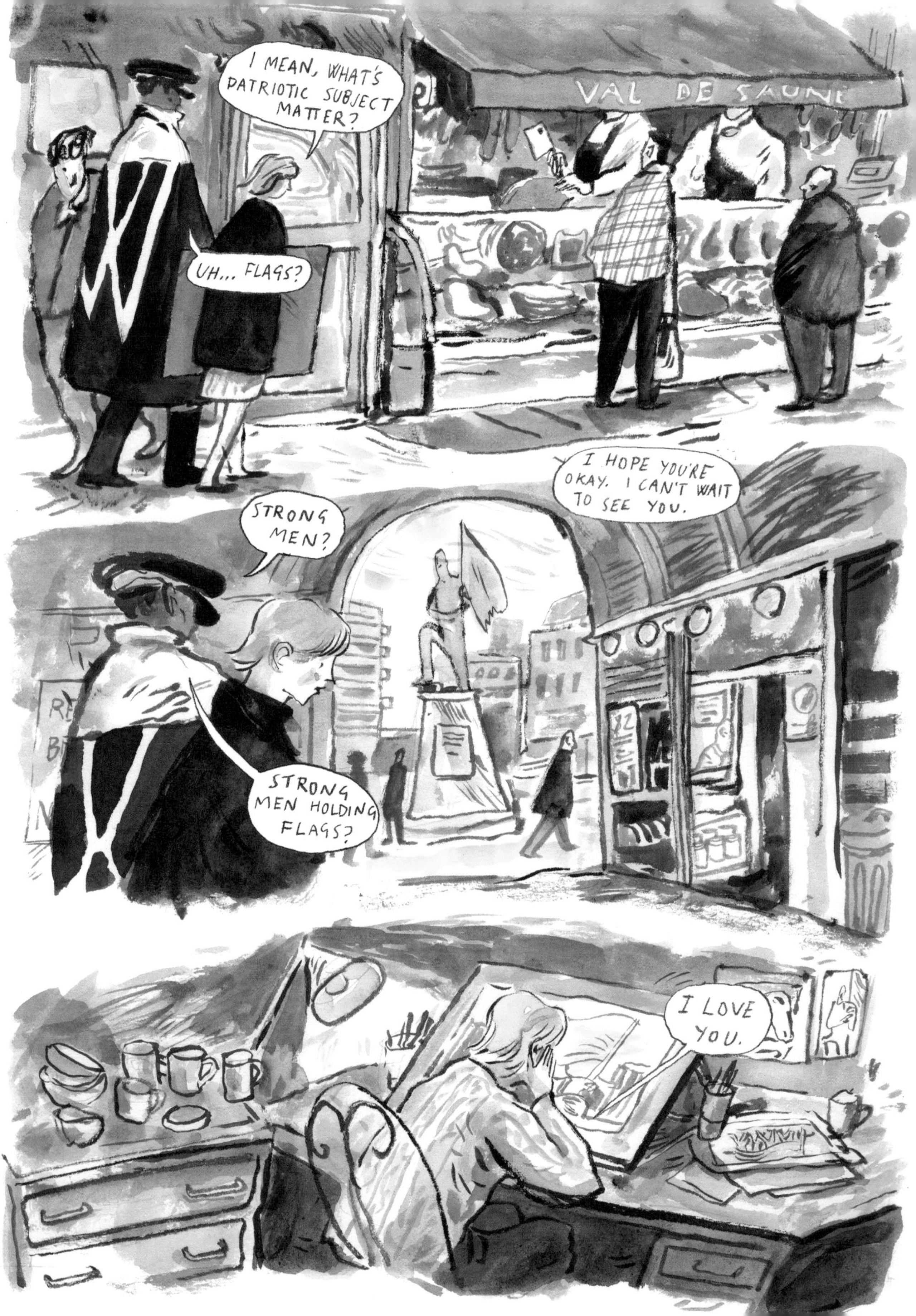
I MEAN, WHAT'S PATRIOTIC SUBJECT MATTER?
VAL DE SAUNE
UH... FLAGS?
STRONG MEN?
I HOPE YOU'RE OKAY. I CAN'T WAIT TO SEE YOU.
STRONG MEN HOLDING FLAGS?
I LOVE YOU.

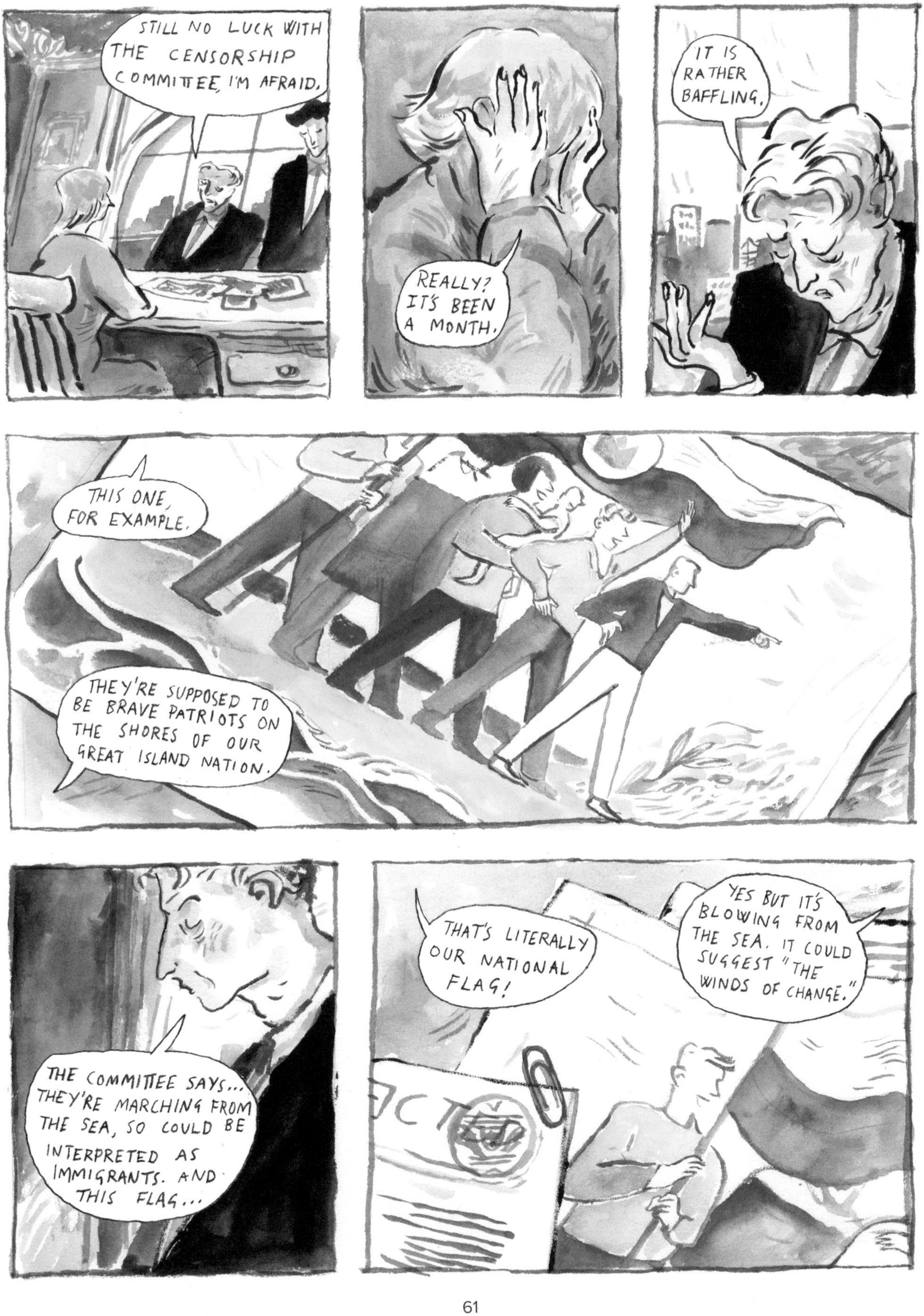
STILL NO LUCK WITH THE CENSORSHIP COMMITTEE, I'M AFRAID.
REALLY? IT'S BEEN A MONTH.
IT IS RATHER BAFFLING.
THIS ONE, FOR EXAMPLE.
THEY'RE SUPPOSED TO BE BRAVE PATRIOTS ON THE SHORES OF OUR GREAT ISLAND NATION.
THE COMMITTEE SAYS... THEY'RE MARCHING FROM THE SEA, SO COULD BE INTERPRETED AS IMMIGRANTS. AND THIS FLAG...
THAT'S LITERALLY OUR NATIONAL FLAG!
YES BUT IT'S BLOWING FROM THE SEA. IT COULD SUGGEST "THE WINDS OF CHANGE."

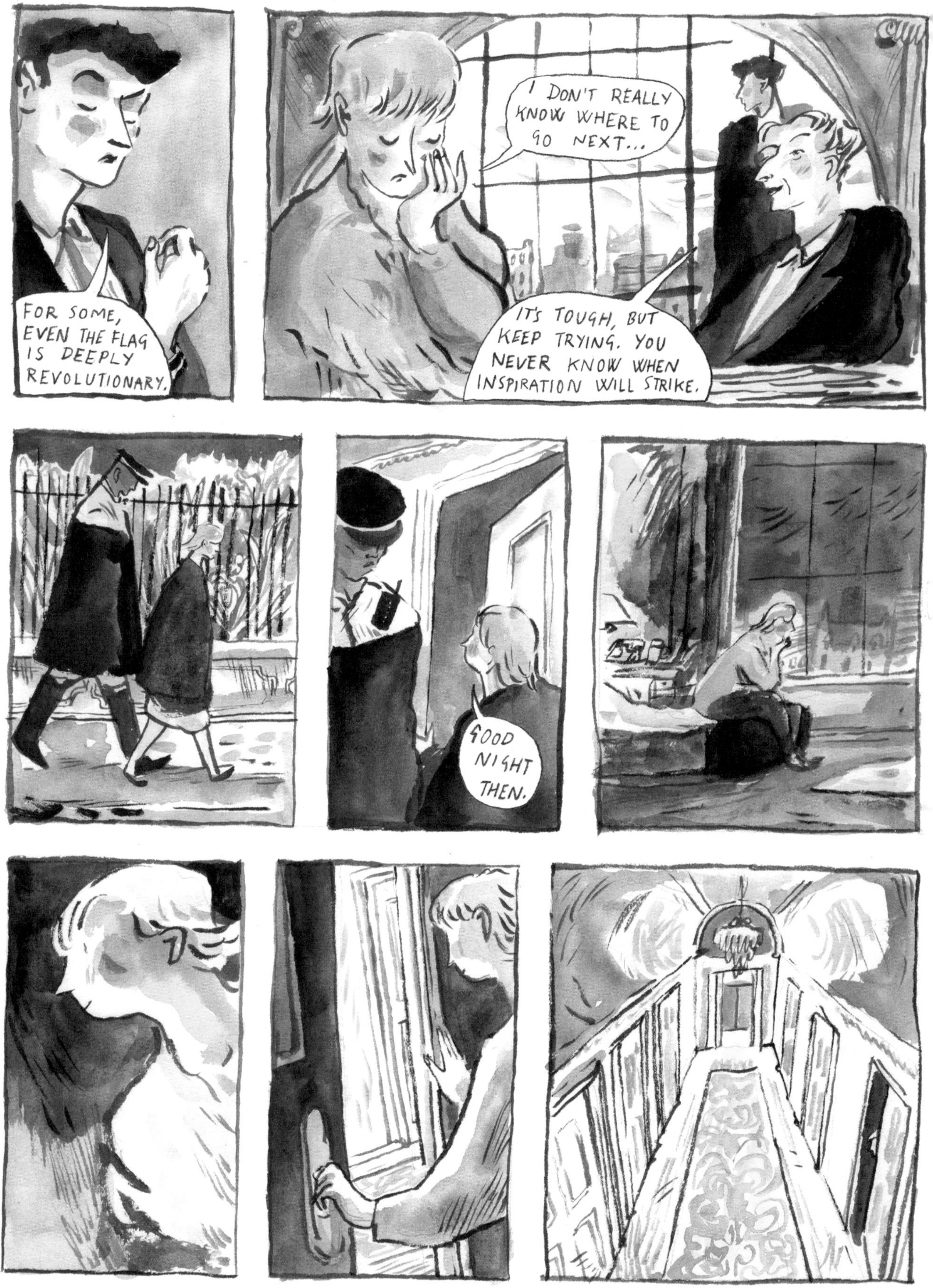
FOR SOME, EVEN THE FLAG IS DEEPLY REVOLUTIONARY.
I DON'T REALLY KNOW WHERE TO GO NEXT...
IT'S TOUGH, BUT KEEP TRYING. YOU NEVER KNOW WHEN INSPIRATION WILL STRIKE.
GOOD NIGHT THEN.

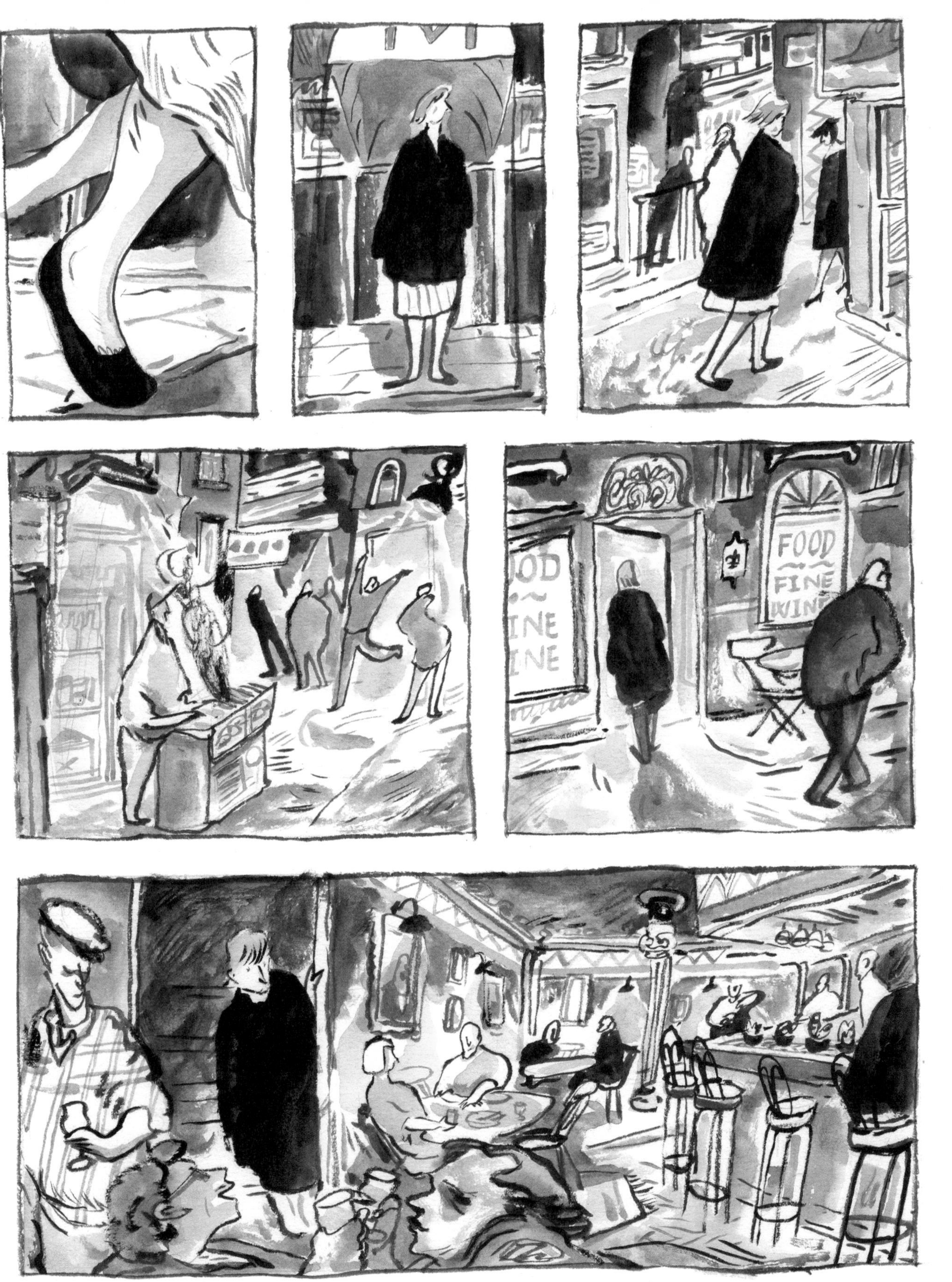
FOOD
FINE

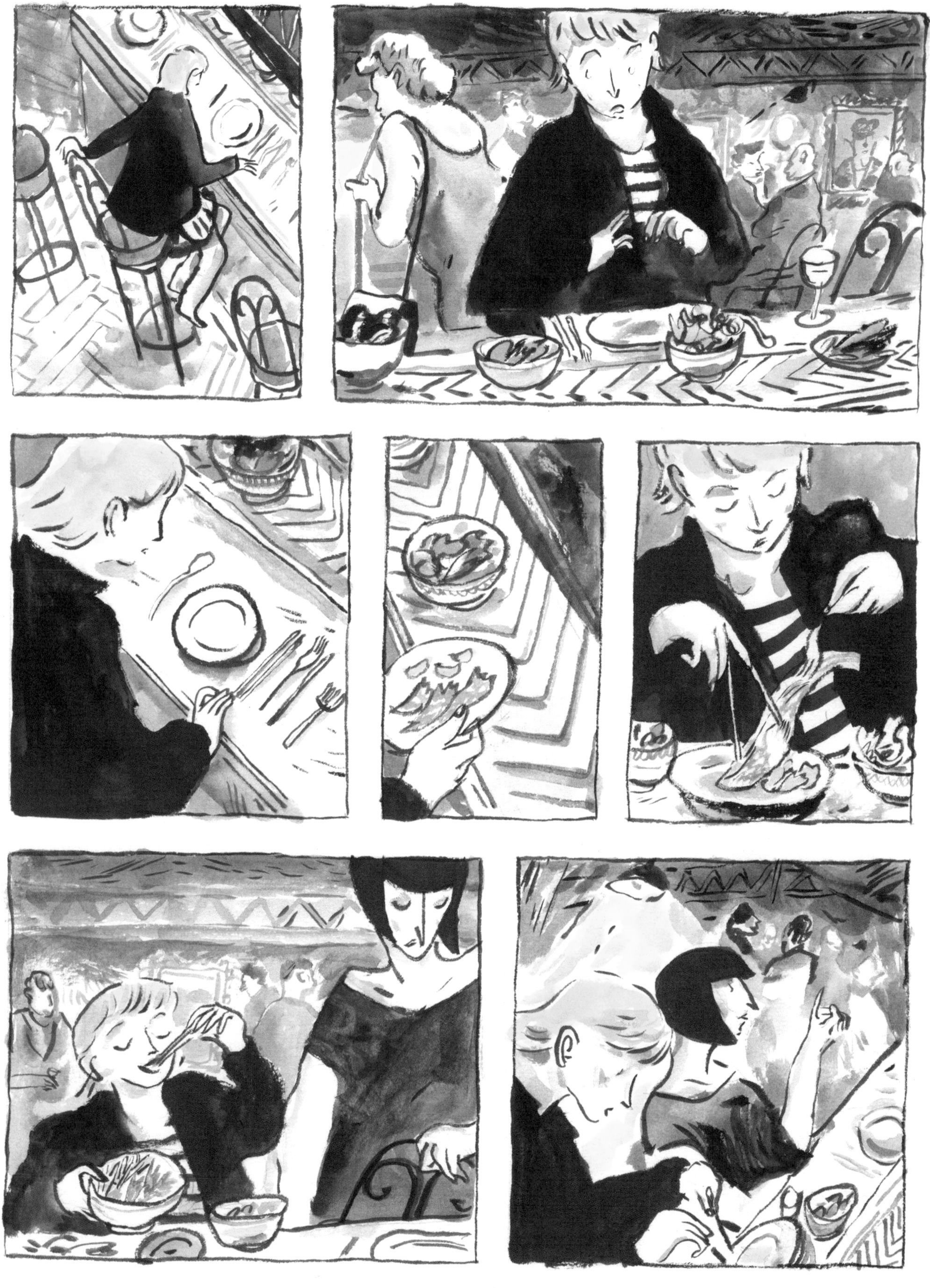

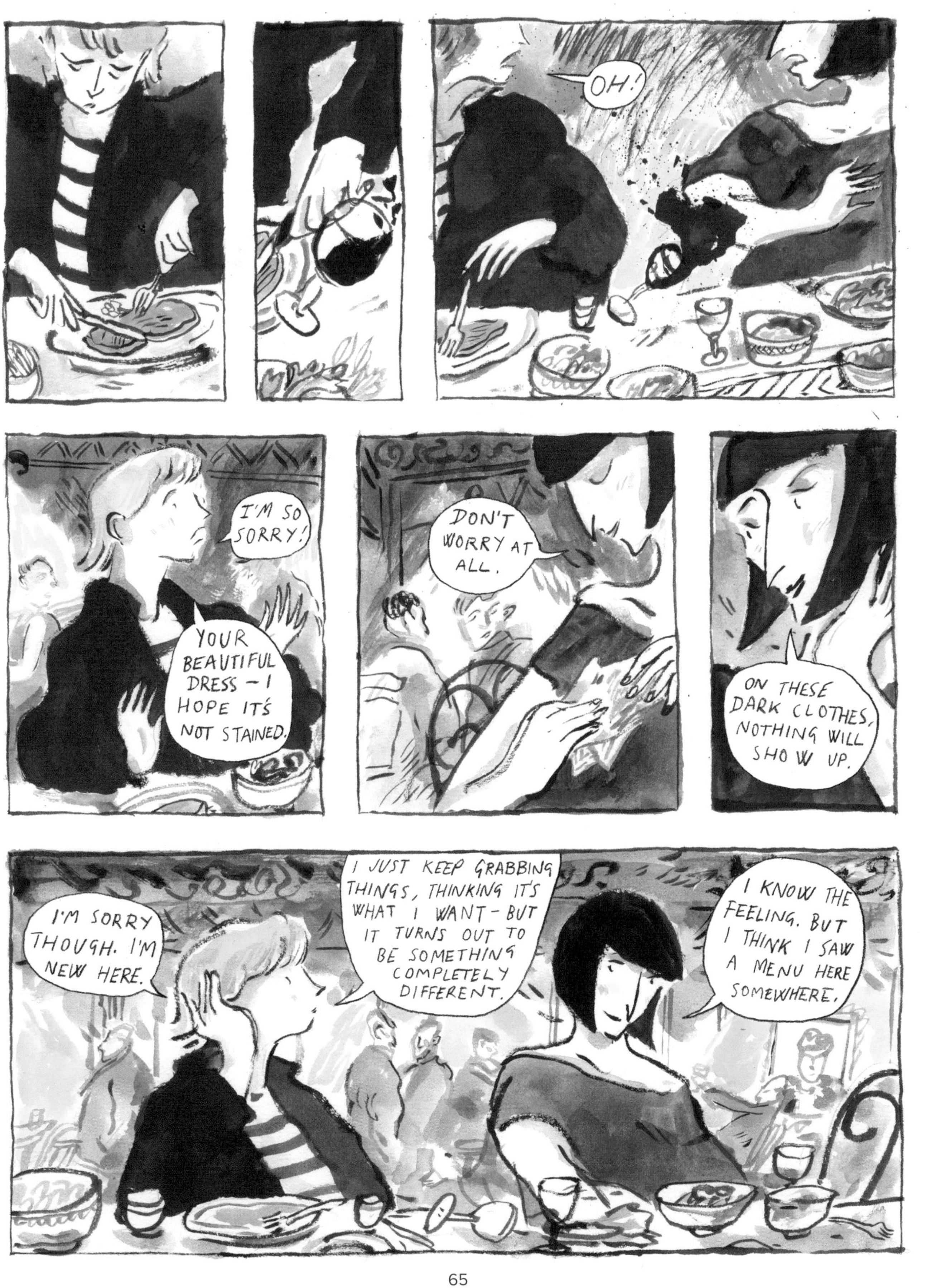
OH!
I'M SO SORRY!
YOUR BEAUTIFUL DRESS – I HOPE IT'S NOT STAINED.
DON'T WORRY AT ALL.
ON THESE DARK CLOTHES, NOTHING WILL SHOW UP.
I'M SORRY THOUGH. I'M NEW HERE.
I JUST KEEP GRABBING THINGS, THINKING IT'S WHAT I WANT – BUT IT TURNS OUT TO BE SOMETHING COMPLETELY DIFFERENT.
I KNOW THE FEELING. BUT I THINK I SAW A MENU HERE SOMEWHERE.

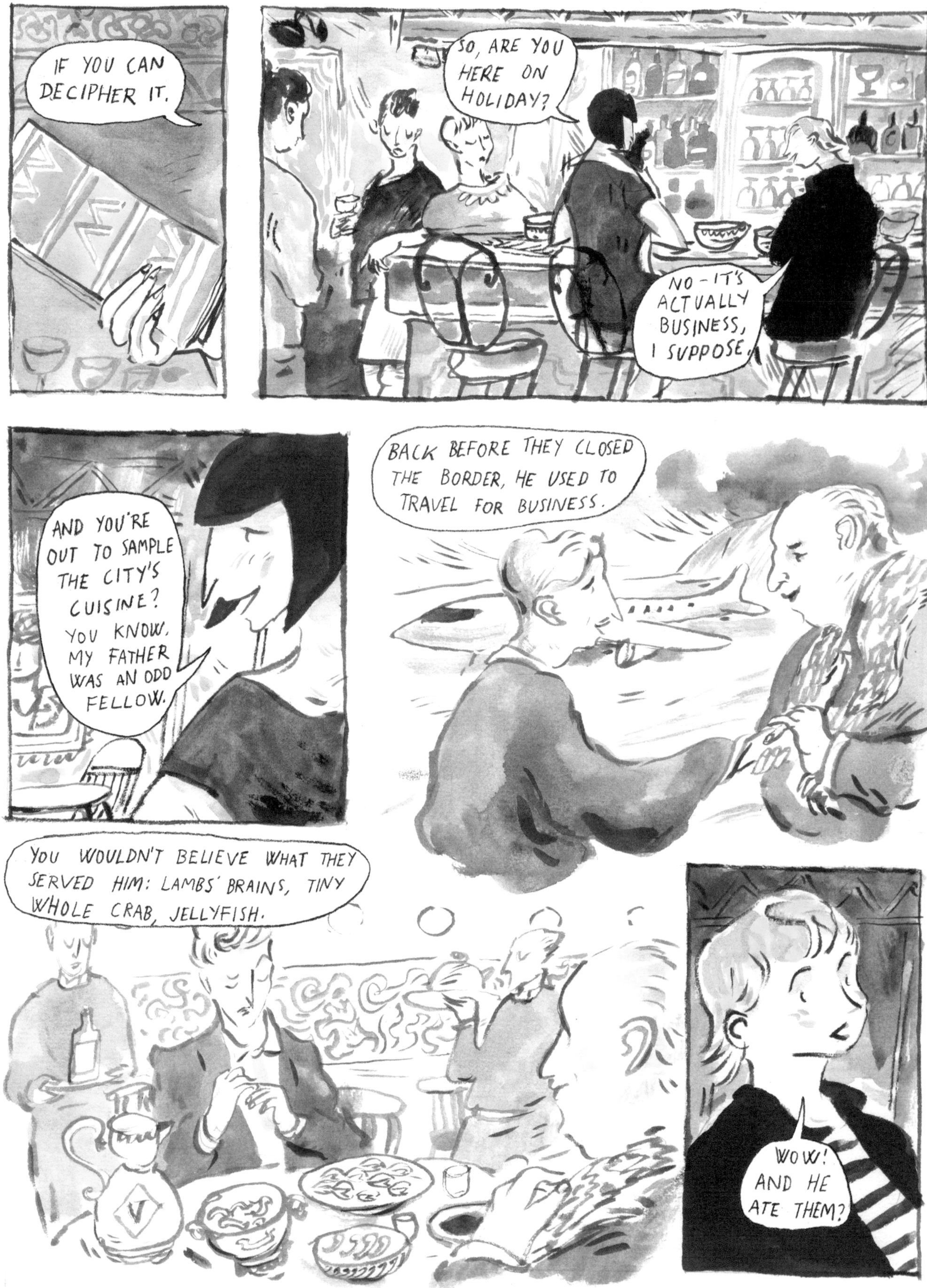
IF YOU CAN DECIPHER IT.
SO, ARE YOU HERE ON HOLIDAY?
NO - IT'S ACTUALLY BUSINESS, I SUPPOSE.
AND YOU'RE OUT TO SAMPLE THE CITY'S CUISINE? YOU KNOW, MY FATHER WAS AN ODD FELLOW.
BACK BEFORE THEY CLOSED THE BORDER, HE USED TO TRAVEL FOR BUSINESS.
YOU WOULDN'T BELIEVE WHAT THEY SERVED HIM: LAMBS' BRAINS, TINY WHOLE CRAB, JELLYFISH.
WOW! AND HE ATE THEM?

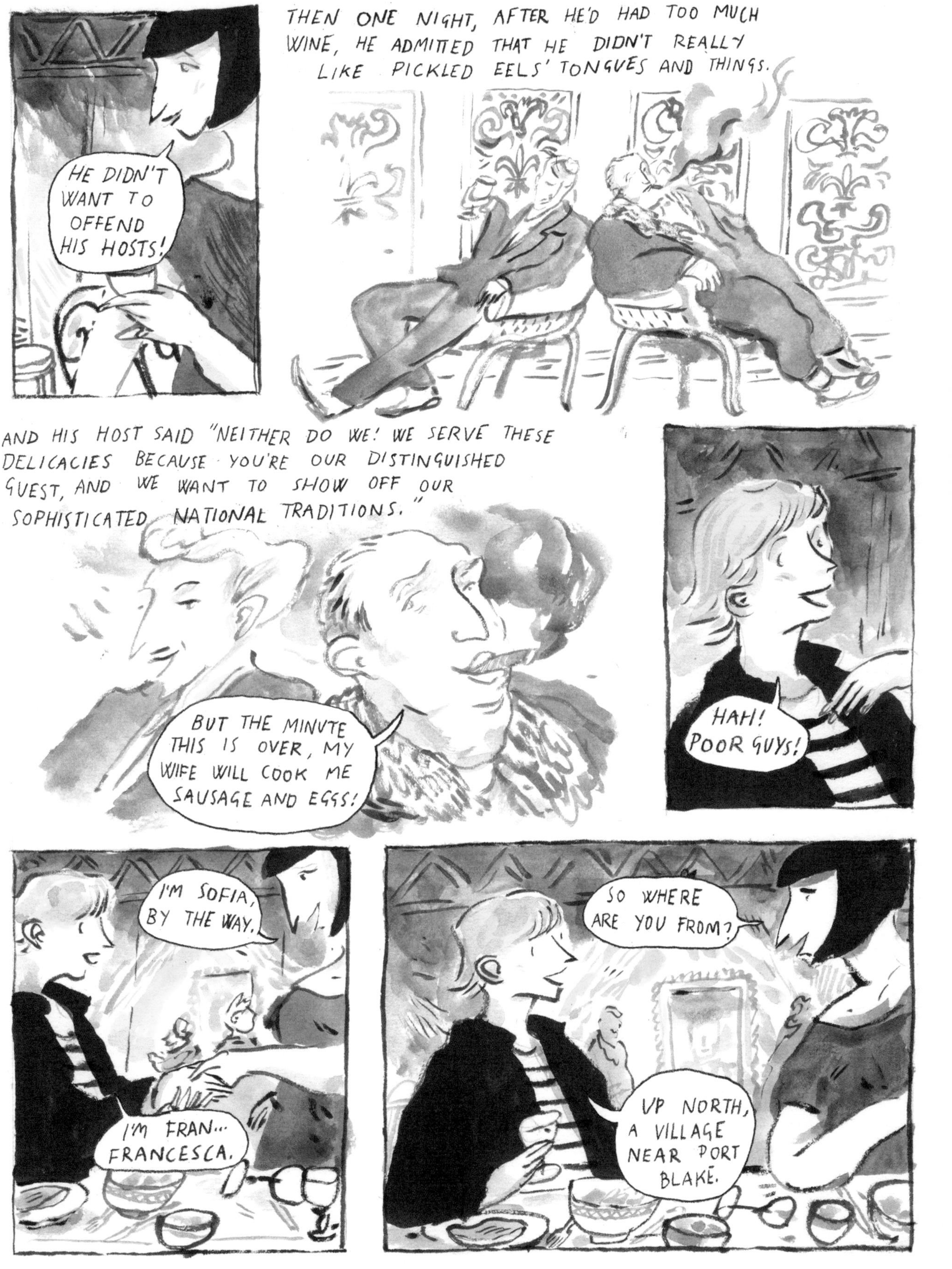
HE DIDN'T WANT TO OFFEND HIS HOSTS!
THEN ONE NIGHT, AFTER HE'D HAD TOO MUCH WINE, HE ADMITTED THAT HE DIDN'T REALLY LIKE PICKLED EELS' TONGUES AND THINGS.
AND HIS HOST SAID "NEITHER DO WE! WE SERVE THESE DELICACIES BECAUSE YOU'RE OUR DISTINGUISHED GUEST, AND WE WANT TO SHOW OFF OUR SOPHISTICATED NATIONAL TRADITIONS."
BUT THE MINUTE THIS IS OVER, MY WIFE WILL COOK ME SAUSAGE AND EGGS!
HAH! POOR GUYS!
I'M SOFIA, BY THE WAY.
I'M FRAN... FRANCESCA.
SO WHERE ARE YOU FROM?
UP NORTH, A VILLAGE NEAR PORT BLAKE.

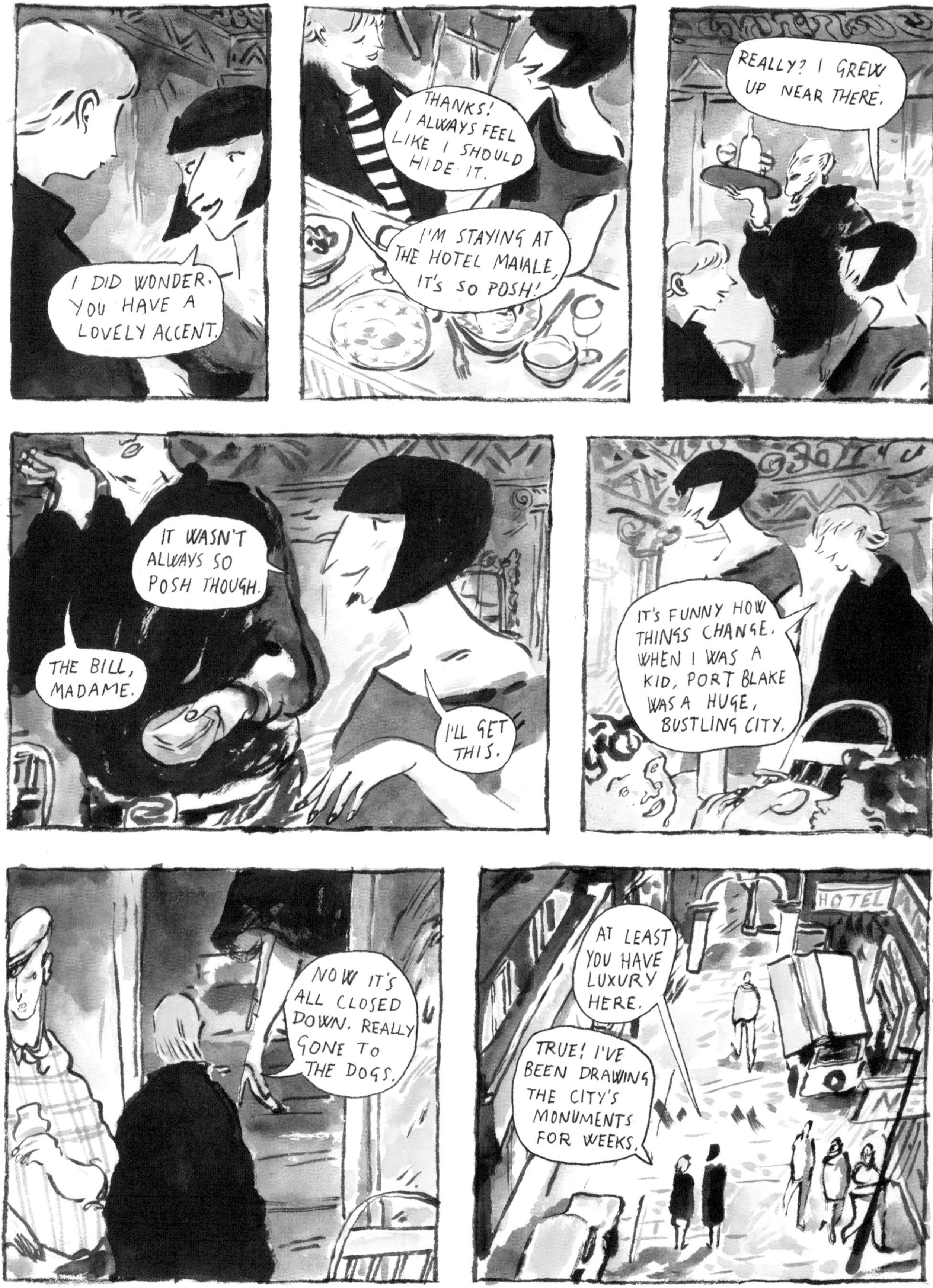
I DID WONDER. YOU HAVE A LOVELY ACCENT.
THANKS! I ALWAYS FEEL LIKE I SHOULD HIDE IT.
I'M STAYING AT THE HOTEL MAIALE, IT'S SO POSH!
REALLY? I GREW UP NEAR THERE.
IT WASN'T ALWAYS SO POSH THOUGH.
THE BILL, MADAME.
I'LL GET THIS.
IT'S FUNNY HOW THINGS CHANGE. WHEN I WAS A KID, PORT BLAKE WAS A HUGE, BUSTLING CITY.
NOW IT'S ALL CLOSED DOWN. REALLY GONE TO THE DOGS.
AT LEAST YOU HAVE LUXURY HERE.
TRUE! I'VE BEEN DRAWING THE CITY'S MONUMENTS FOR WEEKS.
HOTEL

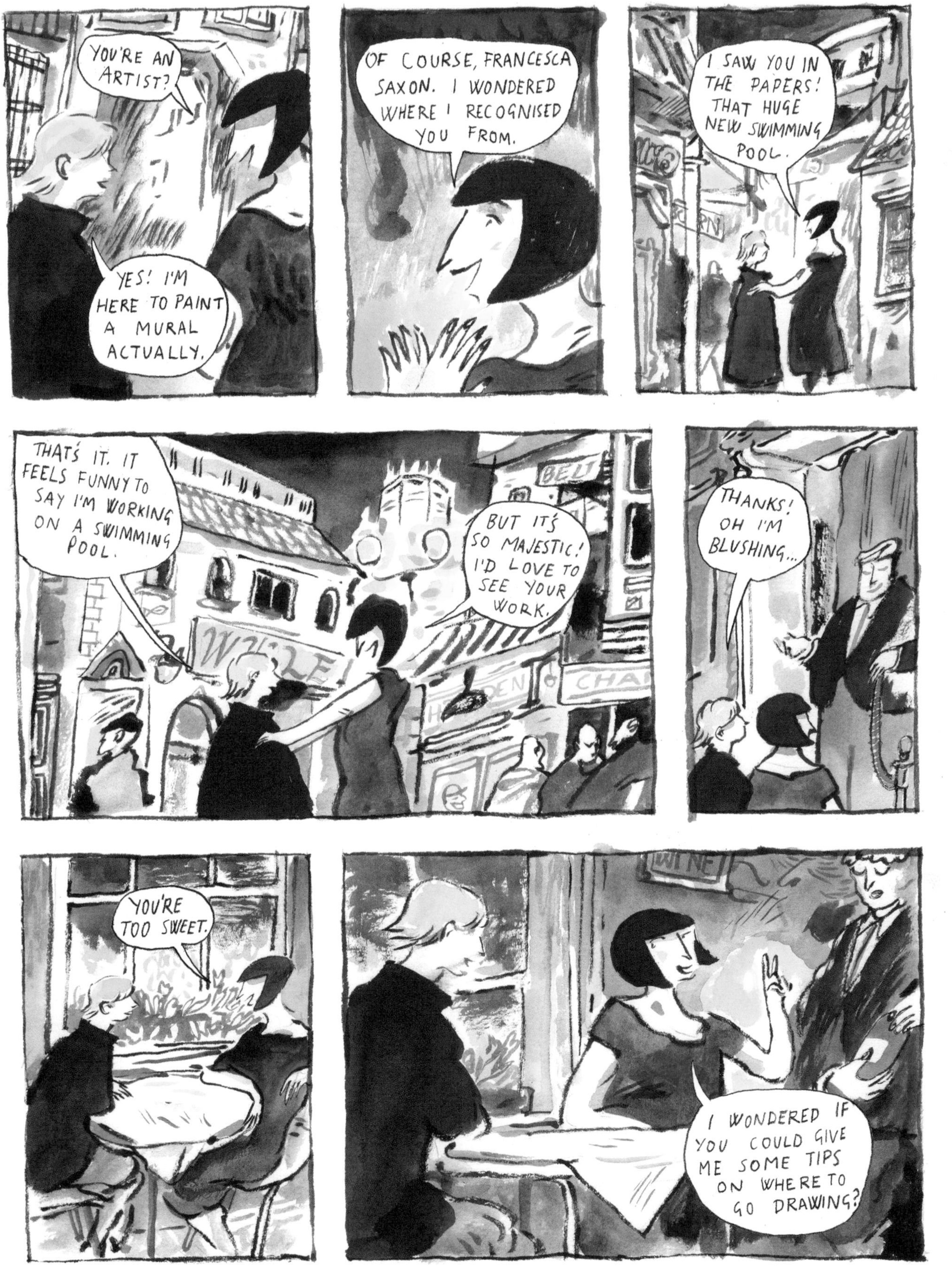

YOU'RE AN ARTIST?
YES! I'M HERE TO PAINT A MURAL ACTUALLY.
OF COURSE, FRANCESCA SAXON. I WONDERED WHERE I RECOGNISED YOU FROM.
I SAW YOU IN THE PAPERS! THAT HUGE NEW SWIMMING POOL.
THAT'S IT. IT FEELS FUNNY TO SAY I'M WORKING ON A SWIMMING POOL.
BUT IT'S SO MAJESTIC! I'D LOVE TO SEE YOUR WORK.
THANKS! OH I'M BLUSHING...
YOU'RE TOO SWEET.
I WONDERED IF YOU COULD GIVE ME SOME TIPS ON WHERE TO GO DRAWING?

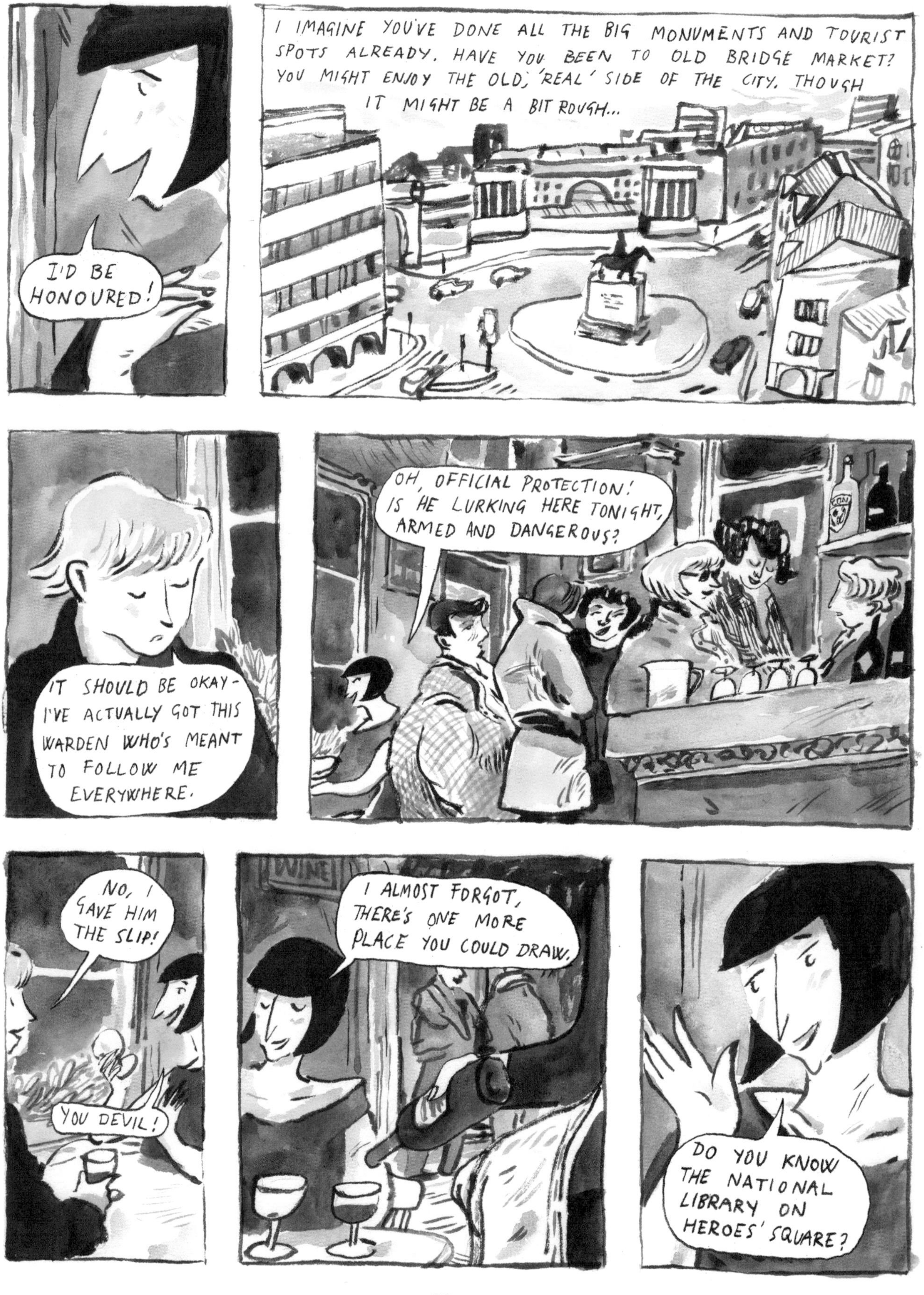
I'D BE HONOURED!
I IMAGINE YOU'VE DONE ALL THE BIG MONUMENTS AND TOURIST SPOTS ALREADY. HAVE YOU BEEN TO OLD BRIDGE MARKET? YOU MIGHT ENJOY THE OLD, 'REAL' SIDE OF THE CITY. THOUGH IT MIGHT BE A BIT ROUGH...
IT SHOULD BE OKAY- I'VE ACTUALLY GOT THIS WARDEN WHO'S MEANT TO FOLLOW ME EVERYWHERE.
OH, OFFICIAL PROTECTION! IS HE LURKING HERE TONIGHT, ARMED AND DANGEROUS?
NO, I GAVE HIM THE SLIP!
YOU DEVIL!
WINE
I ALMOST FORGOT, THERE'S ONE MORE PLACE YOU COULD DRAW.
DO YOU KNOW THE NATIONAL LIBRARY ON HEROES' SQUARE?

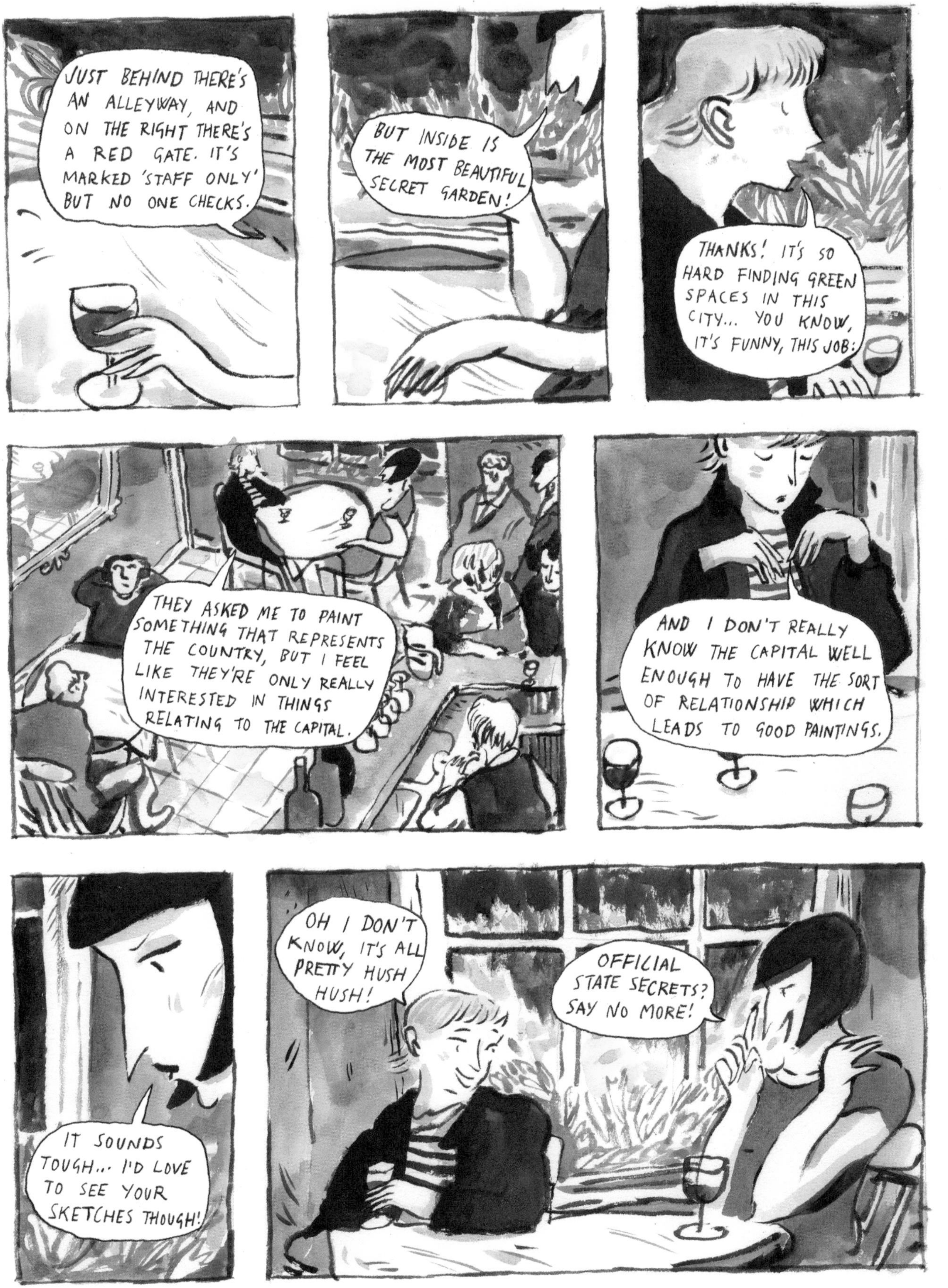
JUST BEHIND THERE'S AN ALLEYWAY, AND ON THE RIGHT THERE'S A RED GATE. IT'S MARKED 'STAFF ONLY' BUT NO ONE CHECKS.
BUT INSIDE IS THE MOST BEAUTIFUL SECRET GARDEN!
THANKS! IT'S SO HARD FINDING GREEN SPACES IN THIS CITY... YOU KNOW, IT'S FUNNY, THIS JOB:
THEY ASKED ME TO PAINT SOMETHING THAT REPRESENTS THE COUNTRY, BUT I FEEL LIKE THEY'RE ONLY REALLY INTERESTED IN THINGS RELATING TO THE CAPITAL.
AND I DON'T REALLY KNOW THE CAPITAL WELL ENOUGH TO HAVE THE SORT OF RELATIONSHIP WHICH LEADS TO GOOD PAINTINGS.
IT SOUNDS TOUGH... I'D LOVE TO SEE YOUR SKETCHES THOUGH!
OH I DON'T KNOW, IT'S ALL PRETTY HUSH HUSH!
OFFICIAL STATE SECRETS? SAY NO MORE!

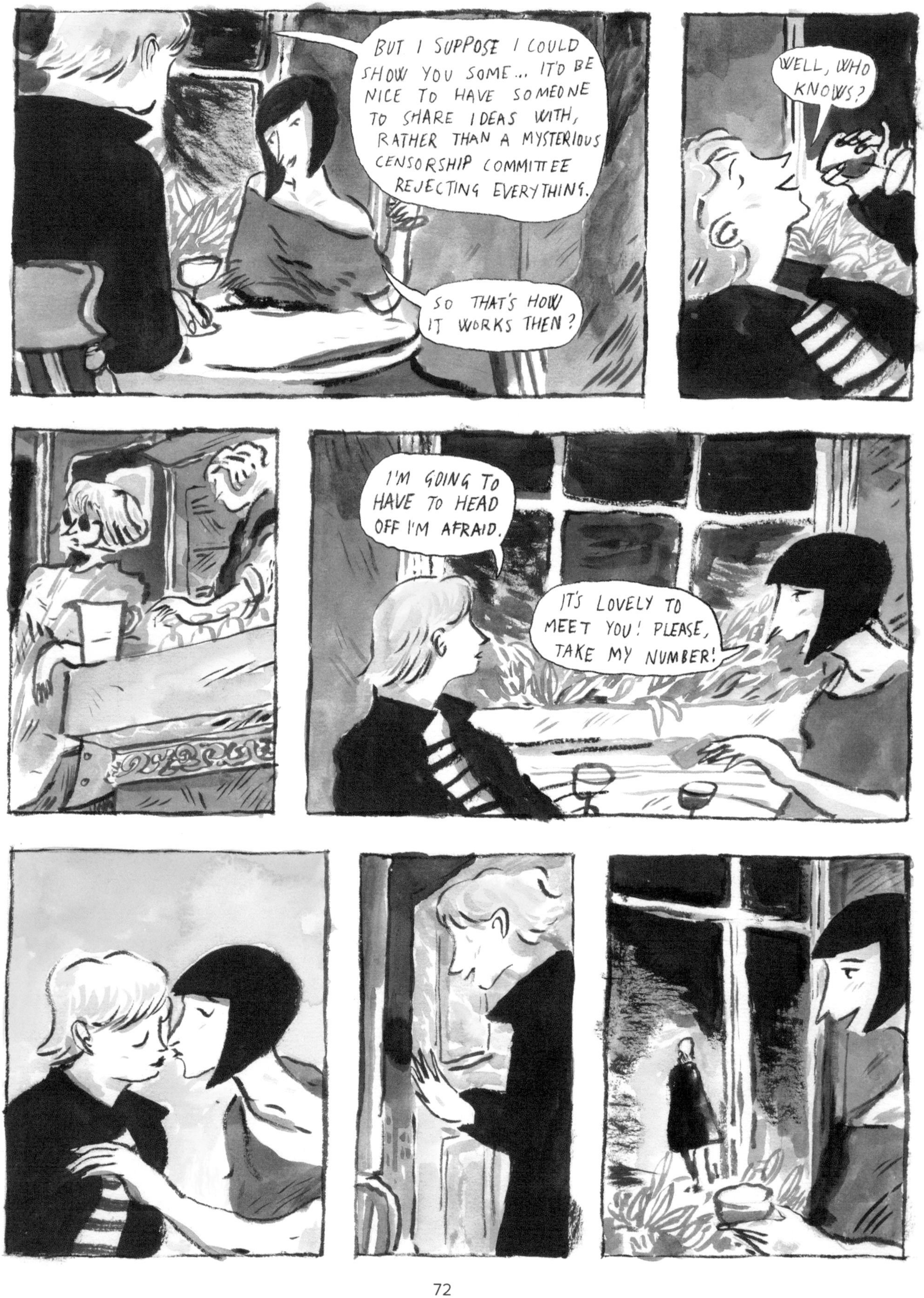
BUT I SUPPOSE I COULD SHOW YOU SOME... IT'D BE NICE TO HAVE SOMEONE TO SHARE IDEAS WITH, RATHER THAN A MYSTERIOUS CENSORSHIP COMMITTEE REJECTING EVERYTHING.
SO THAT'S HOW IT WORKS THEN?
WELL, WHO KNOWS?
I'M GOING TO HAVE TO HEAD OFF I'M AFRAID.
IT'S LOVELY TO MEET YOU! PLEASE, TAKE MY NUMBER!

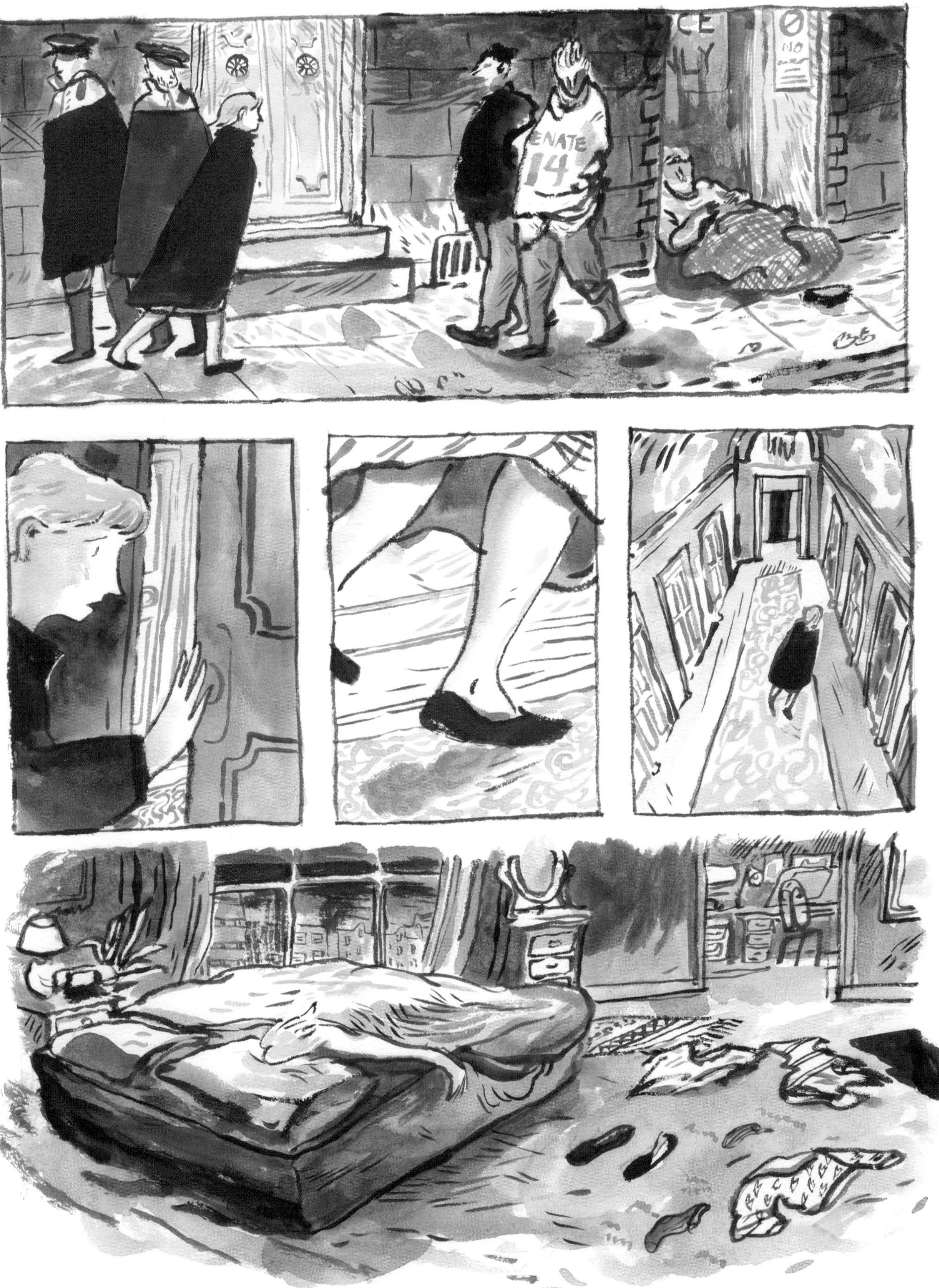
NO
ENATE
14

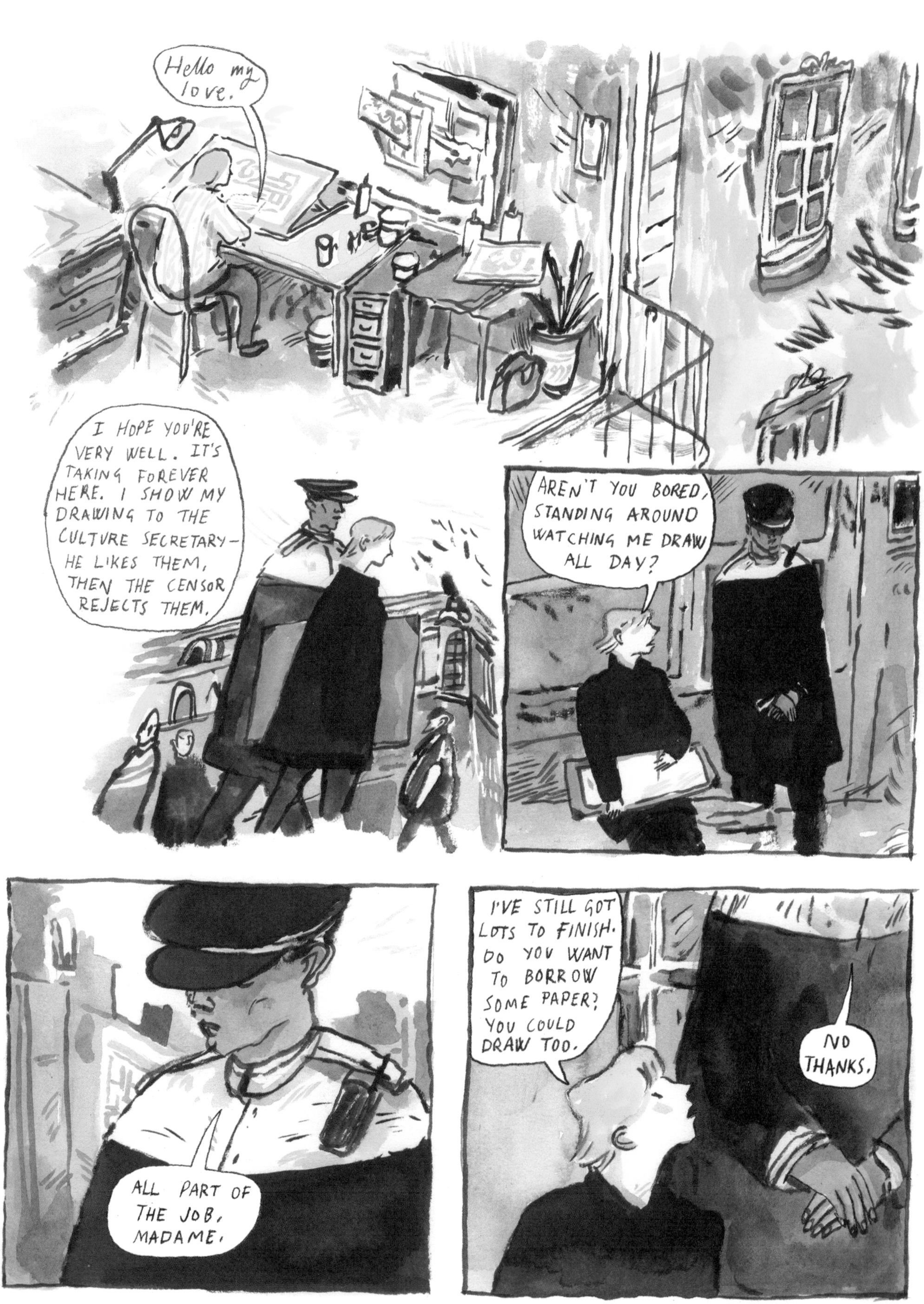
Hello my love.
I HOPE YOU'RE VERY WELL. IT'S TAKING FOREVER HERE. I SHOW MY DRAWING TO THE CULTURE SECRETARY- HE LIKES THEM, THEN THE CENSOR REJECTS THEM.
AREN'T YOU BORED, STANDING AROUND WATCHING ME DRAW ALL DAY?
ALL PART OF THE JOB, MADAME.
I'VE STILL GOT LOTS TO FINISH. DO YOU WANT TO BORROW SOME PAPER? YOU COULD DRAW TOO.
NO THANKS.

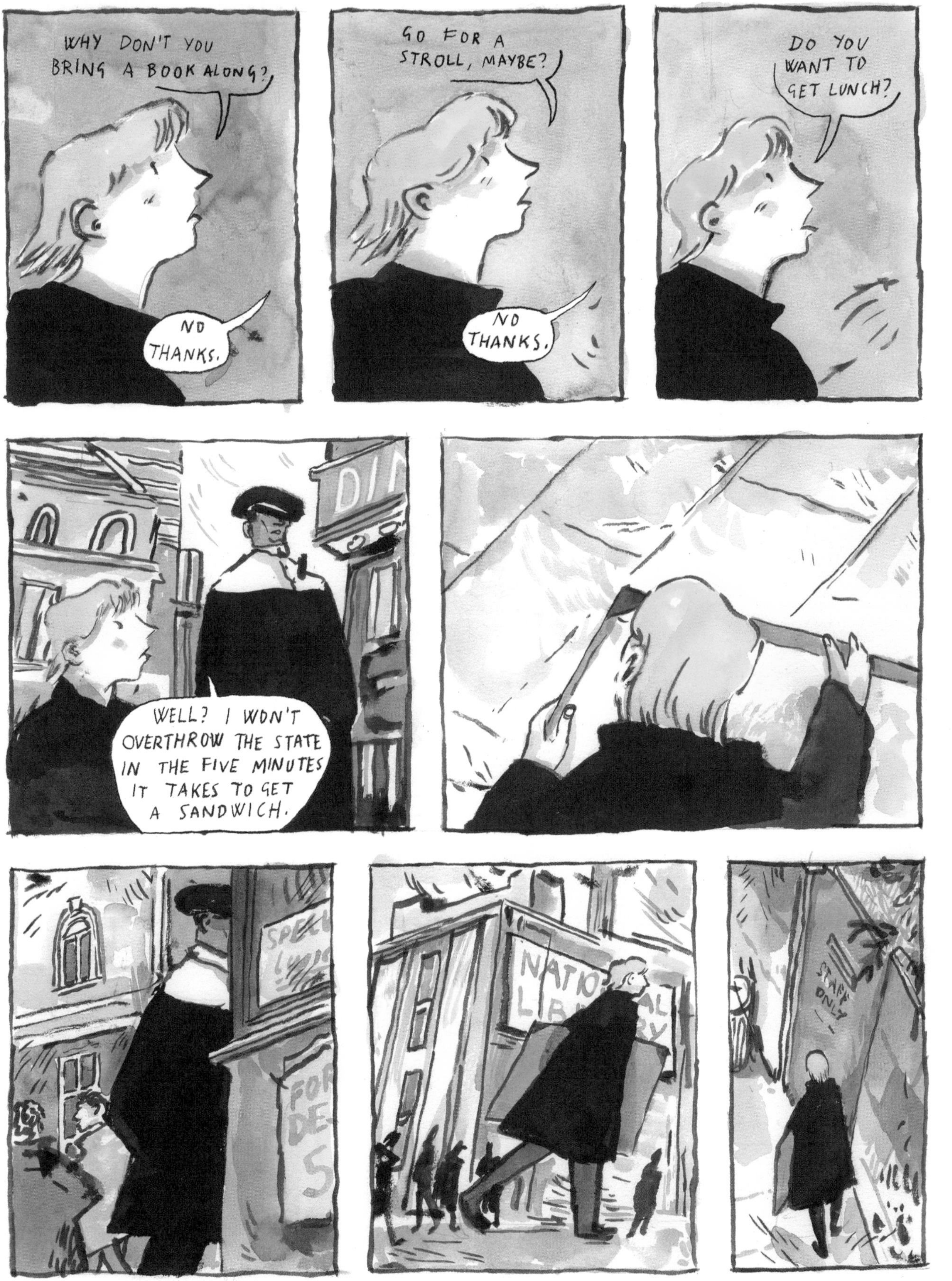
WHY DON'T YOU BRING A BOOK ALONG?
NO THANKS.
GO FOR A STROLL, MAYBE?
NO THANKS.
DO YOU WANT TO GET LUNCH?
WELL? I WON'T OVERTHROW THE STATE IN THE FIVE MINUTES IT TAKES TO GET A SANDWICH.
STAFF ONLY

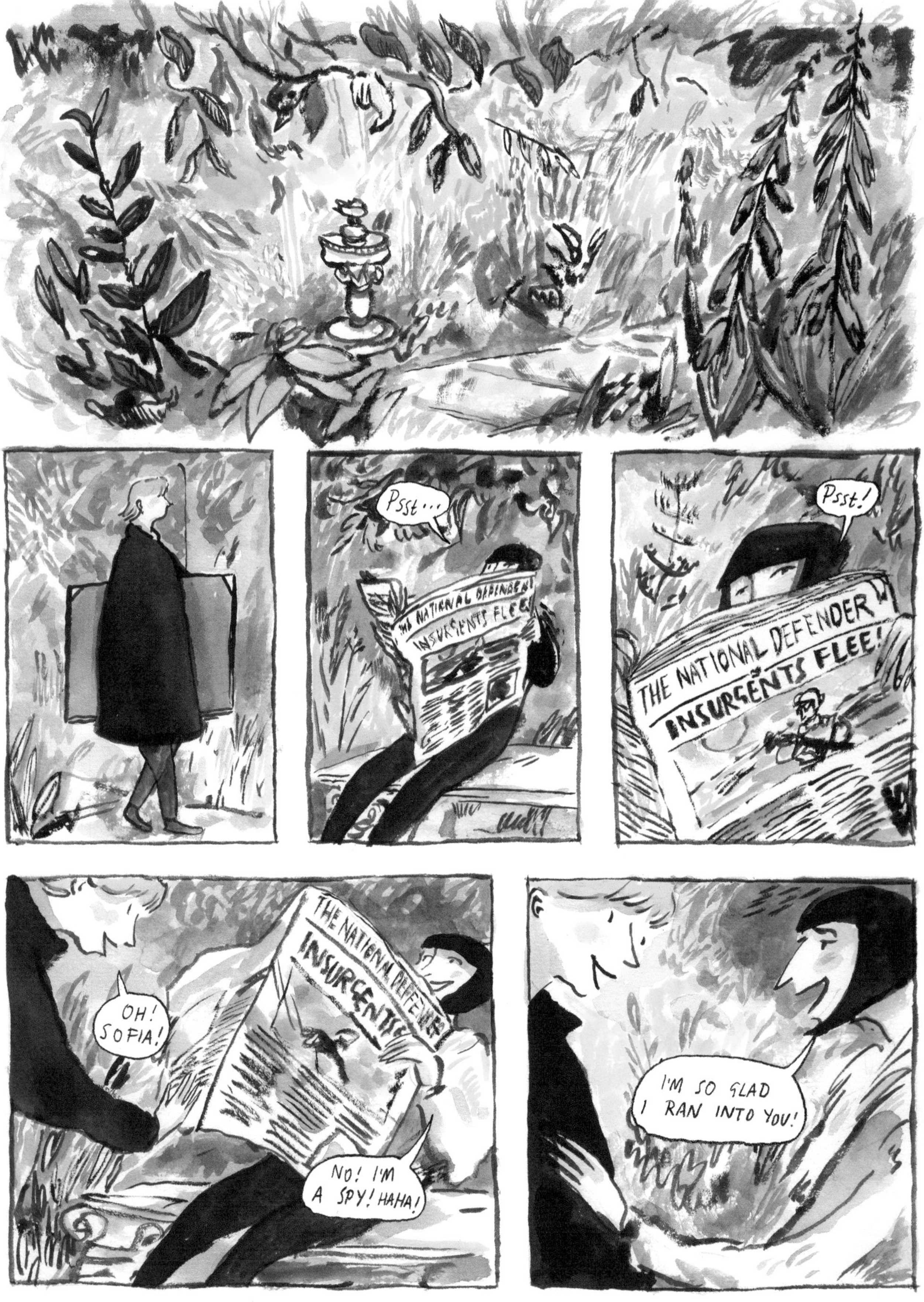
Psst...
THE NATIONAL DEFENDER
INSURGENTS FLEE
Psst!
THE NATIONAL DEFENDER
INSURGENTS FLEE!
THE NATIONAL DEFENDER
INSURGENTS
OH! SOFIA!
NO! I'M A SPY! HAHA!
I'M SO GLAD I RAN INTO YOU!

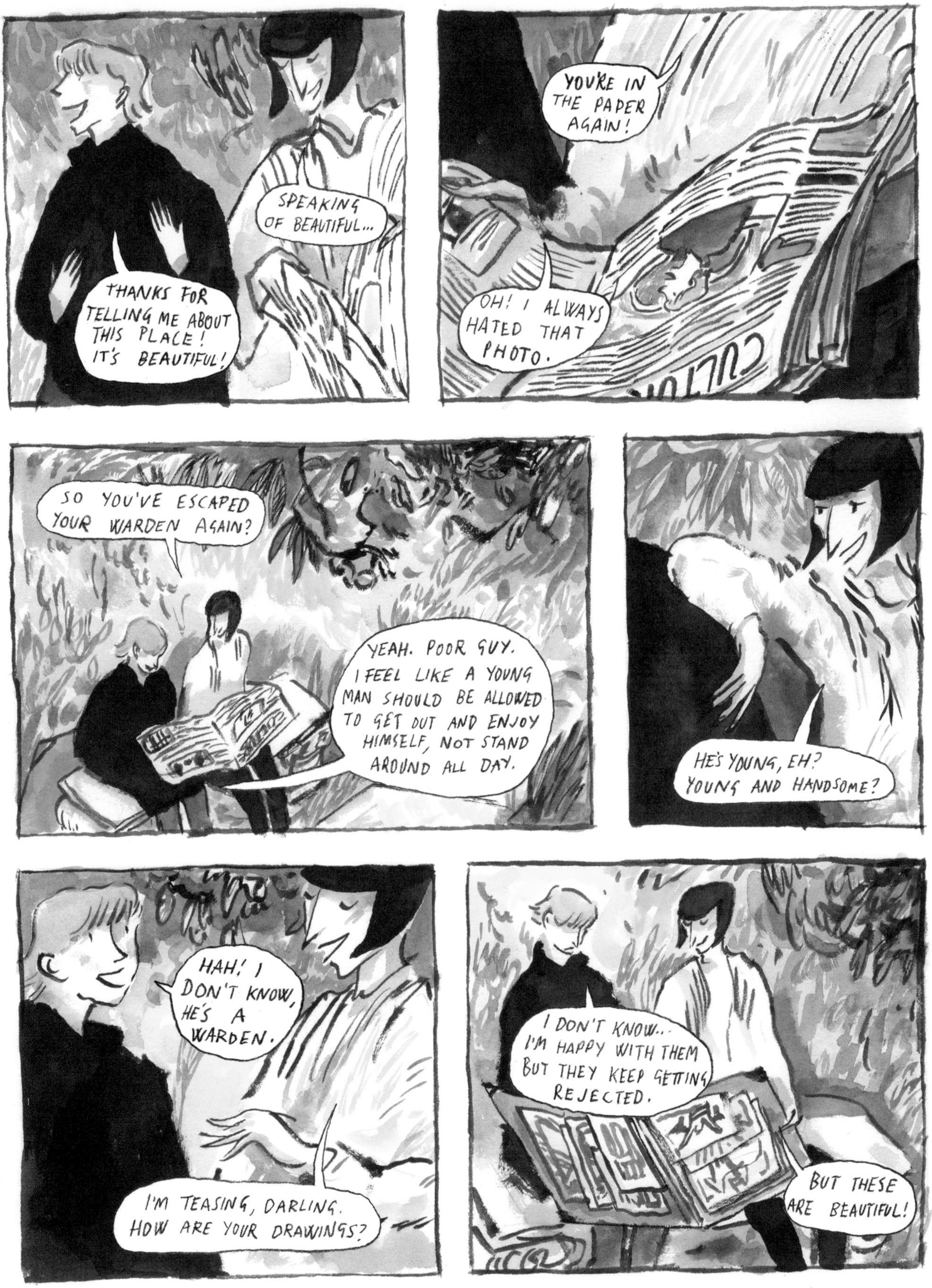
SPEAKING OF BEAUTIFUL...
THANKS FOR TELLING ME ABOUT THIS PLACE! IT'S BEAUTIFUL!
YOU'RE IN THE PAPER AGAIN!
OH! I ALWAYS HATED THAT PHOTO.
SO YOU'VE ESCAPED YOUR WARDEN AGAIN?
YEAH. POOR GUY. I FEEL LIKE A YOUNG MAN SHOULD BE ALLOWED TO GET OUT AND ENJOY HIMSELF, NOT STAND AROUND ALL DAY.
HE'S YOUNG, EH? YOUNG AND HANDSOME?
HAH! I DON'T KNOW, HE'S A WARDEN.
I'M TEASING, DARLING. HOW ARE YOUR DRAWINGS?
I DON'T KNOW... I'M HAPPY WITH THEM BUT THEY KEEP GETTING REJECTED.
BUT THESE ARE BEAUTIFUL!

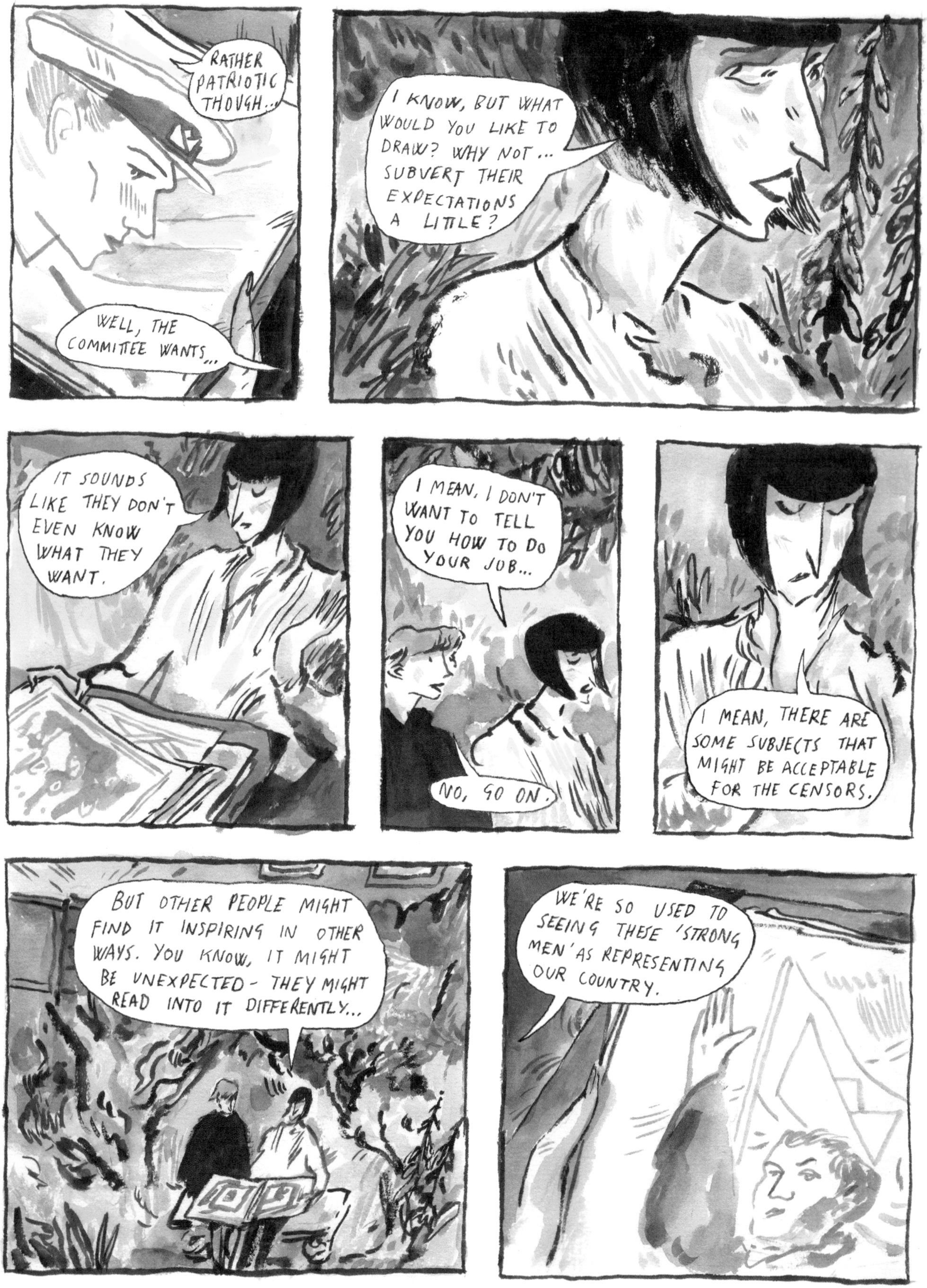
RATHER PATRIOTIC THOUGH...
WELL, THE COMMITTEE WANTS...
I KNOW, BUT WHAT WOULD YOU LIKE TO DRAW? WHY NOT... SUBVERT THEIR EXPECTATIONS A LITTLE?
IT SOUNDS LIKE THEY DON'T EVEN KNOW WHAT THEY WANT.
I MEAN, I DON'T WANT TO TELL YOU HOW TO DO YOUR JOB...
NO, GO ON.
I MEAN, THERE ARE SOME SUBJECTS THAT MIGHT BE ACCEPTABLE FOR THE CENSORS.
BUT OTHER PEOPLE MIGHT FIND IT INSPIRING IN OTHER WAYS. YOU KNOW, IT MIGHT BE UNEXPECTED - THEY MIGHT READ INTO IT DIFFERENTLY...
WE'RE SO USED TO SEEING THESE 'STRONG MEN' AS REPRESENTING OUR COUNTRY.

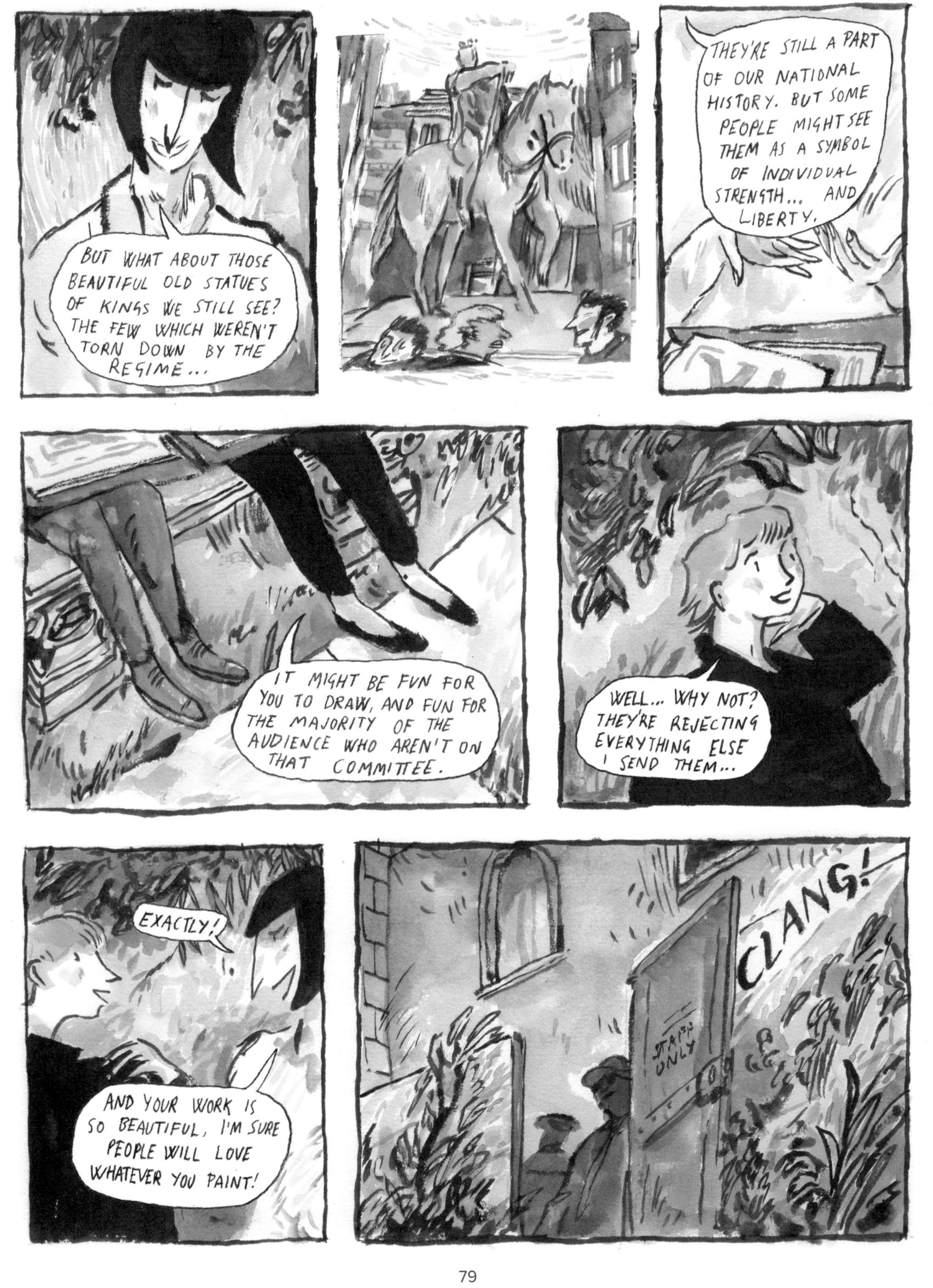
BUT WHAT ABOUT THOSE BEAUTIFUL OLD STATUES OF KINGS WE STILL SEE? THE FEW WHICH WEREN'T TORN DOWN BY THE REGIME...
THEY'RE STILL A PART OF OUR NATIONAL HISTORY. BUT SOME PEOPLE MIGHT SEE THEM AS A SYMBOL OF INDIVIDUAL STRENGTH... AND LIBERTY.
IT MIGHT BE FUN FOR YOU TO DRAW, AND FUN FOR THE MAJORITY OF THE AUDIENCE WHO AREN'T ON THAT COMMITTEE.
WELL... WHY NOT? THEY'RE REJECTING EVERYTHING ELSE I SEND THEM...
EXACTLY!
AND YOUR WORK IS SO BEAUTIFUL, I'M SURE PEOPLE WILL LOVE WHATEVER YOU PAINT!
CLANG!
STAFF ONLY

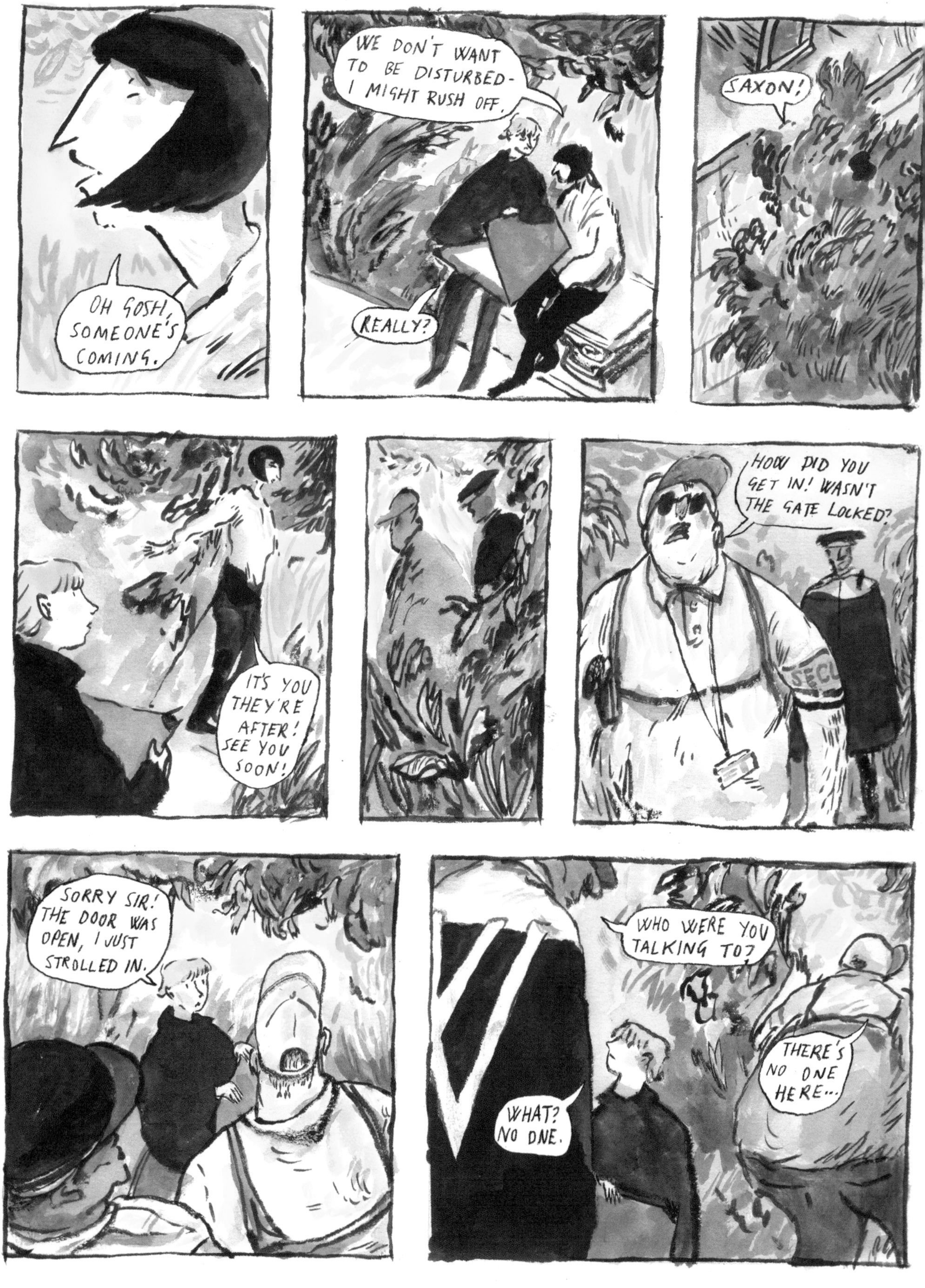

OH GOSH, SOMEONE'S COMING.
WE DON'T WANT TO BE DISTURBED- I MIGHT RUSH OFF.
REALLY?
SAXON!
IT'S YOU THEY'RE AFTER! SEE YOU SOON!
HOW DID YOU GET IN! WASN'T THE GATE LOCKED?
SORRY SIR! THE DOOR WAS OPEN, I JUST STROLLED IN.
WHO WERE YOU TALKING TO?
WHAT? NO ONE.
THERE'S NO ONE HERE...

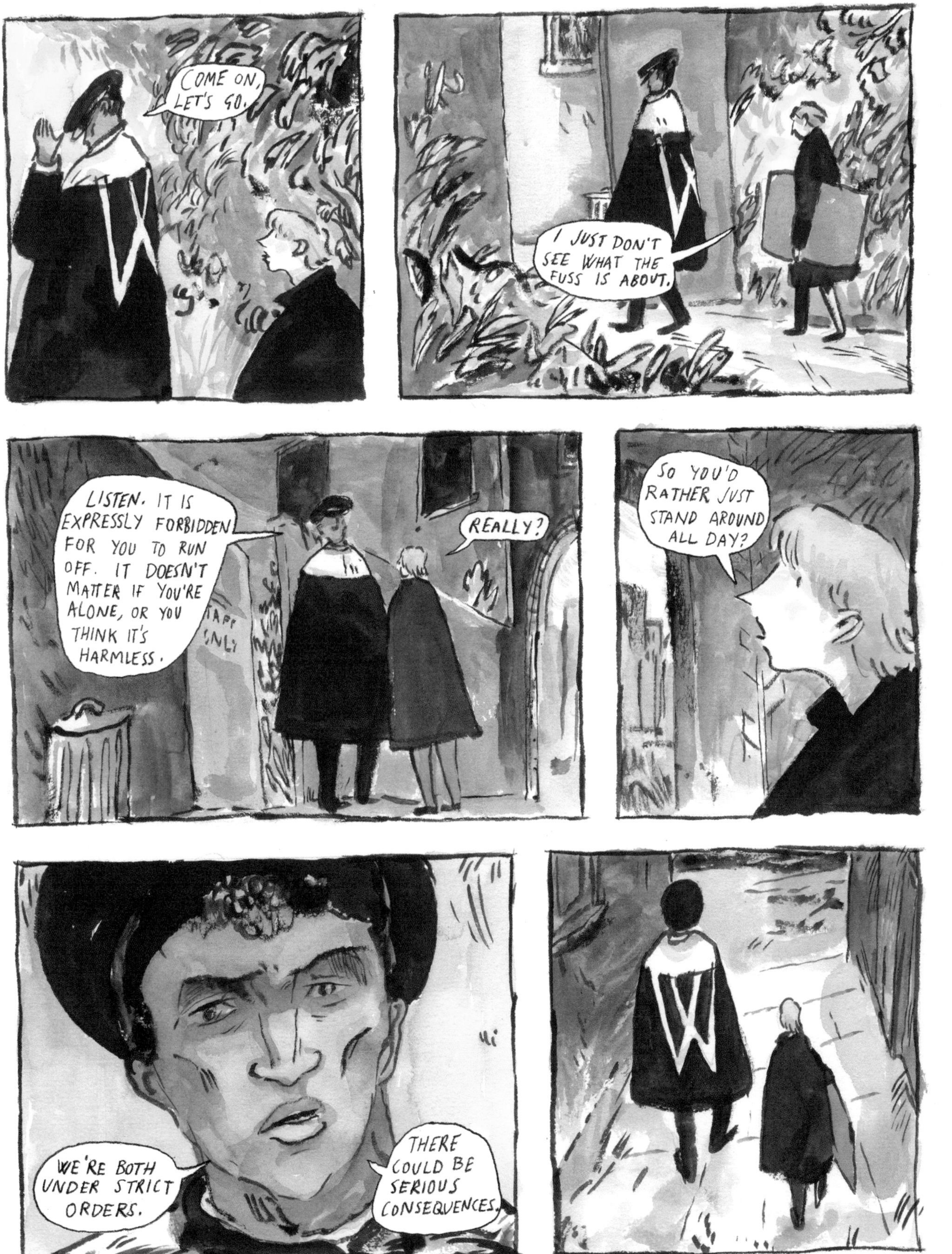
COME ON, LET'S GO.
I JUST DON'T SEE WHAT THE FUSS IS ABOUT.
LISTEN. IT IS EXPRESSLY FORBIDDEN FOR YOU TO RUN OFF. IT DOESN'T MATTER IF YOU'RE ALONE, OR YOU THINK IT'S HARMLESS.
REALLY?
SO YOU'D RATHER JUST STAND AROUND ALL DAY?
WE'RE BOTH UNDER STRICT ORDERS.
THERE COULD BE SERIOUS CONSEQUENCES.

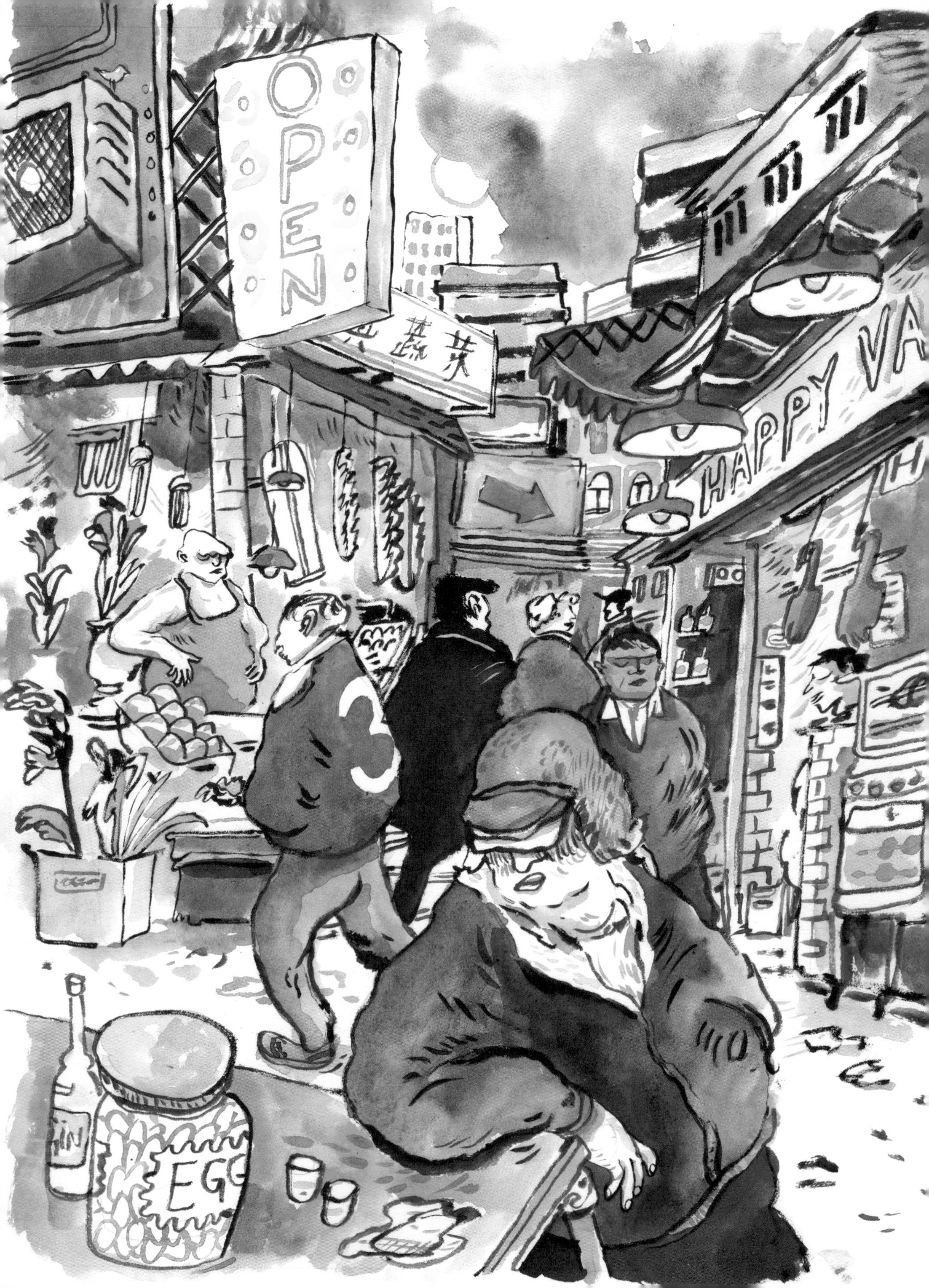
OPEN
HAPPY VA
3

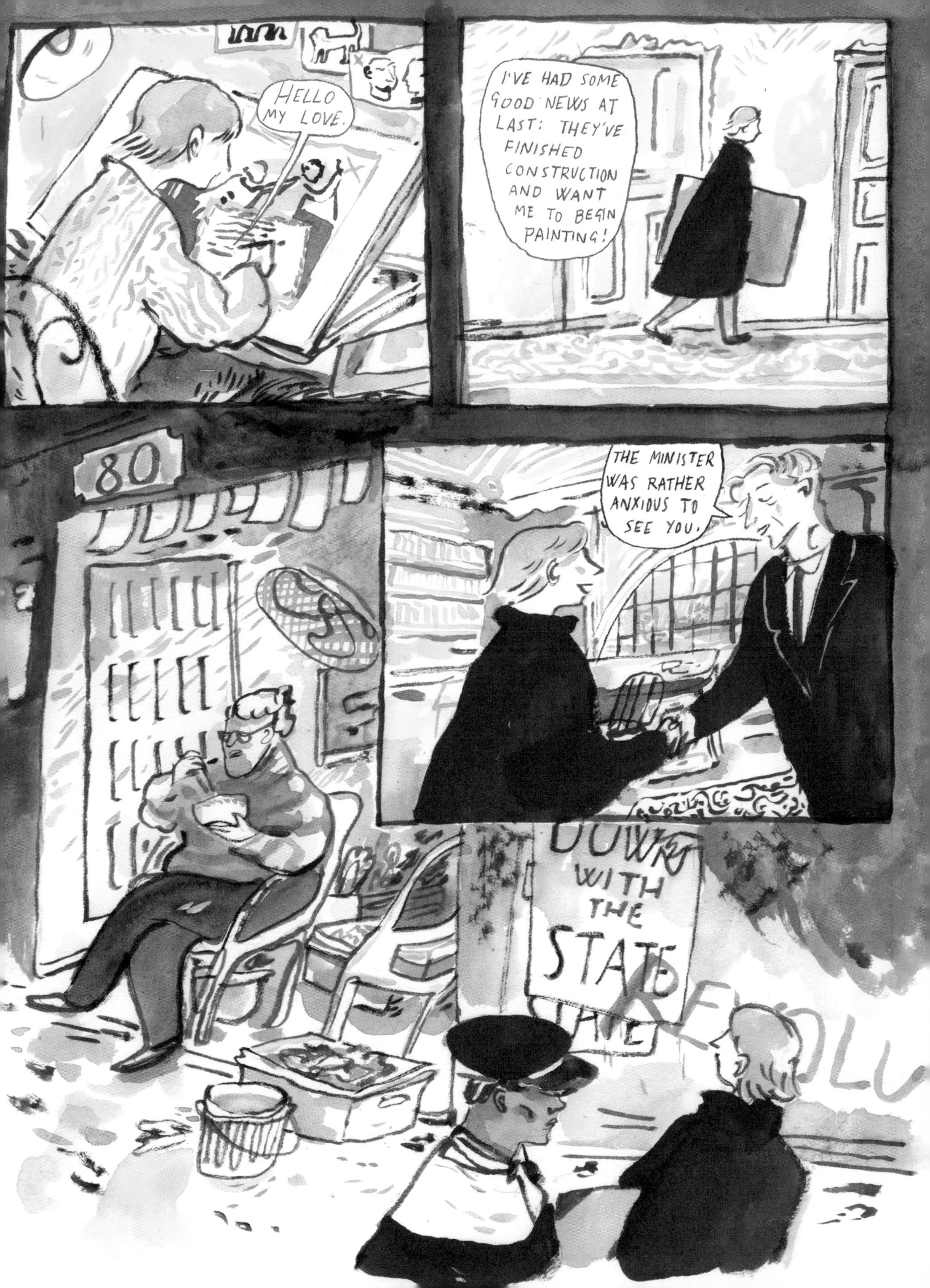
HELLO MY LOVE.
I'VE HAD SOME GOOD NEWS AT LAST: THEY'VE FINISHED CONSTRUCTION AND WANT ME TO BEGIN PAINTING!
80
THE MINISTER WAS RATHER ANXIOUS TO SEE YOU.
WITH THE STATE

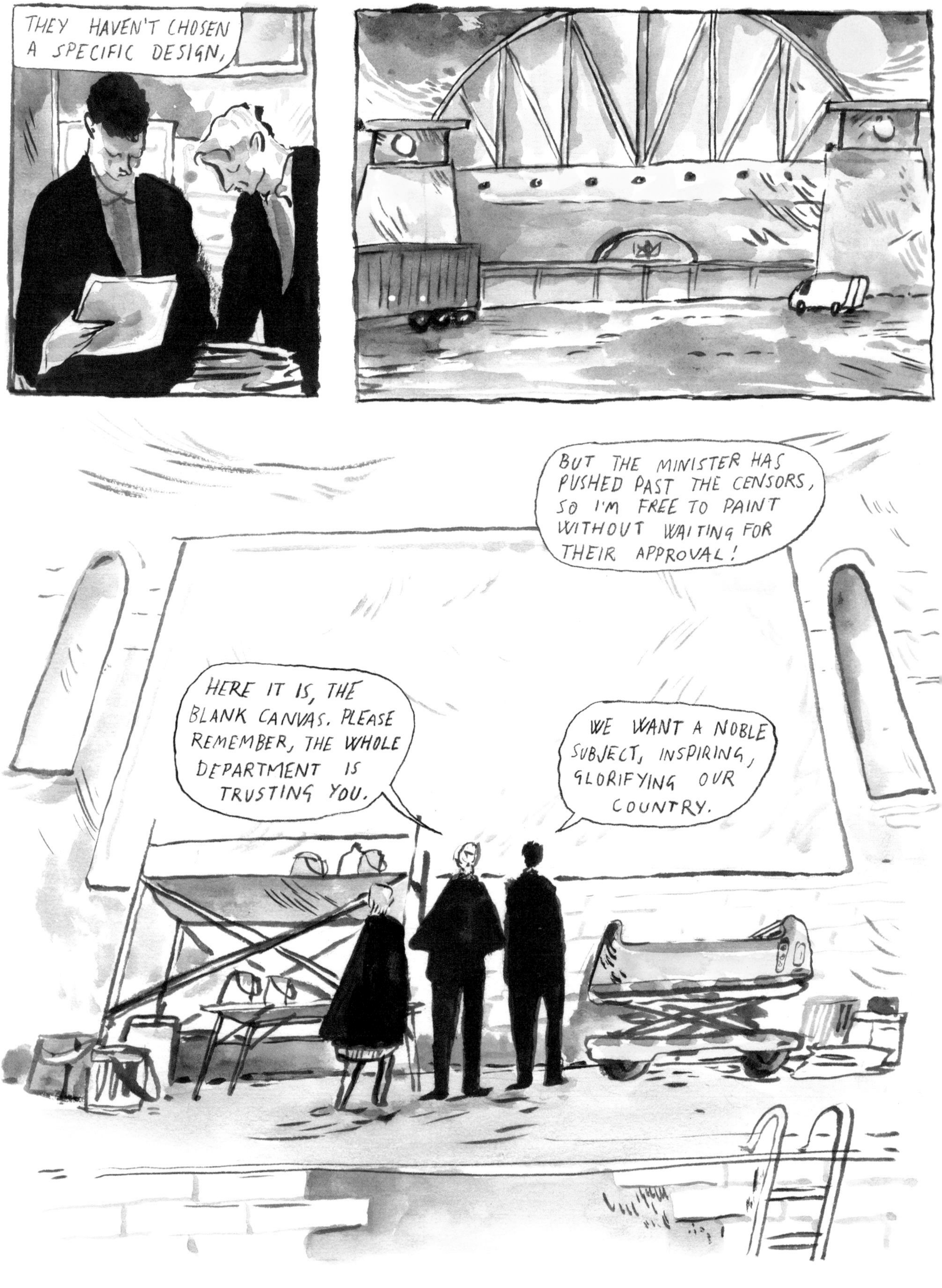
THEY HAVEN'T CHOSEN A SPECIFIC DESIGN,
BUT THE MINISTER HAS PUSHED PAST THE CENSORS, SO I'M FREE TO PAINT WITHOUT WAITING FOR THEIR APPROVAL!
HERE IT IS, THE BLANK CANVAS. PLEASE REMEMBER, THE WHOLE DEPARTMENT IS TRUSTING YOU.
WE WANT A NOBLE SUBJECT, INSPIRING, GLORIFYING OUR COUNTRY.

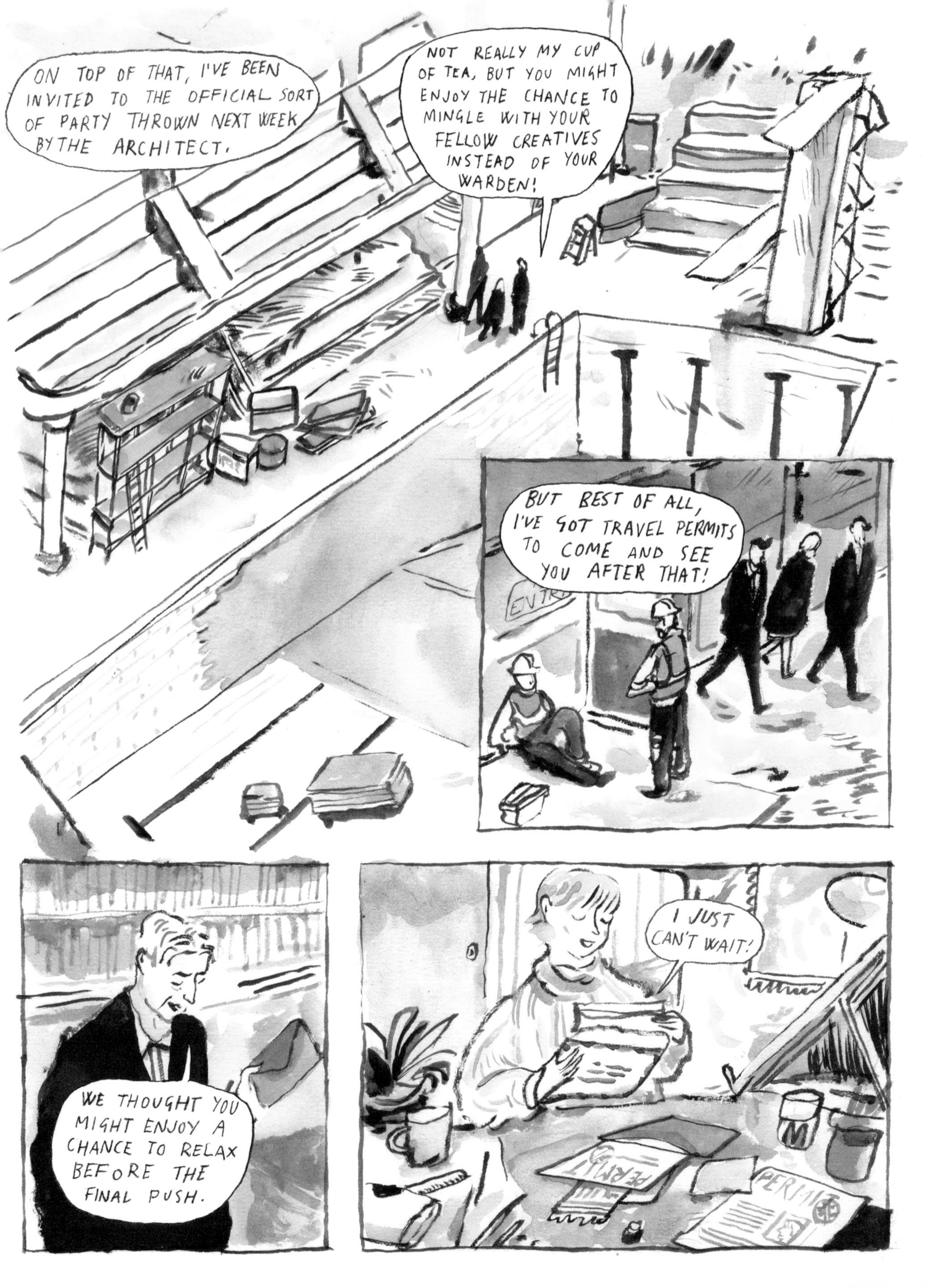
ON TOP OF THAT, I'VE BEEN INVITED TO THE OFFICIAL SORT OF PARTY THROWN NEXT WEEK BY THE ARCHITECT.
NOT REALLY MY CUP OF TEA, BUT YOU MIGHT ENJOY THE CHANCE TO MINGLE WITH YOUR FELLOW CREATIVES INSTEAD OF YOUR WARDEN!
BUT BEST OF ALL, I'VE GOT TRAVEL PERMITS TO COME AND SEE YOU AFTER THAT!
WE THOUGHT YOU MIGHT ENJOY A CHANCE TO RELAX BEFORE THE FINAL PUSH.
I JUST CAN'T WAIT!
PERMIT
PERMIT

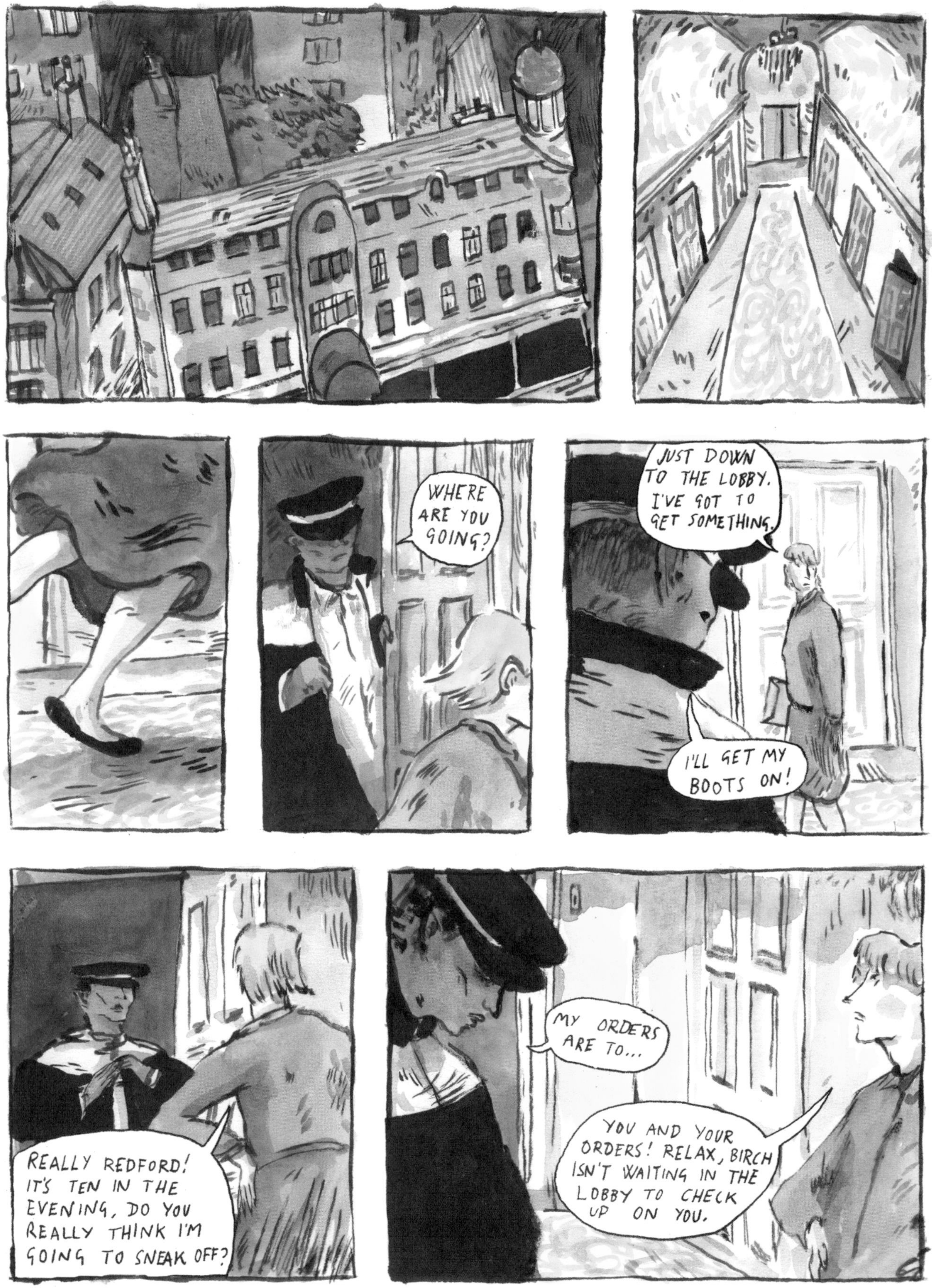
WHERE ARE YOU GOING?
JUST DOWN TO THE LOBBY. I'VE GOT TO GET SOMETHING.
I'LL GET MY BOOTS ON!
REALLY REDFORD! IT'S TEN IN THE EVENING, DO YOU REALLY THINK I'M GOING TO SNEAK OFF?
MY ORDERS ARE TO...
YOU AND YOUR ORDERS! RELAX, BIRCH ISN'T WAITING IN THE LOBBY TO CHECK UP ON YOU.

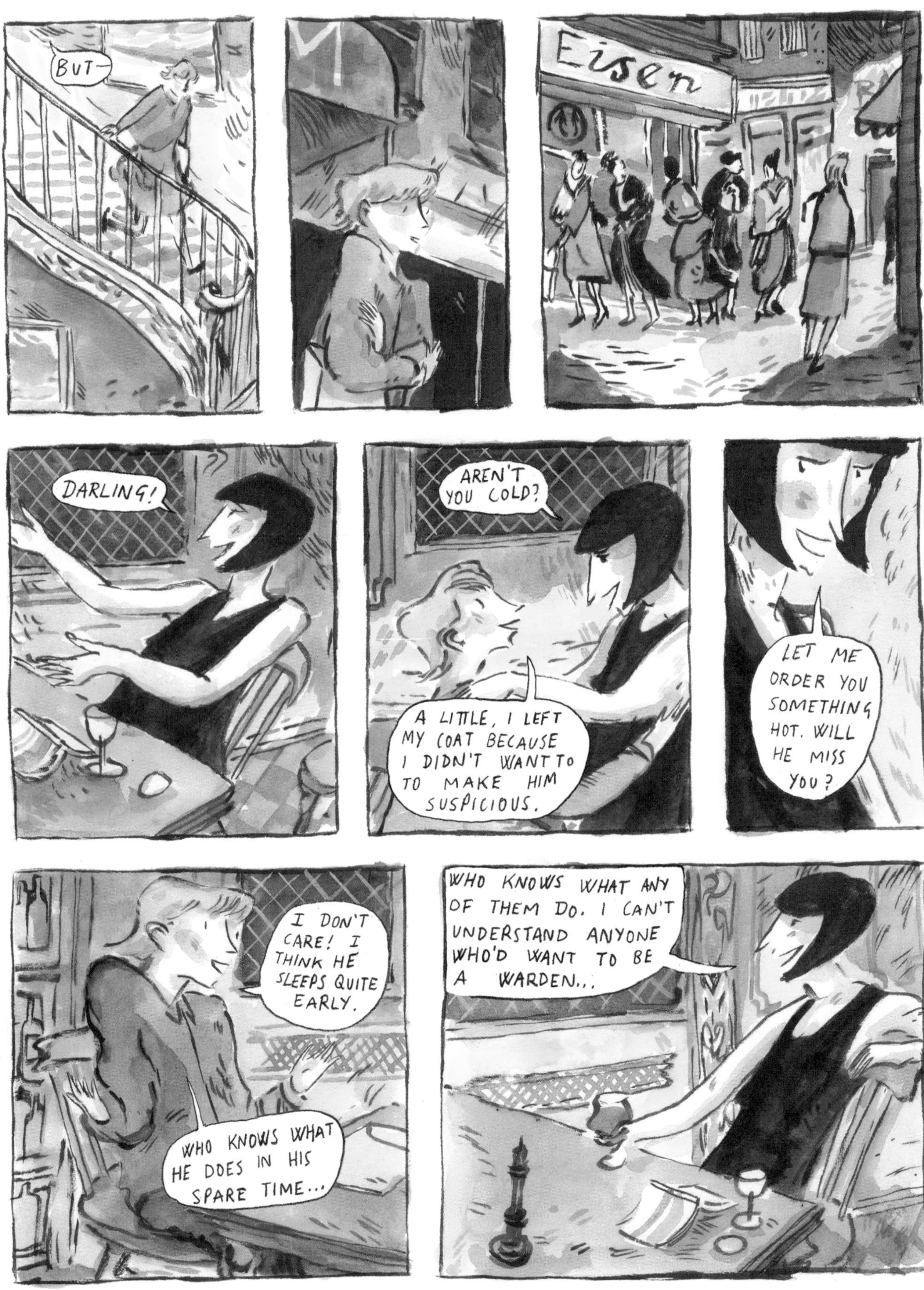
BUT—
Eisen
DARLING!
AREN'T YOU COLD?
A LITTLE, I LEFT MY COAT BECAUSE I DIDN'T WANT TO TO MAKE HIM SUSPICIOUS.
LET ME ORDER YOU SOMETHING HOT. WILL HE MISS YOU?
I DON'T CARE! I THINK HE SLEEPS QUITE EARLY.
WHO KNOWS WHAT HE DOES IN HIS SPARE TIME...
WHO KNOWS WHAT ANY OF THEM DO. I CAN'T UNDERSTAND ANYONE WHO'D WANT TO BE A WARDEN...

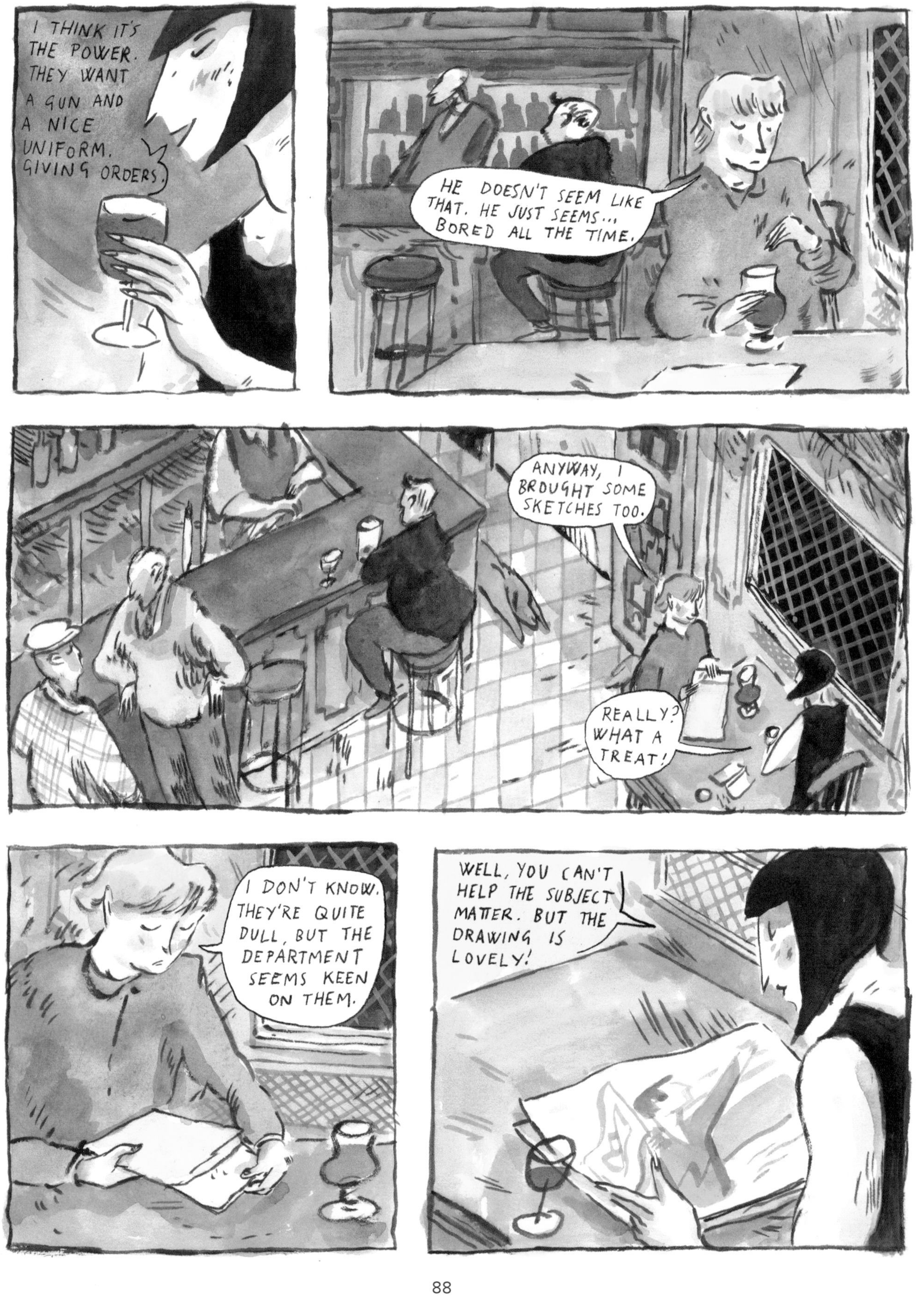

I THINK IT'S THE POWER. THEY WANT A GUN AND A NICE UNIFORM. GIVING ORDERS.
HE DOESN'T SEEM LIKE THAT. HE JUST SEEMS... BORED ALL THE TIME.
ANYWAY, I BROUGHT SOME SKETCHES TOO.
REALLY? WHAT A TREAT!
I DON'T KNOW. THEY'RE QUITE DULL, BUT THE DEPARTMENT SEEMS KEEN ON THEM.
WELL, YOU CAN'T HELP THE SUBJECT MATTER. BUT THE DRAWING IS LOVELY!

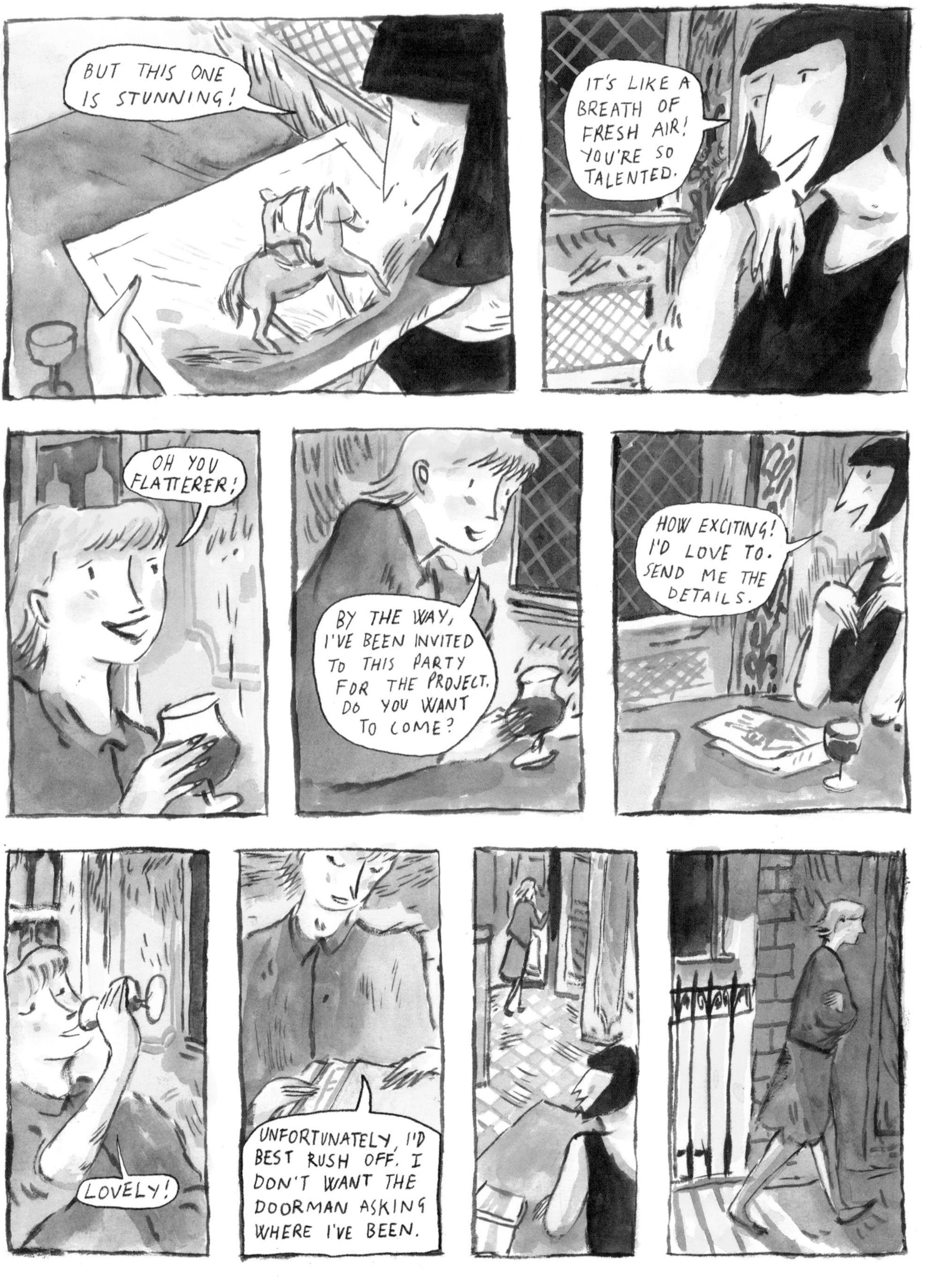

BUT THIS ONE IS STUNNING!
IT'S LIKE A BREATH OF FRESH AIR! YOU'RE SO TALENTED.
OH YOU FLATTERER!
BY THE WAY, I'VE BEEN INVITED TO THIS PARTY FOR THE PROJECT. DO YOU WANT TO COME?
HOW EXCITING! I'D LOVE TO. SEND ME THE DETAILS.
LOVELY!
UNFORTUNATELY, I'D BEST RUSH OFF. I DON'T WANT THE DOORMAN ASKING WHERE I'VE BEEN.

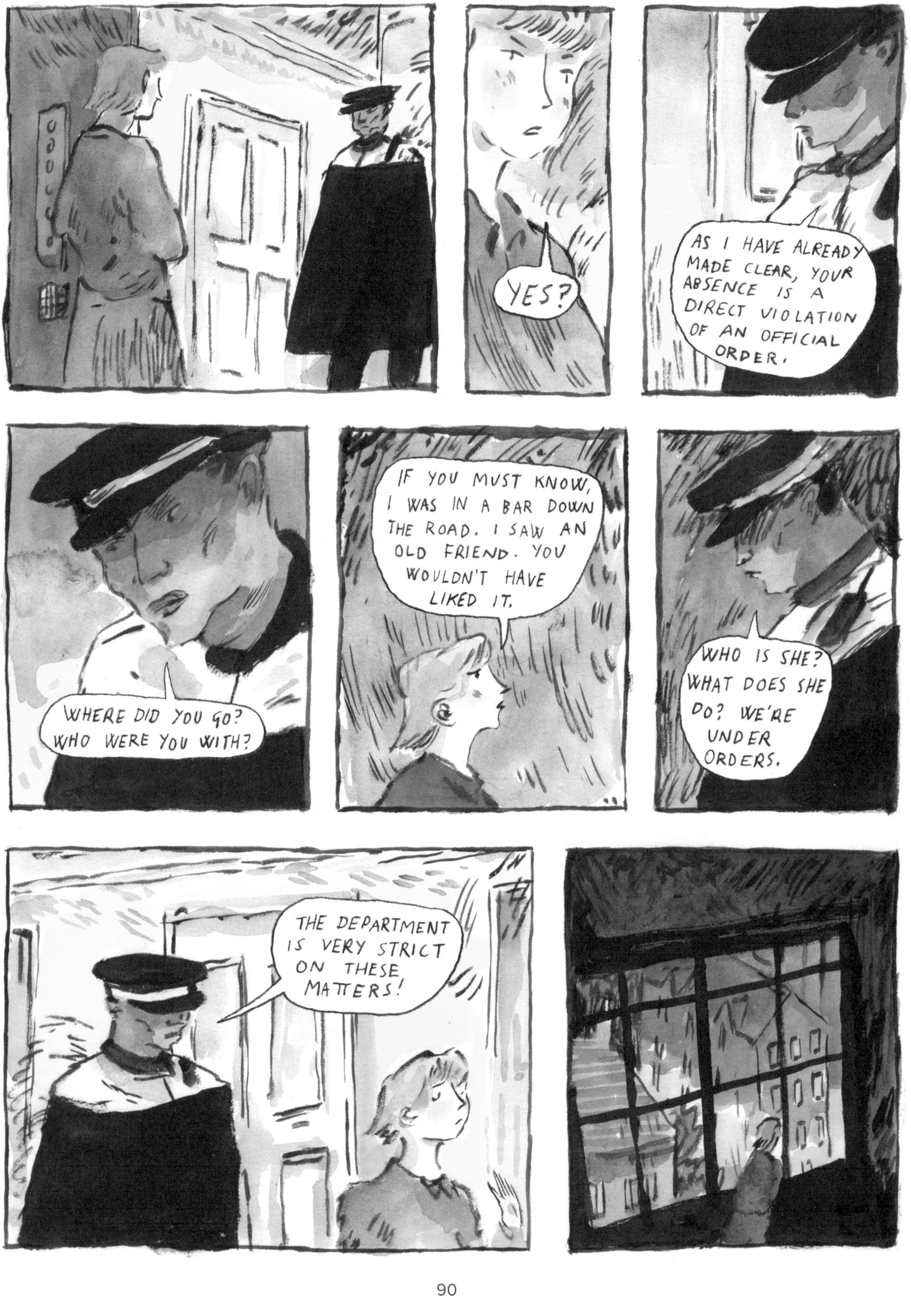
YES?
AS I HAVE ALREADY MADE CLEAR, YOUR ABSENCE IS A DIRECT VIOLATION OF AN OFFICIAL ORDER.
WHERE DID YOU GO? WHO WERE YOU WITH?
IF YOU MUST KNOW, I WAS IN A BAR DOWN THE ROAD. I SAW AN OLD FRIEND. YOU WOULDN'T HAVE LIKED IT.
WHO IS SHE? WHAT DOES SHE DO? WE'RE UNDER ORDERS.
THE DEPARTMENT IS VERY STRICT ON THESE MATTERS!

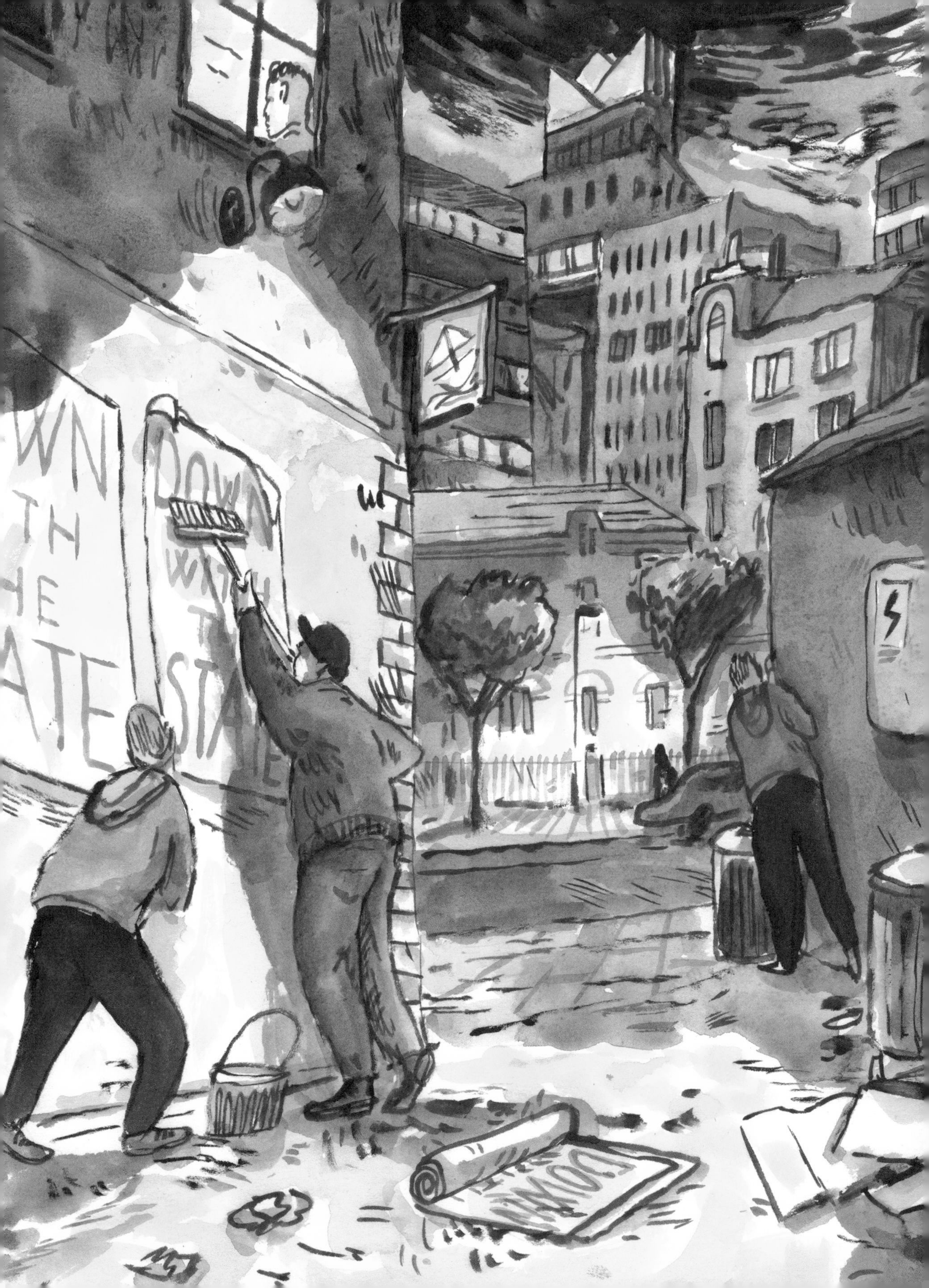
DOWN

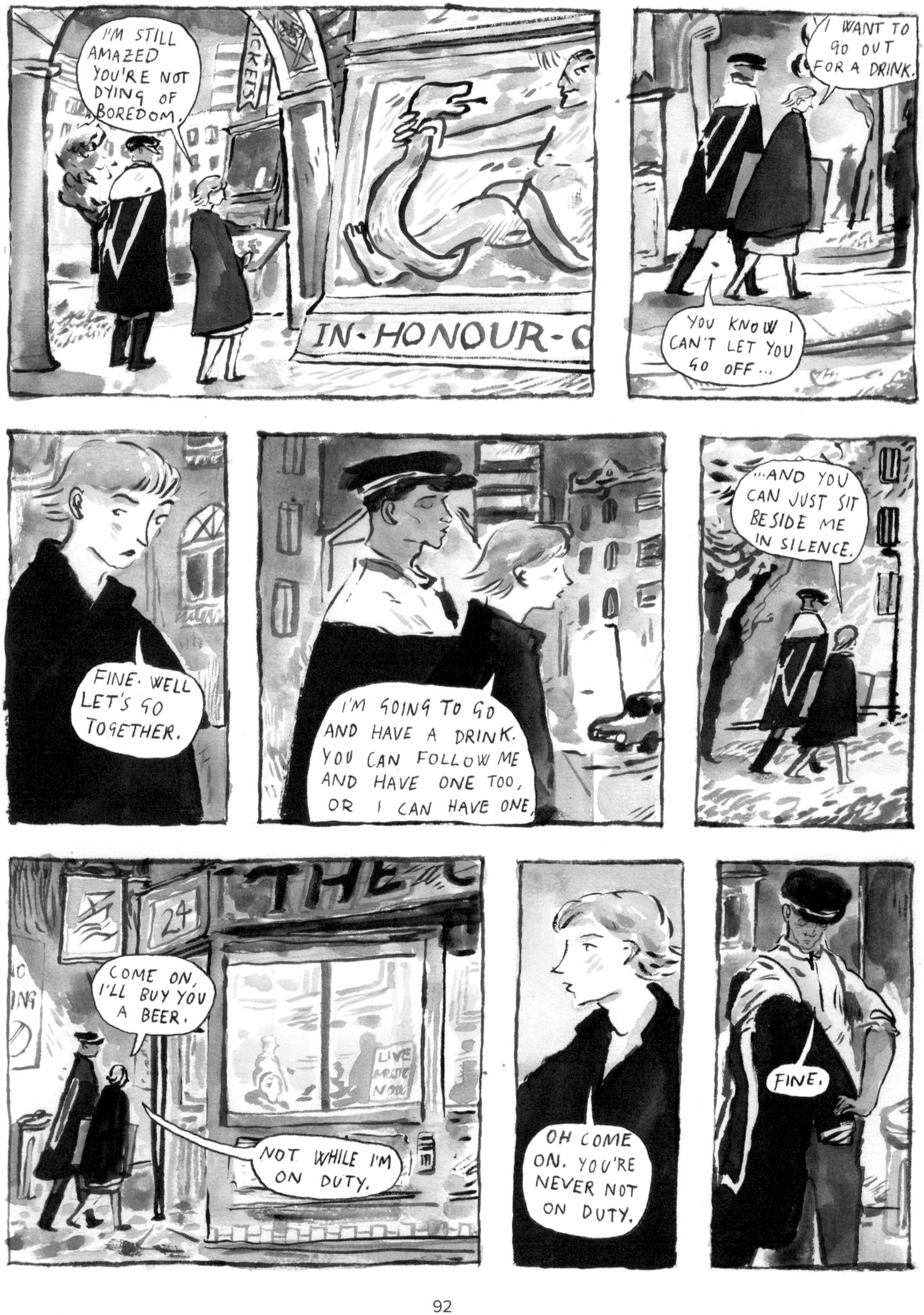
I'M STILL AMAZED YOU'RE NOT DYING OF BOREDOM.
TICKETS
IN-HONOUR-O
I WANT TO GO OUT FOR A DRINK.
YOU KNOW I CAN'T LET YOU GO OFF...
FINE. WELL LET'S GO TOGETHER.
I'M GOING TO GO AND HAVE A DRINK. YOU CAN FOLLOW ME AND HAVE ONE TOO, OR I CAN HAVE ONE,
...AND YOU CAN JUST SIT BESIDE ME IN SILENCE.
THE
24
COME ON, I'LL BUY YOU A BEER.
LIVE MUSIC NOW
NOT WHILE I'M ON DUTY.
OH COME ON. YOU'RE NEVER NOT ON DUTY.
FINE.

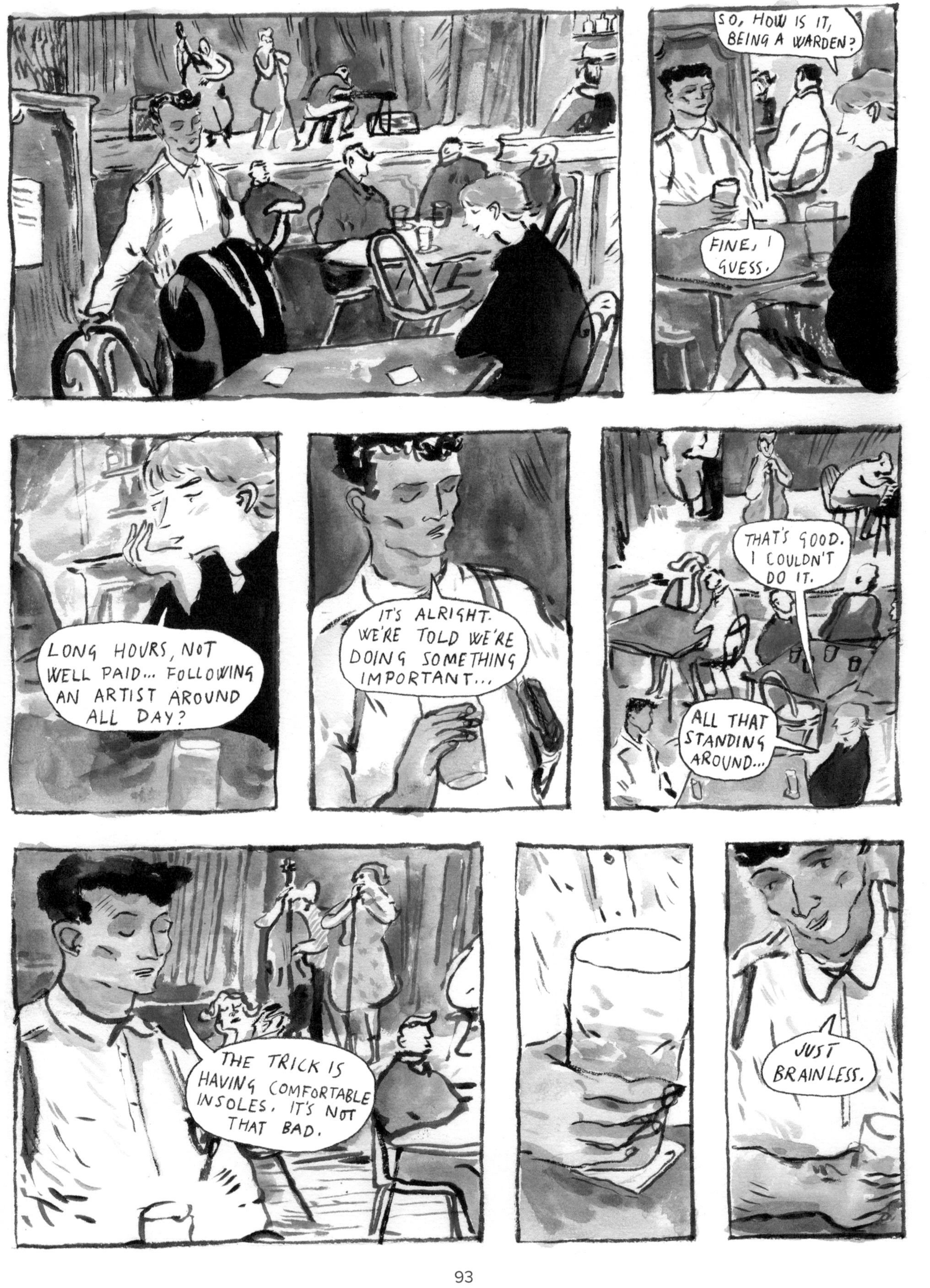
SO, HOW IS IT, BEING A WARDEN?
FINE, I GUESS.
LONG HOURS, NOT WELL PAID... FOLLOWING AN ARTIST AROUND ALL DAY?
IT'S ALRIGHT. WE'RE TOLD WE'RE DOING SOMETHING IMPORTANT...
THAT'S GOOD. I COULDN'T DO IT.
ALL THAT STANDING AROUND...
THE TRICK IS HAVING COMFORTABLE INSOLES. IT'S NOT THAT BAD.
JUST BRAINLESS.

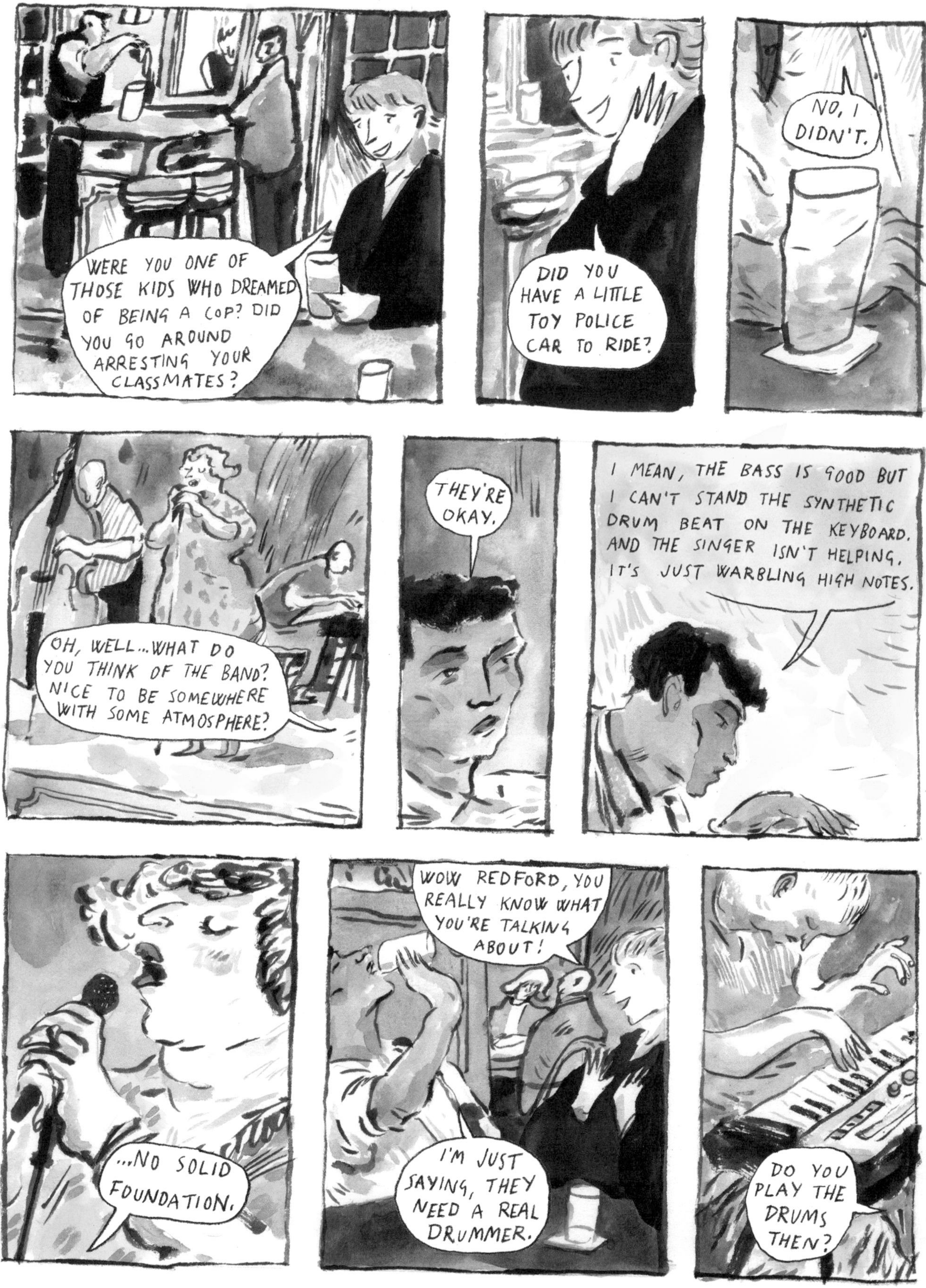
WERE YOU ONE OF THOSE KIDS WHO DREAMED OF BEING A COP? DID YOU GO AROUND ARRESTING YOUR CLASSMATES?
DID YOU HAVE A LITTLE TOY POLICE CAR TO RIDE?
NO, I DIDN'T.
OH, WELL... WHAT DO YOU THINK OF THE BAND? NICE TO BE SOMEWHERE WITH SOME ATMOSPHERE?
THEY'RE OKAY.
I MEAN, THE BASS IS GOOD BUT I CAN'T STAND THE SYNTHETIC DRUM BEAT ON THE KEYBOARD. AND THE SINGER ISN'T HELPING. IT'S JUST WARBLING HIGH NOTES.
...NO SOLID FOUNDATION.
WOW REDFORD, YOU REALLY KNOW WHAT YOU'RE TALKING ABOUT!
I'M JUST SAYING, THEY NEED A REAL DRUMMER.
DO YOU PLAY THE DRUMS THEN?

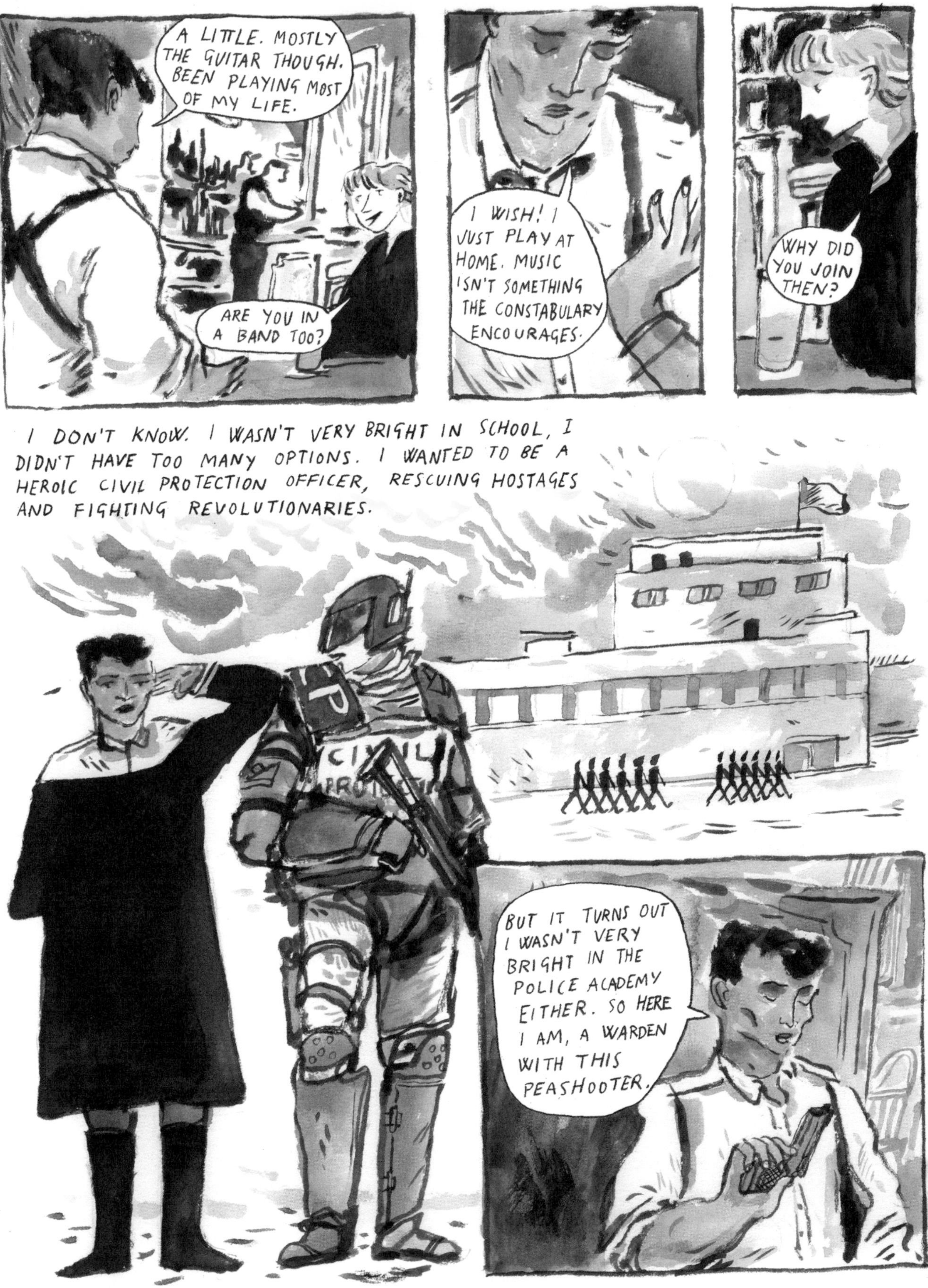
A LITTLE. MOSTLY THE GUITAR THOUGH. BEEN PLAYING MOST OF MY LIFE.
ARE YOU IN A BAND TOO?
I WISH! I JUST PLAY AT HOME. MUSIC ISN'T SOMETHING THE CONSTABULARY ENCOURAGES.
WHY DID YOU JOIN THEN?
I DON'T KNOW. I WASN'T VERY BRIGHT IN SCHOOL, I DIDN'T HAVE TOO MANY OPTIONS. I WANTED TO BE A HEROIC CIVIL PROTECTION OFFICER, RESCUING HOSTAGES AND FIGHTING REVOLUTIONARIES.
BUT IT TURNS OUT I WASN'T VERY BRIGHT IN THE POLICE ACADEMY EITHER. SO HERE I AM, A WARDEN WITH THIS PEASHOOTER.

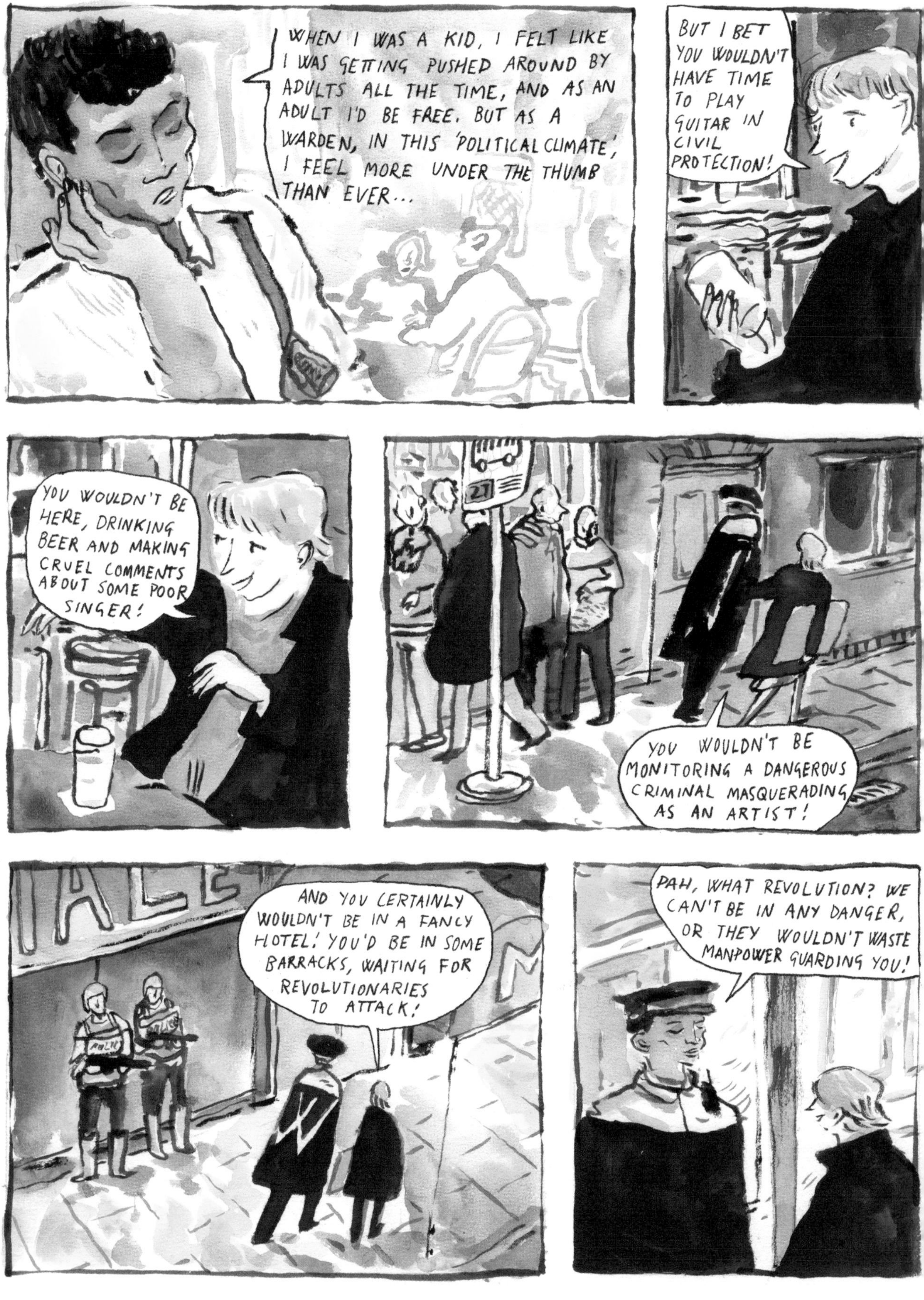

WHEN I WAS A KID, I FELT LIKE I WAS GETTING PUSHED AROUND BY ADULTS ALL THE TIME, AND AS AN ADULT I'D BE FREE. BUT AS A WARDEN, IN THIS 'POLITICAL CLIMATE', I FEEL MORE UNDER THE THUMB THAN EVER...
BUT I BET YOU WOULDN'T HAVE TIME TO PLAY GUITAR IN CIVIL PROTECTION!
YOU WOULDN'T BE HERE, DRINKING BEER AND MAKING CRUEL COMMENTS ABOUT SOME POOR SINGER!
YOU WOULDN'T BE MONITORING A DANGEROUS CRIMINAL MASQUERADING AS AN ARTIST!
AND YOU CERTAINLY WOULDN'T BE IN A FANCY HOTEL! YOU'D BE IN SOME BARRACKS, WAITING FOR REVOLUTIONARIES TO ATTACK!
PAH, WHAT REVOLUTION? WE CAN'T BE IN ANY DANGER, OR THEY WOULDN'T WASTE MANPOWER GUARDING YOU!

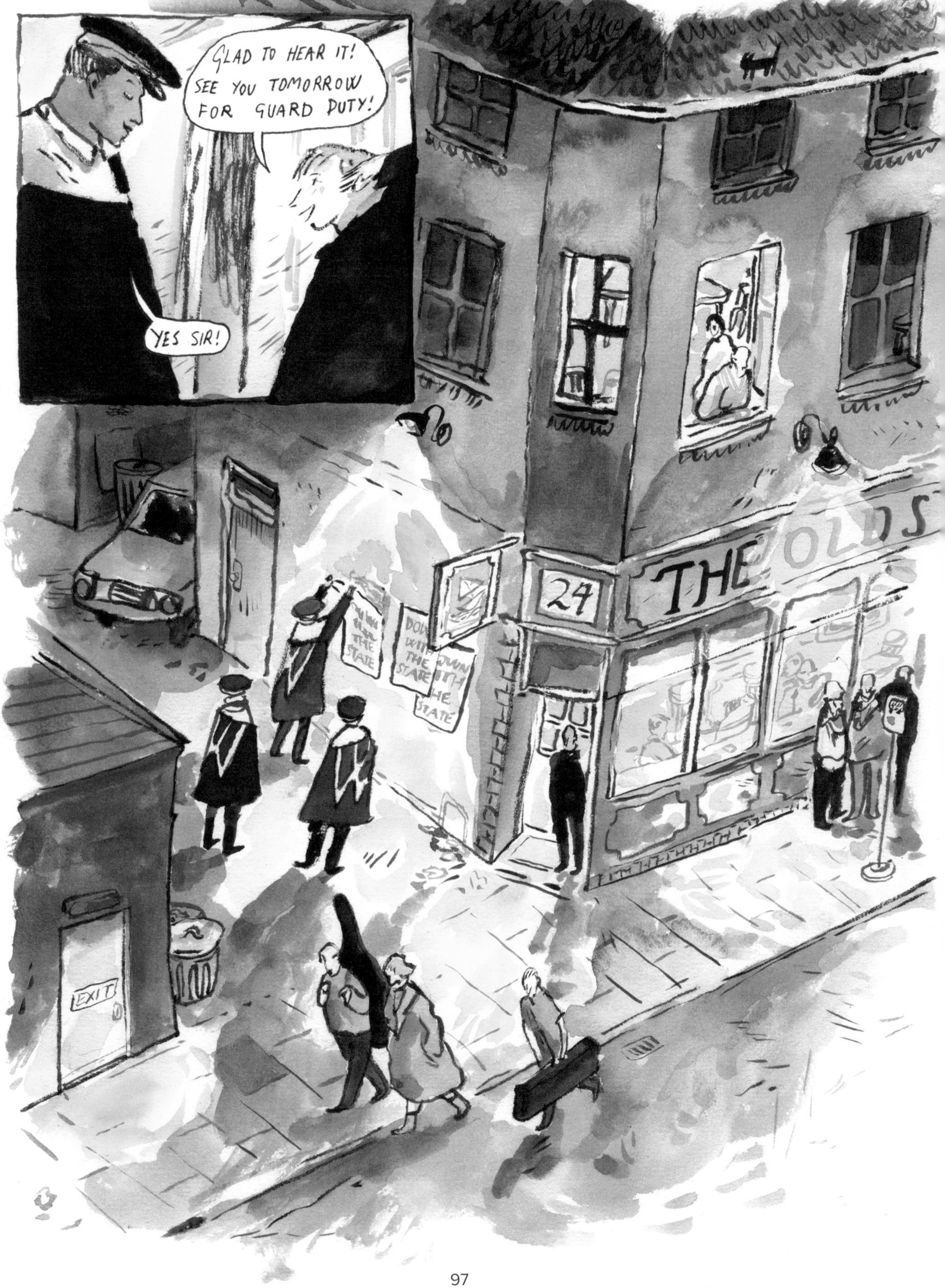
GLAD TO HEAR IT! SEE YOU TOMORROW FOR GUARD DUTY!
YES SIR!
DOWN WITH THE STATE
24
THE
EXIT

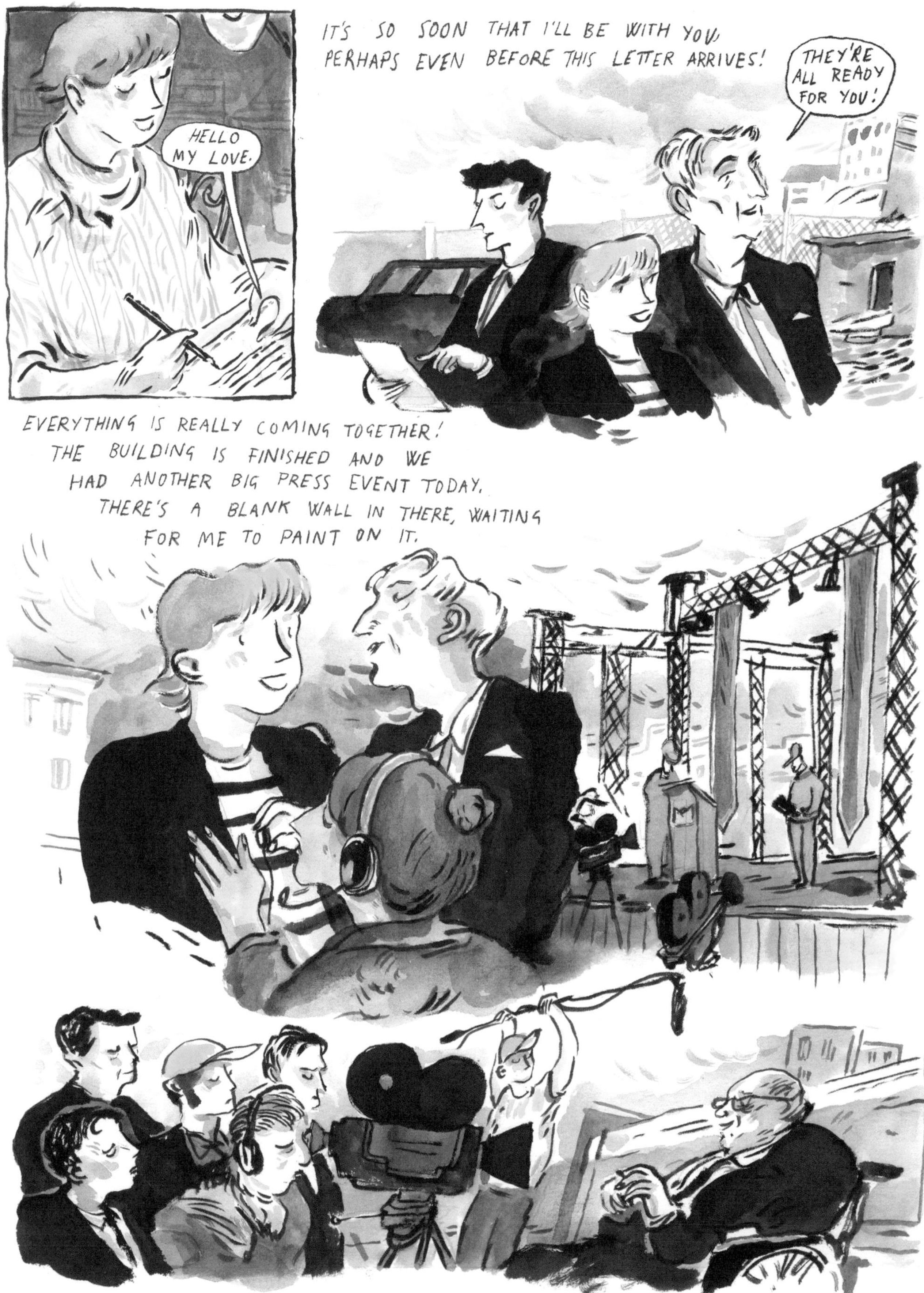
IT'S SO SOON THAT I'LL BE WITH YOU, PERHAPS EVEN BEFORE THIS LETTER ARRIVES!
HELLO MY LOVE.
THEY'RE ALL READY FOR YOU!
EVERYTHING IS REALLY COMING TOGETHER! THE BUILDING IS FINISHED AND WE HAD ANOTHER BIG PRESS EVENT TODAY. THERE'S A BLANK WALL IN THERE, WAITING FOR ME TO PAINT ON IT.

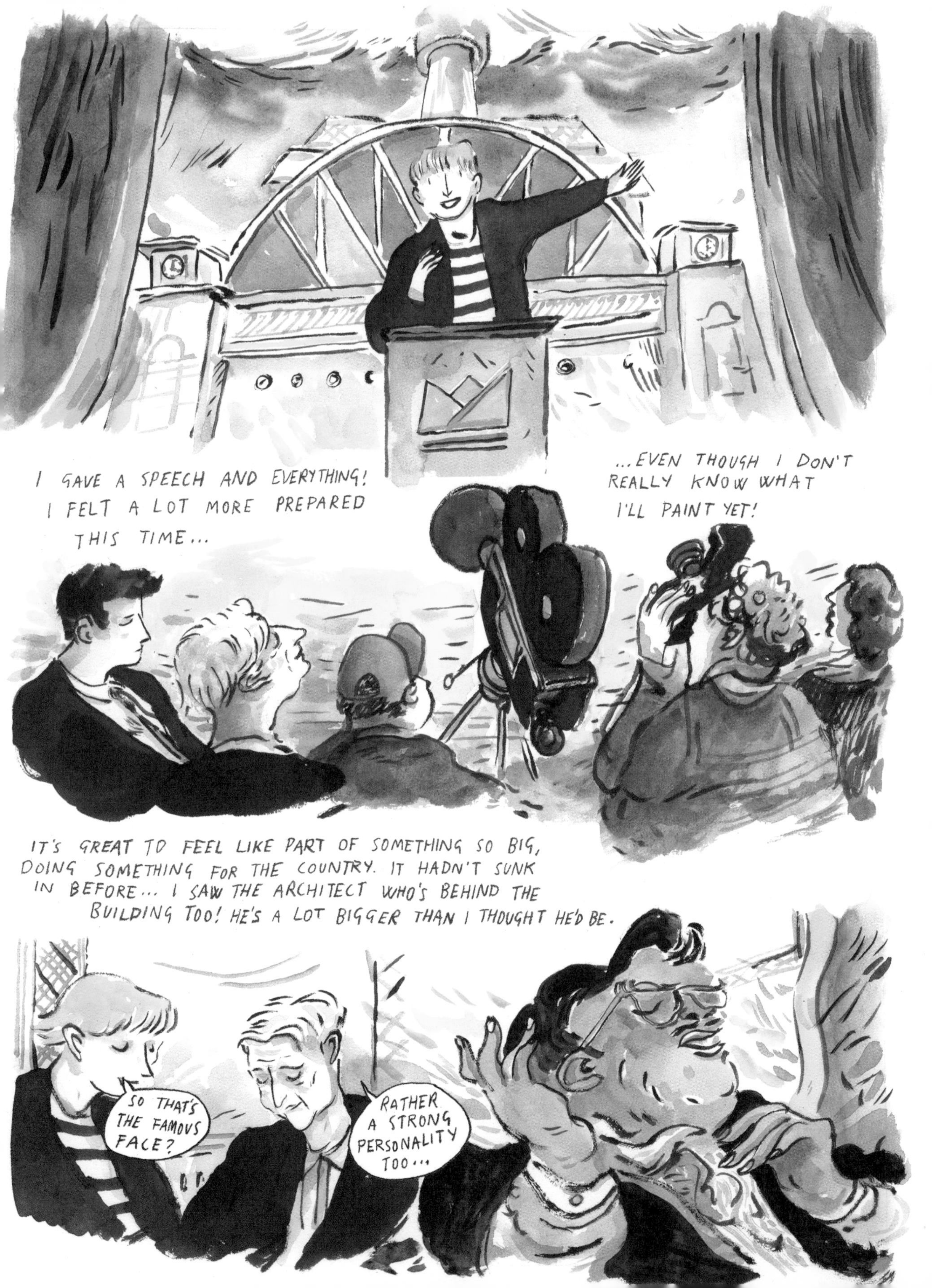
I GAVE A SPEECH AND EVERYTHING! I FELT A LOT MORE PREPARED THIS TIME...
...EVEN THOUGH I DON'T REALLY KNOW WHAT I'LL PAINT YET!
IT'S GREAT TO FEEL LIKE PART OF SOMETHING SO BIG, DOING SOMETHING FOR THE COUNTRY. IT HADN'T SUNK IN BEFORE... I SAW THE ARCHITECT WHO'S BEHIND THE BUILDING TOO! HE'S A LOT BIGGER THAN I THOUGHT HE'D BE.
SO THAT'S THE FAMOUS FACE?
RATHER A STRONG PERSONALITY TOO...

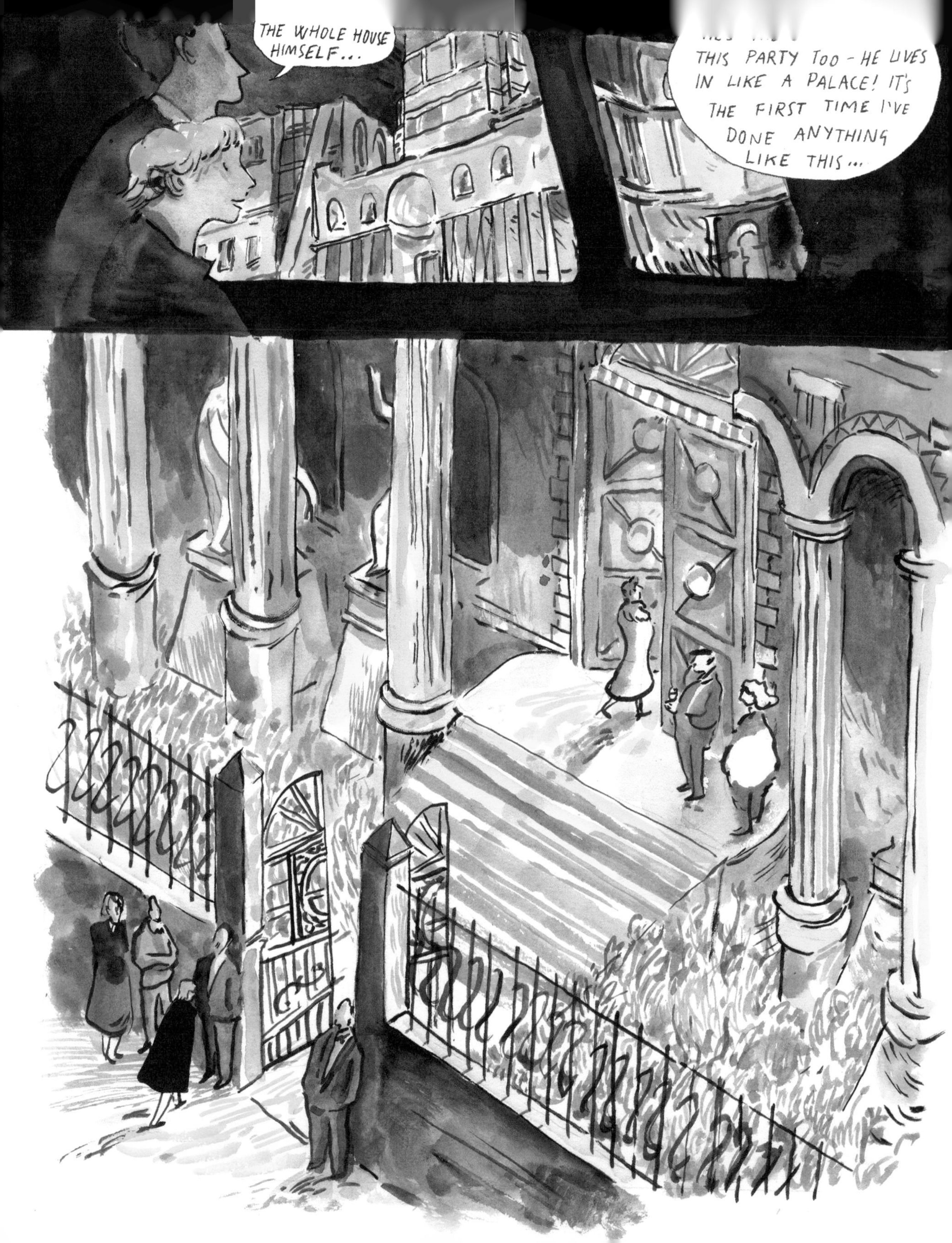
THE WHOLE HOUSE HIMSELF...
THIS PARTY TOO - HE LIVES IN LIKE A PALACE! IT'S THE FIRST TIME I'VE DONE ANYTHING LIKE THIS...

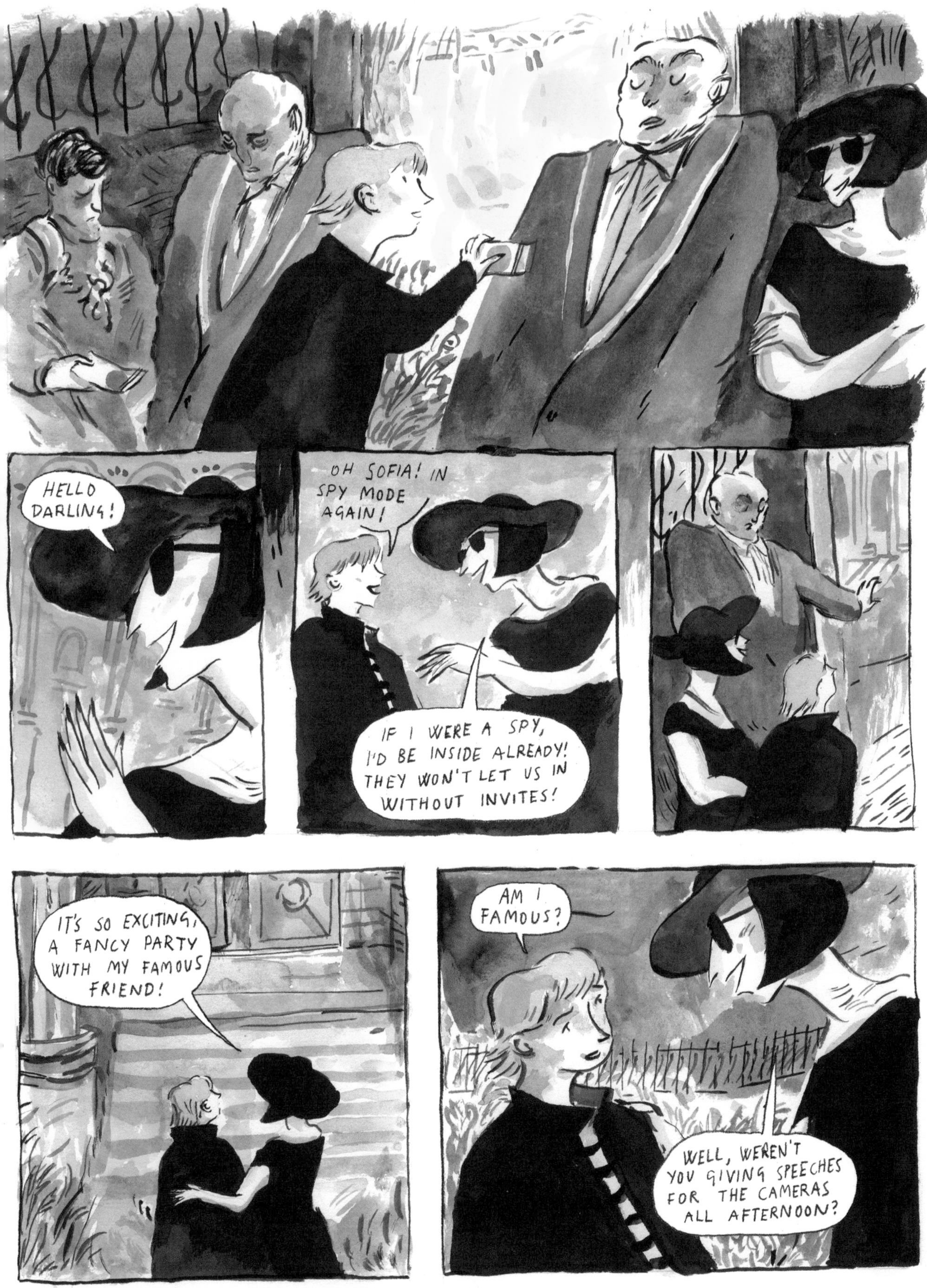
HELLO DARLING!
OH SOFIA! IN SPY MODE AGAIN!
IF I WERE A SPY, I'D BE INSIDE ALREADY! THEY WON'T LET US IN WITHOUT INVITES!
IT'S SO EXCITING, A FANCY PARTY WITH MY FAMOUS FRIEND!
AM I FAMOUS?
WELL, WEREN'T YOU GIVING SPEECHES FOR THE CAMERAS ALL AFTERNOON?

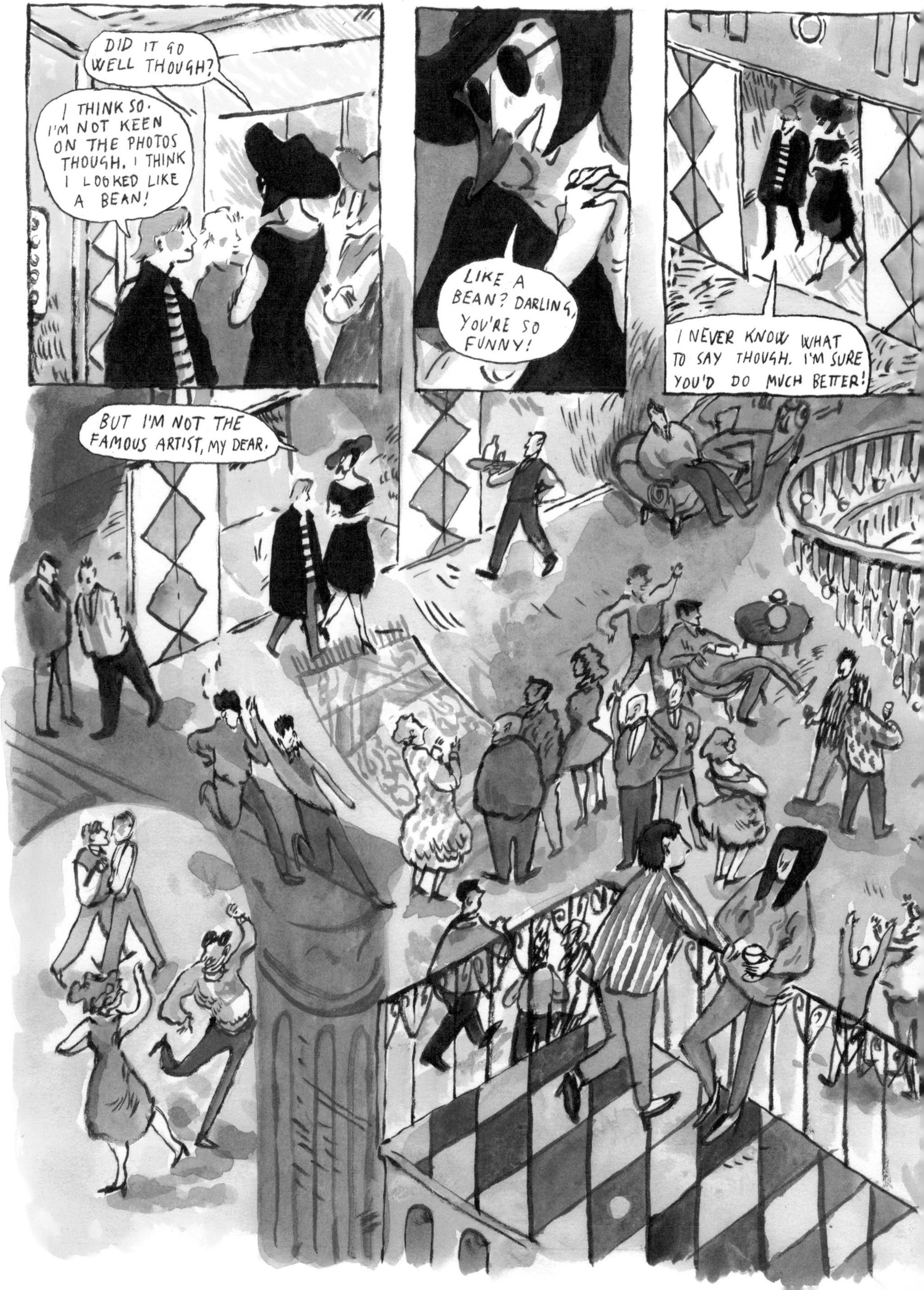
DID IT GO WELL THOUGH?
I THINK SO. I'M NOT KEEN ON THE PHOTOS THOUGH. I THINK I LOOKED LIKE A BEAN!
LIKE A BEAN? DARLING, YOU'RE SO FUNNY!
I NEVER KNOW WHAT TO SAY THOUGH. I'M SURE YOU'D DO MUCH BETTER!
BUT I'M NOT THE FAMOUS ARTIST, MY DEAR.

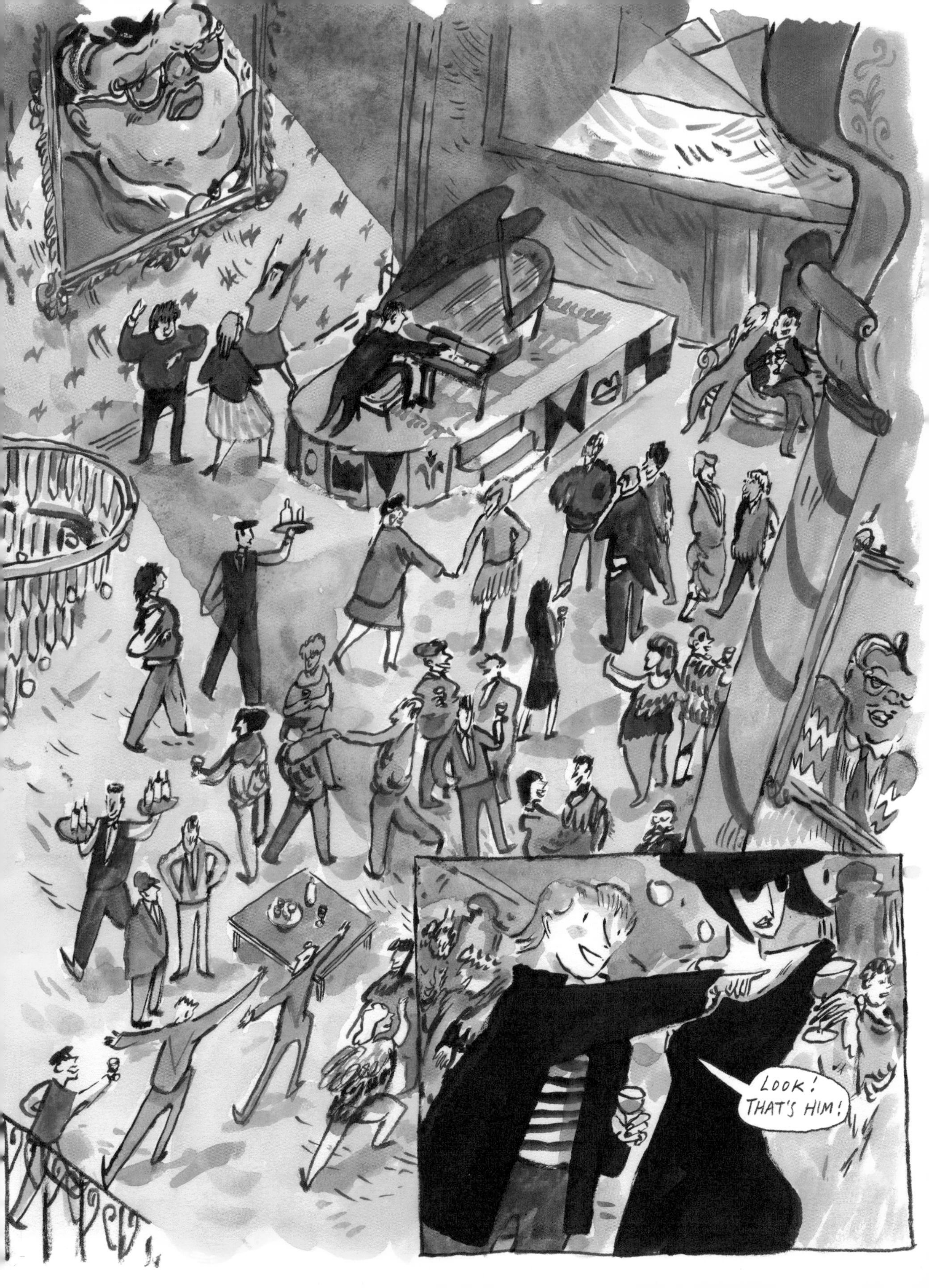
LOOK! THAT'S HIM!

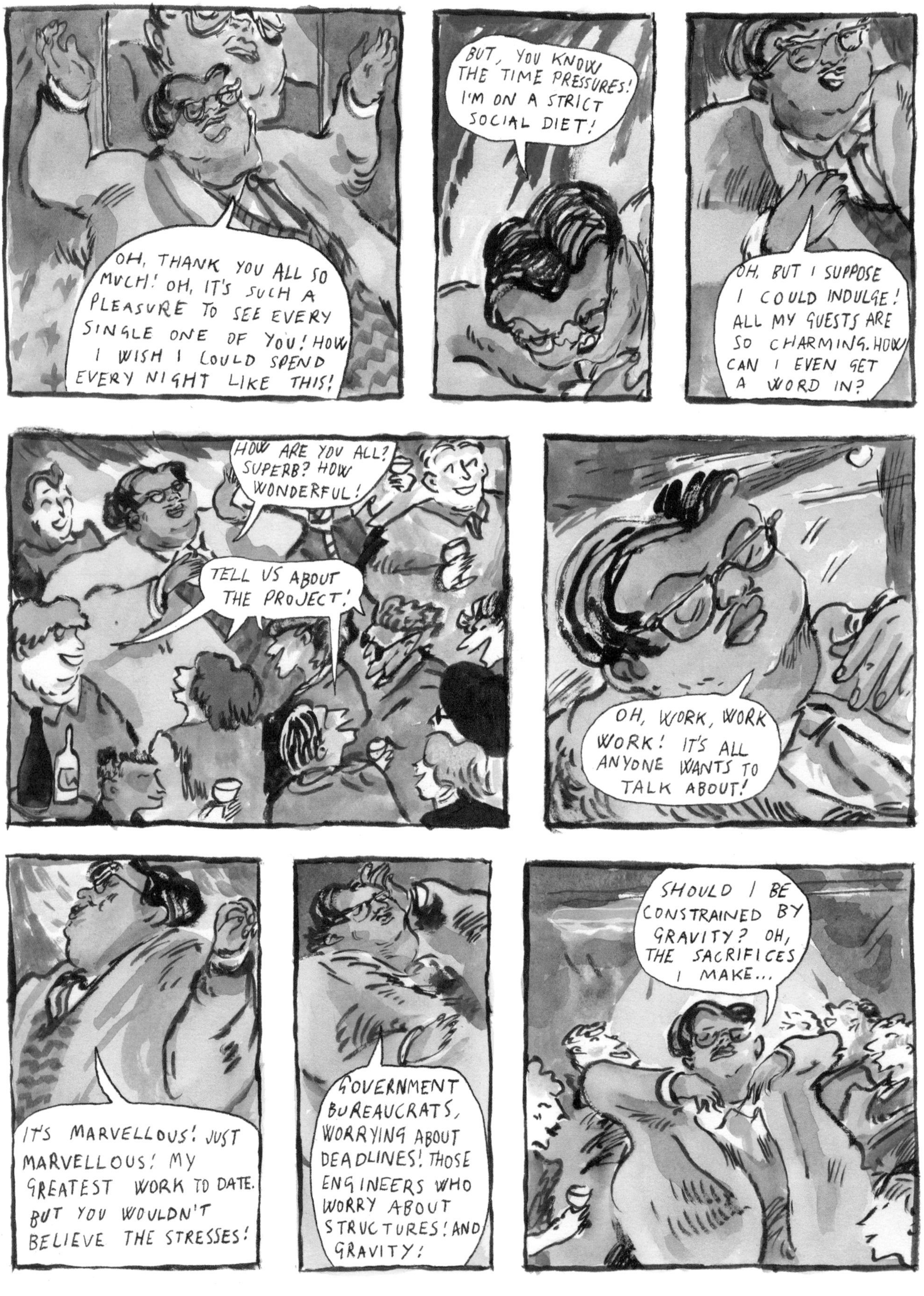
OH, THANK YOU ALL SO MUCH! OH, IT'S SUCH A PLEASURE TO SEE EVERY SINGLE ONE OF YOU! HOW I WISH I COULD SPEND EVERY NIGHT LIKE THIS!
BUT, YOU KNOW THE TIME PRESSURES! I'M ON A STRICT SOCIAL DIET!
OH, BUT I SUPPOSE I COULD INDULGE! ALL MY GUESTS ARE SO CHARMING. HOW CAN I EVEN GET A WORD IN?
HOW ARE YOU ALL? SUPERB? HOW WONDERFUL!
TELL US ABOUT THE PROJECT!
OH, WORK, WORK WORK! IT'S ALL ANYONE WANTS TO TALK ABOUT!
IT'S MARVELLOUS! JUST MARVELLOUS! MY GREATEST WORK TO DATE. BUT YOU WOULDN'T BELIEVE THE STRESSES!
GOVERNMENT BUREAUCRATS, WORRYING ABOUT DEADLINES! THOSE ENGINEERS WHO WORRY ABOUT STRUCTURES! AND GRAVITY!
SHOULD I BE CONSTRAINED BY GRAVITY? OH, THE SACRIFICES I MAKE...

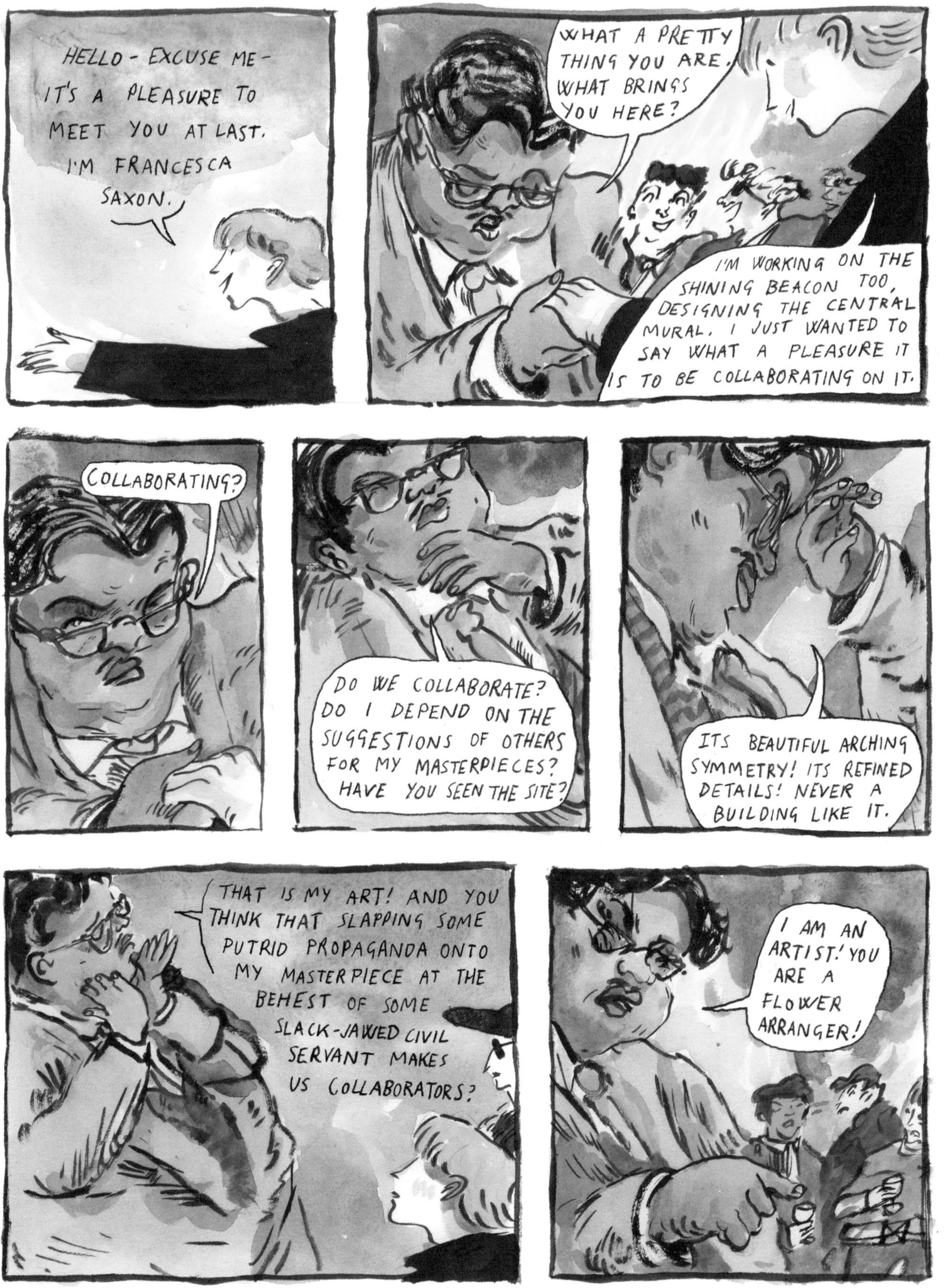
HELLO - EXCUSE ME - IT'S A PLEASURE TO MEET YOU AT LAST. I'M FRANCESCA SAXON.
WHAT A PRETTY THING YOU ARE. WHAT BRINGS YOU HERE?
I'M WORKING ON THE SHINING BEACON TOO, DESIGNING THE CENTRAL MURAL. I JUST WANTED TO SAY WHAT A PLEASURE IT IS TO BE COLLABORATING ON IT.
COLLABORATING?
DO WE COLLABORATE? DO I DEPEND ON THE SUGGESTIONS OF OTHERS FOR MY MASTERPIECES? HAVE YOU SEEN THE SITE?
ITS BEAUTIFUL ARCHING SYMMETRY! ITS REFINED DETAILS! NEVER A BUILDING LIKE IT.
THAT IS MY ART! AND YOU THINK THAT SLAPPING SOME PUTRID PROPAGANDA ONTO MY MASTERPIECE AT THE BEHEST OF SOME SLACK-JAWED CIVIL SERVANT MAKES US COLLABORATORS?
I AM AN ARTIST! YOU ARE A FLOWER ARRANGER!

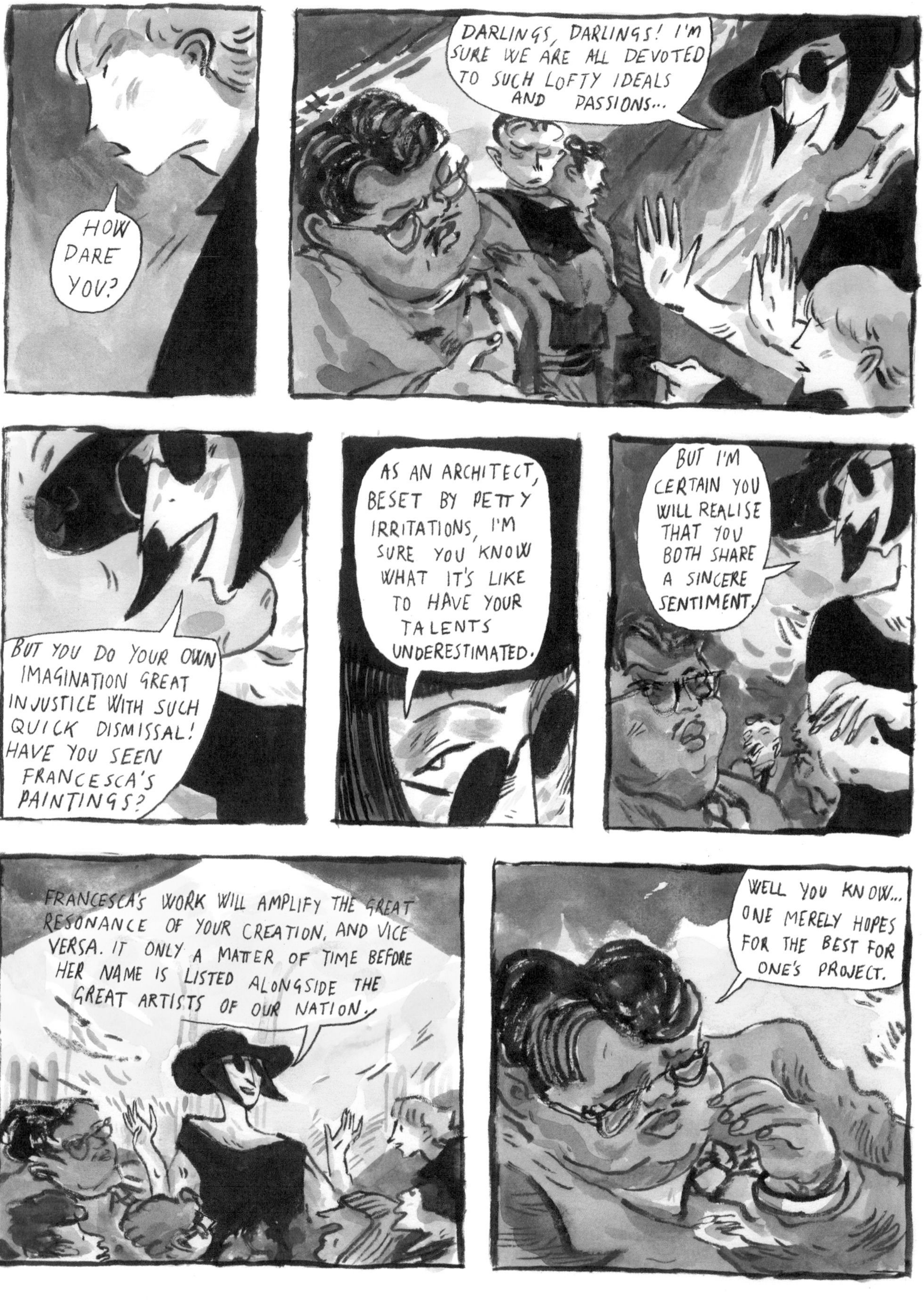
HOW DARE YOU?
DARLINGS, DARLINGS! I'M SURE WE ARE ALL DEVOTED TO SUCH LOFTY IDEALS AND PASSIONS...
BUT YOU DO YOUR OWN IMAGINATION GREAT INJUSTICE WITH SUCH QUICK DISMISSAL! HAVE YOU SEEN FRANCESCA'S PAINTINGS?
AS AN ARCHITECT, BESET BY PETTY IRRITATIONS, I'M SURE YOU KNOW WHAT IT'S LIKE TO HAVE YOUR TALENTS UNDERESTIMATED.
BUT I'M CERTAIN YOU WILL REALISE THAT YOU BOTH SHARE A SINCERE SENTIMENT.
FRANCESCA'S WORK WILL AMPLIFY THE GREAT RESONANCE OF YOUR CREATION, AND VICE VERSA. IT ONLY A MATTER OF TIME BEFORE HER NAME IS LISTED ALONGSIDE THE GREAT ARTISTS OF OUR NATION.
WELL YOU KNOW... ONE MERELY HOPES FOR THE BEST FOR ONE'S PROJECT.

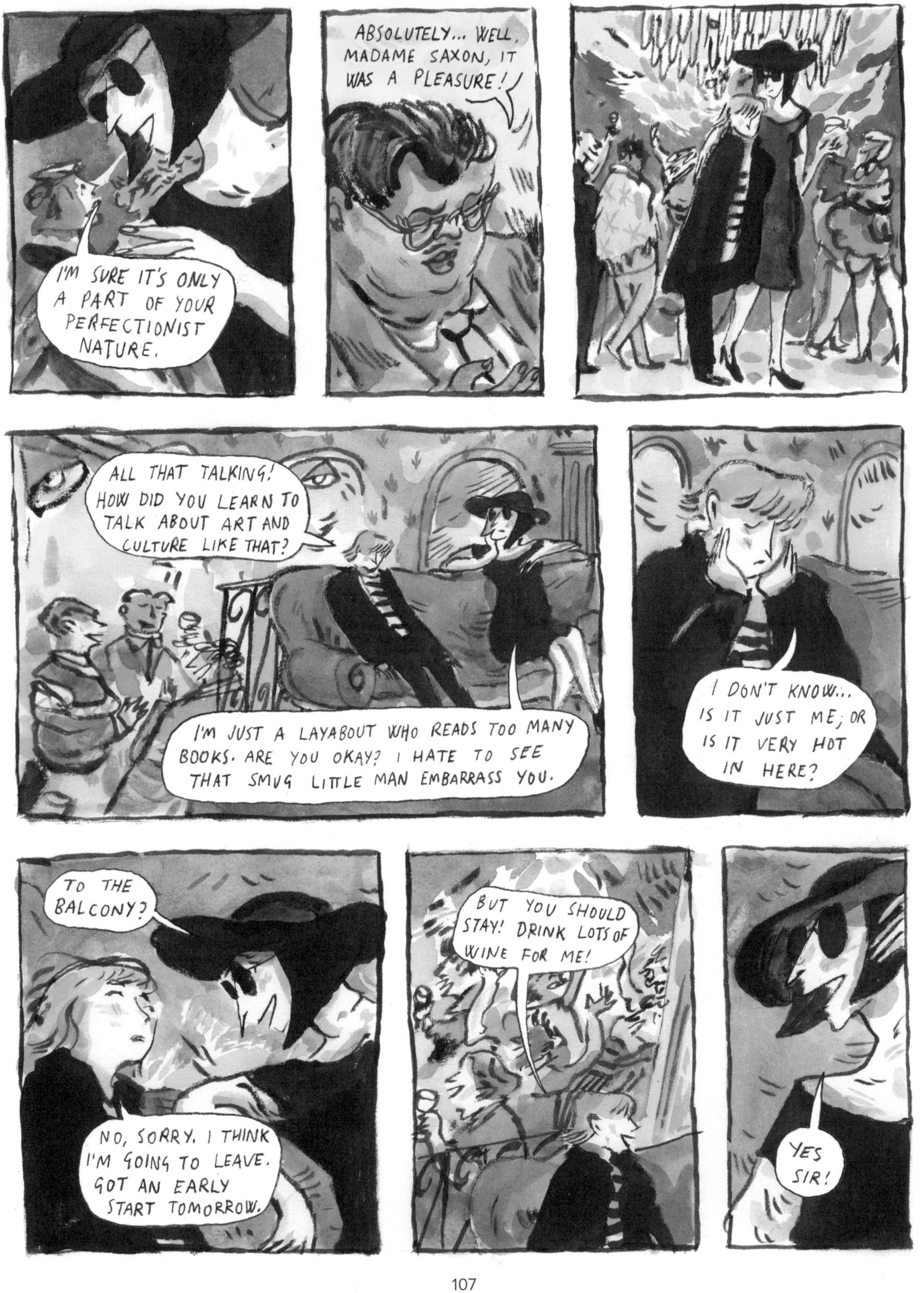
I'M SURE IT'S ONLY A PART OF YOUR PERFECTIONIST NATURE.
ABSOLUTELY... WELL, MADAME SAXON, IT WAS A PLEASURE!
ALL THAT TALKING! HOW DID YOU LEARN TO TALK ABOUT ART AND CULTURE LIKE THAT?
I'M JUST A LAYABOUT WHO READS TOO MANY BOOKS. ARE YOU OKAY? I HATE TO SEE THAT SMUG LITTLE MAN EMBARRASS YOU.
I DON'T KNOW... IS IT JUST ME, OR IS IT VERY HOT IN HERE?
TO THE BALCONY?
NO, SORRY. I THINK I'M GOING TO LEAVE. GOT AN EARLY START TOMORROW.
BUT YOU SHOULD STAY! DRINK LOTS OF WINE FOR ME!
YES SIR!

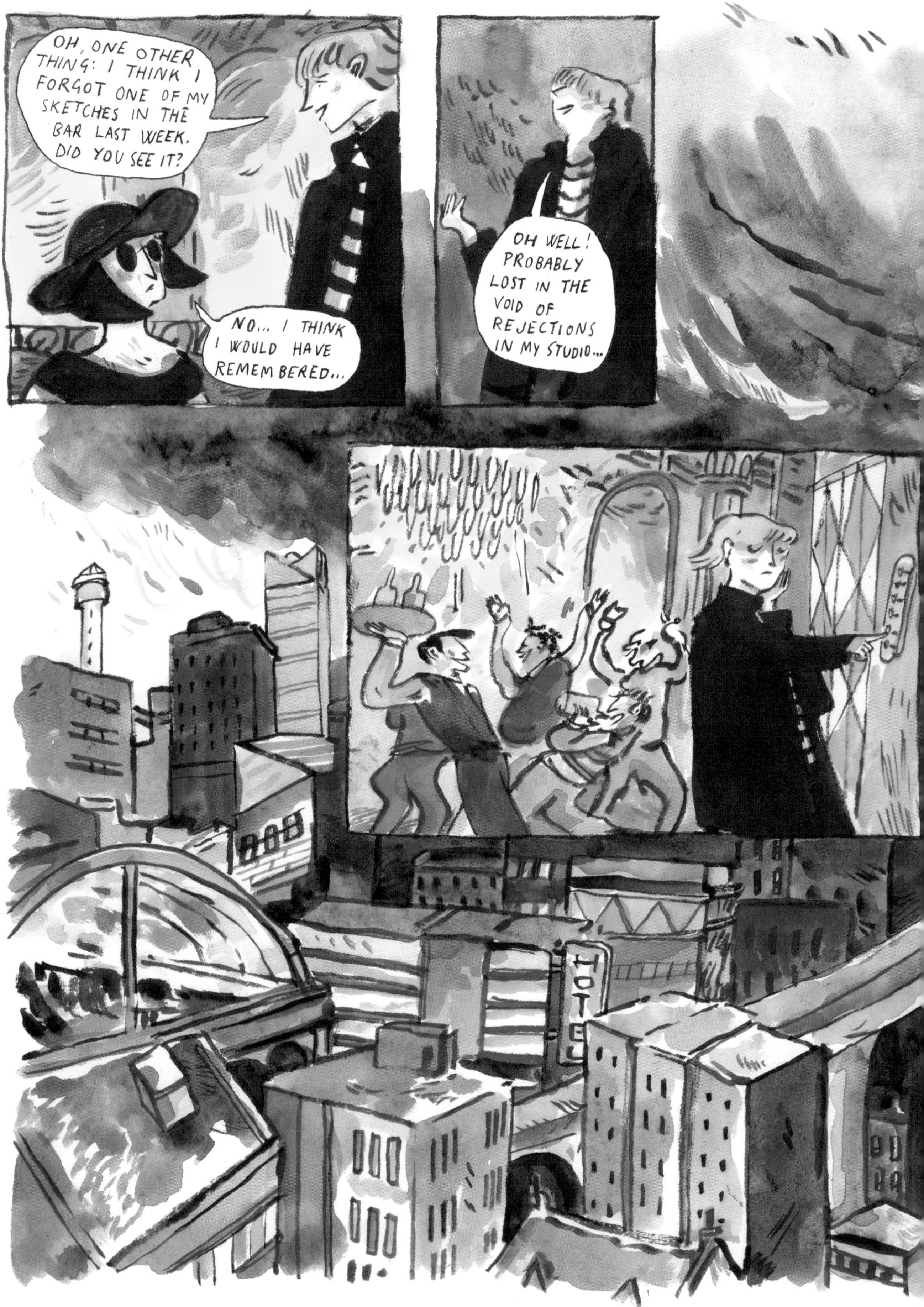
OH, ONE OTHER THING: I THINK I FORGOT ONE OF MY SKETCHES IN THE BAR LAST WEEK. DID YOU SEE IT?
NO... I THINK I WOULD HAVE REMEMBERED...
OH WELL! PROBABLY LOST IN THE VOID OF REJECTIONS IN MY STUDIO...
HOTEL

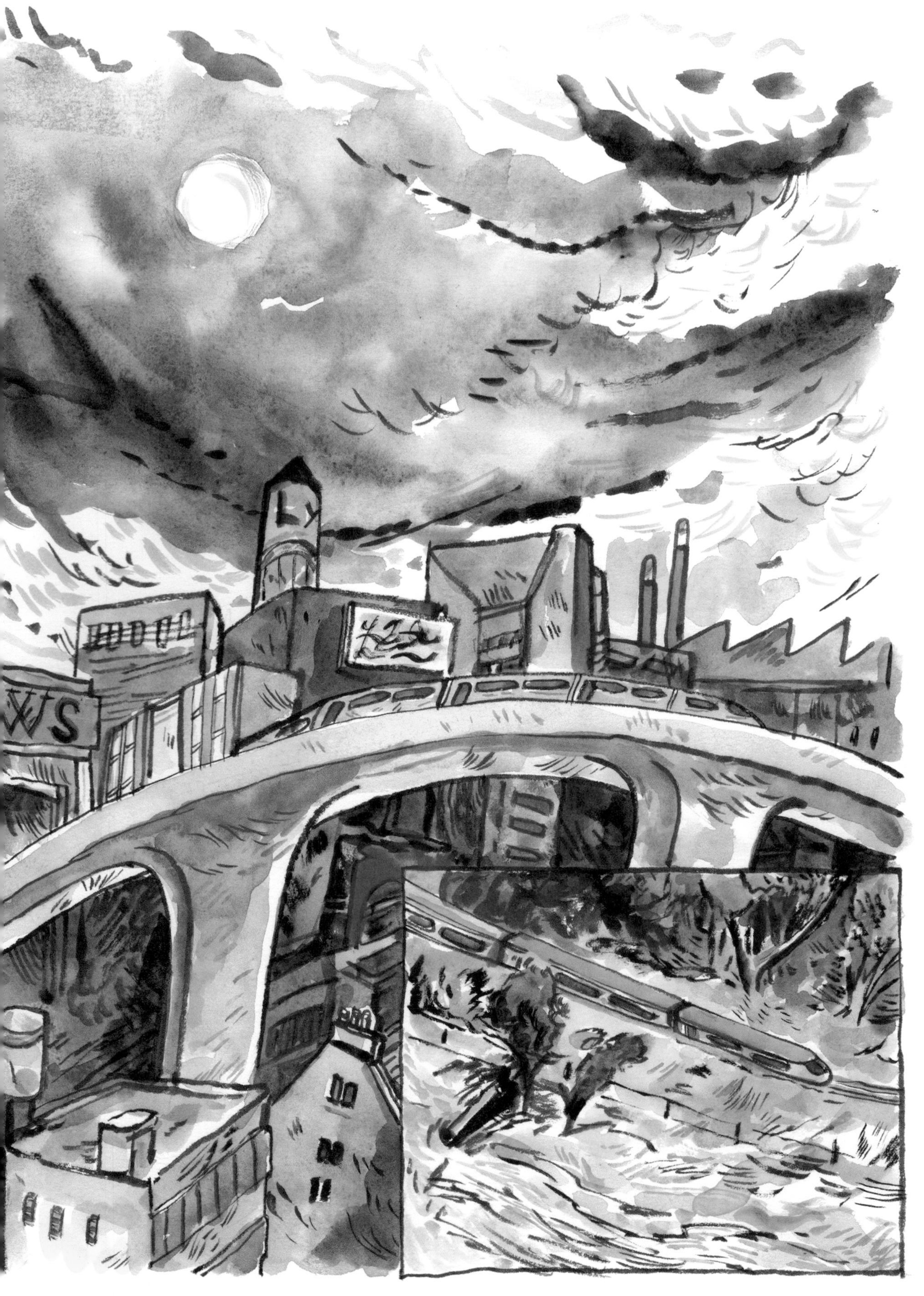

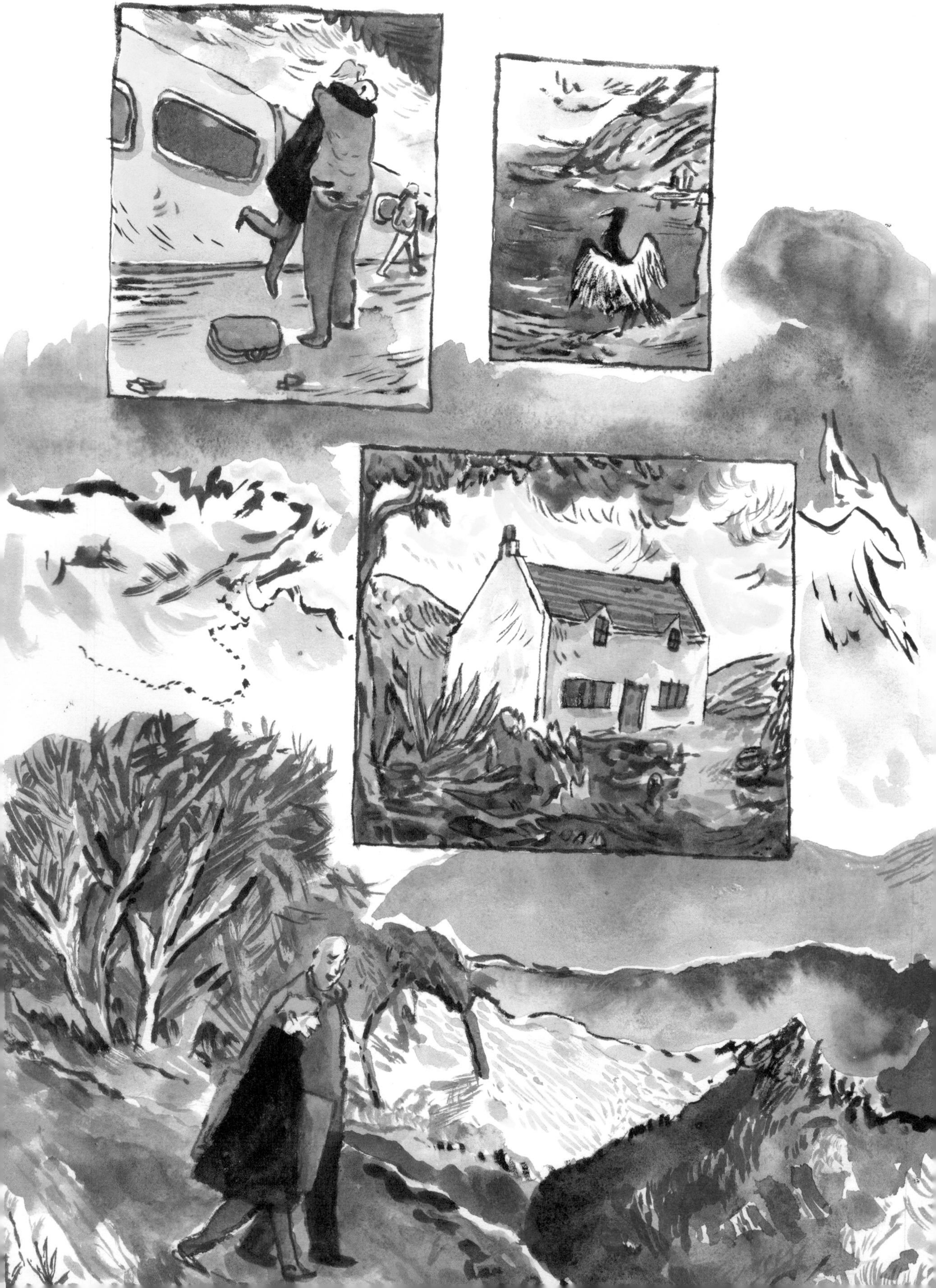

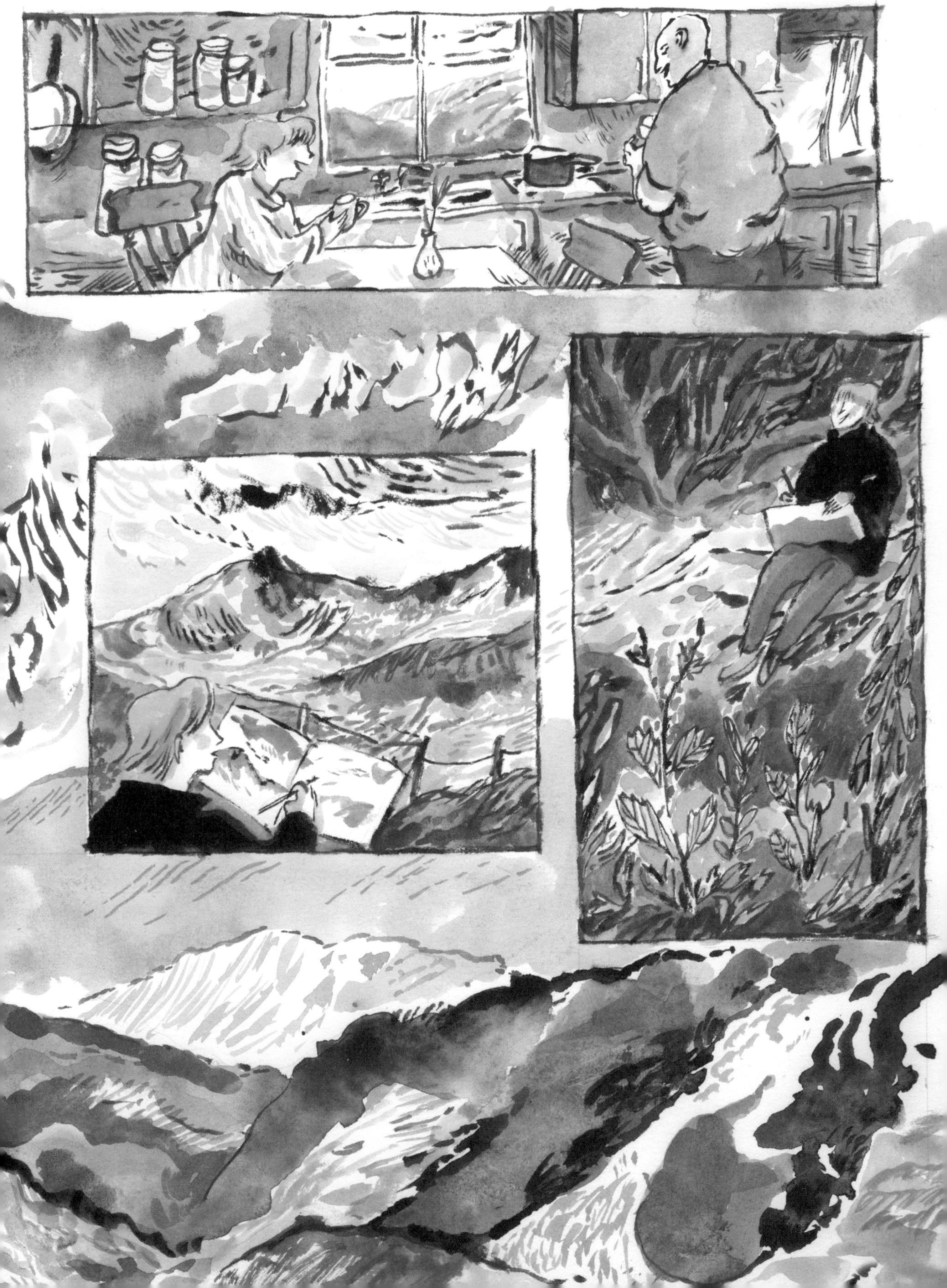

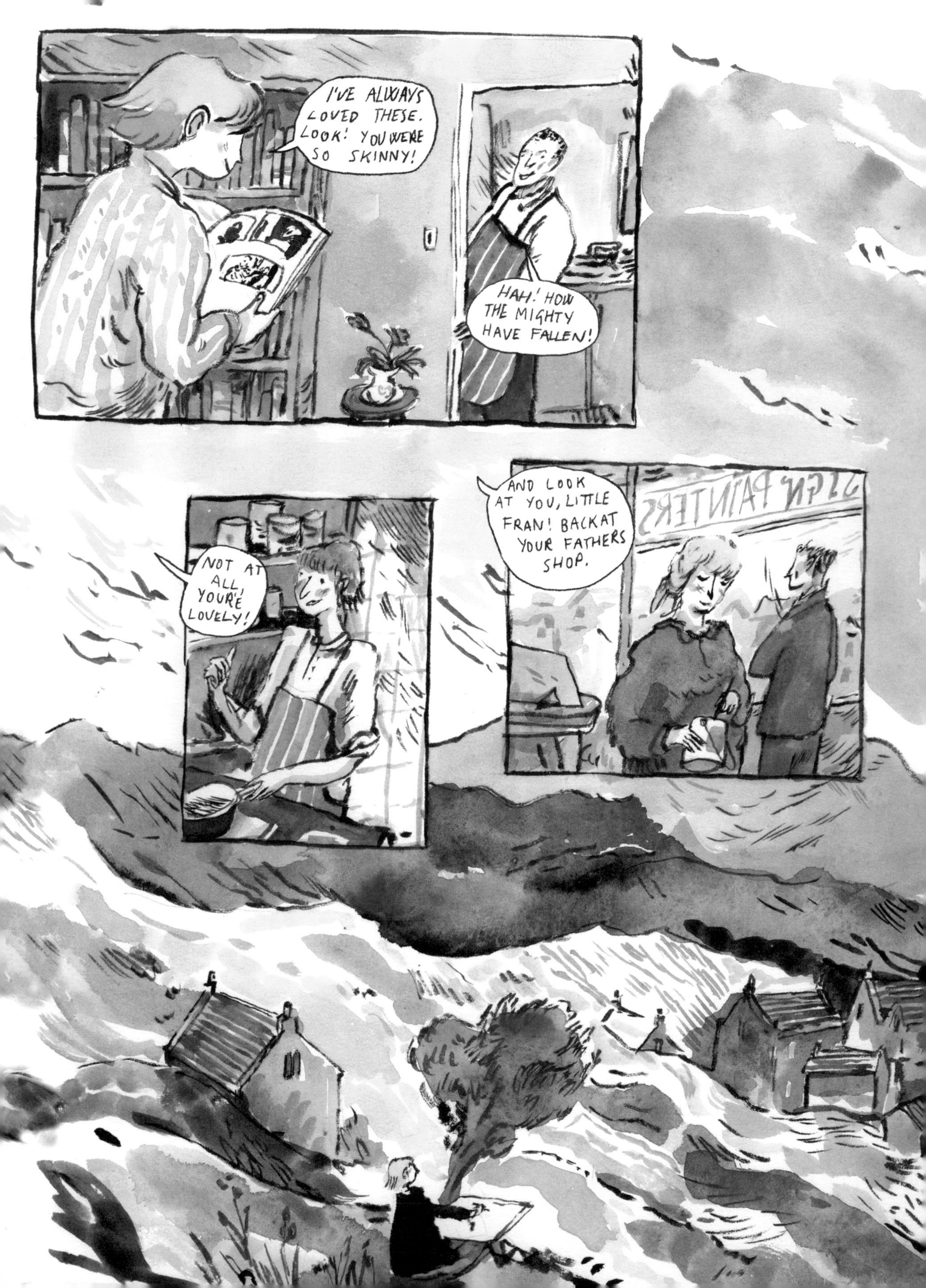
I'VE ALWAYS LOVED THESE. LOOK! YOU WERE SO SKINNY!
HAH! HOW THE MIGHTY HAVE FALLEN!
AND LOOK AT YOU, LITTLE FRAN! BACK AT YOUR FATHERS SHOP.
SIGN PAINTERS
NOT AT ALL, YOU'RE LOVELY!

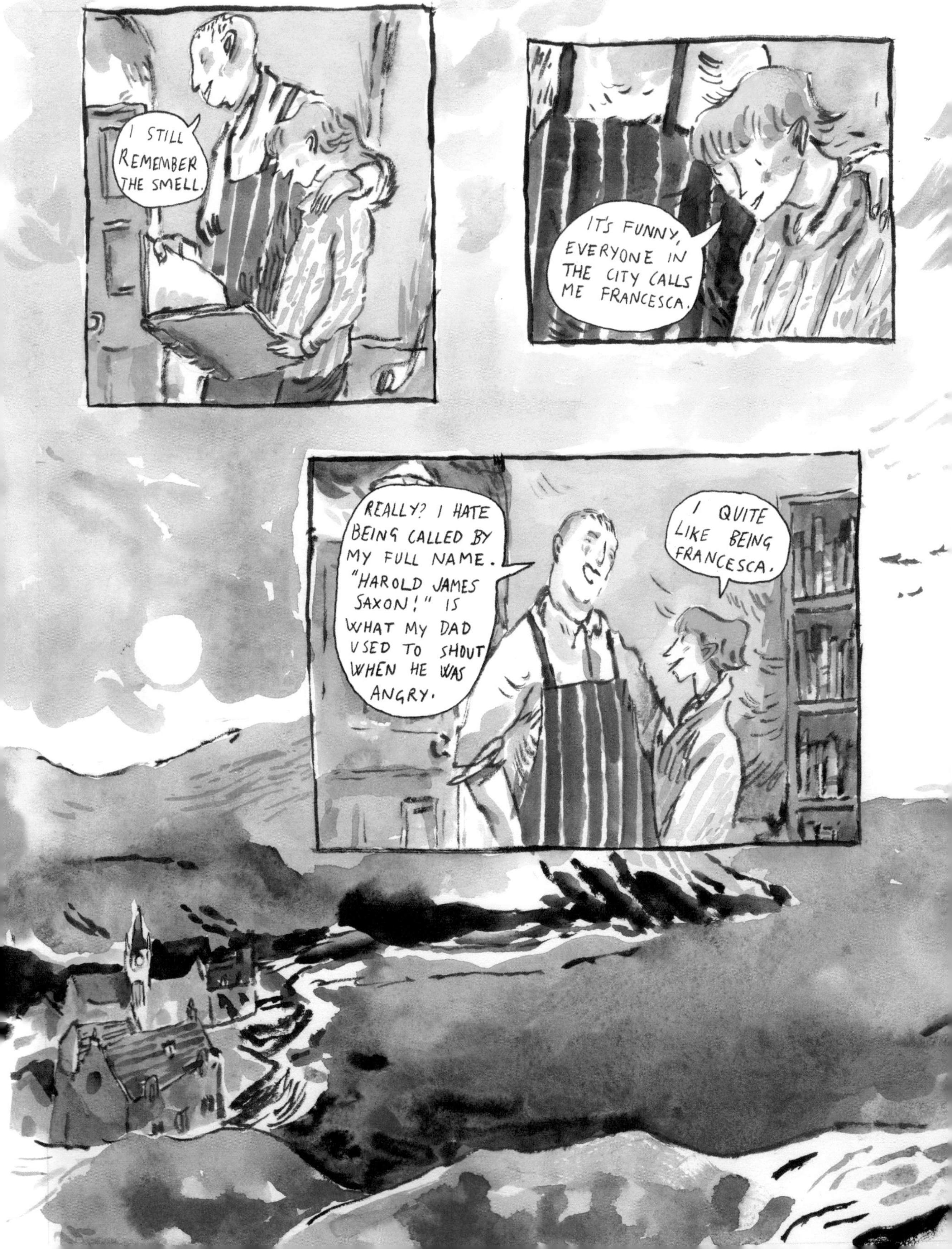
I STILL REMEMBER THE SMELL.
IT'S FUNNY, EVERYONE IN THE CITY CALLS ME FRANCESCA.
REALLY? I HATE BEING CALLED BY MY FULL NAME. "HAROLD JAMES SAXON!" IS WHAT MY DAD USED TO SHOUT WHEN HE WAS ANGRY.
I QUITE LIKE BEING FRANCESCA.

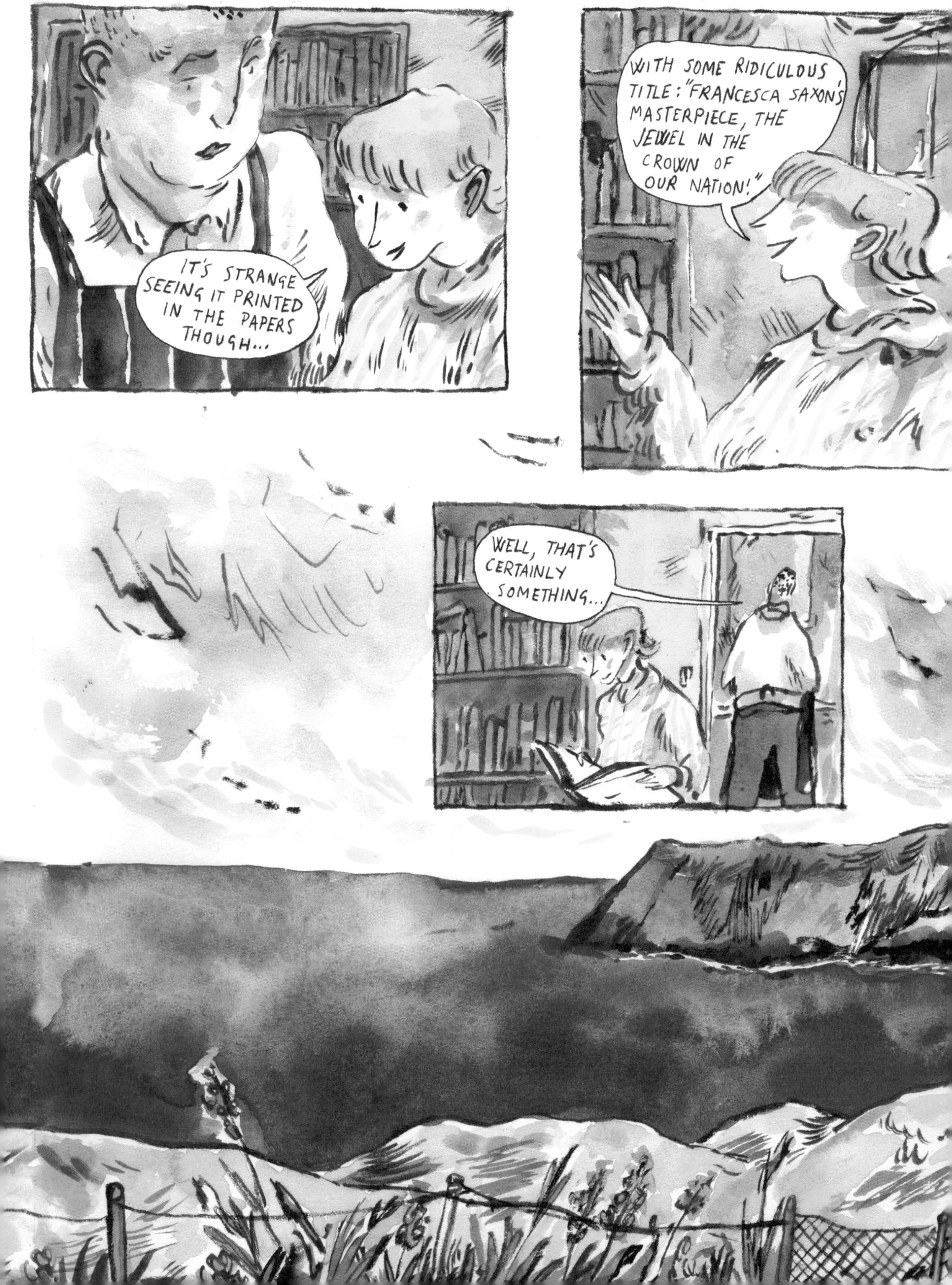
IT'S STRANGE SEEING IT PRINTED IN THE PAPERS THOUGH...
WITH SOME RIDICULOUS TITLE: "FRANCESCA SAXON'S MASTERPIECE, THE JEWEL IN THE CROWN OF OUR NATION!"
WELL, THAT'S CERTAINLY SOMETHING...

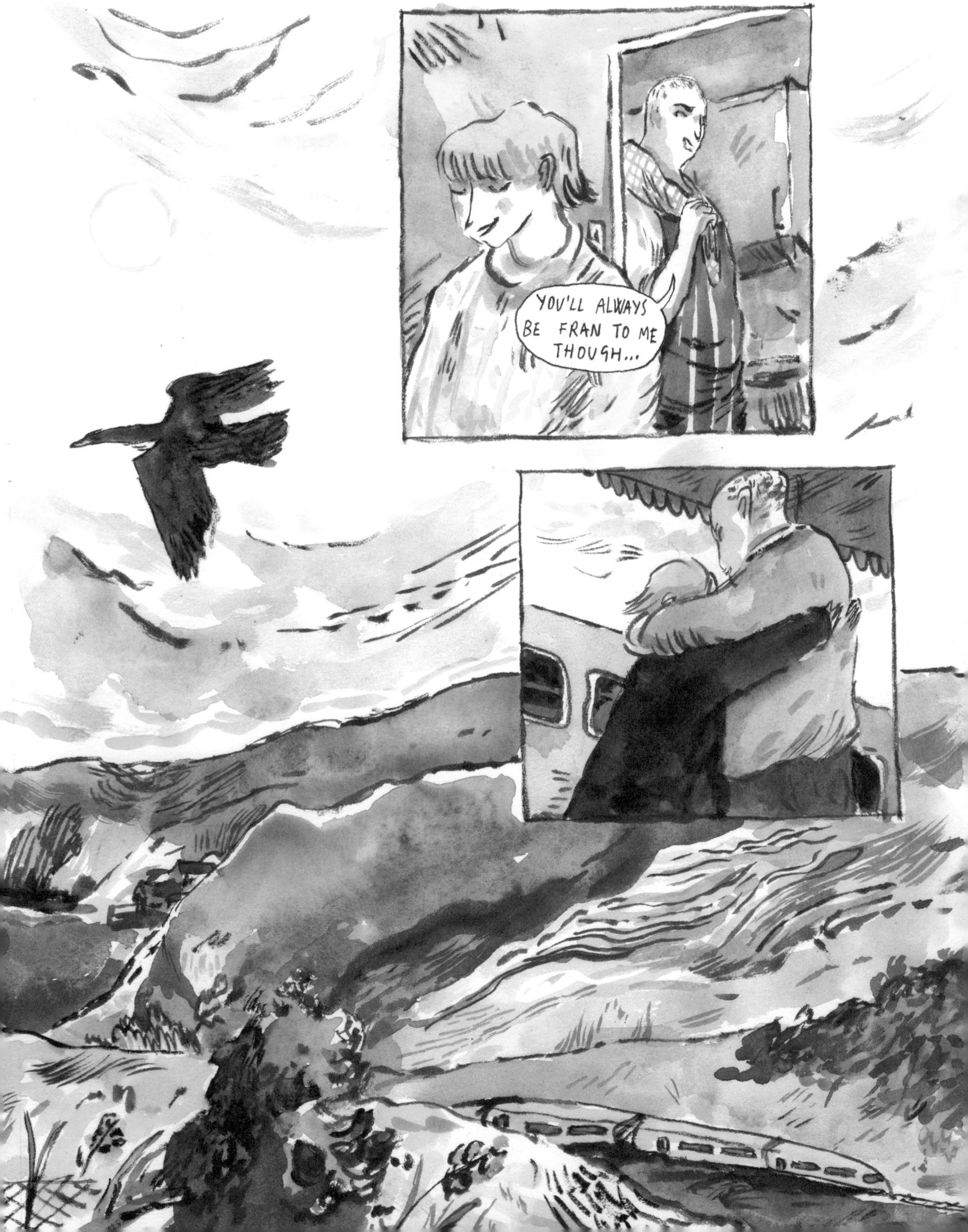
YOU'LL ALWAYS BE FRAN TO ME THOUGH...

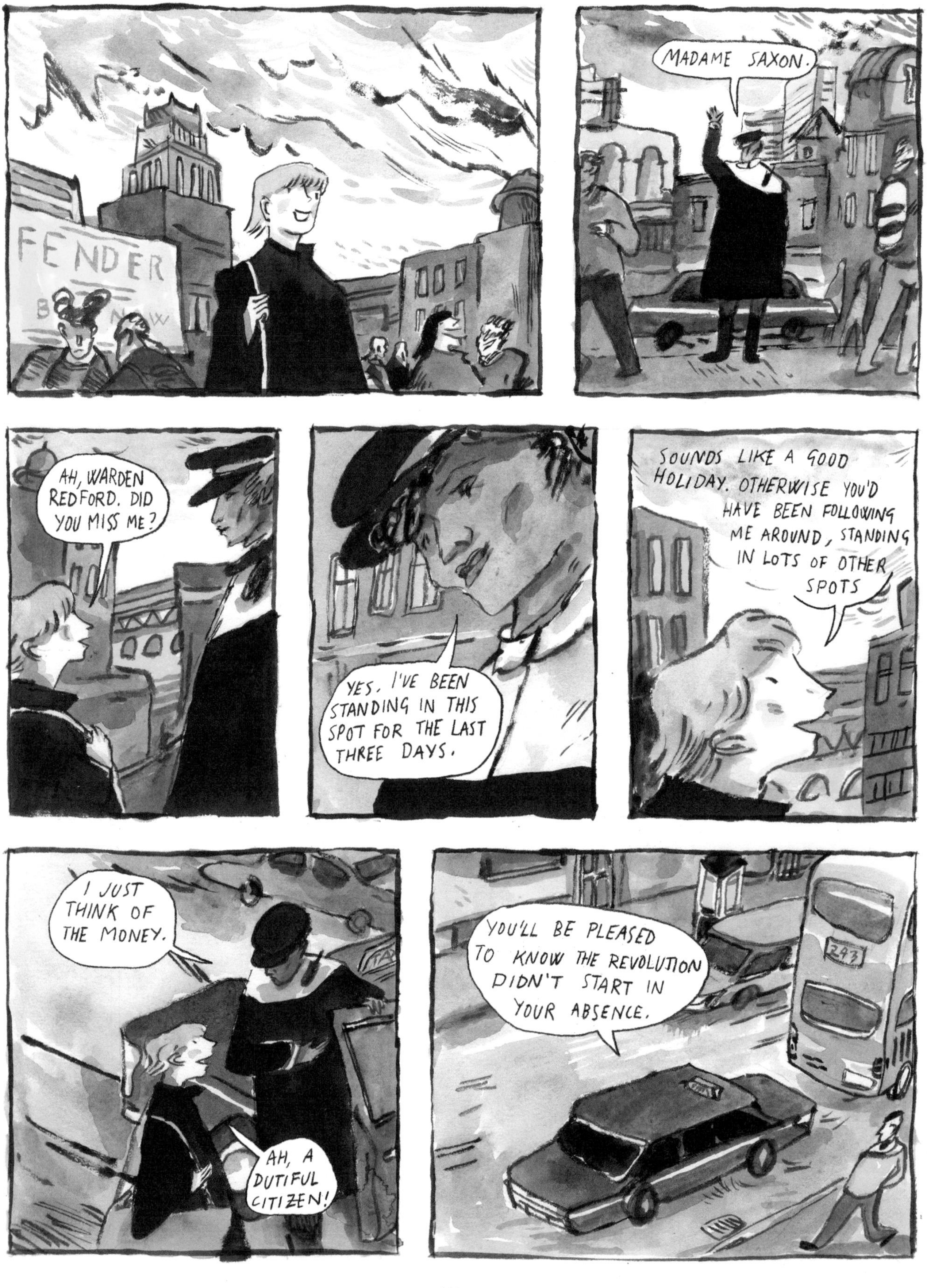
FENDER
MADAME SAXON.
AH, WARDEN REDFORD. DID YOU MISS ME?
YES. I'VE BEEN STANDING IN THIS SPOT FOR THE LAST THREE DAYS.
SOUNDS LIKE A GOOD HOLIDAY. OTHERWISE YOU'D HAVE BEEN FOLLOWING ME AROUND, STANDING IN LOTS OF OTHER SPOTS
I JUST THINK OF THE MONEY.
AH, A DUTIFUL CITIZEN!
YOU'LL BE PLEASED TO KNOW THE REVOLUTION DIDN'T START IN YOUR ABSENCE.
243

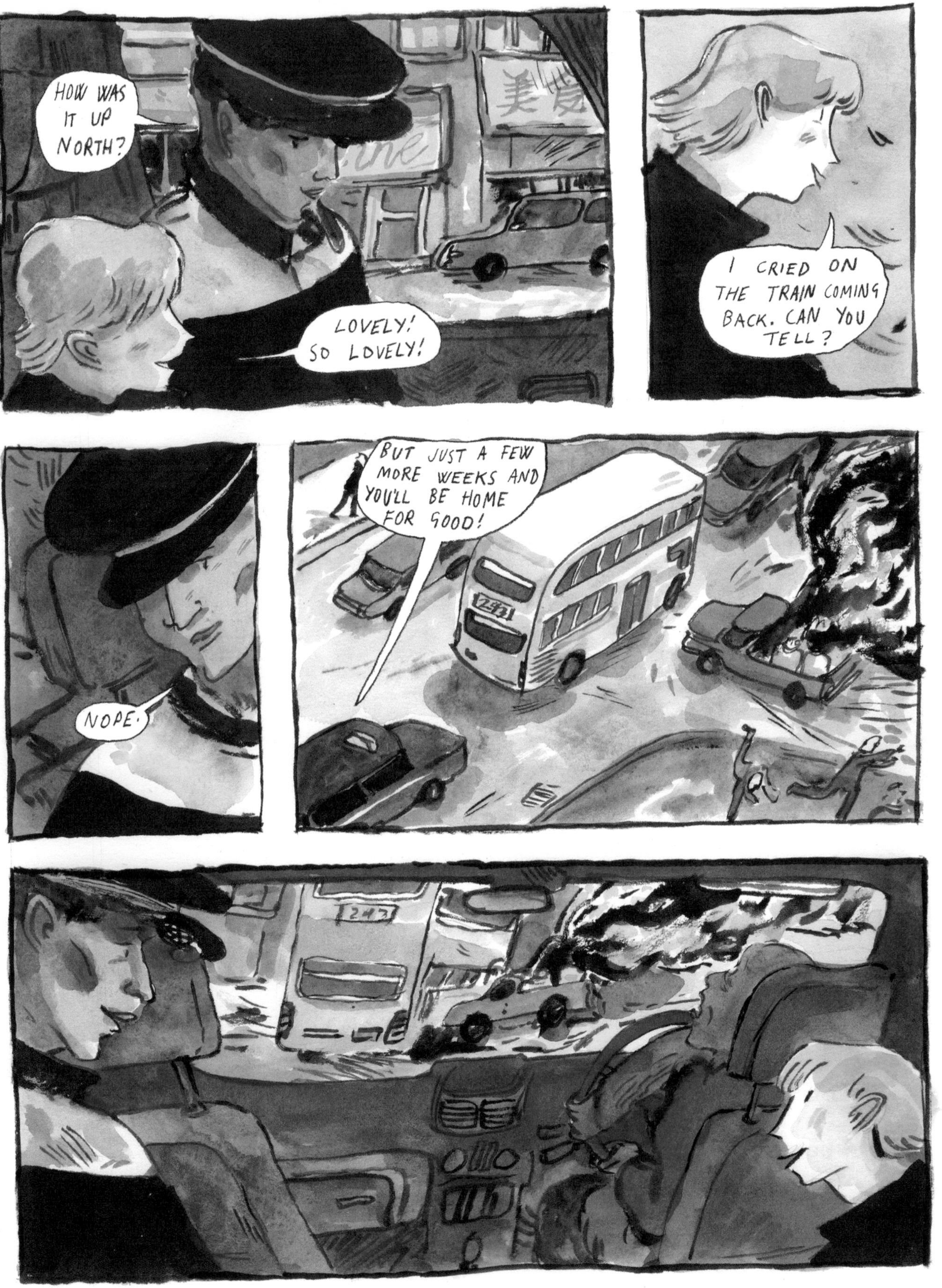
HOW WAS IT UP NORTH?
LOVELY! SO LOVELY!
I CRIED ON THE TRAIN COMING BACK. CAN YOU TELL?
NOPE.
BUT JUST A FEW MORE WEEKS AND YOU'LL BE HOME FOR GOOD!

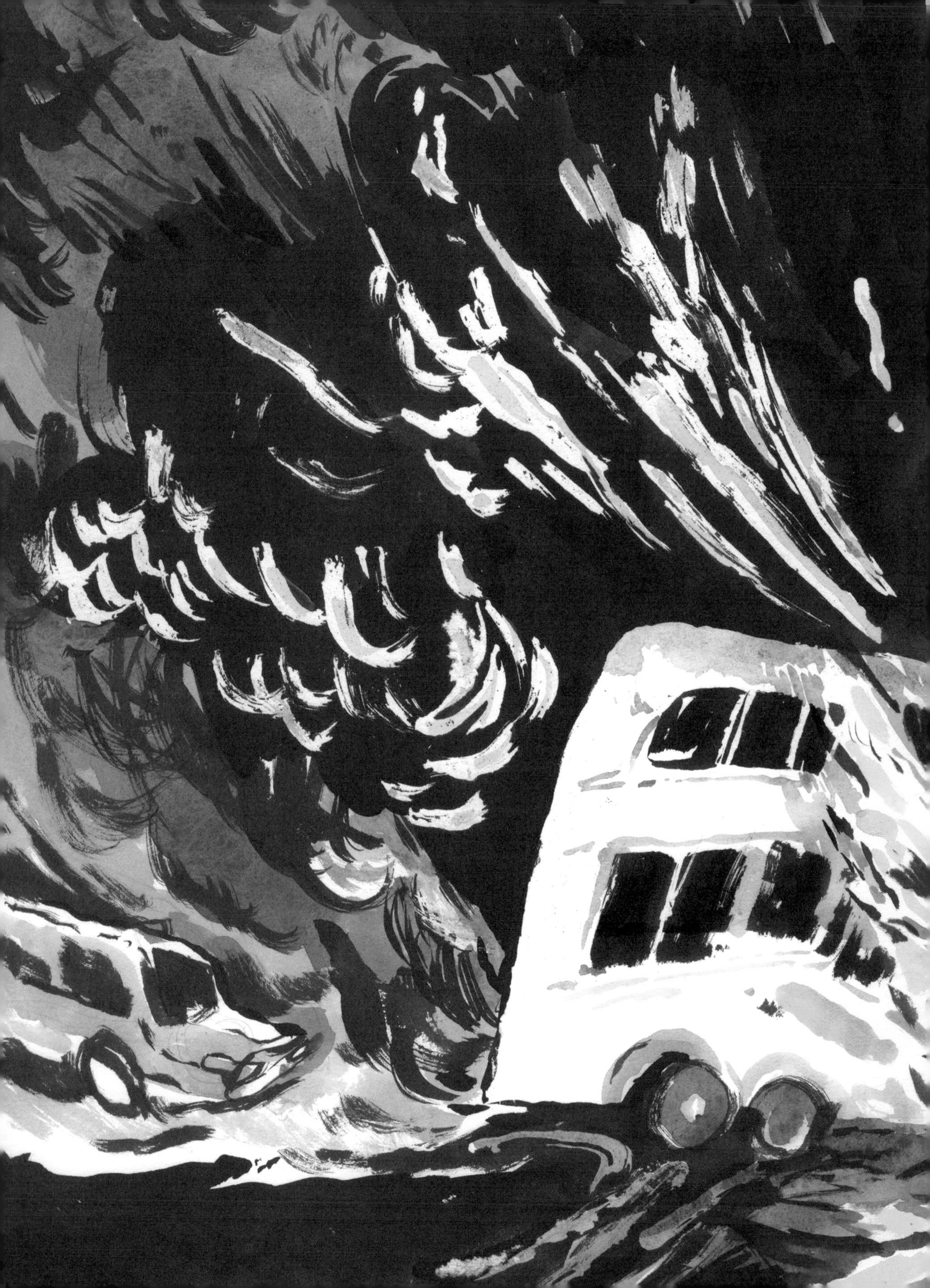

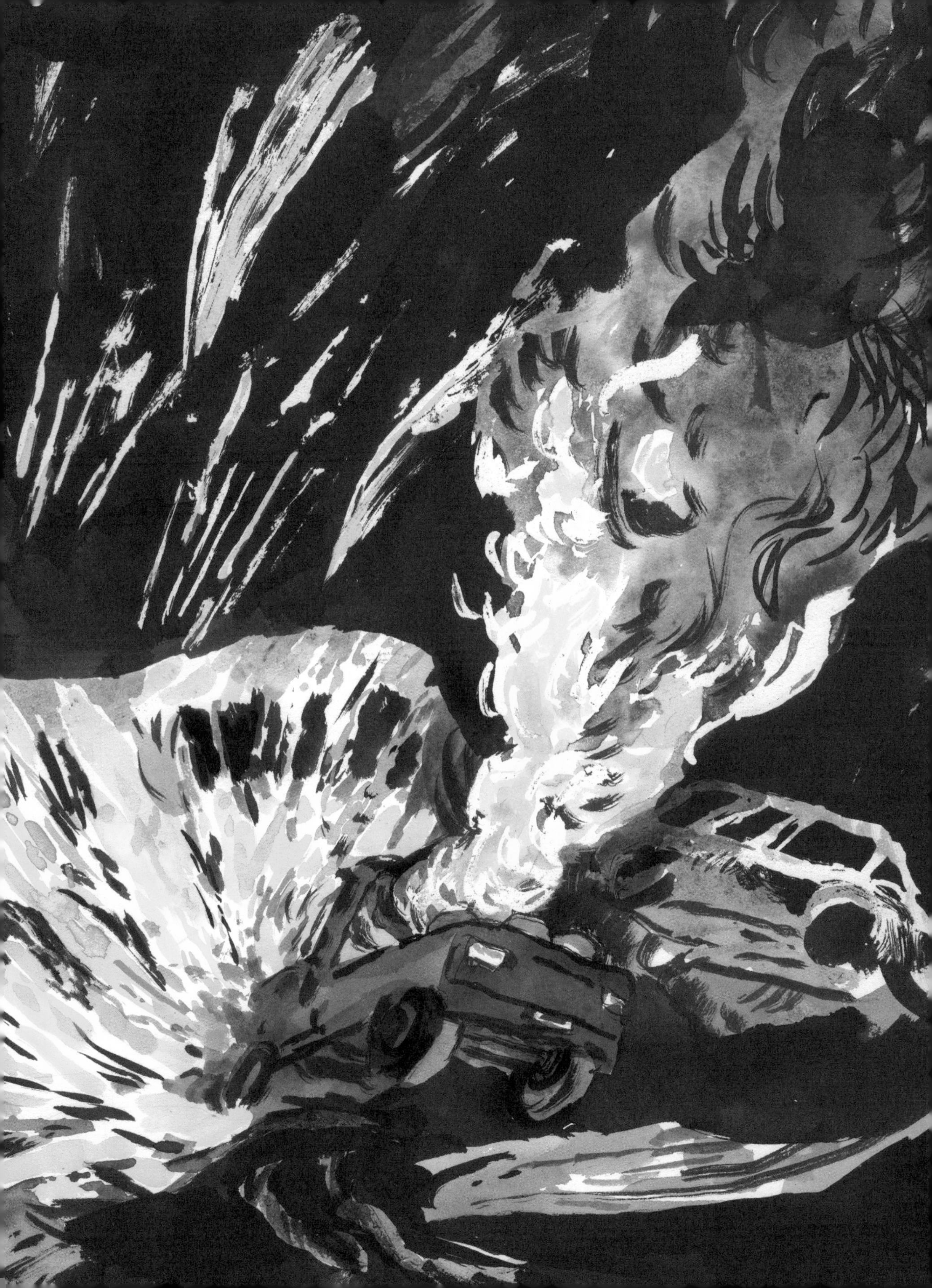

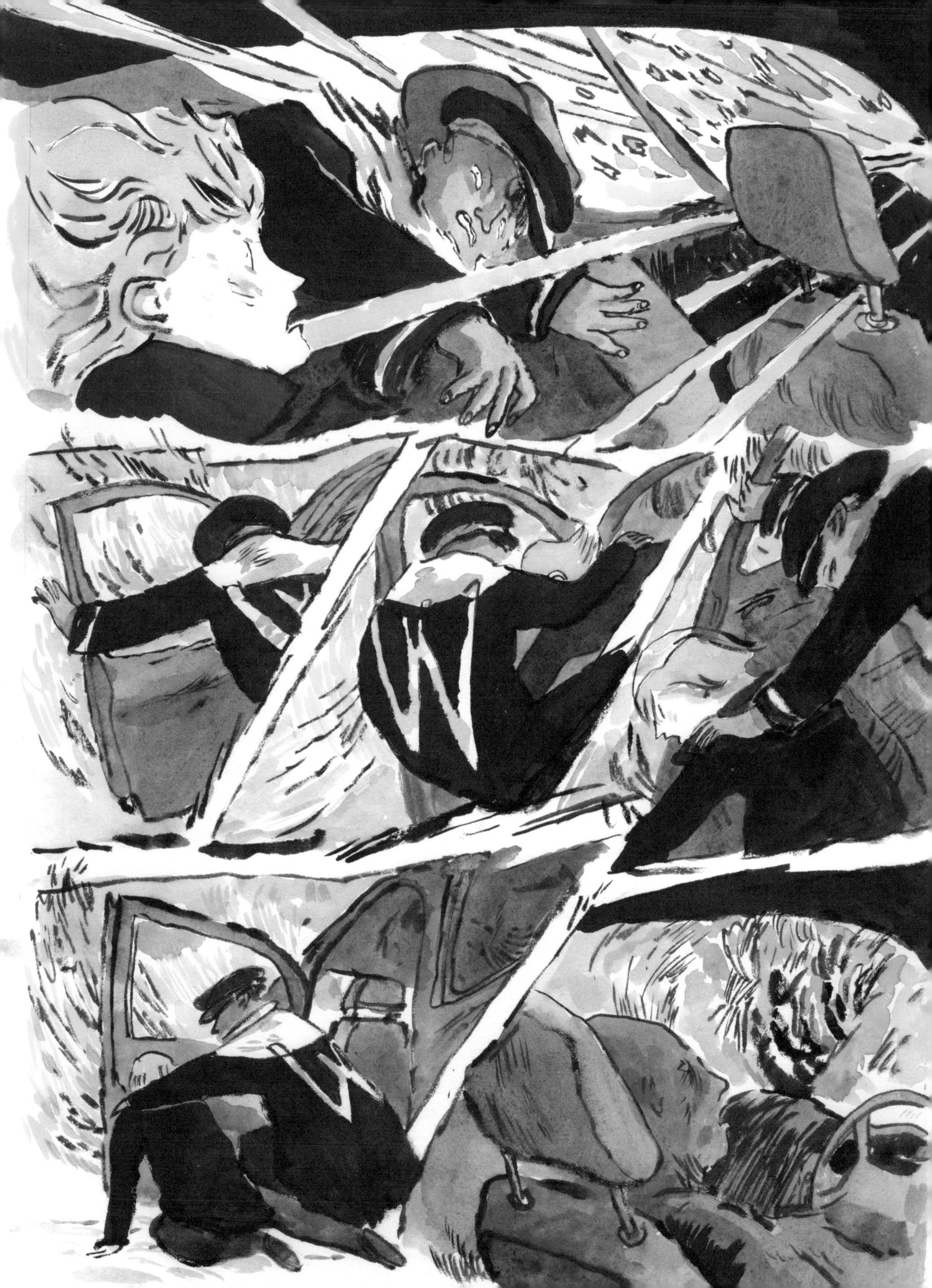

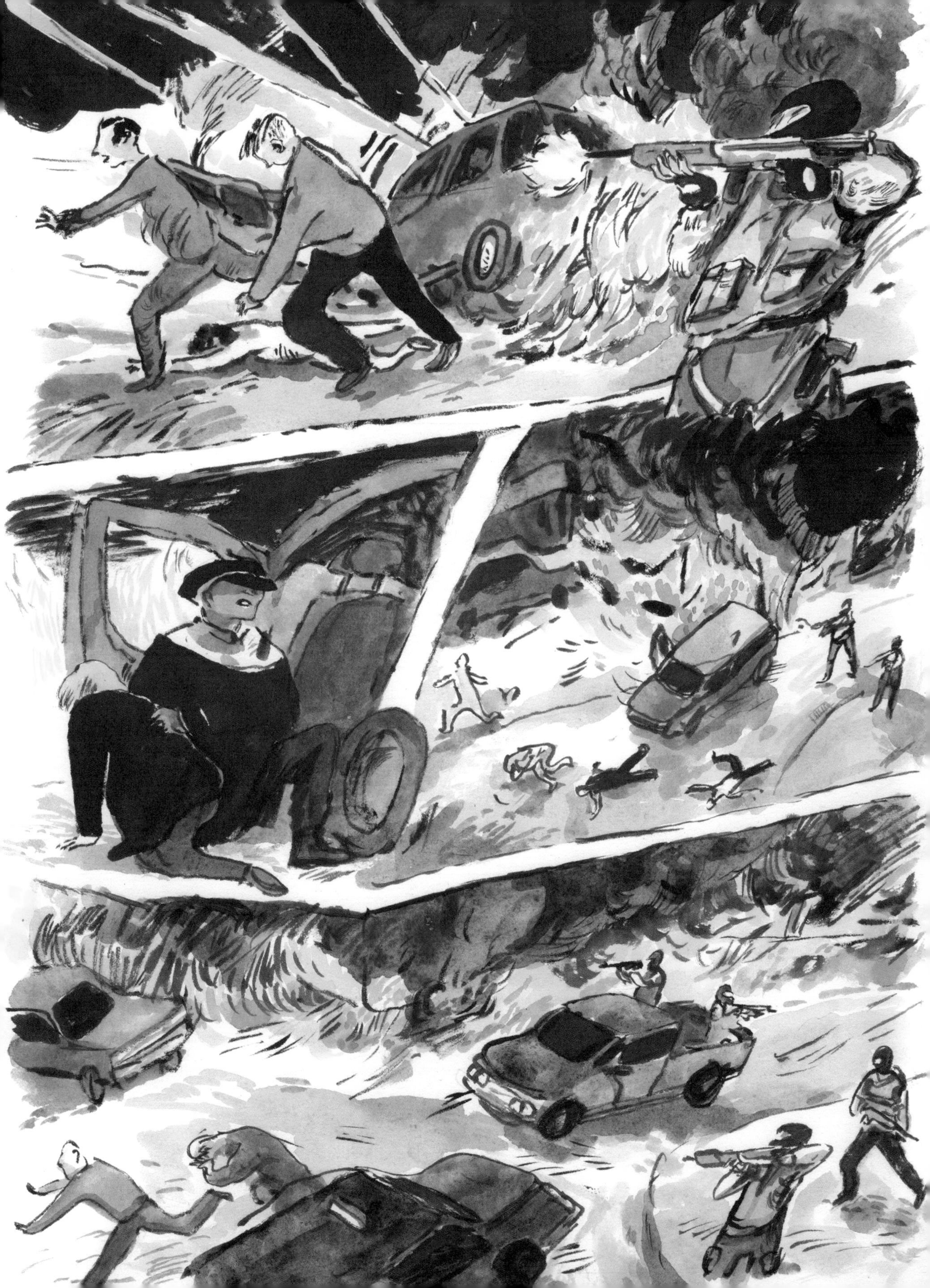

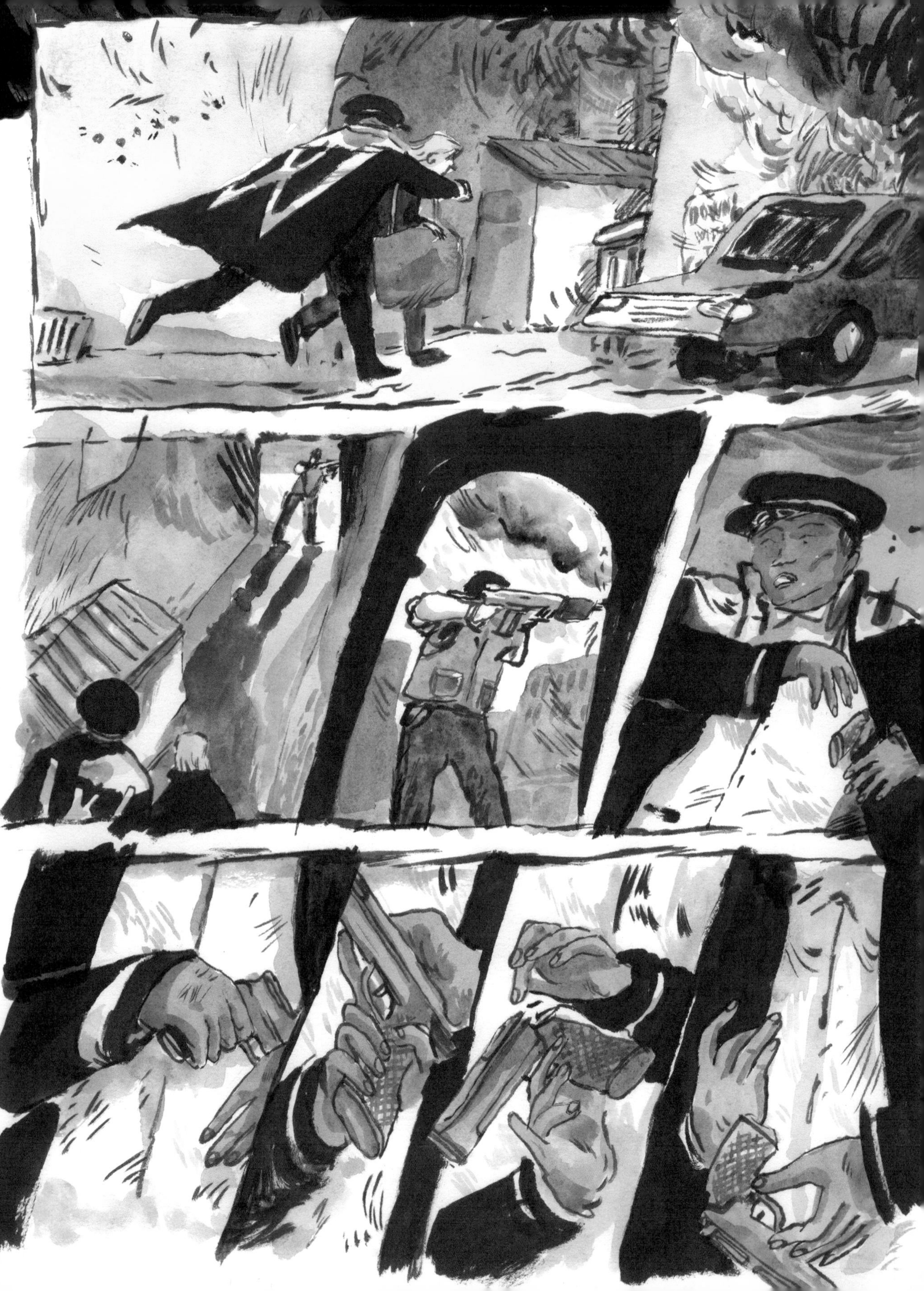

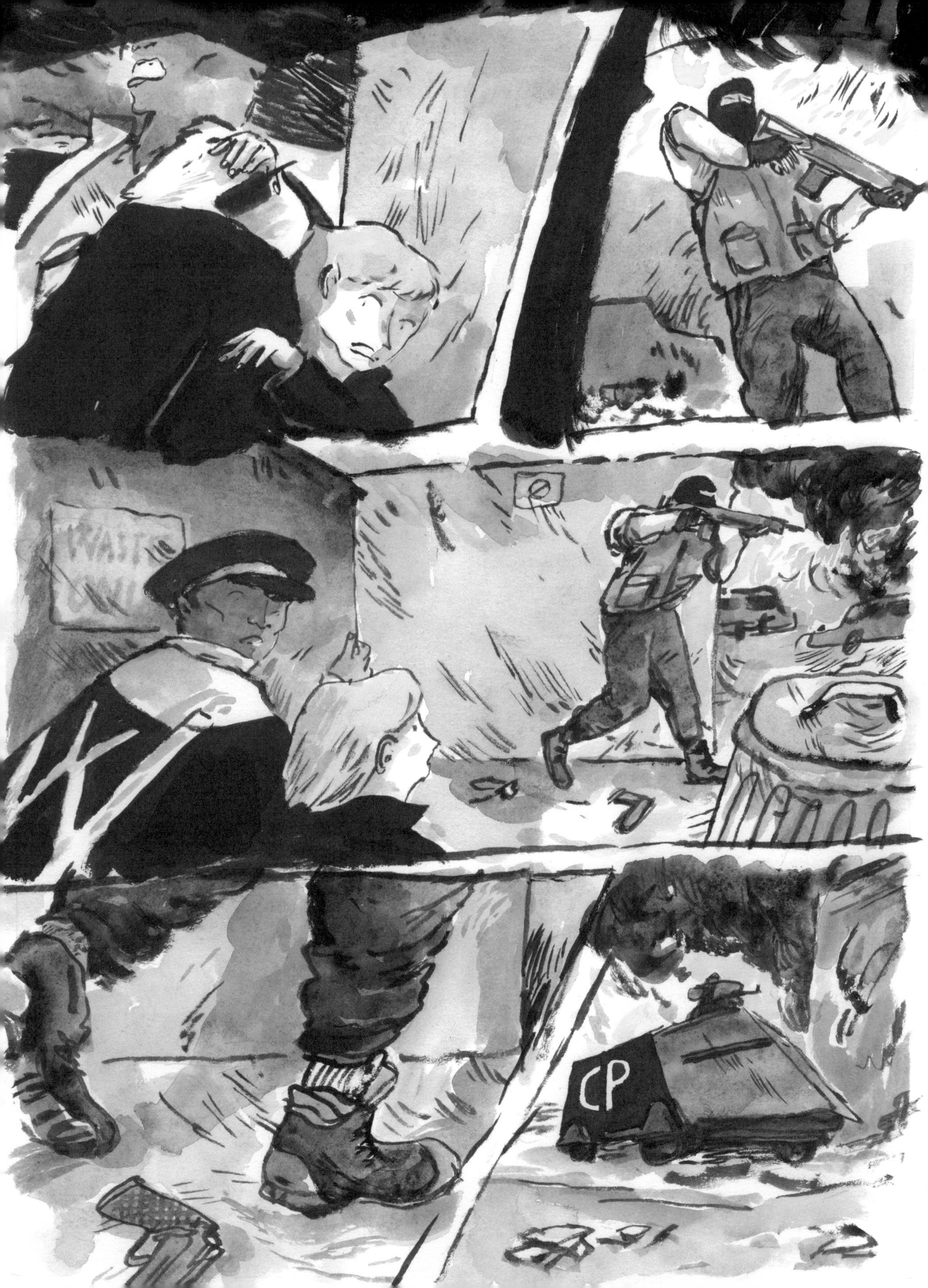
CP

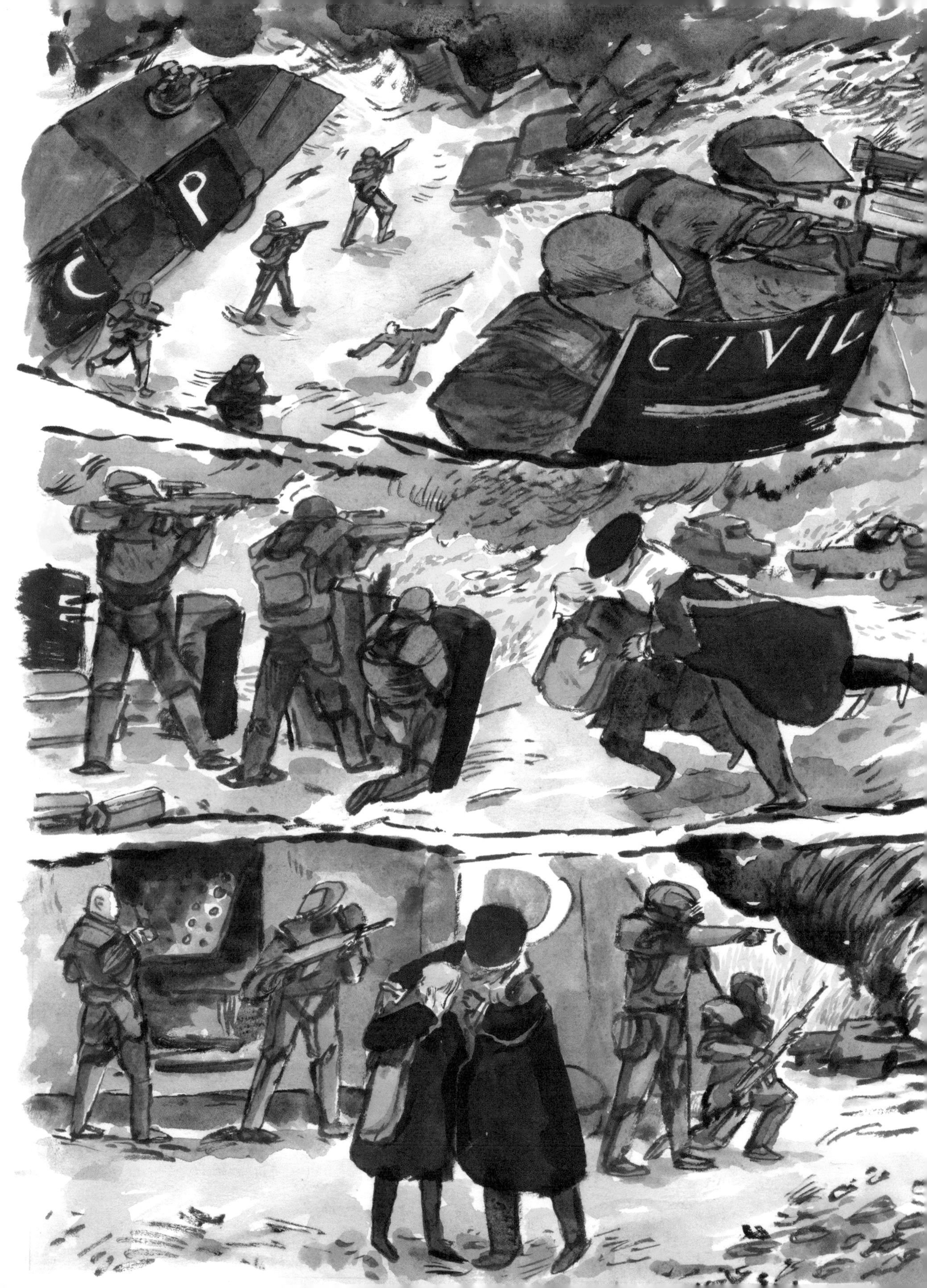
CIVIL

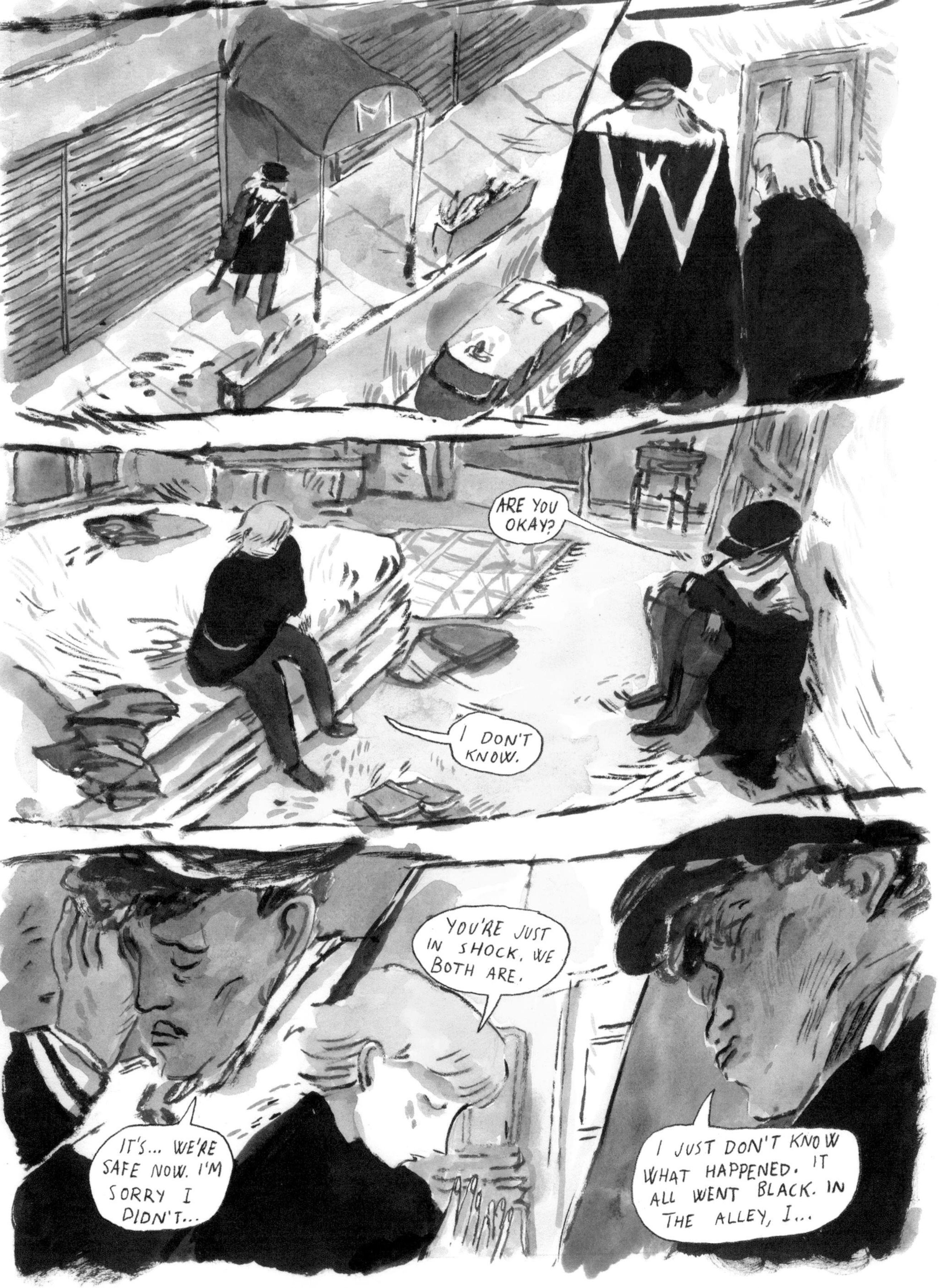
ARE YOU OKAY?
I DON'T KNOW.
YOU'RE JUST IN SHOCK. WE BOTH ARE.
IT'S... WE'RE SAFE NOW. I'M SORRY I DIDN'T...
I JUST DON'T KNOW WHAT HAPPENED. IT ALL WENT BLACK. IN THE ALLEY, I...

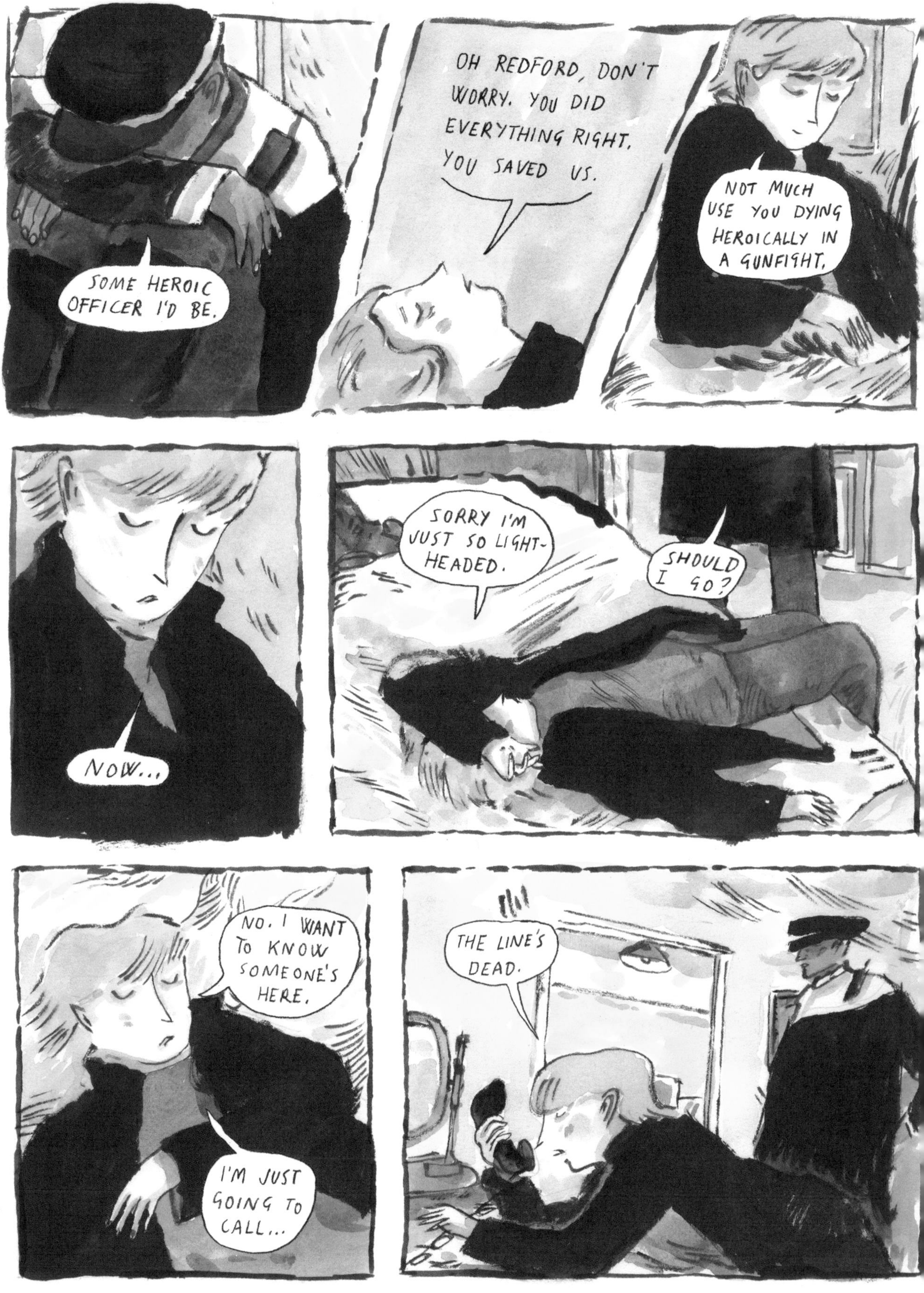
SOME HEROIC OFFICER I'D BE.
OH REDFORD, DON'T WORRY. YOU DID EVERYTHING RIGHT. YOU SAVED US.
NOT MUCH USE YOU DYING HEROICALLY IN A GUNFIGHT.
NOW...
SORRY I'M JUST SO LIGHT-HEADED.
SHOULD I GO?
NO. I WANT TO KNOW SOMEONE'S HERE.
I'M JUST GOING TO CALL...
THE LINE'S DEAD.

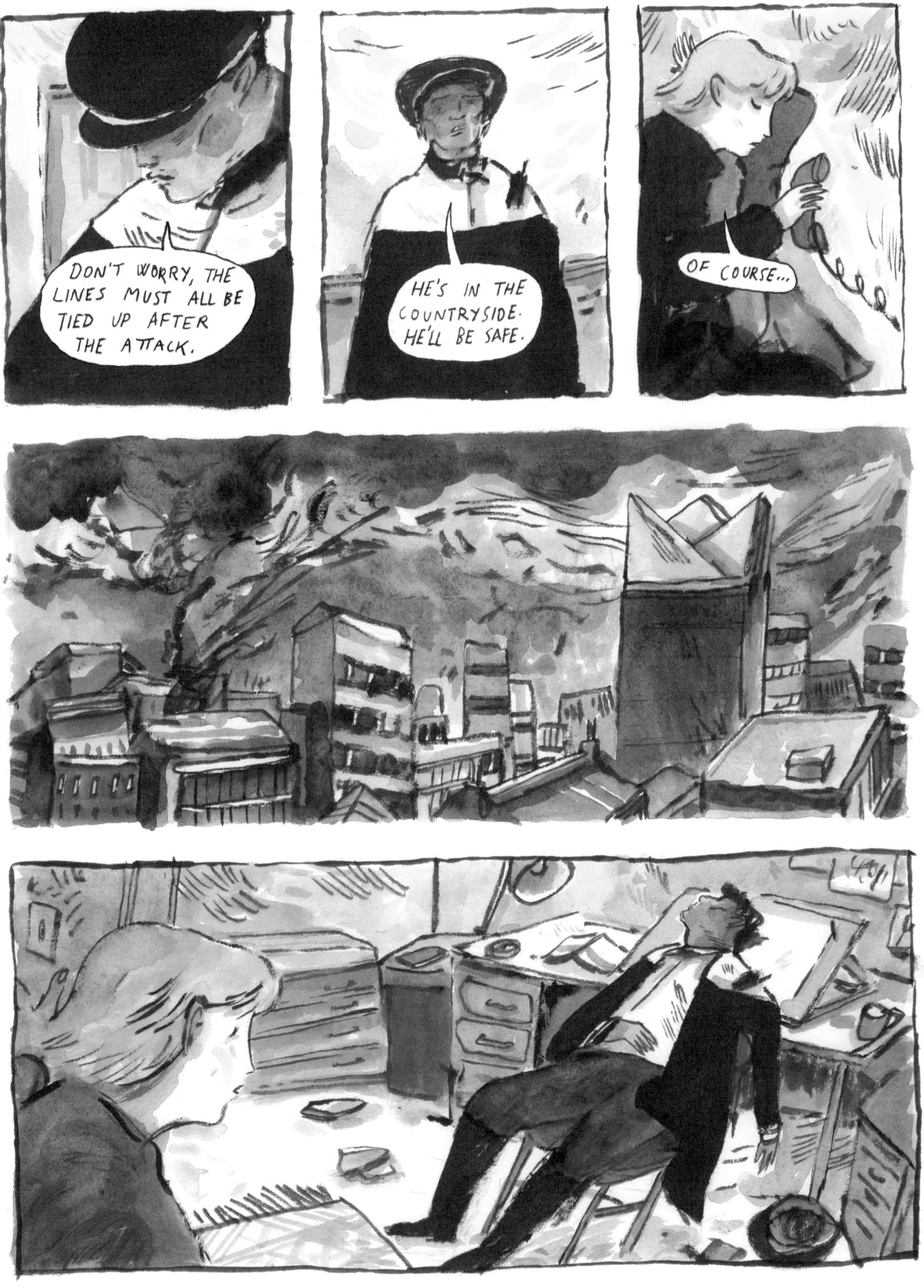
DON'T WORRY, THE LINES MUST ALL BE TIED UP AFTER THE ATTACK.
HE'S IN THE COUNTRYSIDE. HE'LL BE SAFE.
OF COURSE...

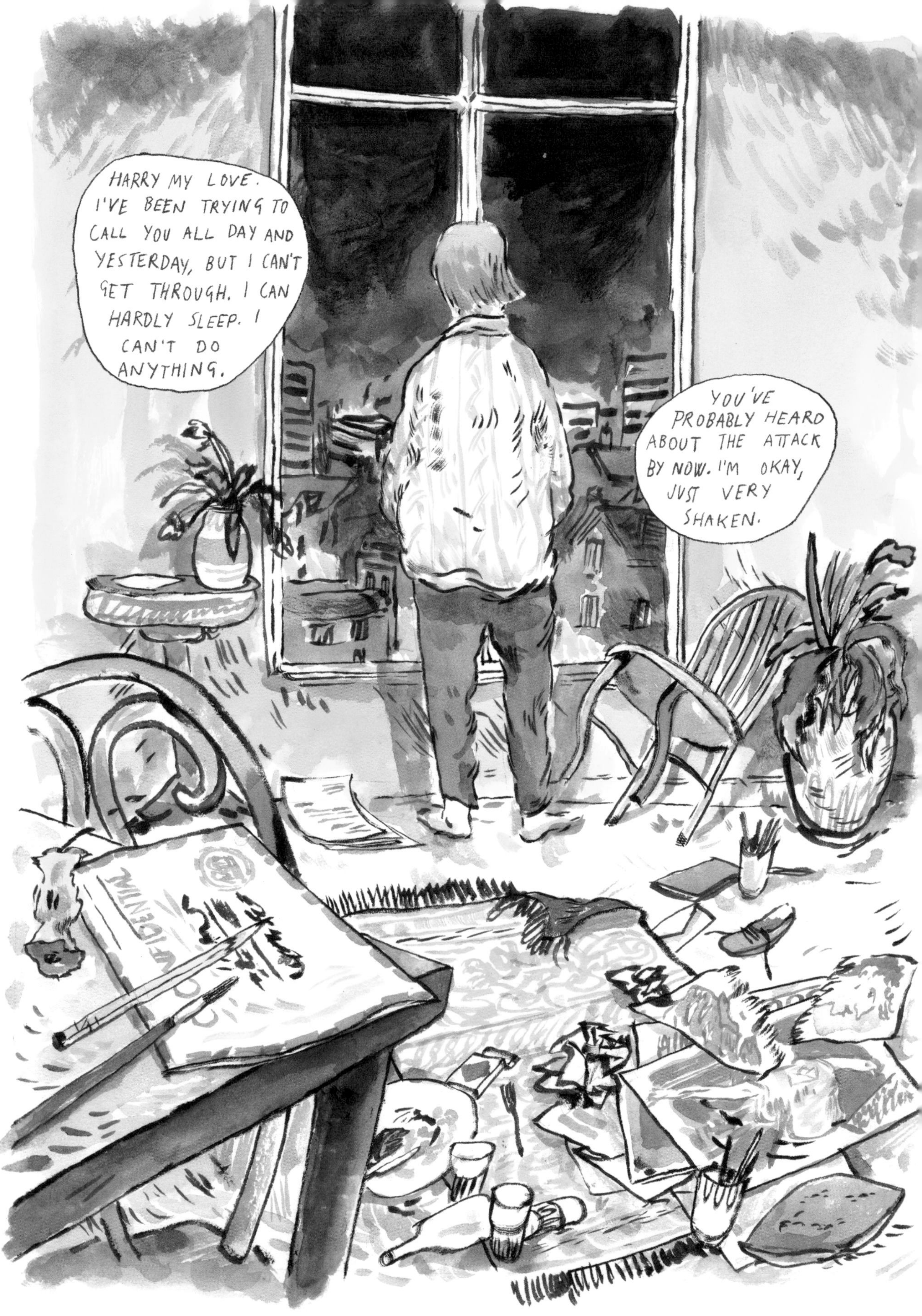
HARRY MY LOVE. I'VE BEEN TRYING TO CALL YOU ALL DAY AND YESTERDAY, BUT I CAN'T GET THROUGH. I CAN HARDLY SLEEP. I CAN'T DO ANYTHING.
YOU'VE PROBABLY HEARD ABOUT THE ATTACK BY NOW. I'M OKAY, JUST VERY SHAKEN.
CONFIDENTIAL

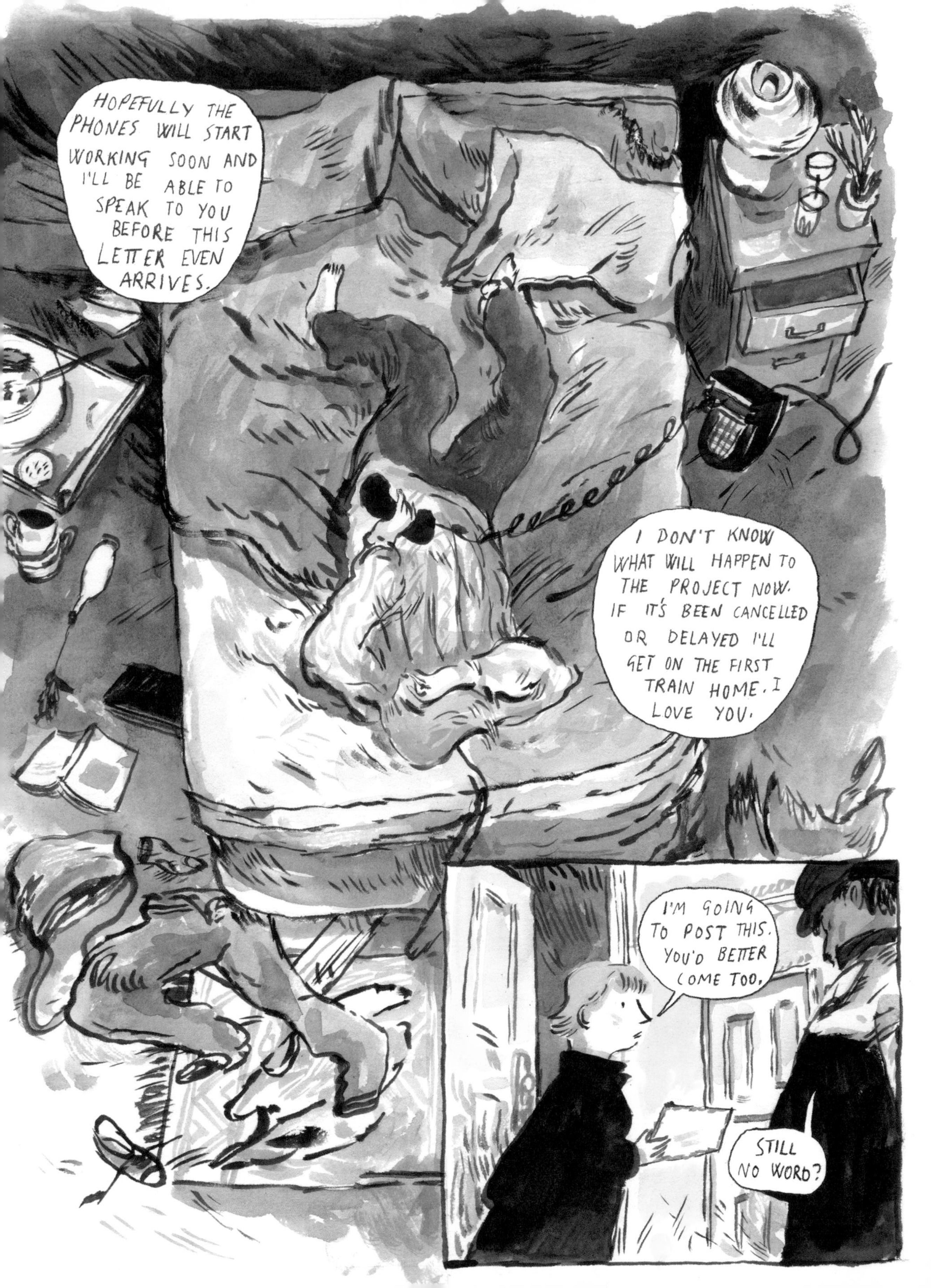
HOPEFULLY THE PHONES WILL START WORKING SOON AND I'LL BE ABLE TO SPEAK TO YOU BEFORE THIS LETTER EVEN ARRIVES.
I DON'T KNOW WHAT WILL HAPPEN TO THE PROJECT NOW. IF IT'S BEEN CANCELLED OR DELAYED I'LL GET ON THE FIRST TRAIN HOME. I LOVE YOU.
I'M GOING TO POST THIS. YOU'D BETTER COME TOO.
STILL NO WORD?

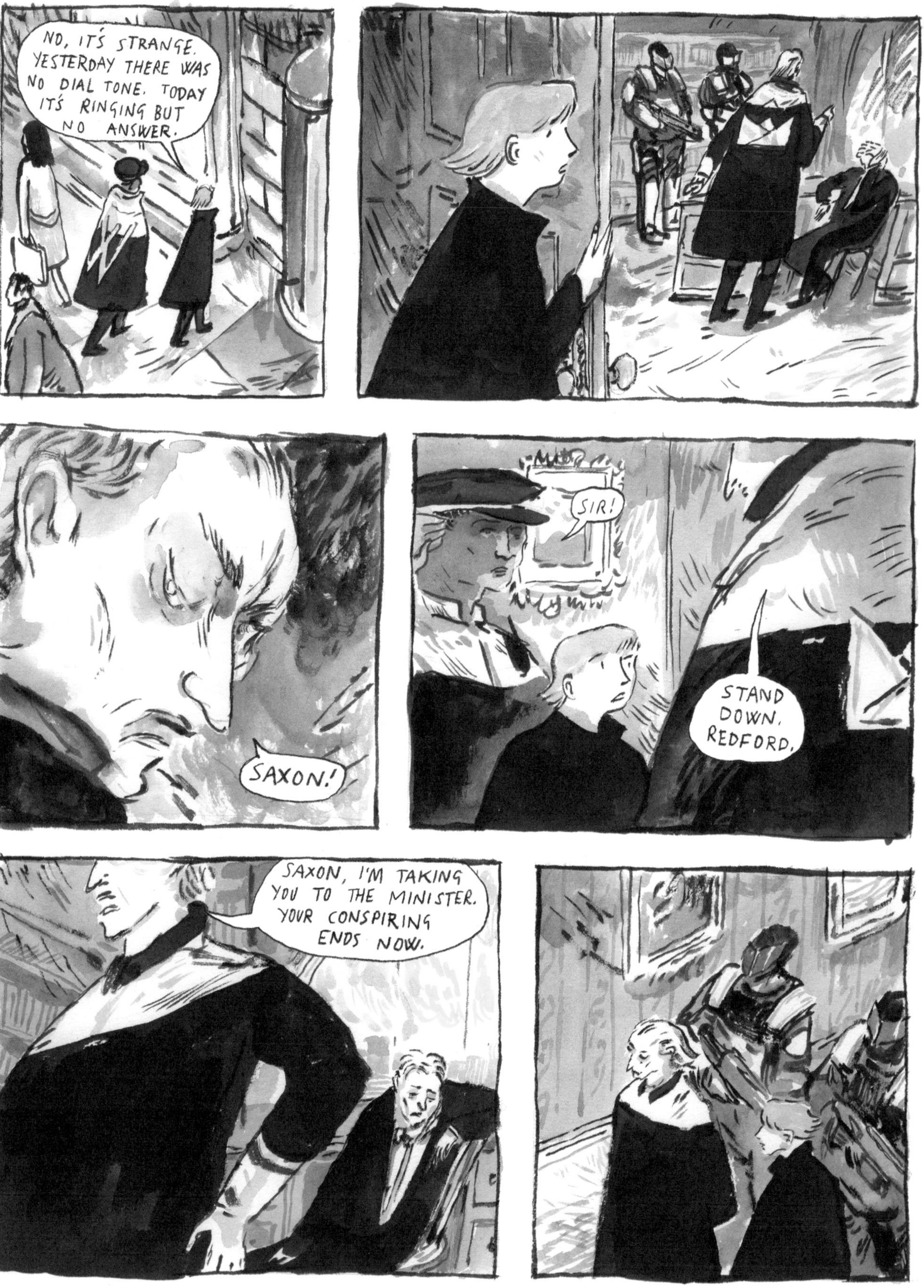
NO, IT'S STRANGE. YESTERDAY THERE WAS NO DIAL TONE. TODAY IT'S RINGING BUT NO ANSWER.
SAXON!
SIR!
STAND DOWN, REDFORD.
SAXON, I'M TAKING YOU TO THE MINISTER. YOUR CONSPIRING ENDS NOW.

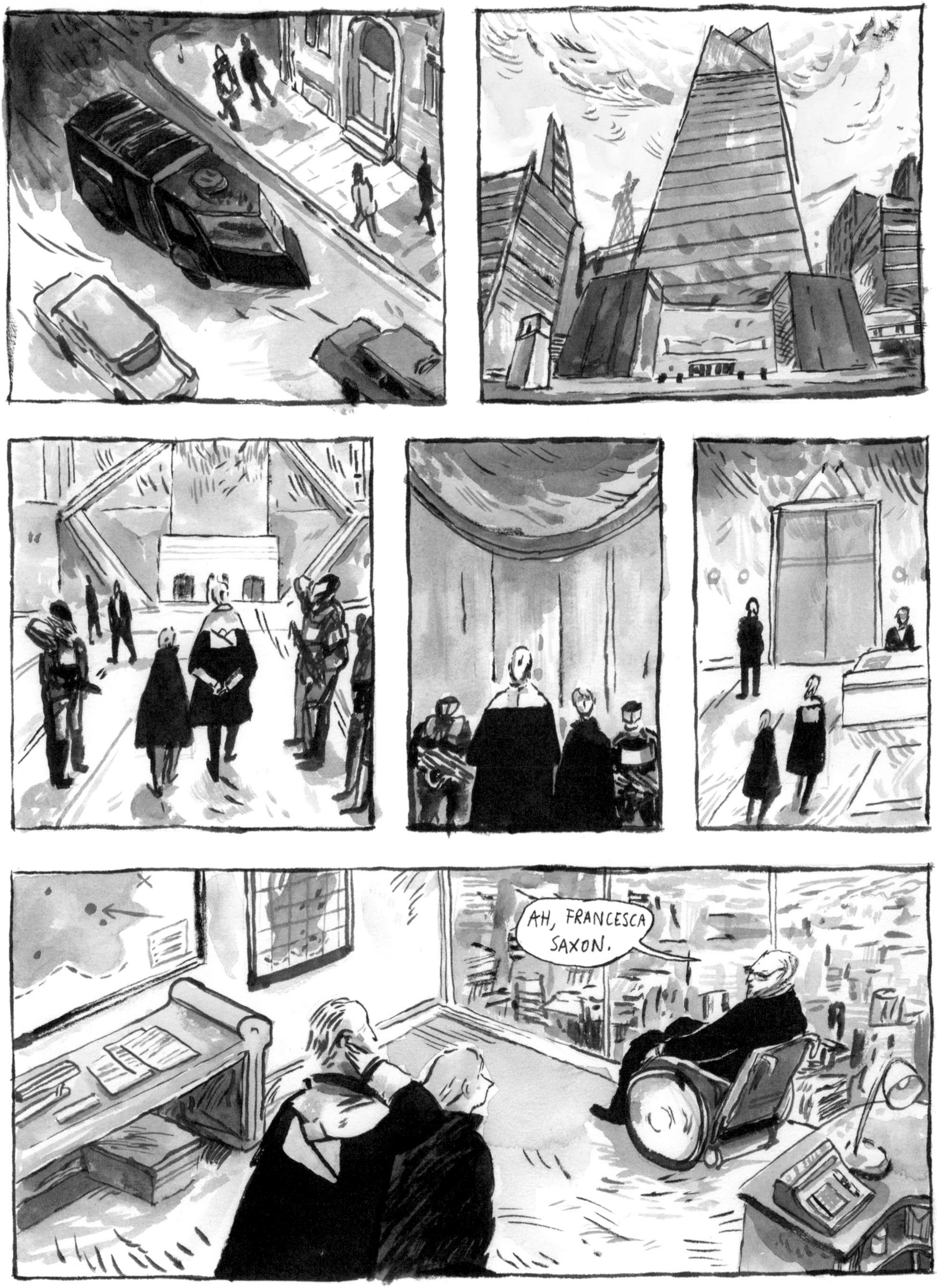
AH, FRANCESCA
SAXON.

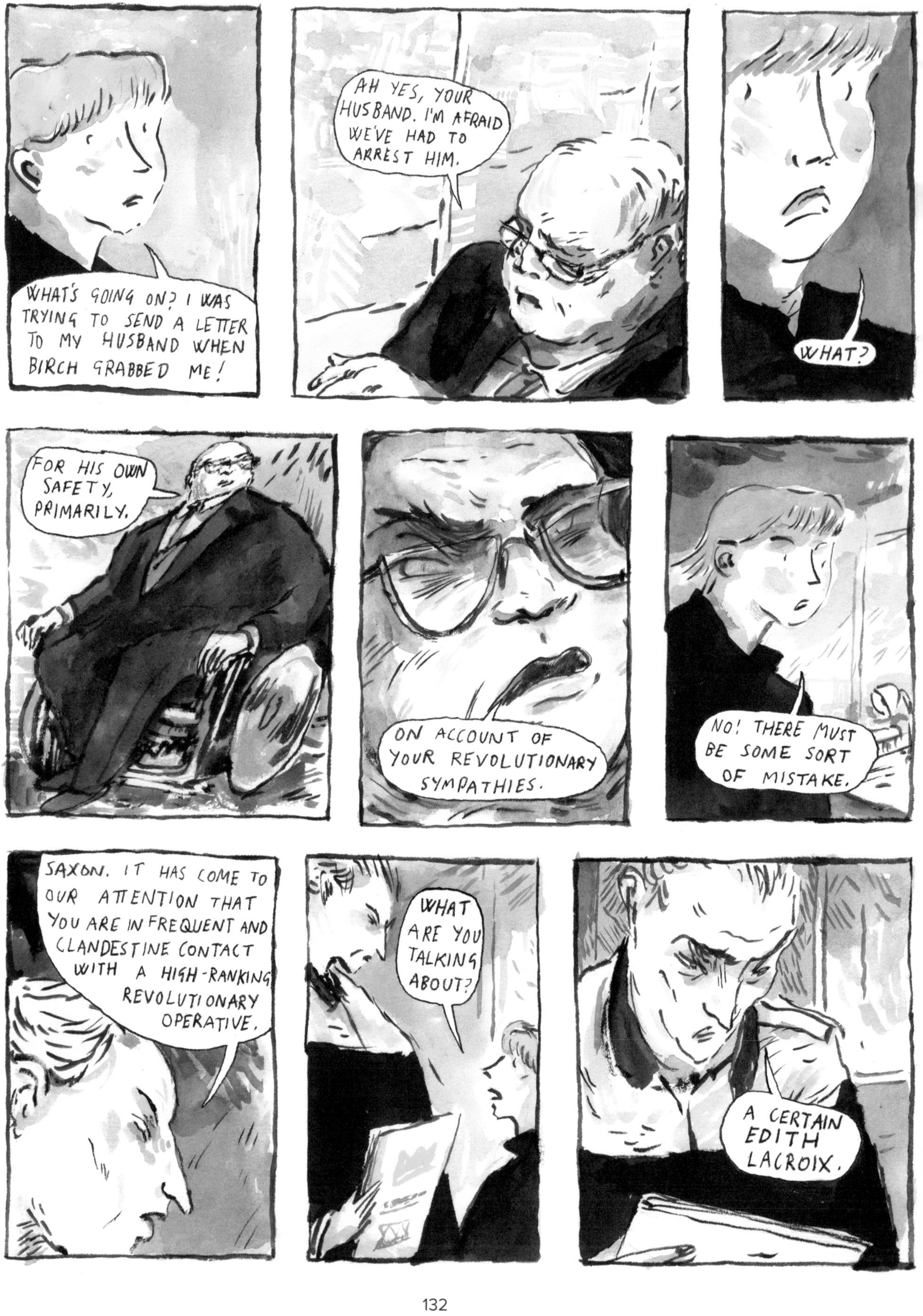
WHAT'S GOING ON? I WAS TRYING TO SEND A LETTER TO MY HUSBAND WHEN BIRCH GRABBED ME!
AH YES, YOUR HUSBAND. I'M AFRAID WE'VE HAD TO ARREST HIM.
WHAT?
FOR HIS OWN SAFETY, PRIMARILY.
ON ACCOUNT OF YOUR REVOLUTIONARY SYMPATHIES.
NO! THERE MUST BE SOME SORT OF MISTAKE.
SAXON. IT HAS COME TO OUR ATTENTION THAT YOU ARE IN FREQUENT AND CLANDESTINE CONTACT WITH A HIGH-RANKING REVOLUTIONARY OPERATIVE.
WHAT ARE YOU TALKING ABOUT?
A CERTAIN EDITH LACROIX.

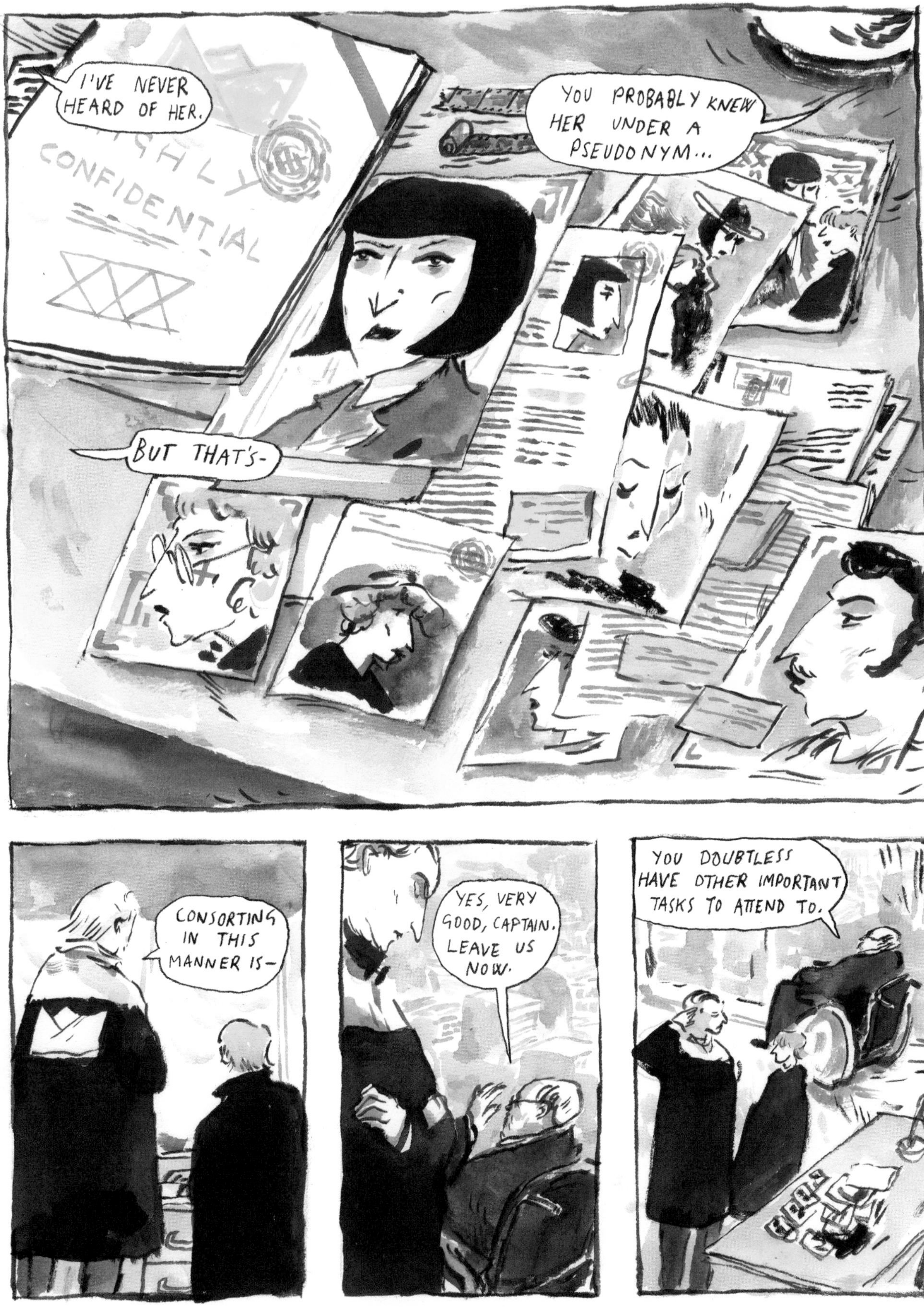
I'VE NEVER HEARD OF HER.
YOU PROBABLY KNEW HER UNDER A PSEUDONYM...
CONFIDENTIAL
BUT THAT'S-
CONSORTING IN THIS MANNER IS—
YES, VERY GOOD, CAPTAIN. LEAVE US NOW.
YOU DOUBTLESS HAVE OTHER IMPORTANT TASKS TO ATTEND TO.

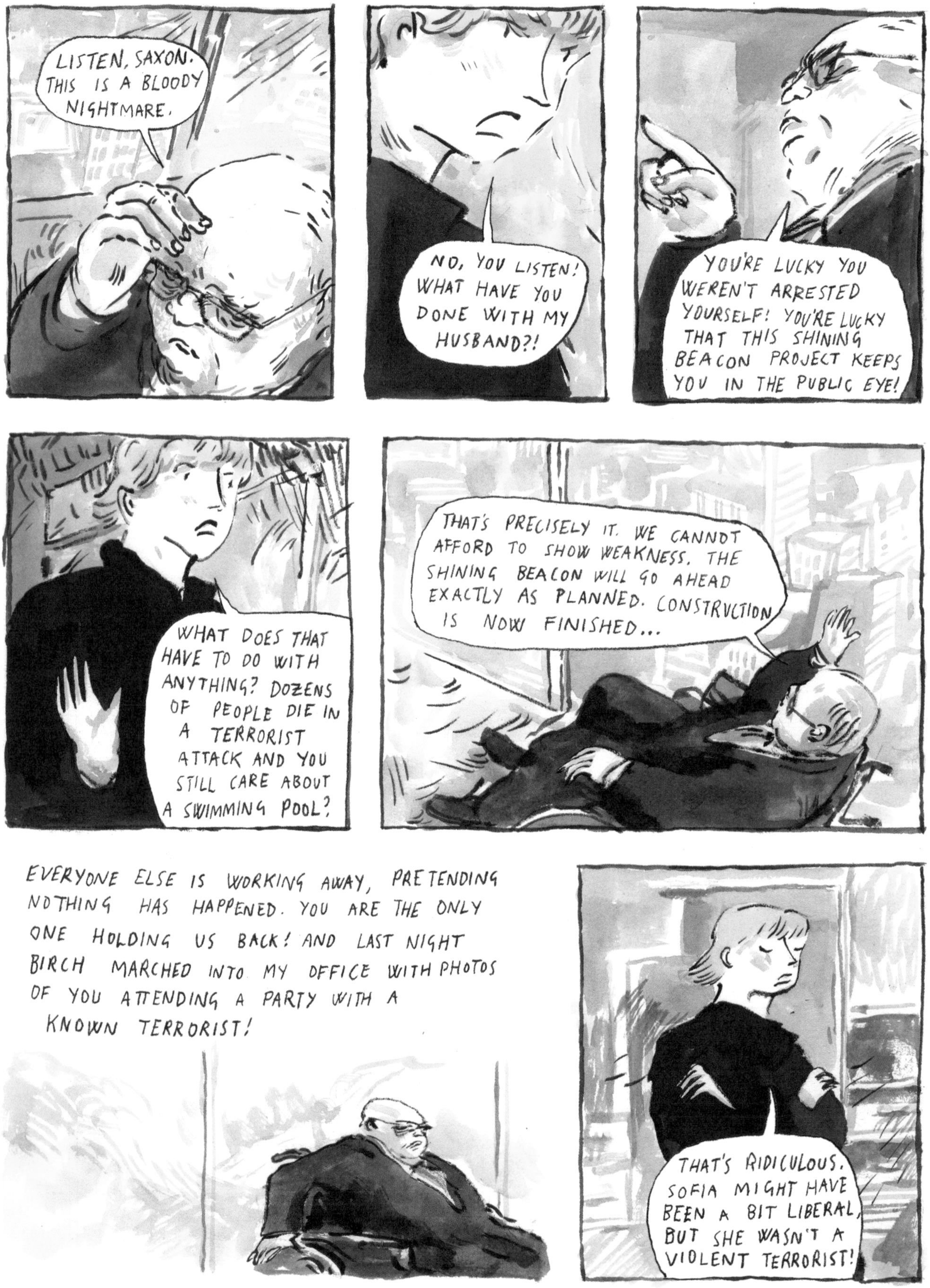
LISTEN, SAXON. THIS IS A BLOODY NIGHTMARE.
NO, YOU LISTEN! WHAT HAVE YOU DONE WITH MY HUSBAND?!
YOU'RE LUCKY YOU WEREN'T ARRESTED YOURSELF! YOU'RE LUCKY THAT THIS SHINING BEACON PROJECT KEEPS YOU IN THE PUBLIC EYE!
WHAT DOES THAT HAVE TO DO WITH ANYTHING? DOZENS OF PEOPLE DIE IN A TERRORIST ATTACK AND YOU STILL CARE ABOUT A SWIMMING POOL?
THAT'S PRECISELY IT. WE CANNOT AFFORD TO SHOW WEAKNESS. THE SHINING BEACON WILL GO AHEAD EXACTLY AS PLANNED. CONSTRUCTION IS NOW FINISHED...
EVERYONE ELSE IS WORKING AWAY, PRETENDING NOTHING HAS HAPPENED. YOU ARE THE ONLY ONE HOLDING US BACK! AND LAST NIGHT BIRCH MARCHED INTO MY OFFICE WITH PHOTOS OF YOU ATTENDING A PARTY WITH A KNOWN TERRORIST!
THAT'S RIDICULOUS. SOFIA MIGHT HAVE BEEN A BIT LIBERAL, BUT SHE WASN'T A VIOLENT TERRORIST!

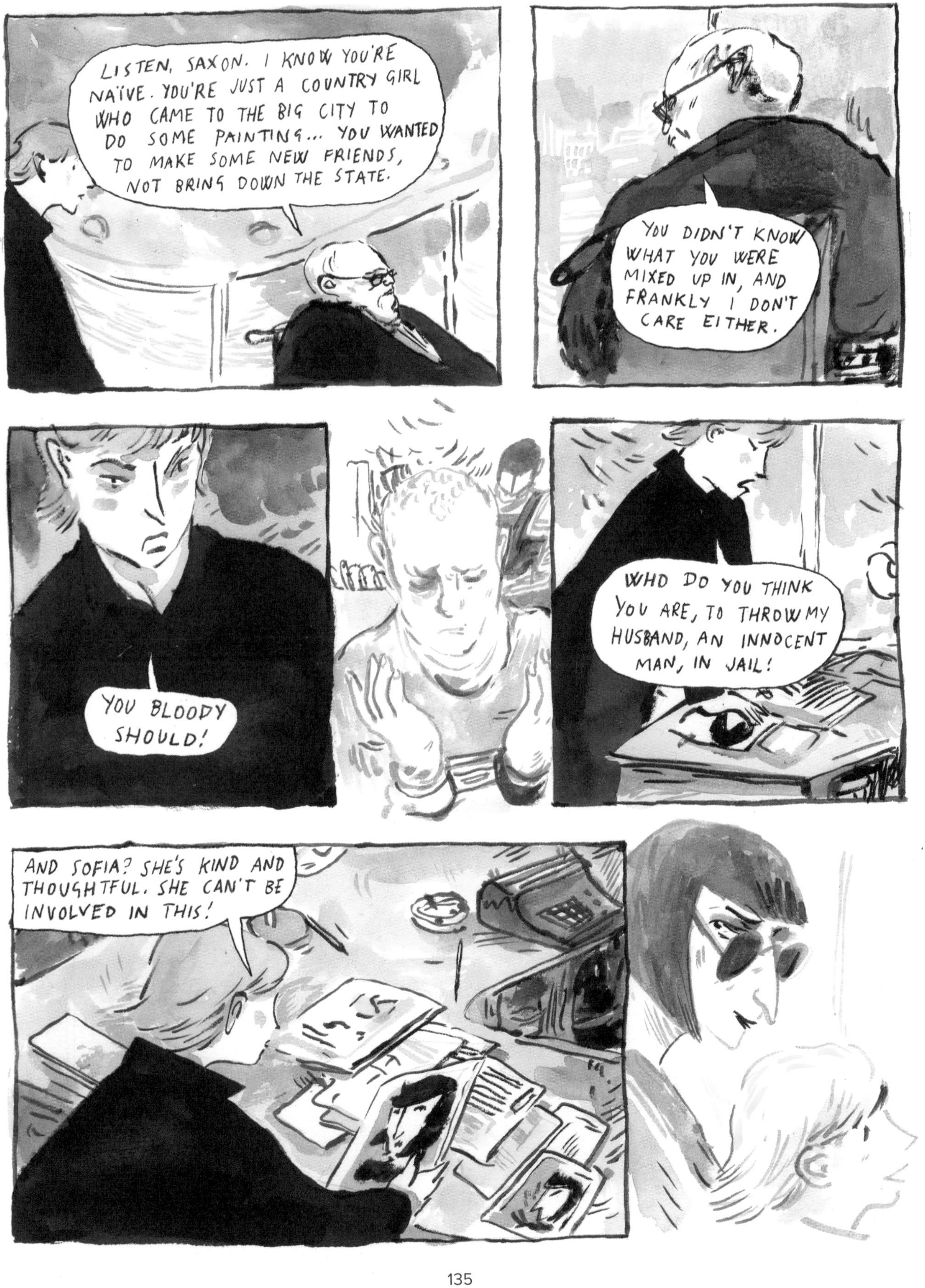
LISTEN, SAXON. I KNOW YOU'RE NAÏVE. YOU'RE JUST A COUNTRY GIRL WHO CAME TO THE BIG CITY TO DO SOME PAINTING... YOU WANTED TO MAKE SOME NEW FRIENDS, NOT BRING DOWN THE STATE.
YOU DIDN'T KNOW WHAT YOU WERE MIXED UP IN, AND FRANKLY I DON'T CARE EITHER.
YOU BLOODY SHOULD!
WHO DO YOU THINK YOU ARE, TO THROW MY HUSBAND, AN INNOCENT MAN, IN JAIL!
AND SOFIA? SHE'S KIND AND THOUGHTFUL. SHE CAN'T BE INVOLVED IN THIS!

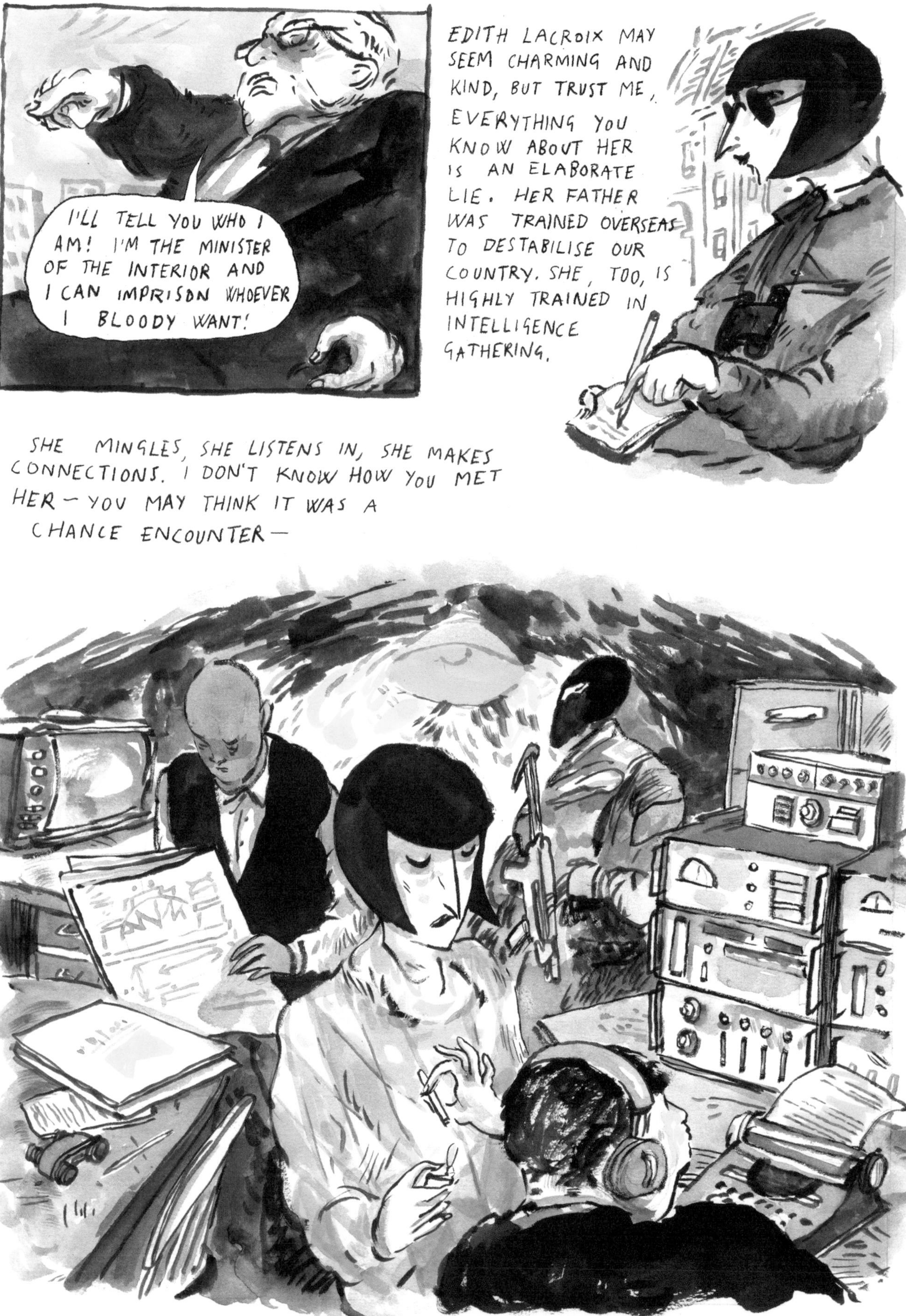
I'LL TELL YOU WHO I AM! I'M THE MINISTER OF THE INTERIOR AND I CAN IMPRISON WHOEVER I BLOODY WANT!
EDITH LACROIX MAY SEEM CHARMING AND KIND, BUT TRUST ME,
EVERYTHING YOU KNOW ABOUT HER IS AN ELABORATE LIE. HER FATHER WAS TRAINED OVERSEAS TO DESTABILISE OUR COUNTRY. SHE, TOO, IS HIGHLY TRAINED IN INTELLIGENCE GATHERING.
SHE MINGLES, SHE LISTENS IN, SHE MAKES CONNECTIONS. I DON'T KNOW HOW YOU MET HER — YOU MAY THINK IT WAS A CHANCE ENCOUNTER —

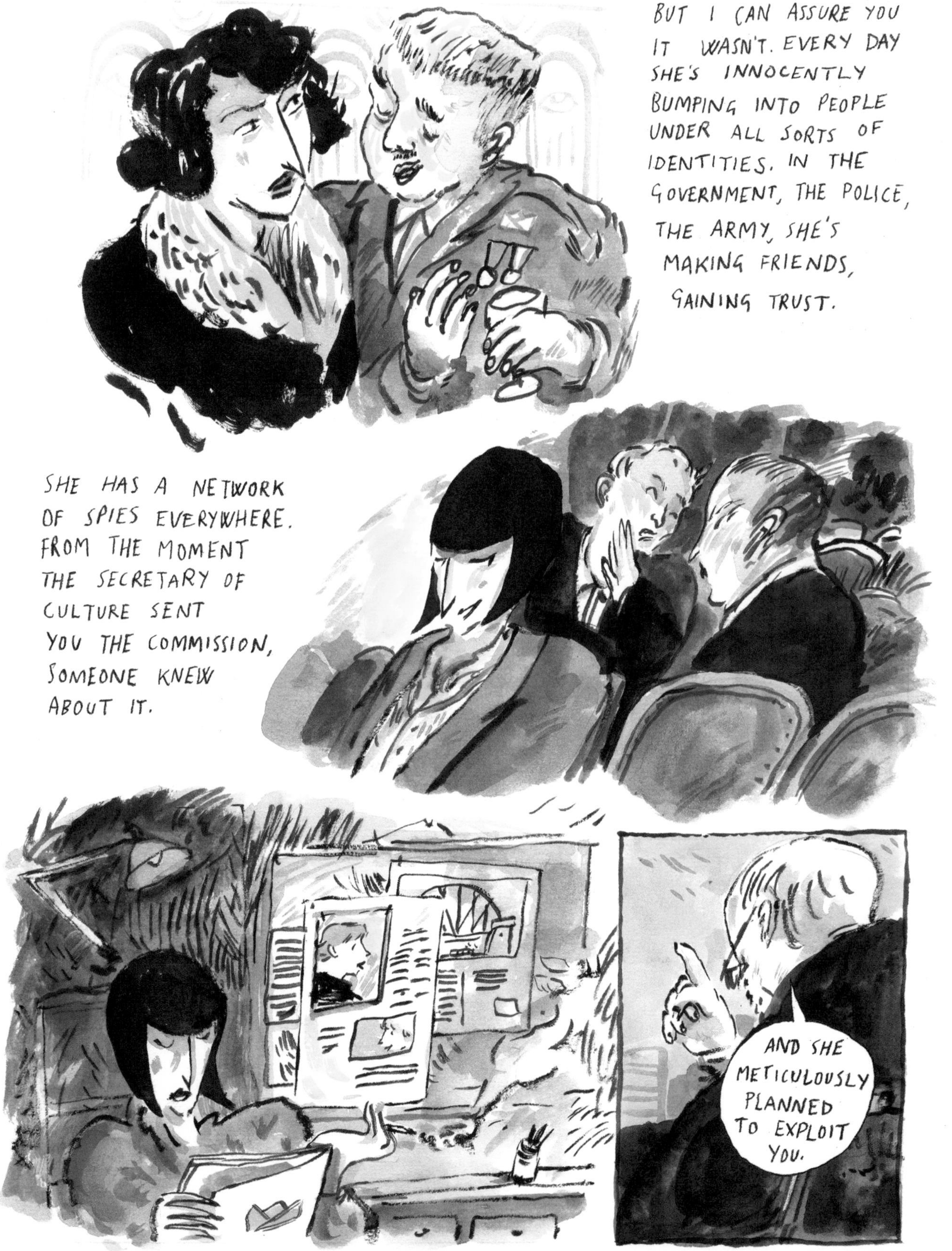
BUT I CAN ASSURE YOU IT WASN'T. EVERY DAY SHE'S INNOCENTLY BUMPING INTO PEOPLE UNDER ALL SORTS OF IDENTITIES. IN THE GOVERNMENT, THE POLICE, THE ARMY, SHE'S MAKING FRIENDS, GAINING TRUST.
SHE HAS A NETWORK OF SPIES EVERYWHERE. FROM THE MOMENT THE SECRETARY OF CULTURE SENT YOU THE COMMISSION, SOMEONE KNEW ABOUT IT.
AND SHE METICULOUSLY PLANNED TO EXPLOIT YOU.

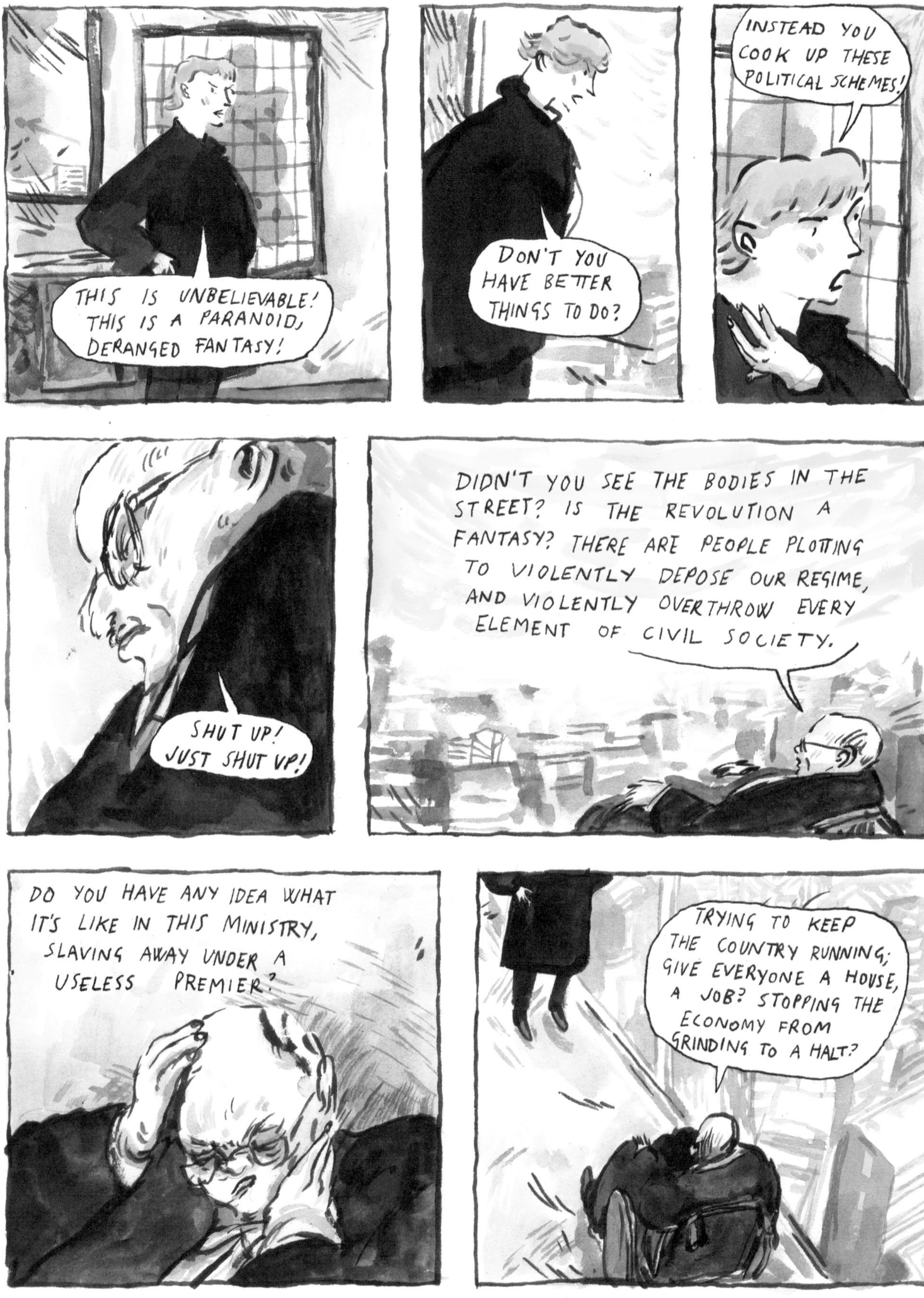
THIS IS UNBELIEVABLE! THIS IS A PARANOID, DERANGED FANTASY!
DON'T YOU HAVE BETTER THINGS TO DO?
INSTEAD YOU COOK UP THESE POLITICAL SCHEMES!
SHUT UP! JUST SHUT UP!
DIDN'T YOU SEE THE BODIES IN THE STREET? IS THE REVOLUTION A FANTASY? THERE ARE PEOPLE PLOTTING TO VIOLENTLY DEPOSE OUR REGIME, AND VIOLENTLY OVERTHROW EVERY ELEMENT OF CIVIL SOCIETY.
DO YOU HAVE ANY IDEA WHAT IT'S LIKE IN THIS MINISTRY, SLAVING AWAY UNDER A USELESS PREMIER?
TRYING TO KEEP THE COUNTRY RUNNING; GIVE EVERYONE A HOUSE, A JOB? STOPPING THE ECONOMY FROM GRINDING TO A HALT?

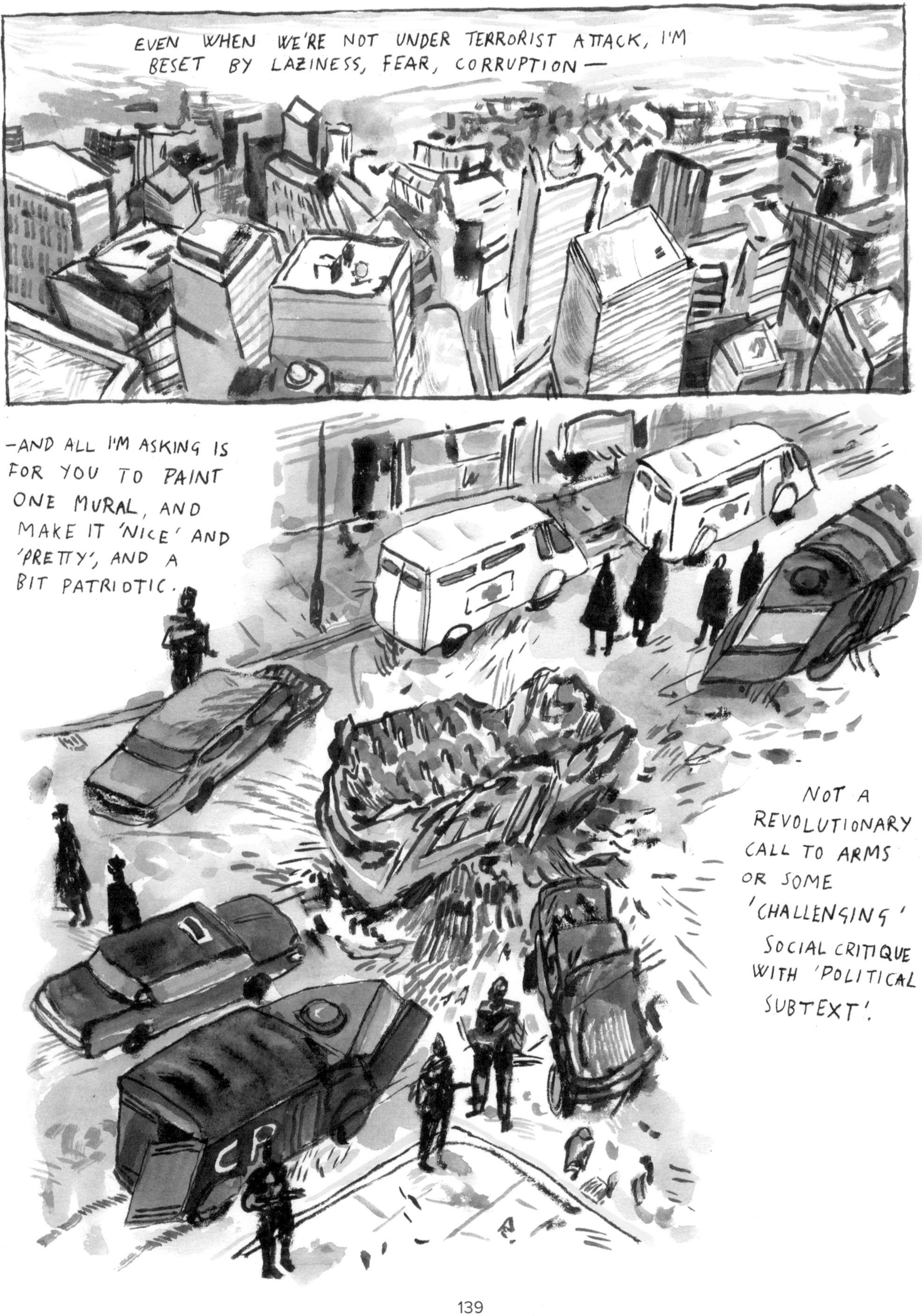
EVEN WHEN WE'RE NOT UNDER TERRORIST ATTACK, I'M BESET BY LAZINESS, FEAR, CORRUPTION—
—AND ALL I'M ASKING IS FOR YOU TO PAINT ONE MURAL, AND MAKE IT 'NICE' AND 'PRETTY', AND A BIT PATRIOTIC.
NOT A REVOLUTIONARY CALL TO ARMS OR SOME 'CHALLENGING' SOCIAL CRITIQUE WITH 'POLITICAL SUBTEXT'.

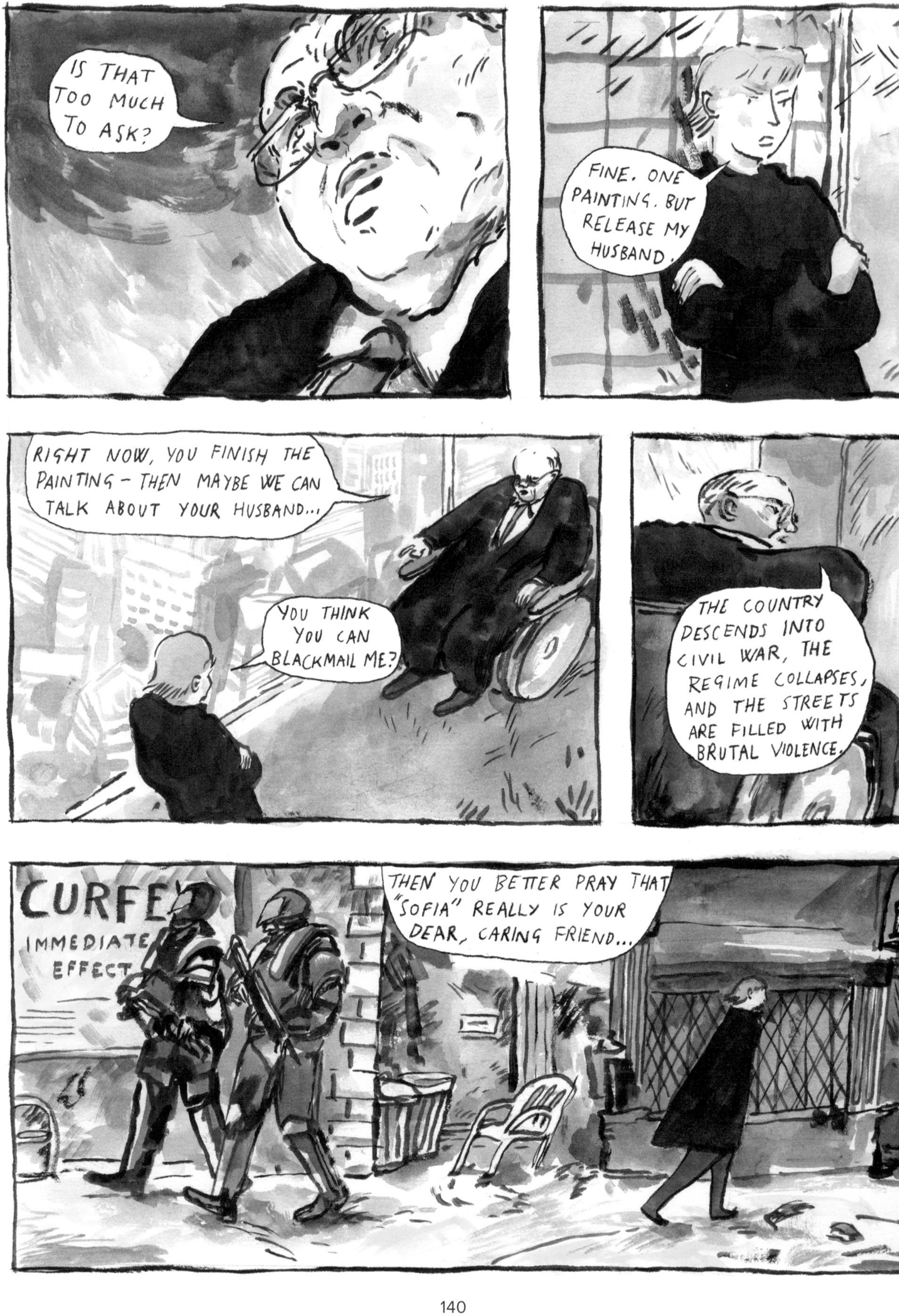
IS THAT TOO MUCH TO ASK?
FINE. ONE PAINTING. BUT RELEASE MY HUSBAND.
RIGHT NOW, YOU FINISH THE PAINTING - THEN MAYBE WE CAN TALK ABOUT YOUR HUSBAND...
YOU THINK YOU CAN BLACKMAIL ME?
THE COUNTRY DESCENDS INTO CIVIL WAR, THE REGIME COLLAPSES, AND THE STREETS ARE FILLED WITH BRUTAL VIOLENCE.
CURFE
IMMEDIATE
EFFECT
THEN YOU BETTER PRAY THAT "SOFIA" REALLY IS YOUR DEAR, CARING FRIEND...

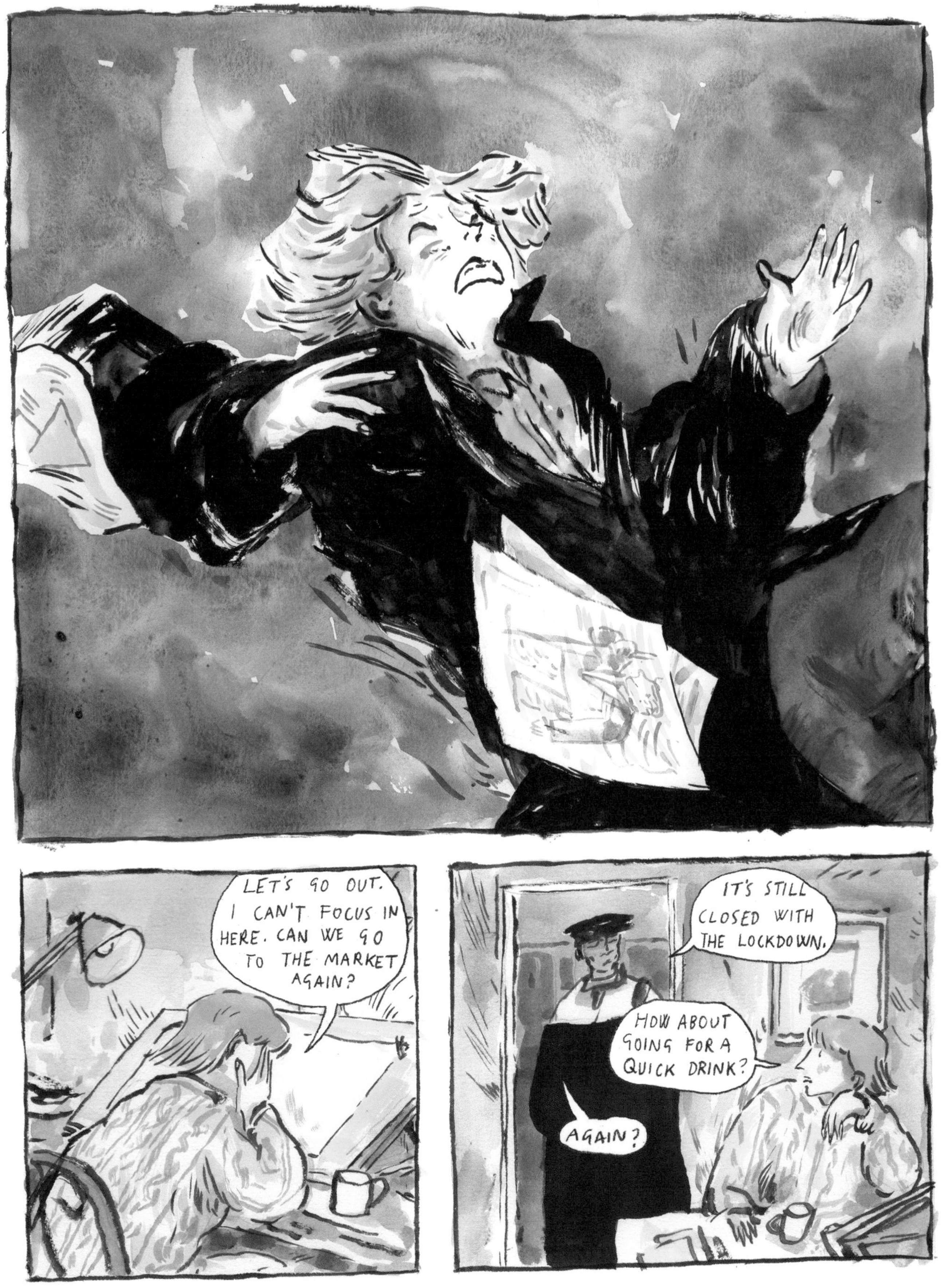
LET'S GO OUT. I CAN'T FOCUS IN HERE. CAN WE GO TO THE MARKET AGAIN?
IT'S STILL CLOSED WITH THE LOCKDOWN.
HOW ABOUT GOING FOR A QUICK DRINK?
AGAIN?

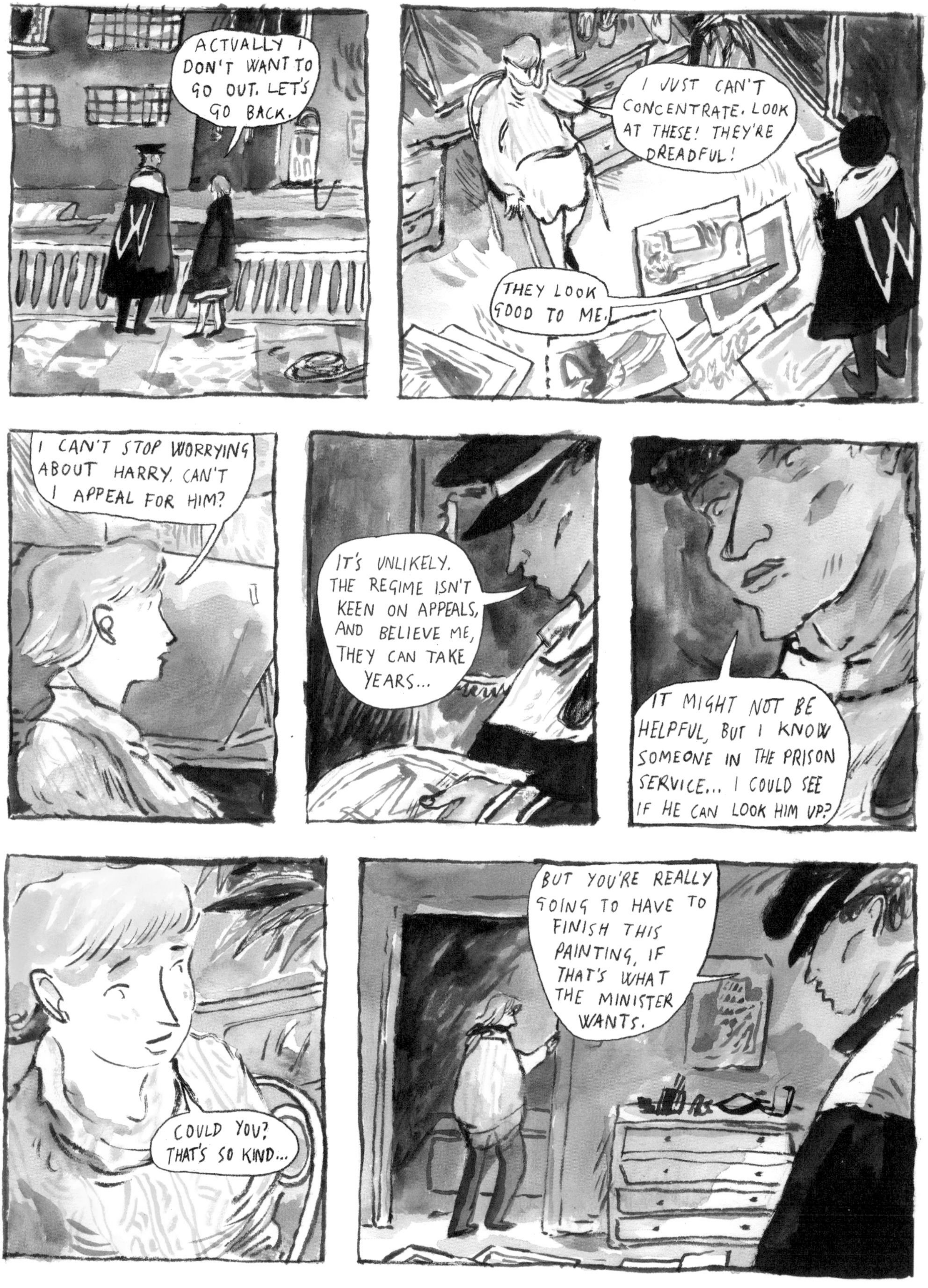
ACTUALLY I DON'T WANT TO GO OUT. LET'S GO BACK.
I JUST CAN'T CONCENTRATE. LOOK AT THESE! THEY'RE DREADFUL!
THEY LOOK GOOD TO ME.
I CAN'T STOP WORRYING ABOUT HARRY. CAN'T I APPEAL FOR HIM?
IT'S UNLIKELY. THE REGIME ISN'T KEEN ON APPEALS, AND BELIEVE ME, THEY CAN TAKE YEARS...
IT MIGHT NOT BE HELPFUL, BUT I KNOW SOMEONE IN THE PRISON SERVICE... I COULD SEE IF HE CAN LOOK HIM UP?
COULD YOU? THAT'S SO KIND...
BUT YOU'RE REALLY GOING TO HAVE TO FINISH THIS PAINTING, IF THAT'S WHAT THE MINISTER WANTS.

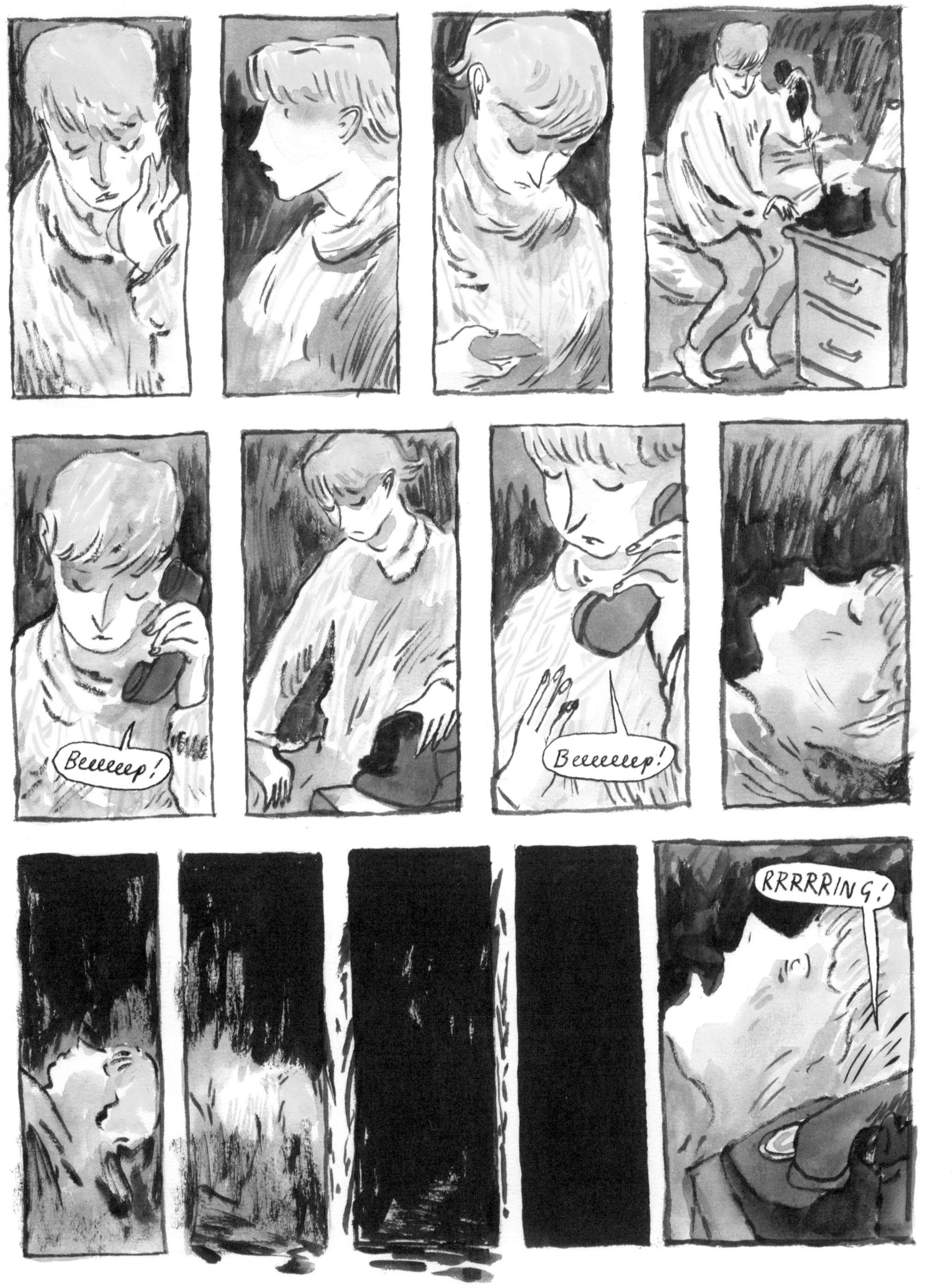
Beeeeeep!
Beeeeeep!
RRRRRING!

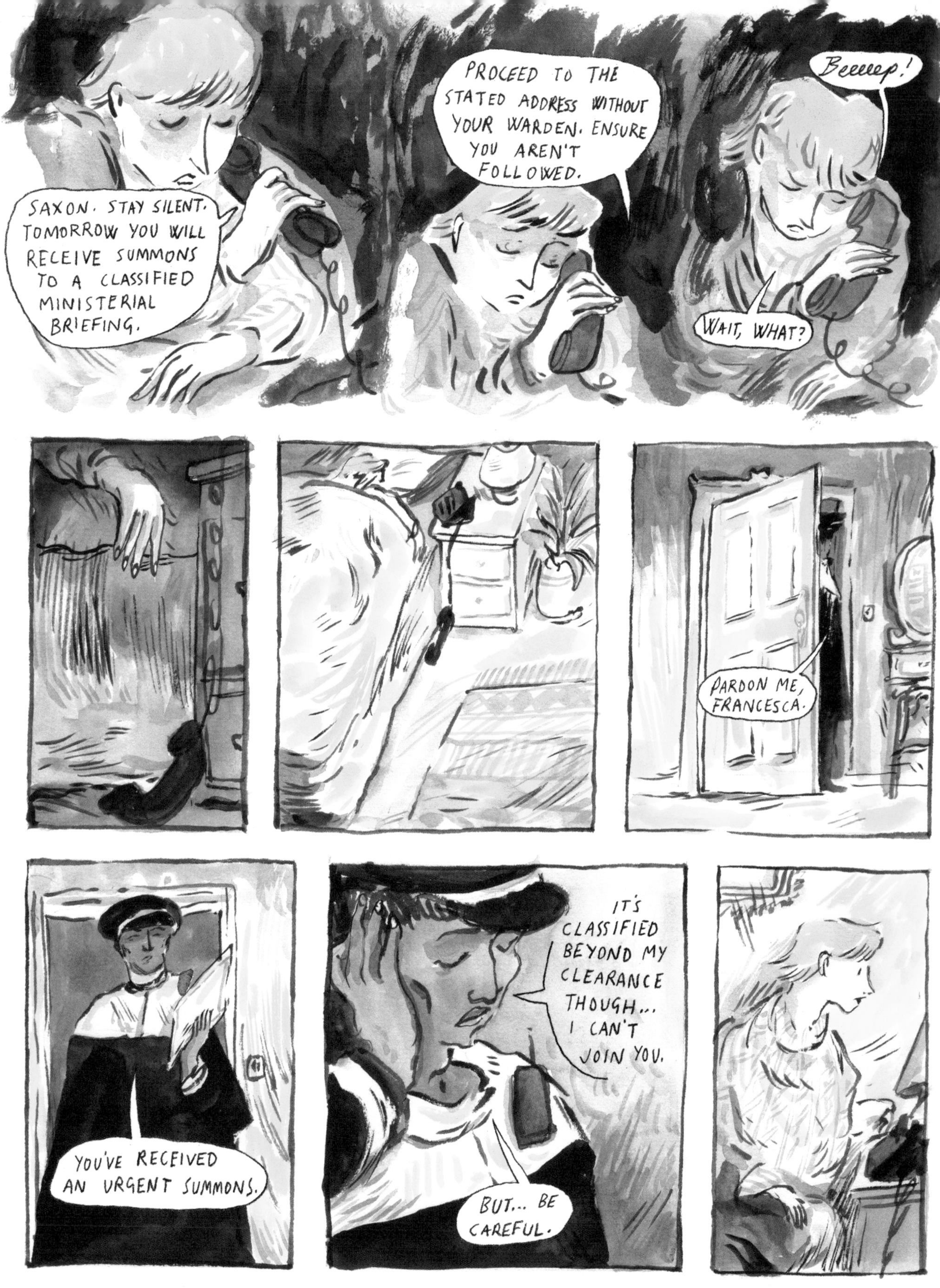
SAXON. STAY SILENT. TOMORROW YOU WILL RECEIVE SUMMONS TO A CLASSIFIED MINISTERIAL BRIEFING.
PROCEED TO THE STATED ADDRESS WITHOUT YOUR WARDEN. ENSURE YOU AREN'T FOLLOWED.
Beeeep!
WAIT, WHAT?
PARDON ME, FRANCESCA.
YOU'VE RECEIVED AN URGENT SUMMONS.
IT'S CLASSIFIED BEYOND MY CLEARANCE THOUGH... I CAN'T JOIN YOU.
BUT... BE CAREFUL.

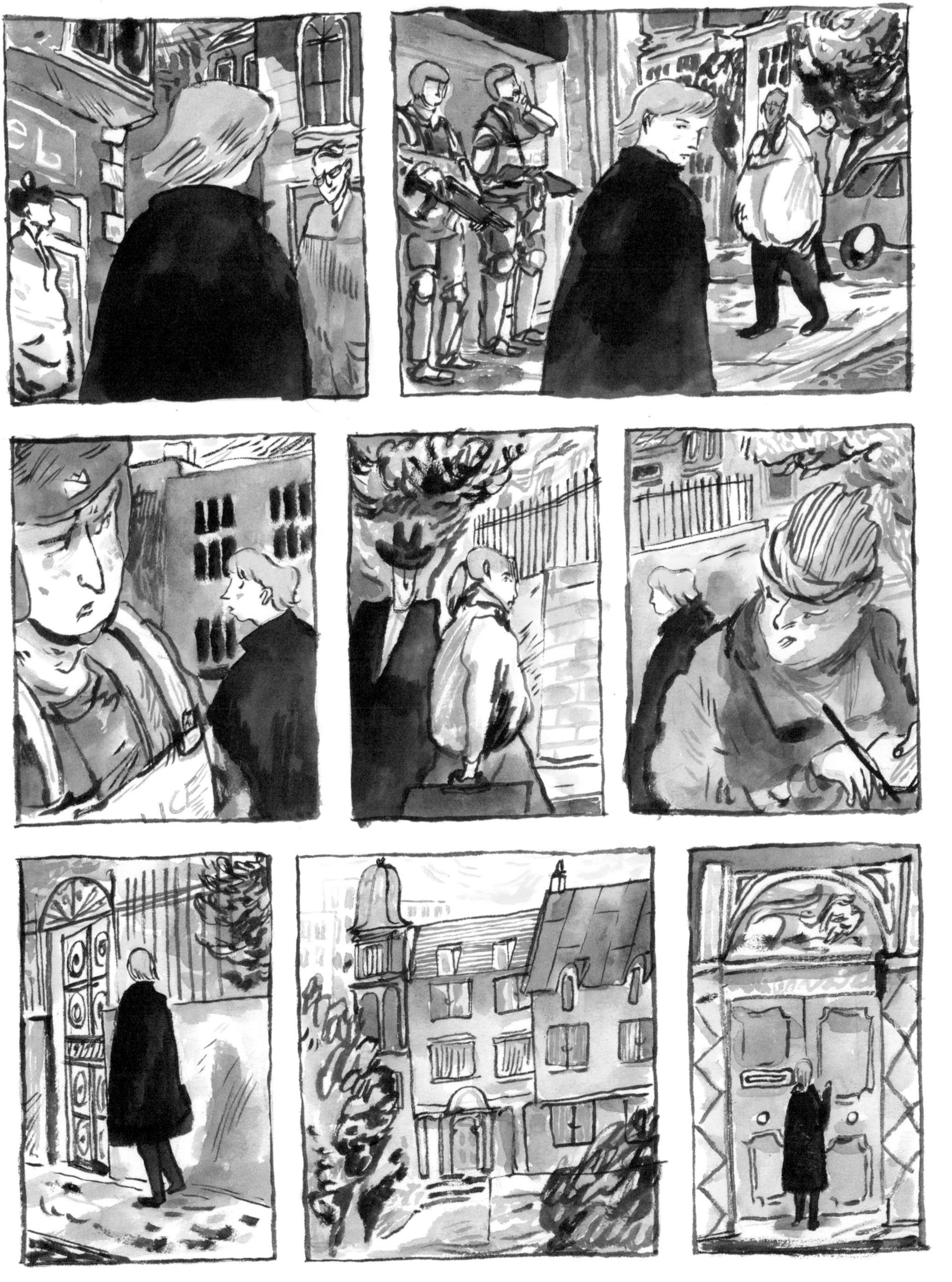

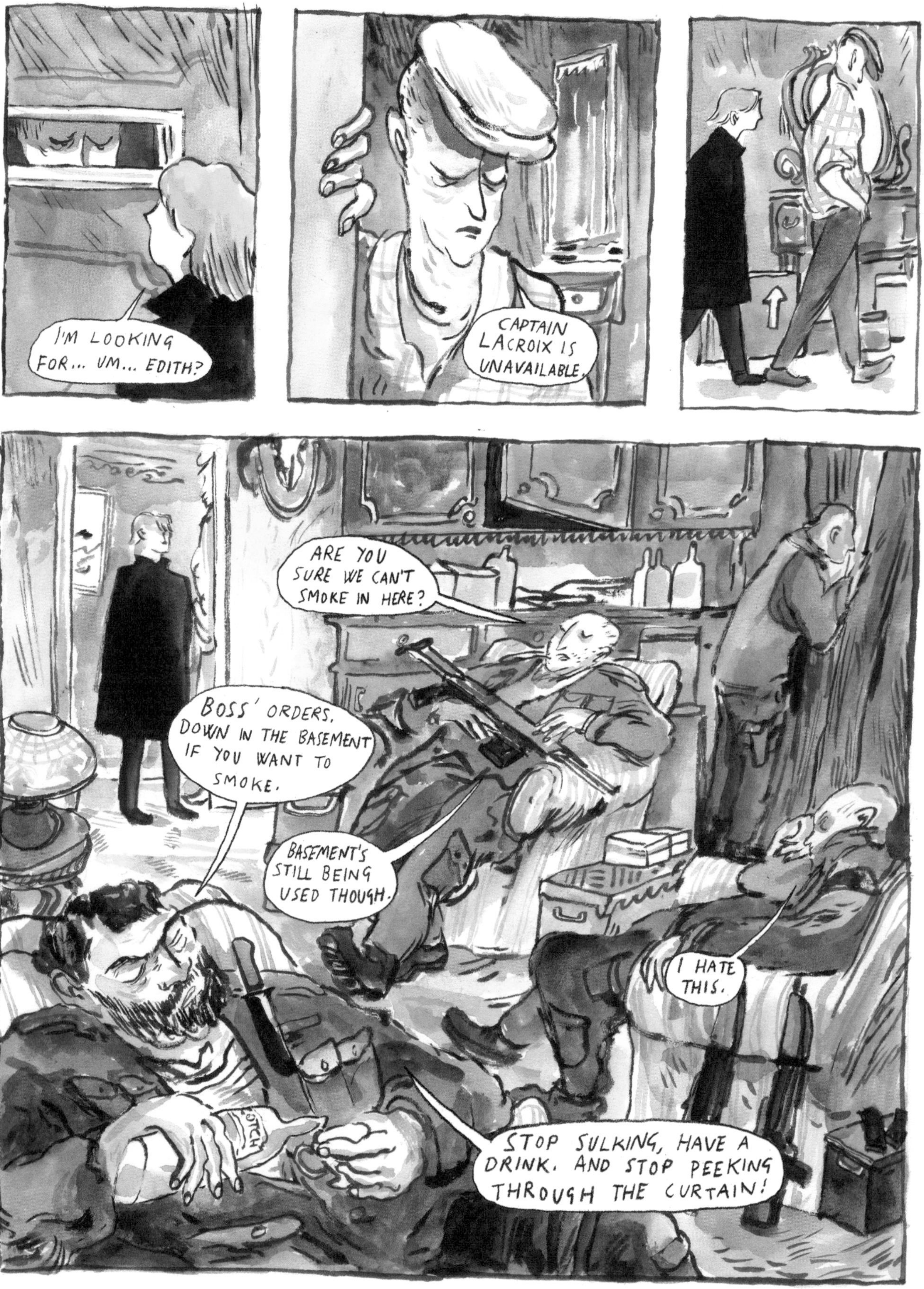
I'M LOOKING FOR... UM... EDITH?
CAPTAIN LACROIX IS UNAVAILABLE.
ARE YOU SURE WE CAN'T SMOKE IN HERE?
BOSS' ORDERS. DOWN IN THE BASEMENT IF YOU WANT TO SMOKE.
BASEMENT'S STILL BEING USED THOUGH.
I HATE THIS.
STOP SULKING, HAVE A DRINK. AND STOP PEEKING THROUGH THE CURTAIN!

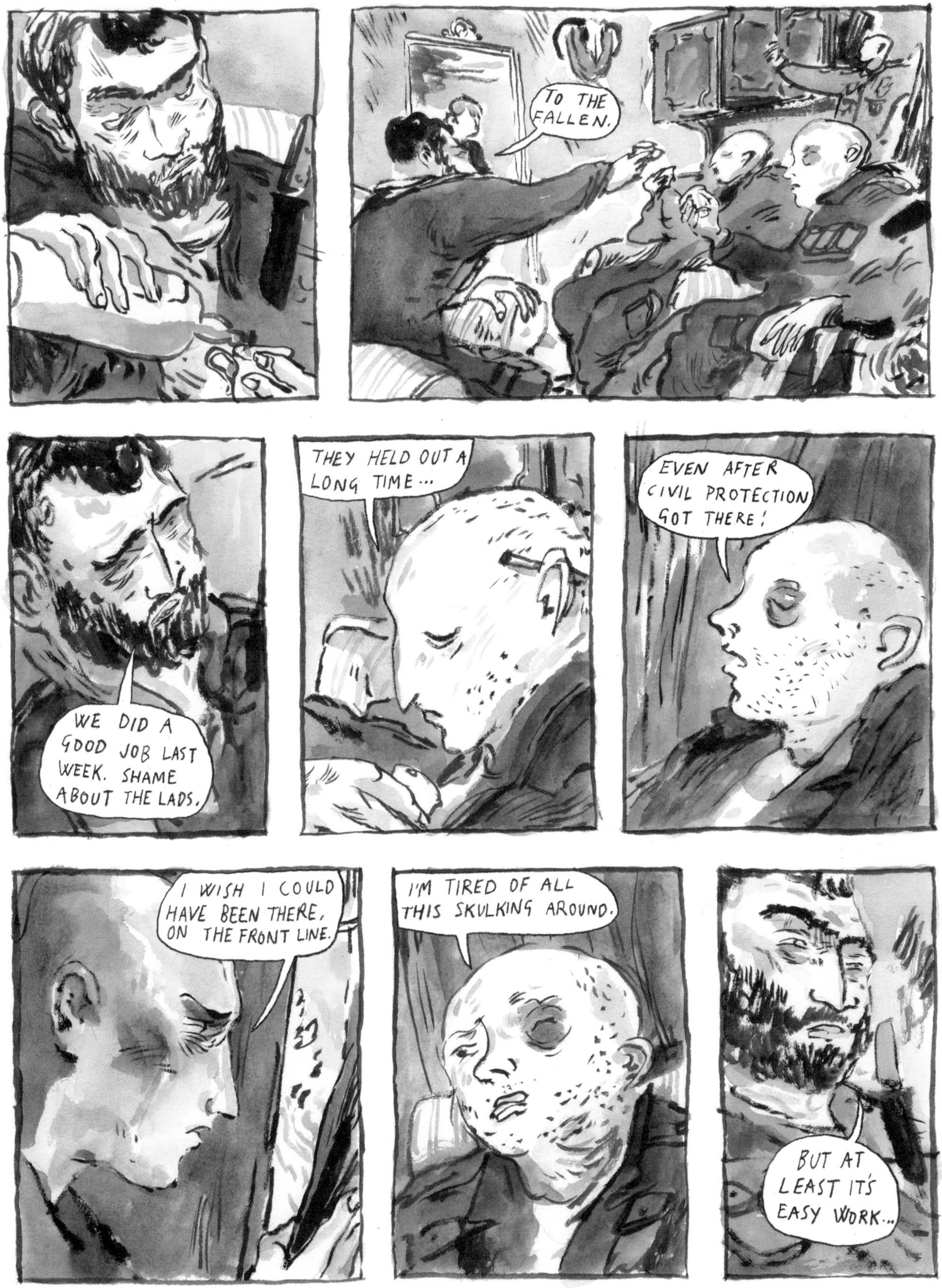
TO THE FALLEN.
WE DID A GOOD JOB LAST WEEK. SHAME ABOUT THE LADS.
THEY HELD OUT A LONG TIME...
EVEN AFTER CIVIL PROTECTION GOT THERE!
I WISH I COULD HAVE BEEN THERE, ON THE FRONT LINE.
I'M TIRED OF ALL THIS SKULKING AROUND.
BUT AT LEAST IT'S EASY WORK...

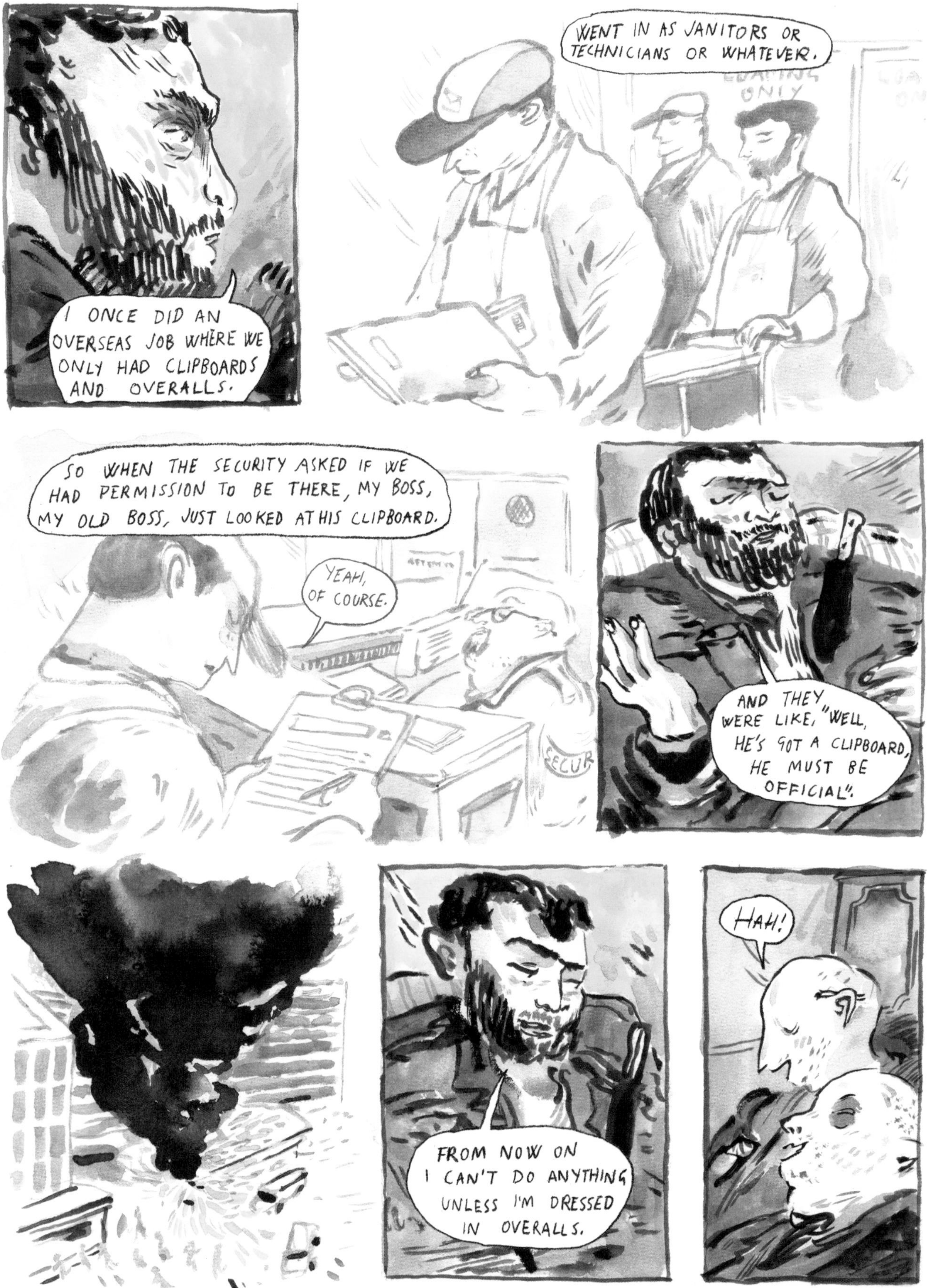
I ONCE DID AN OVERSEAS JOB WHERE WE ONLY HAD CLIPBOARDS AND OVERALLS.
WENT IN AS JANITORS OR TECHNICIANS OR WHATEVER.
LOADING ONLY
SO WHEN THE SECURITY ASKED IF WE HAD PERMISSION TO BE THERE, MY BOSS, MY OLD BOSS, JUST LOOKED AT HIS CLIPBOARD.
YEAH, OF COURSE.
SECUR
AND THEY WERE LIKE, "WELL, HE'S GOT A CLIPBOARD, HE MUST BE OFFICIAL".
FROM NOW ON I CAN'T DO ANYTHING UNLESS I'M DRESSED IN OVERALLS.
HAH!

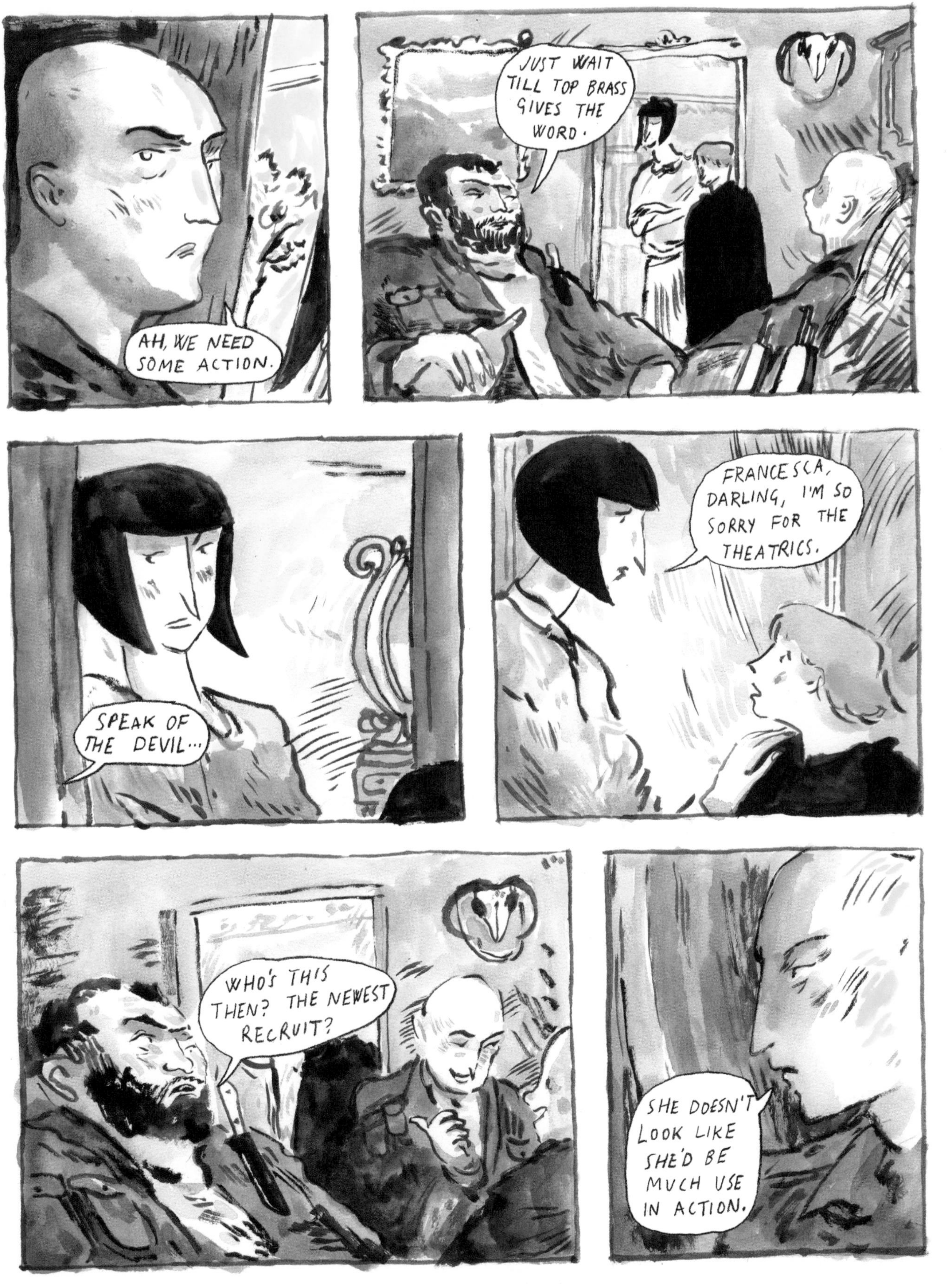
AH, WE NEED SOME ACTION.
JUST WAIT TILL TOP BRASS GIVES THE WORD.
SPEAK OF THE DEVIL...
FRANCESCA, DARLING, I'M SO SORRY FOR THE THEATRICS.
WHO'S THIS THEN? THE NEWEST RECRUIT?
SHE DOESN'T LOOK LIKE SHE'D BE MUCH USE IN ACTION.

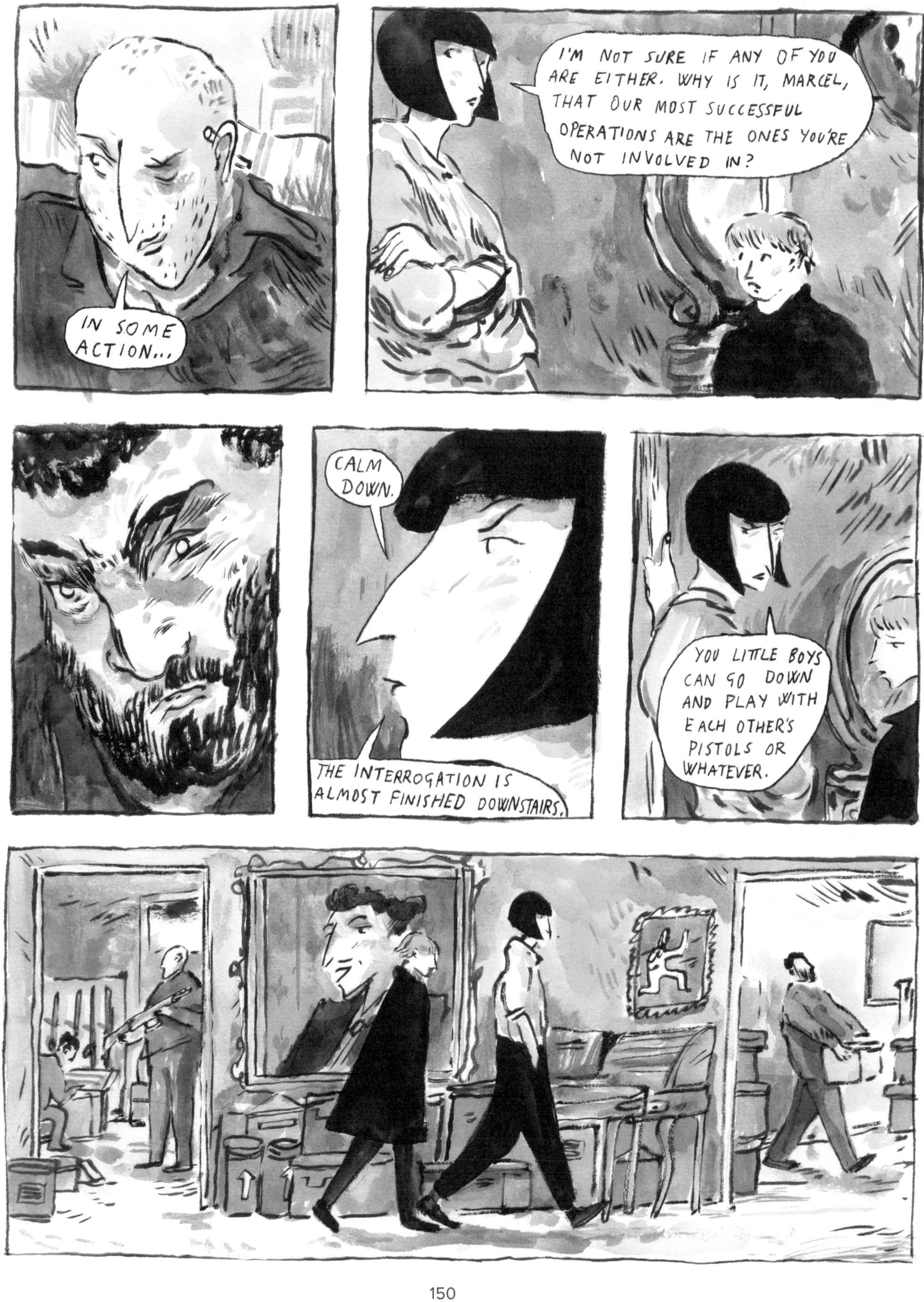
IN SOME ACTION...
I'M NOT SURE IF ANY OF YOU ARE EITHER. WHY IS IT, MARCEL, THAT OUR MOST SUCCESSFUL OPERATIONS ARE THE ONES YOU'RE NOT INVOLVED IN?
CALM DOWN.
THE INTERROGATION IS ALMOST FINISHED DOWNSTAIRS.
YOU LITTLE BOYS CAN GO DOWN AND PLAY WITH EACH OTHER'S PISTOLS OR WHATEVER.

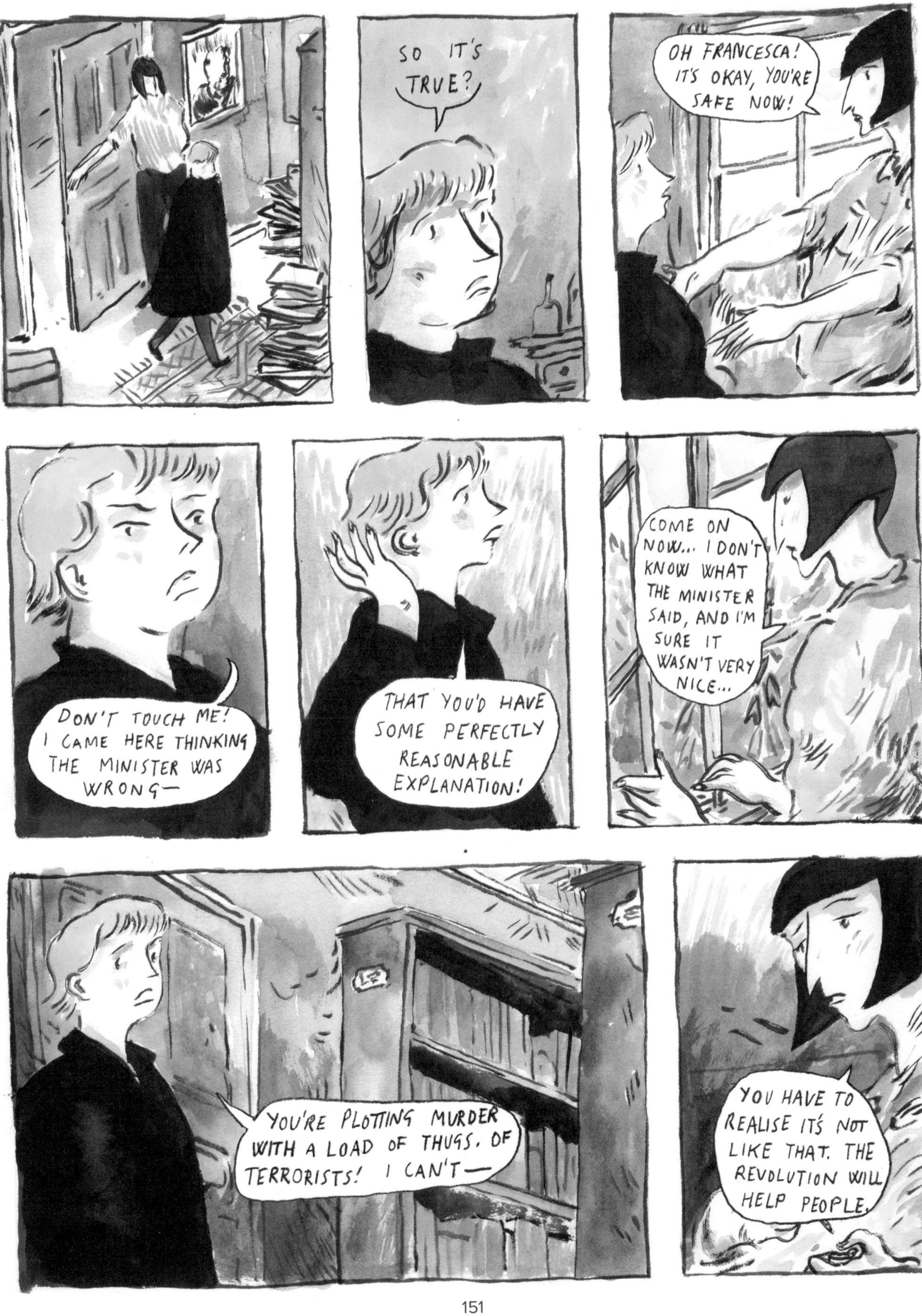
SO IT'S TRUE?
OH FRANCESCA! IT'S OKAY, YOU'RE SAFE NOW!
DON'T TOUCH ME! I CAME HERE THINKING THE MINISTER WAS WRONG—
THAT YOU'D HAVE SOME PERFECTLY REASONABLE EXPLANATION!
COME ON NOW... I DON'T KNOW WHAT THE MINISTER SAID, AND I'M SURE IT WASN'T VERY NICE...
YOU'RE PLOTTING MURDER WITH A LOAD OF THUGS. OF TERRORISTS! I CAN'T—
YOU HAVE TO REALISE IT'S NOT LIKE THAT. THE REVOLUTION WILL HELP PEOPLE.

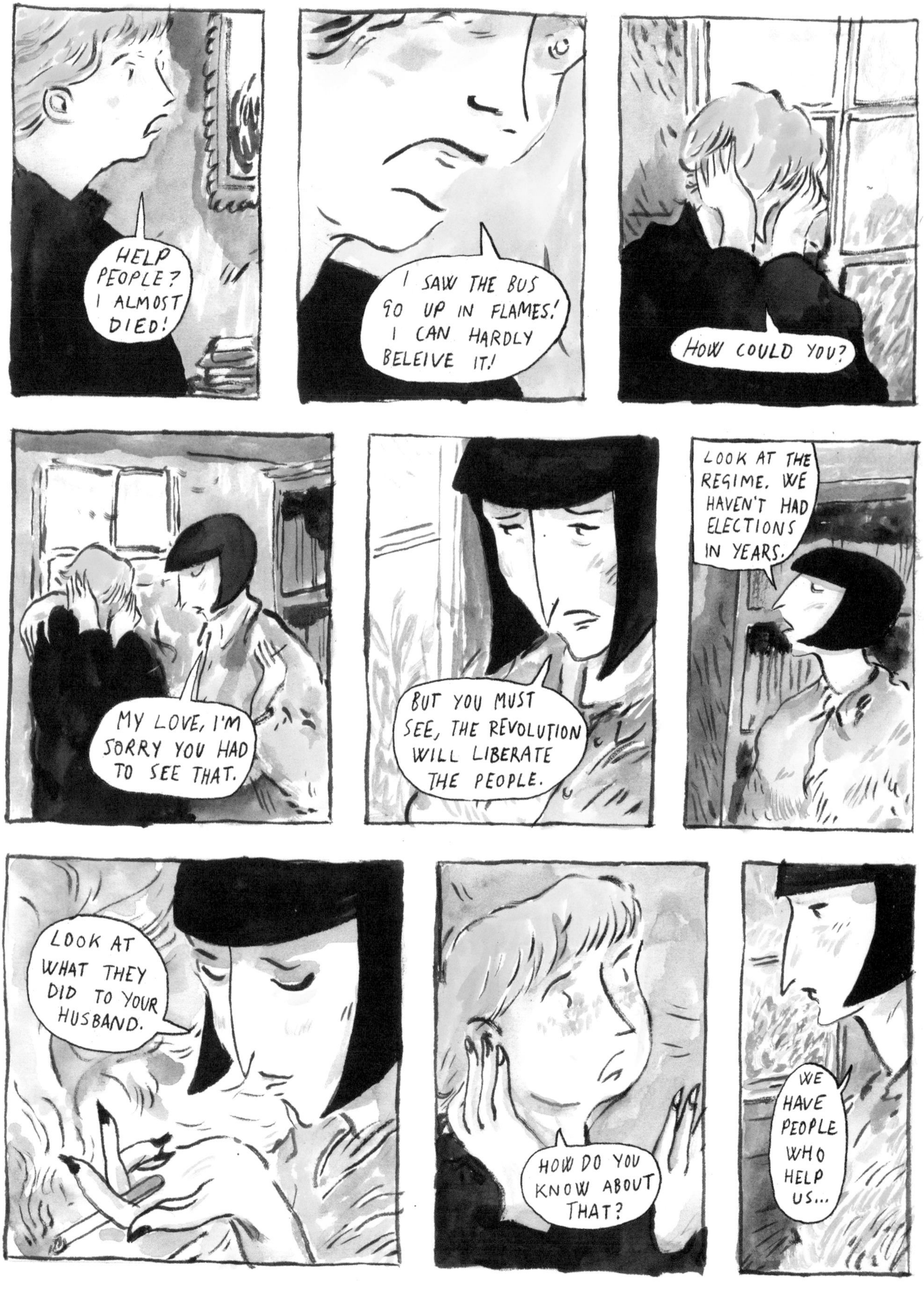
HELP PEOPLE? I ALMOST DIED!
I SAW THE BUS GO UP IN FLAMES! I CAN HARDLY BELEIVE IT!
HOW COULD YOU?
MY LOVE, I'M SORRY YOU HAD TO SEE THAT.
BUT YOU MUST SEE, THE REVOLUTION WILL LIBERATE THE PEOPLE.
LOOK AT THE REGIME. WE HAVEN'T HAD ELECTIONS IN YEARS.
LOOK AT WHAT THEY DID TO YOUR HUSBAND.
HOW DO YOU KNOW ABOUT THAT?
WE HAVE PEOPLE WHO HELP US...

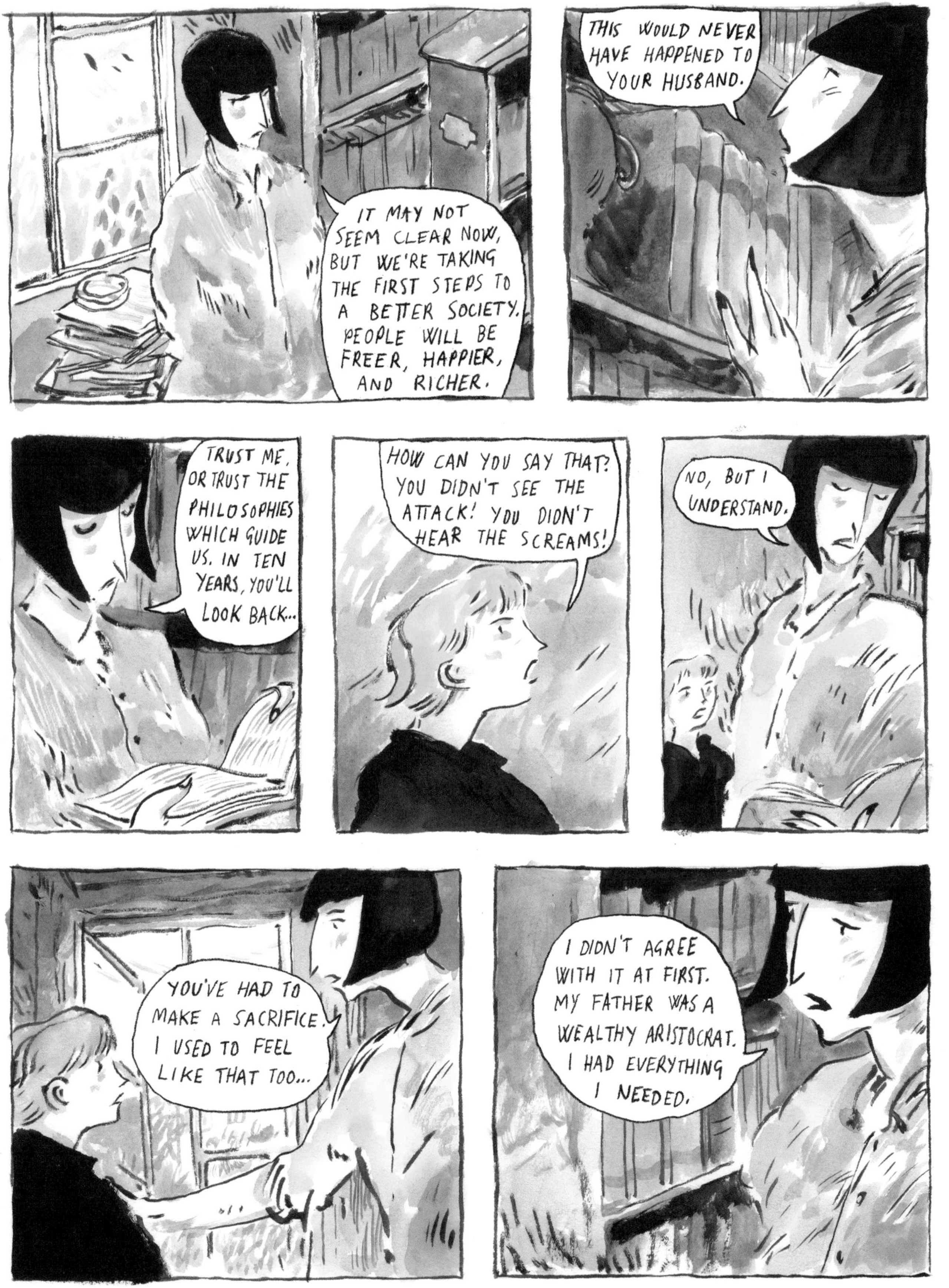
IT MAY NOT SEEM CLEAR NOW, BUT WE'RE TAKING THE FIRST STEPS TO A BETTER SOCIETY. PEOPLE WILL BE FREER, HAPPIER, AND RICHER.
THIS WOULD NEVER HAVE HAPPENED TO YOUR HUSBAND.
TRUST ME, OR TRUST THE PHILOSOPHIES WHICH GUIDE US. IN TEN YEARS, YOU'LL LOOK BACK...
HOW CAN YOU SAY THAT? YOU DIDN'T SEE THE ATTACK! YOU DIDN'T HEAR THE SCREAMS!
NO, BUT I UNDERSTAND.
YOU'VE HAD TO MAKE A SACRIFICE. I USED TO FEEL LIKE THAT TOO...
I DIDN'T AGREE WITH IT AT FIRST. MY FATHER WAS A WEALTHY ARISTOCRAT. I HAD EVERYTHING I NEEDED.

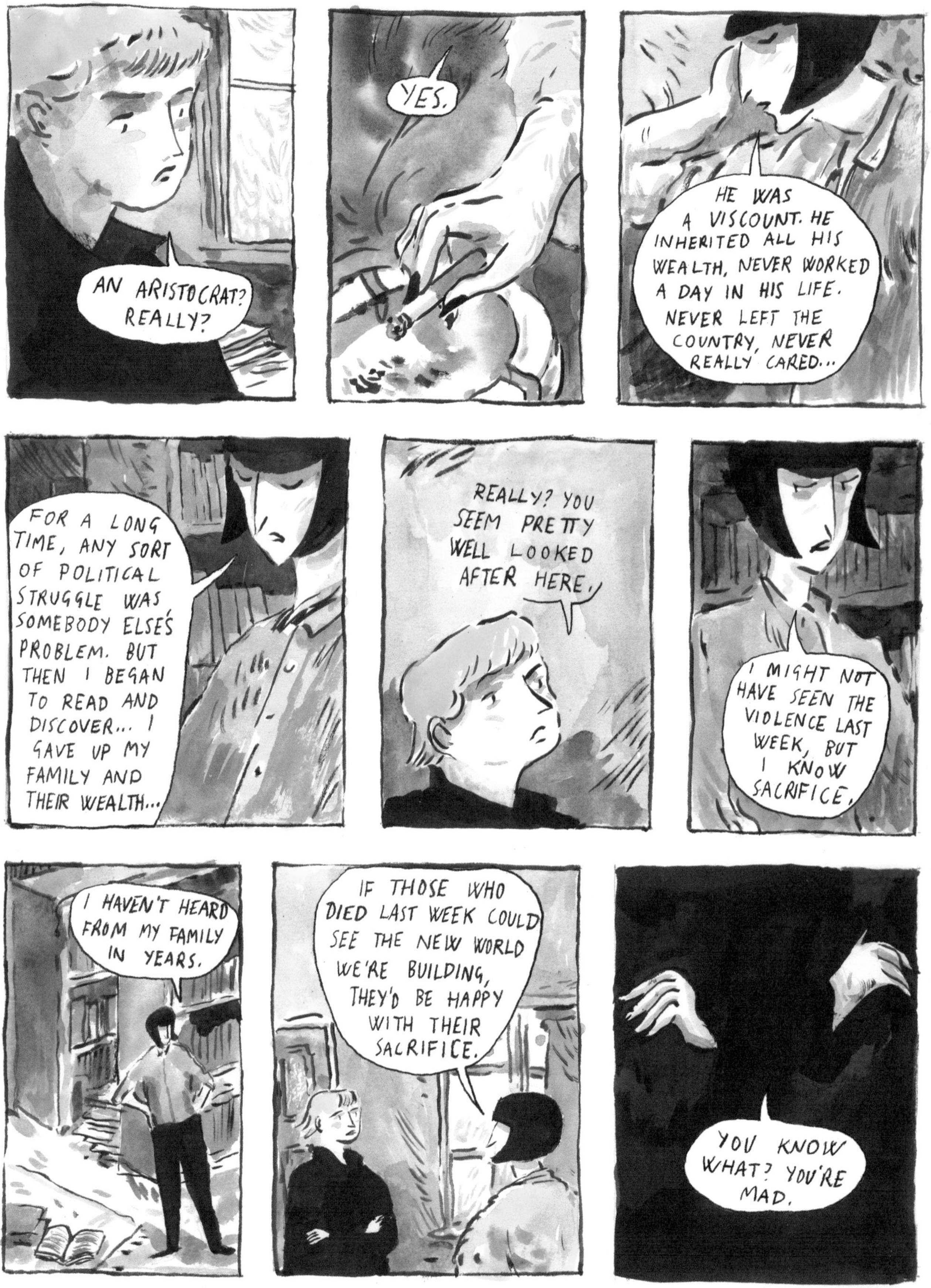
AN ARISTOCRAT? REALLY?
YES.
HE WAS A VISCOUNT. HE INHERITED ALL HIS WEALTH, NEVER WORKED A DAY IN HIS LIFE. NEVER LEFT THE COUNTRY, NEVER REALLY CARED...
FOR A LONG TIME, ANY SORT OF POLITICAL STRUGGLE WAS SOMEBODY ELSE'S PROBLEM. BUT THEN I BEGAN TO READ AND DISCOVER... I GAVE UP MY FAMILY AND THEIR WEALTH...
REALLY? YOU SEEM PRETTY WELL LOOKED AFTER HERE.
I MIGHT NOT HAVE SEEN THE VIOLENCE LAST WEEK, BUT I KNOW SACRIFICE.
I HAVEN'T HEARD FROM MY FAMILY IN YEARS.
IF THOSE WHO DIED LAST WEEK COULD SEE THE NEW WORLD WE'RE BUILDING, THEY'D BE HAPPY WITH THEIR SACRIFICE.
YOU KNOW WHAT? YOU'RE MAD.

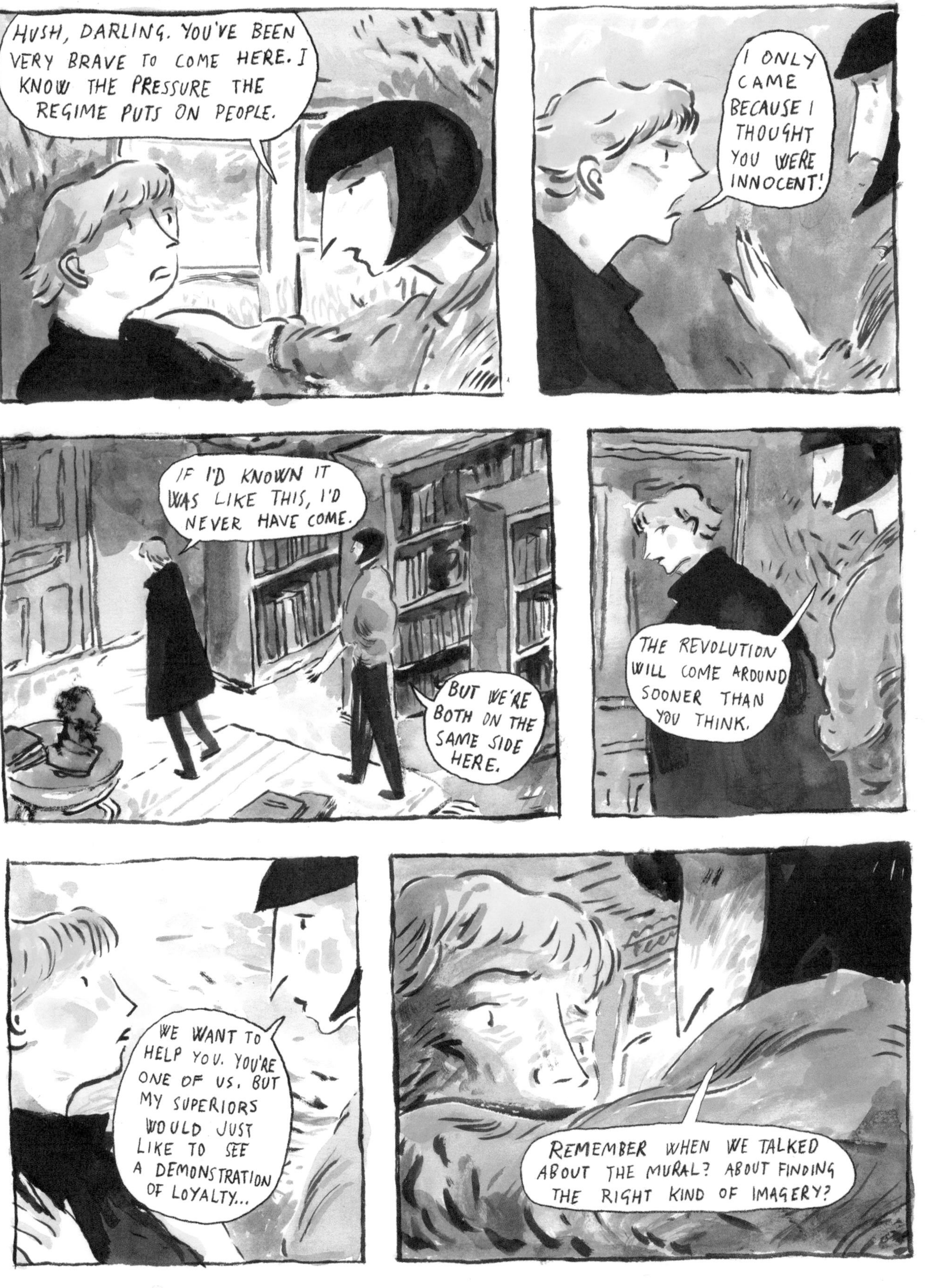

HUSH, DARLING. YOU'VE BEEN VERY BRAVE TO COME HERE. I KNOW THE PRESSURE THE REGIME PUTS ON PEOPLE.
I ONLY CAME BECAUSE I THOUGHT YOU WERE INNOCENT!
IF I'D KNOWN IT WAS LIKE THIS, I'D NEVER HAVE COME.
BUT WE'RE BOTH ON THE SAME SIDE HERE.
THE REVOLUTION WILL COME AROUND SOONER THAN YOU THINK.
WE WANT TO HELP YOU. YOU'RE ONE OF US. BUT MY SUPERIORS WOULD JUST LIKE TO SEE A DEMONSTRATION OF LOYALTY...
REMEMBER WHEN WE TALKED ABOUT THE MURAL? ABOUT FINDING THE RIGHT KIND OF IMAGERY?

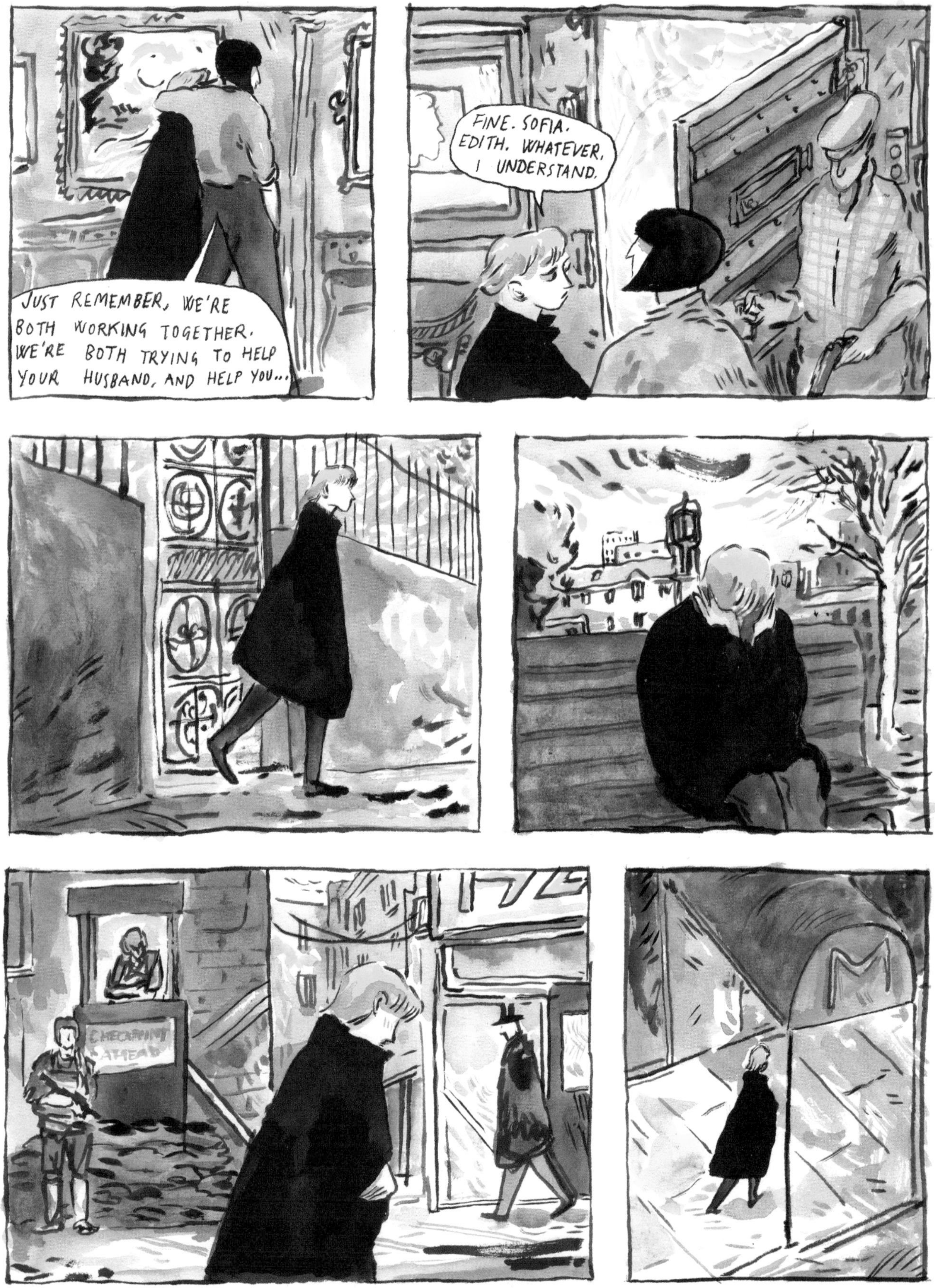
JUST REMEMBER, WE'RE BOTH WORKING TOGETHER. WE'RE BOTH TRYING TO HELP YOUR HUSBAND, AND HELP YOU...
FINE. SOFIA. EDITH. WHATEVER. I UNDERSTAND.

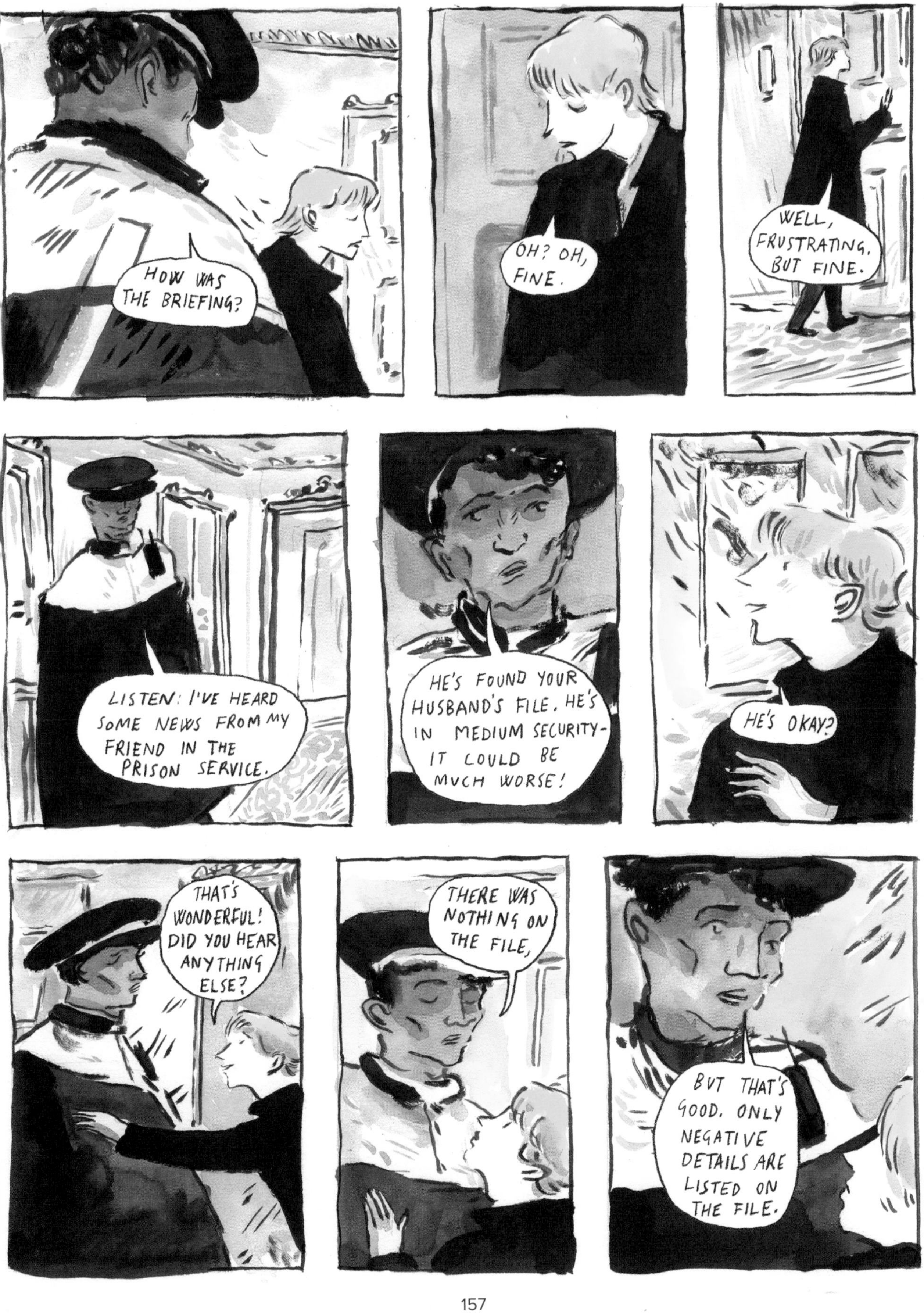
HOW WAS THE BRIEFING?
OH? OH, FINE.
WELL, FRUSTRATING. BUT FINE.
LISTEN: I'VE HEARD SOME NEWS FROM MY FRIEND IN THE PRISON SERVICE.
HE'S FOUND YOUR HUSBAND'S FILE. HE'S IN MEDIUM SECURITY- IT COULD BE MUCH WORSE!
HE'S OKAY?
THAT'S WONDERFUL! DID YOU HEAR ANYTHING ELSE?
THERE WAS NOTHING ON THE FILE,
BUT THAT'S GOOD. ONLY NEGATIVE DETAILS ARE LISTED ON THE FILE.

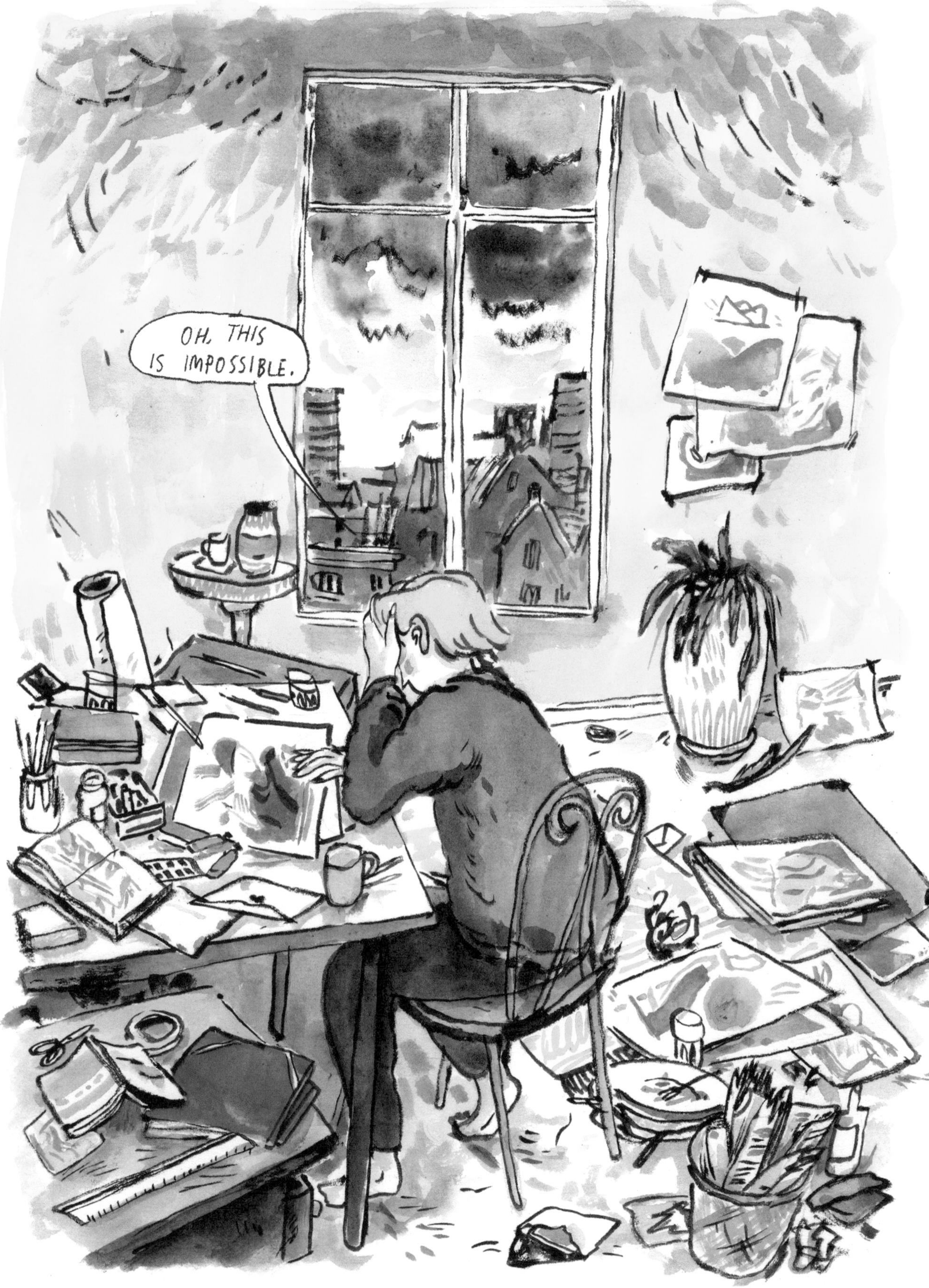
OH, THIS IS IMPOSSIBLE.

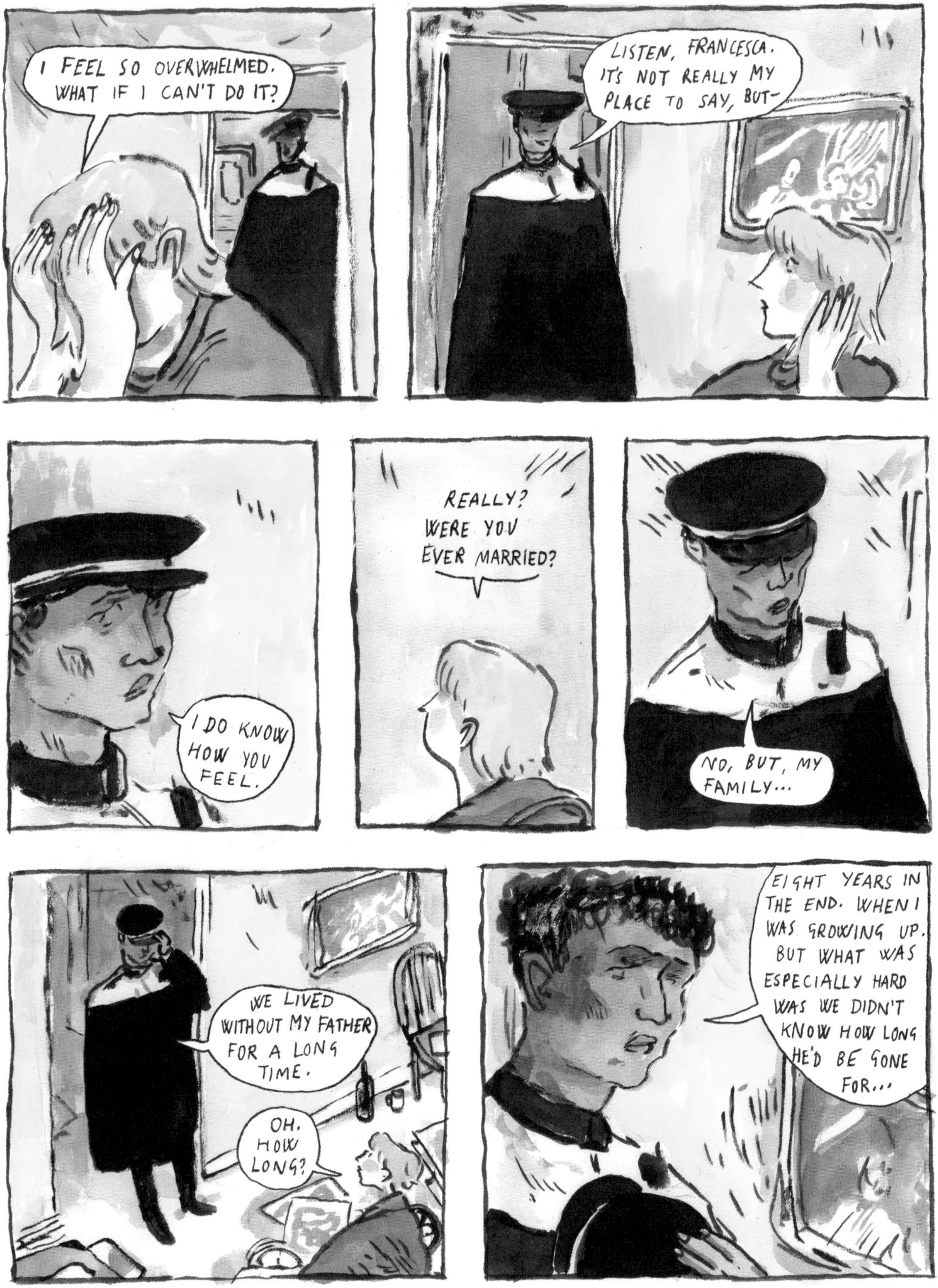
I FEEL SO OVERWHELMED. WHAT IF I CAN'T DO IT?
LISTEN, FRANCESCA. IT'S NOT REALLY MY PLACE TO SAY, BUT-
I DO KNOW HOW YOU FEEL.
REALLY? WERE YOU EVER MARRIED?
NO, BUT, MY FAMILY...
WE LIVED WITHOUT MY FATHER FOR A LONG TIME.
OH. HOW LONG?
EIGHT YEARS IN THE END. WHEN I WAS GROWING UP. BUT WHAT WAS ESPECIALLY HARD WAS WE DIDN'T KNOW HOW LONG HE'D BE GONE FOR...

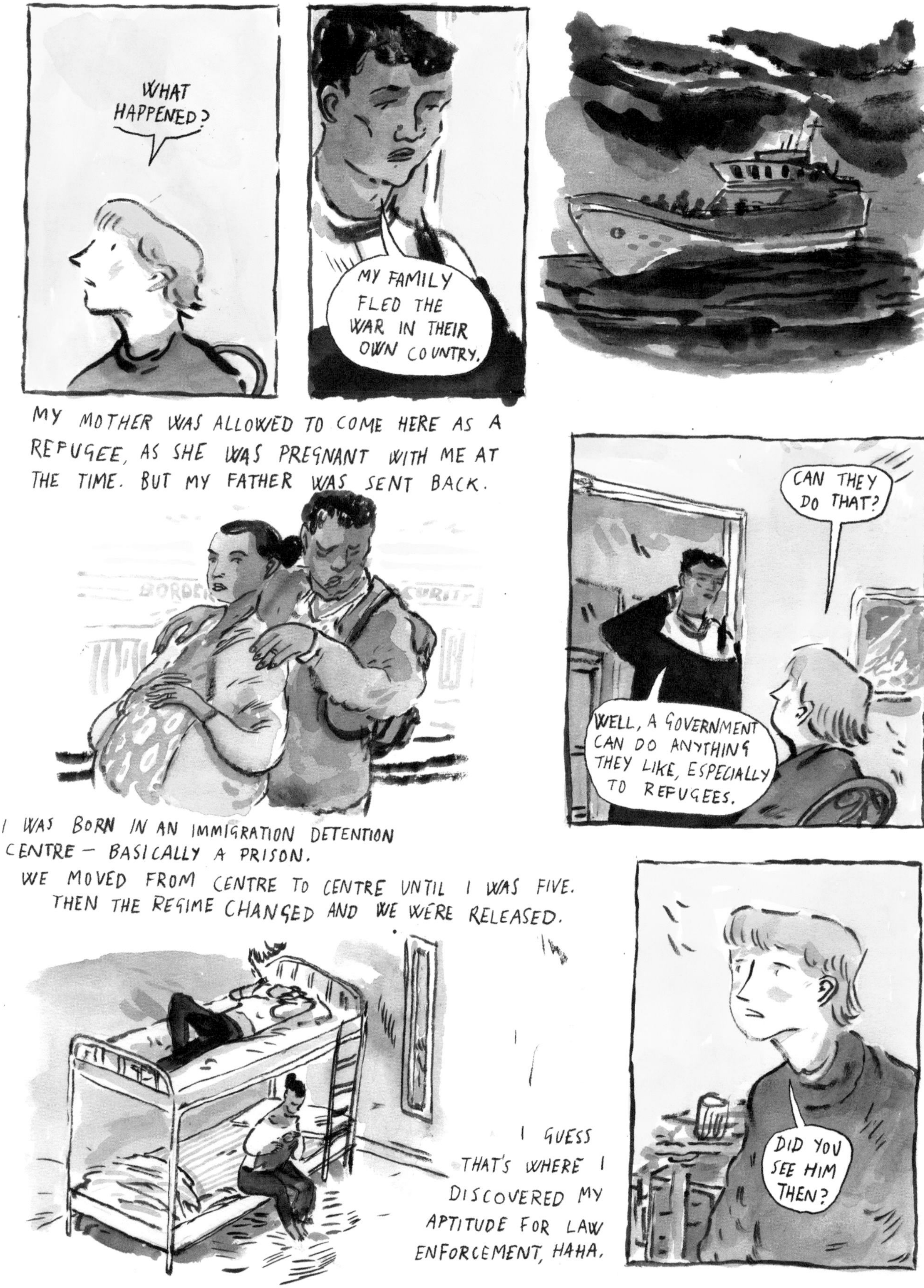
WHAT HAPPENED?
MY FAMILY FLED THE WAR IN THEIR OWN COUNTRY.
MY MOTHER WAS ALLOWED TO COME HERE AS A REFUGEE, AS SHE WAS PREGNANT WITH ME AT THE TIME. BUT MY FATHER WAS SENT BACK.
CAN THEY DO THAT?
WELL, A GOVERNMENT CAN DO ANYTHING THEY LIKE, ESPECIALLY TO REFUGEES.
I WAS BORN IN AN IMMIGRATION DETENTION CENTRE – BASICALLY A PRISON.
WE MOVED FROM CENTRE TO CENTRE UNTIL I WAS FIVE. THEN THE REGIME CHANGED AND WE WERE RELEASED.
I GUESS THAT'S WHERE I DISCOVERED MY APTITUDE FOR LAW ENFORCEMENT, HAHA.
DID YOU SEE HIM THEN?

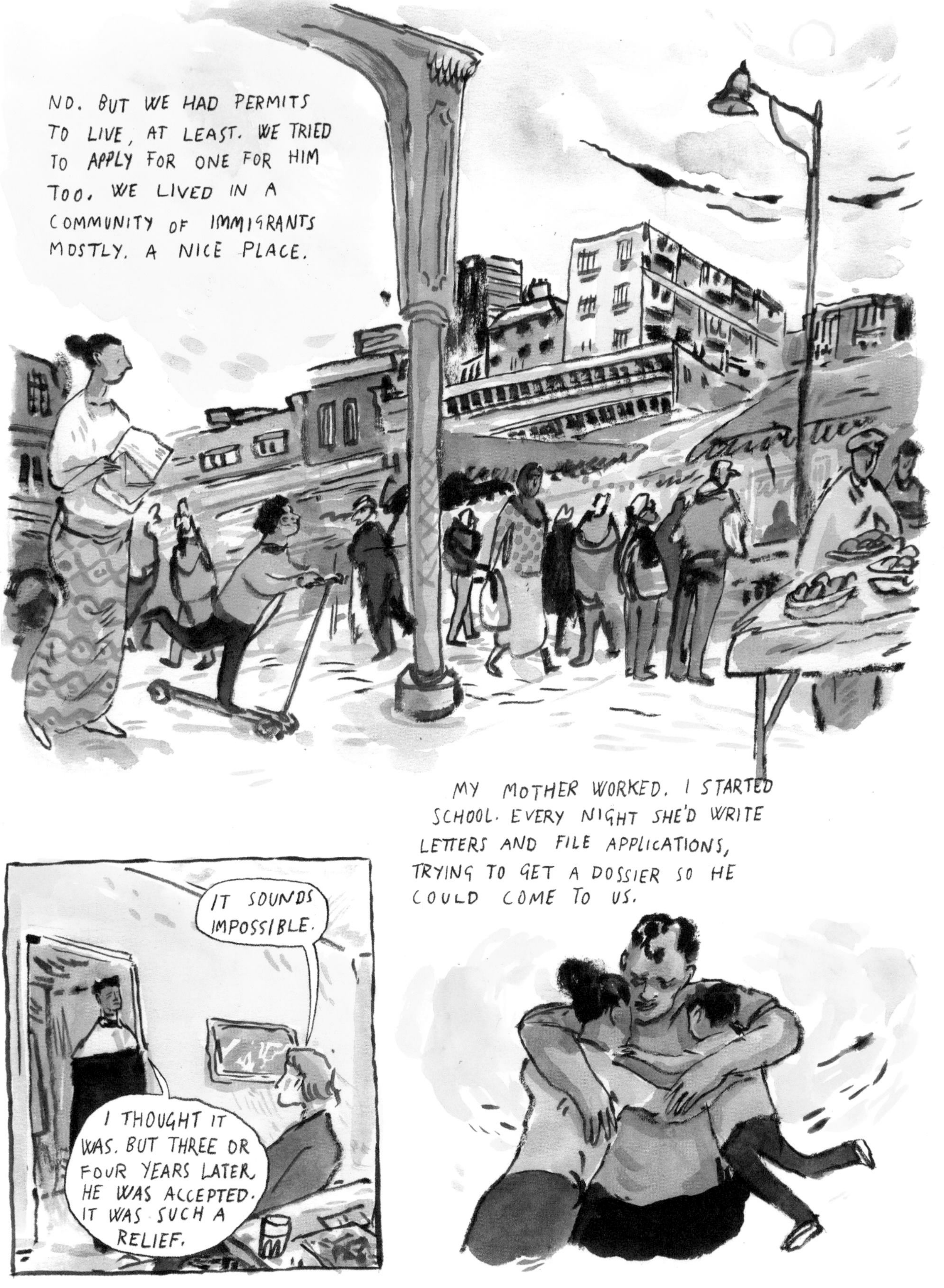
NO. BUT WE HAD PERMITS TO LIVE, AT LEAST. WE TRIED TO APPLY FOR ONE FOR HIM TOO. WE LIVED IN A COMMUNITY OF IMMIGRANTS MOSTLY. A NICE PLACE.
MY MOTHER WORKED. I STARTED SCHOOL. EVERY NIGHT SHE'D WRITE LETTERS AND FILE APPLICATIONS, TRYING TO GET A DOSSIER SO HE COULD COME TO US.
IT SOUNDS IMPOSSIBLE.
I THOUGHT IT WAS. BUT THREE OR FOUR YEARS LATER, HE WAS ACCEPTED. IT WAS SUCH A RELIEF.

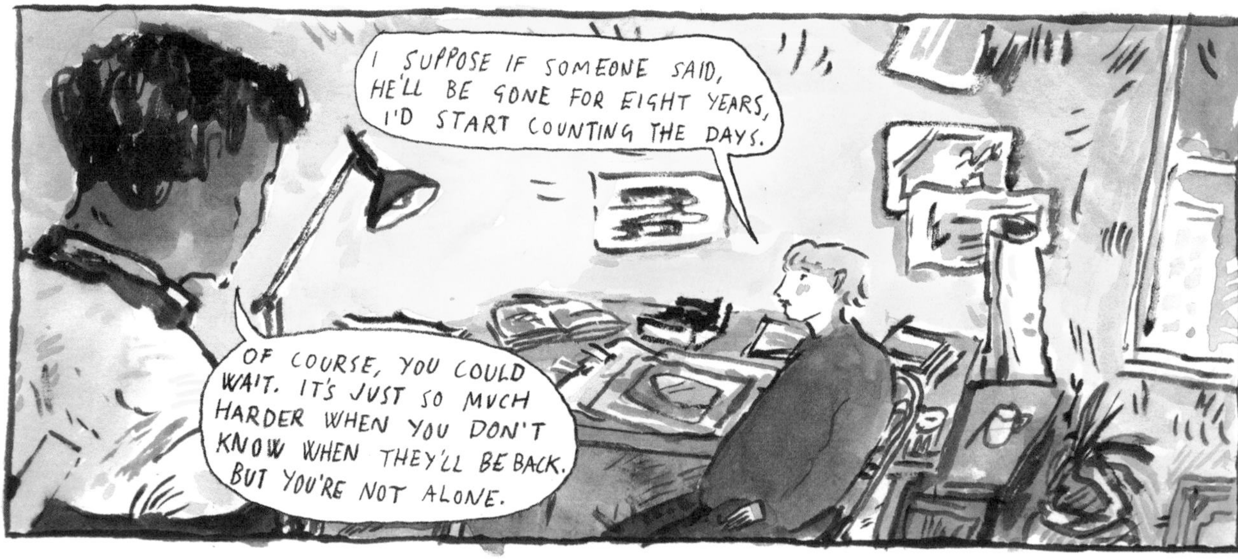
I SUPPOSE IF SOMEONE SAID, HE'LL BE GONE FOR EIGHT YEARS, I'D START COUNTING THE DAYS.
OF COURSE, YOU COULD WAIT. IT'S JUST SO MUCH HARDER WHEN YOU DON'T KNOW WHEN THEY'LL BE BACK. BUT YOU'RE NOT ALONE.

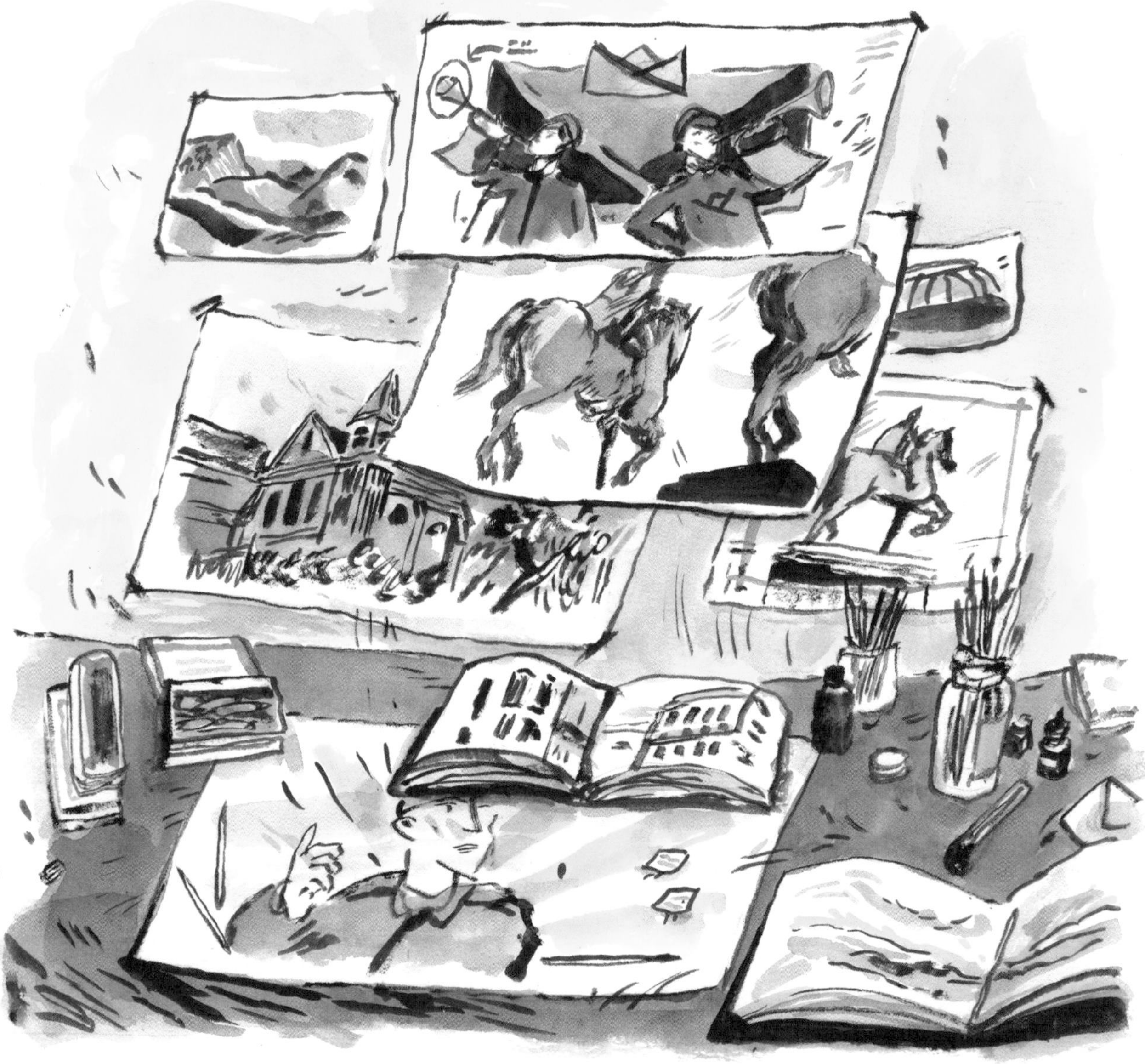

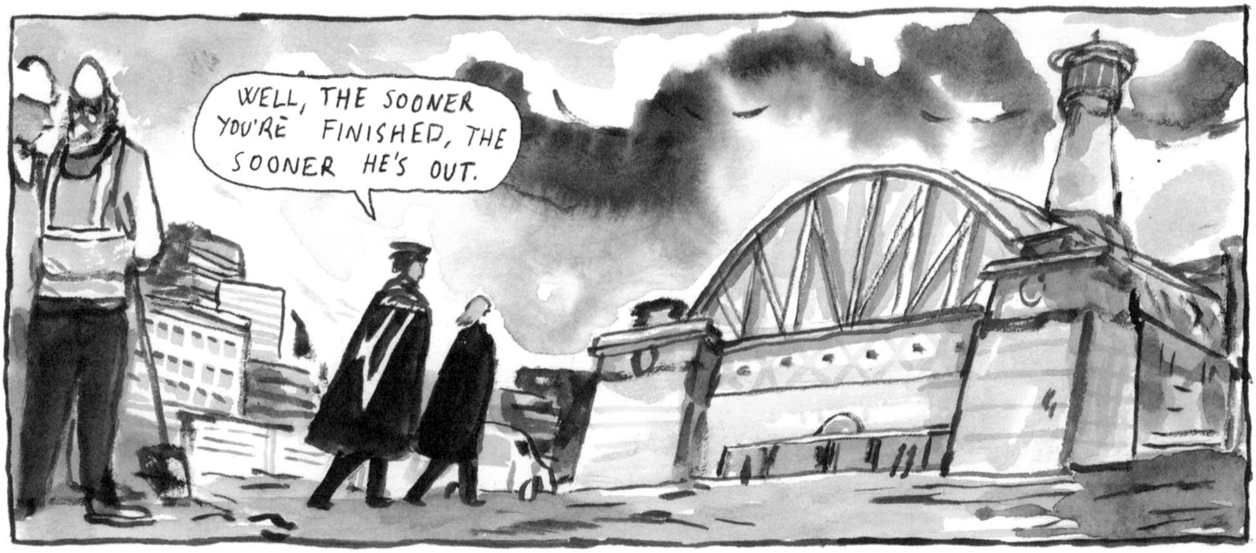
WELL, THE SOONER YOU'RE FINISHED, THE SOONER HE'S OUT.

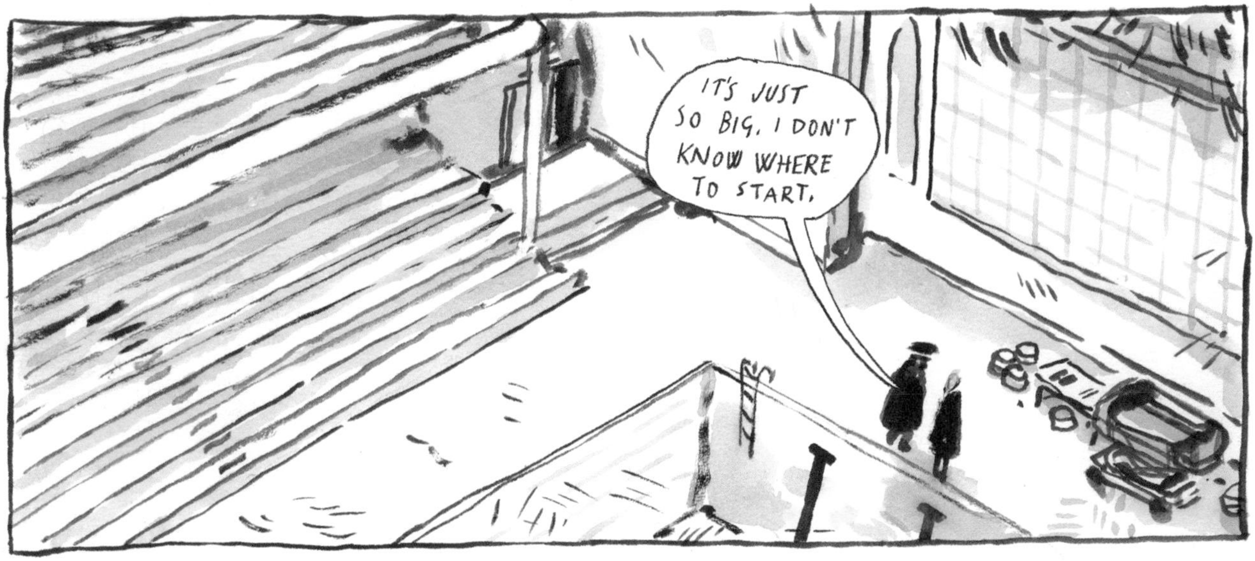
IT'S JUST SO BIG. I DON'T KNOW WHERE TO START.

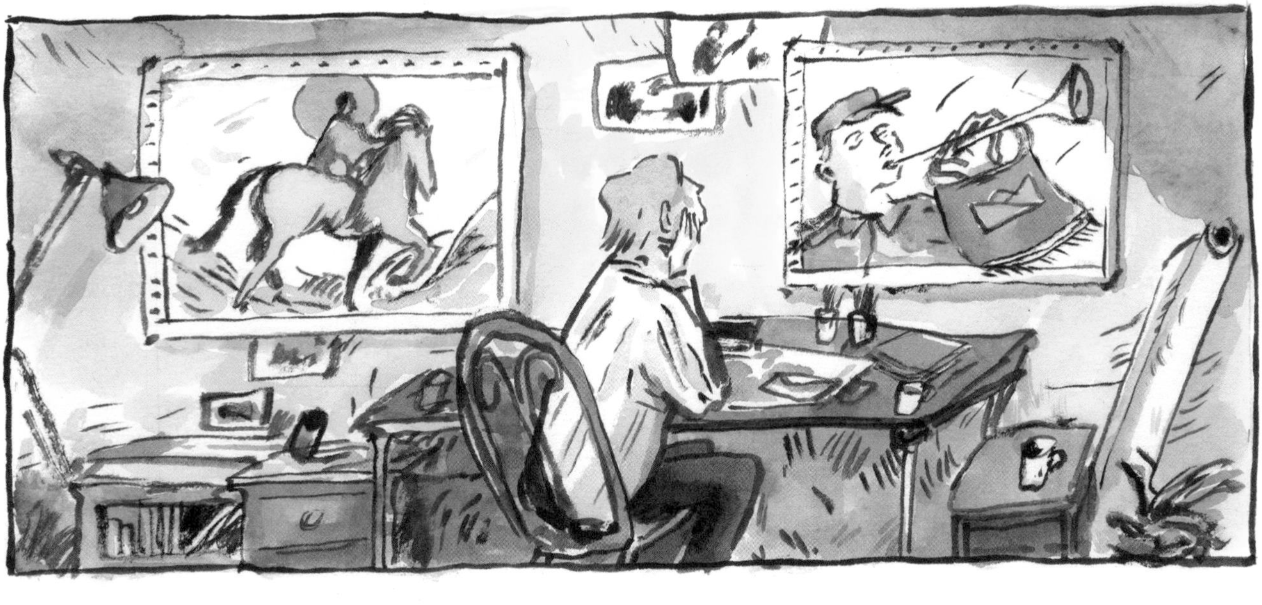

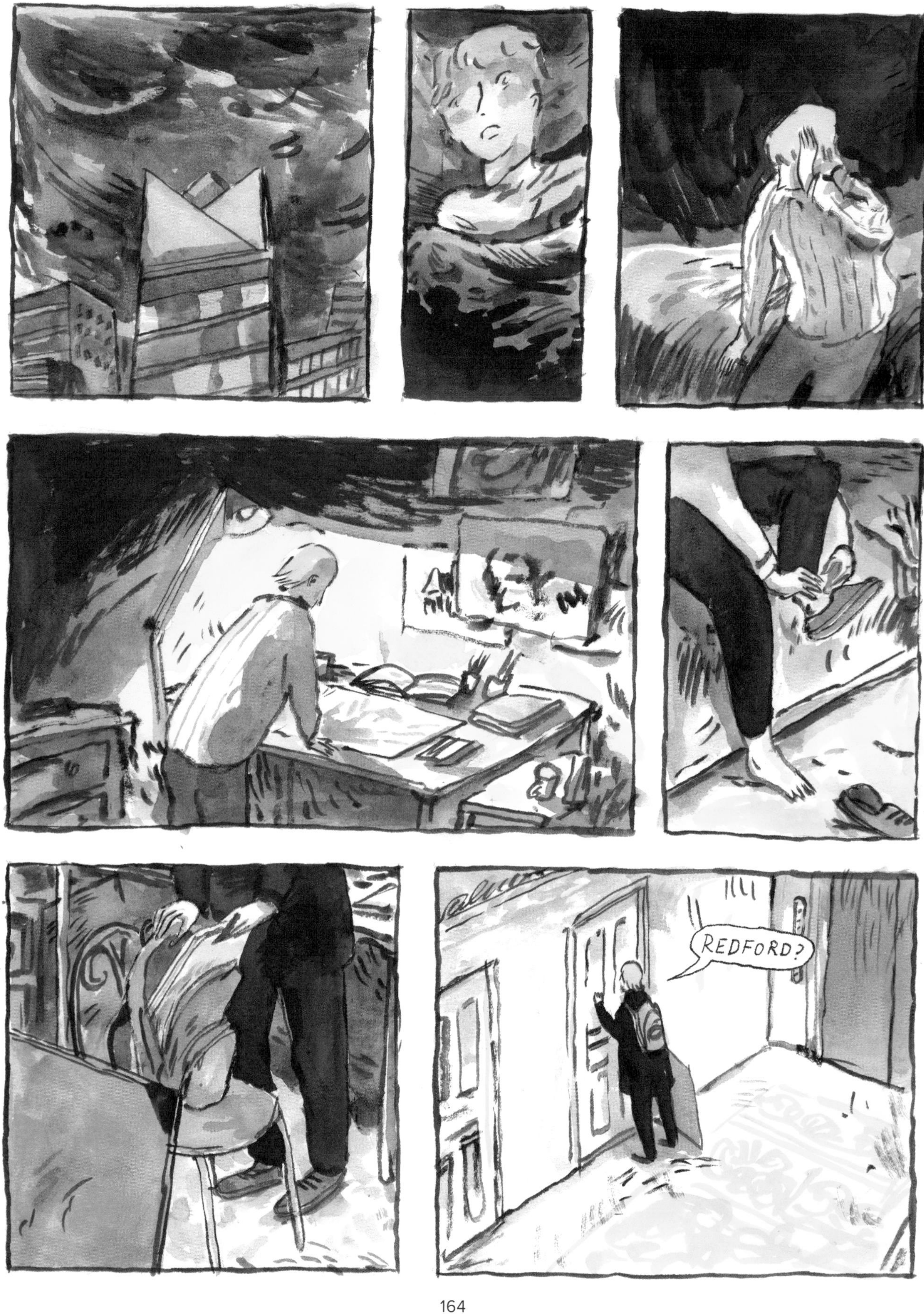
REDFORD?

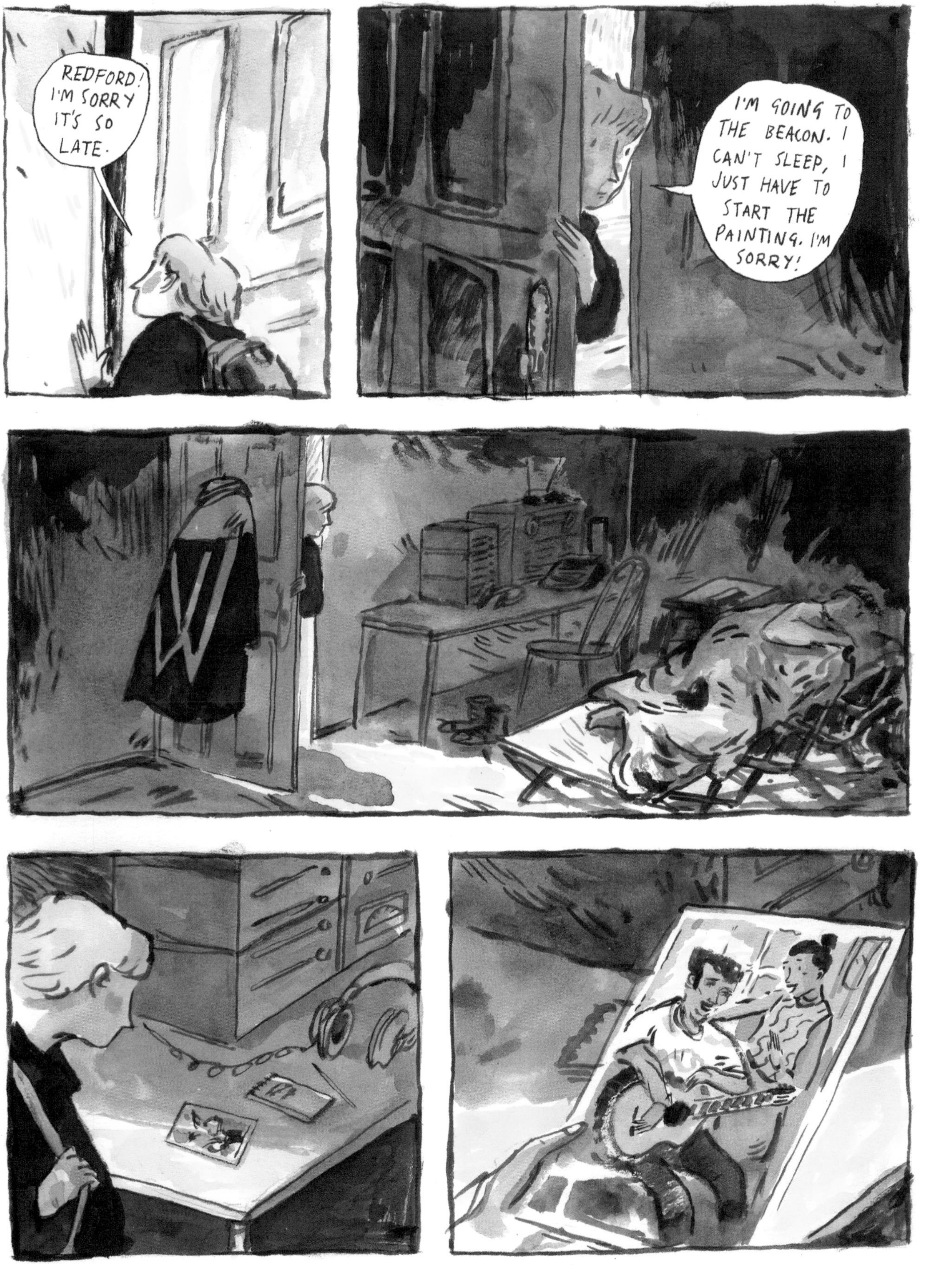
REDFORD! I'M SORRY IT'S SO LATE.
I'M GOING TO THE BEACON. I CAN'T SLEEP, I JUST HAVE TO START THE PAINTING. I'M SORRY!

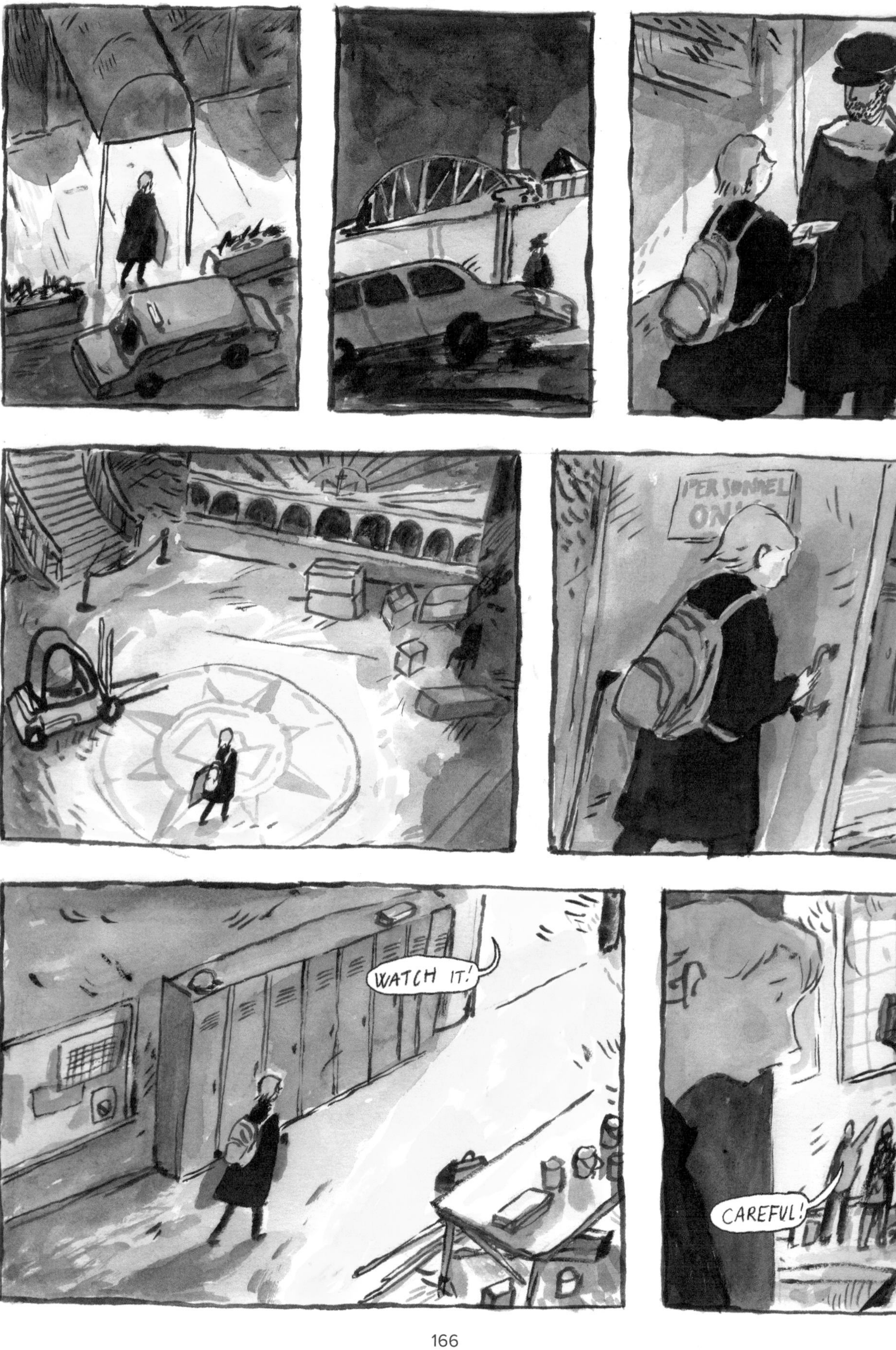
PERSONNEL
WATCH IT!
CAREFUL!

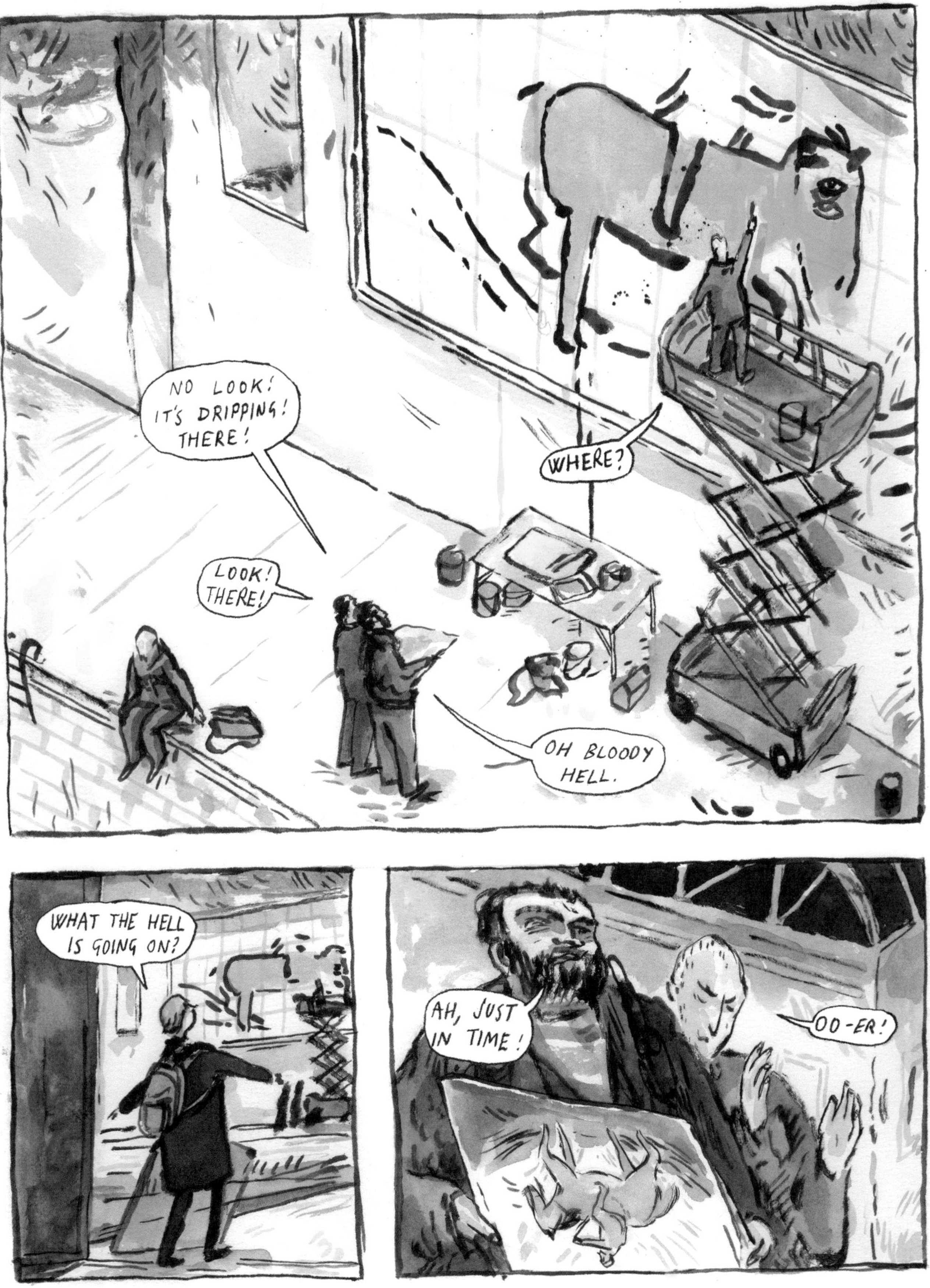
NO LOOK! IT'S DRIPPING! THERE!
WHERE?
LOOK! THERE!
OH BLOODY HELL.
WHAT THE HELL IS GOING ON?
AH, JUST IN TIME!
OO-ER!

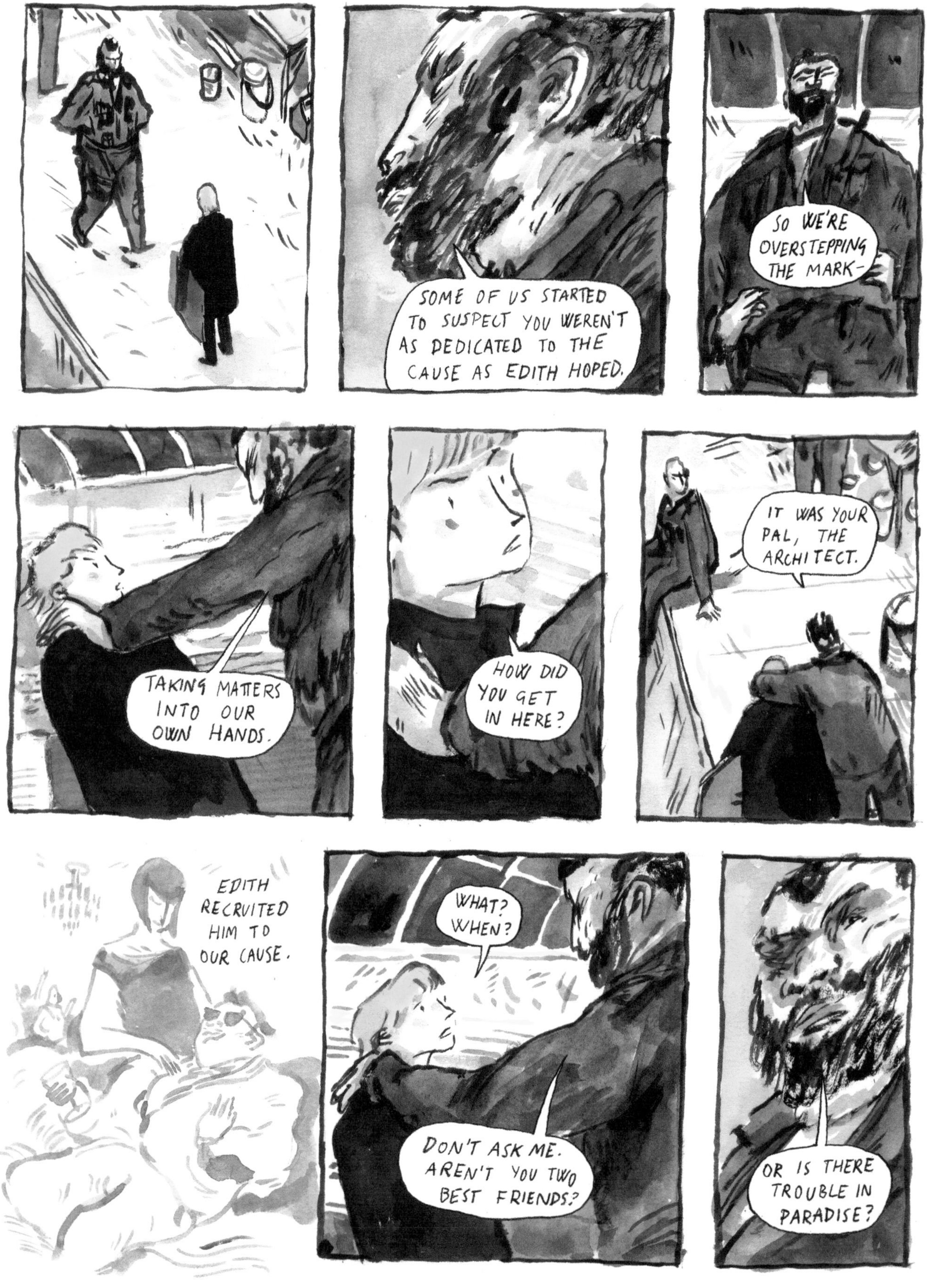
SOME OF US STARTED TO SUSPECT YOU WEREN'T AS DEDICATED TO THE CAUSE AS EDITH HOPED.
SO WE'RE OVERSTEPPING THE MARK-
TAKING MATTERS INTO OUR OWN HANDS.
HOW DID YOU GET IN HERE?
IT WAS YOUR PAL, THE ARCHITECT.
EDITH RECRUITED HIM TO OUR CAUSE.
WHAT? WHEN?
DON'T ASK ME. AREN'T YOU TWO BEST FRIENDS?
OR IS THERE TROUBLE IN PARADISE?

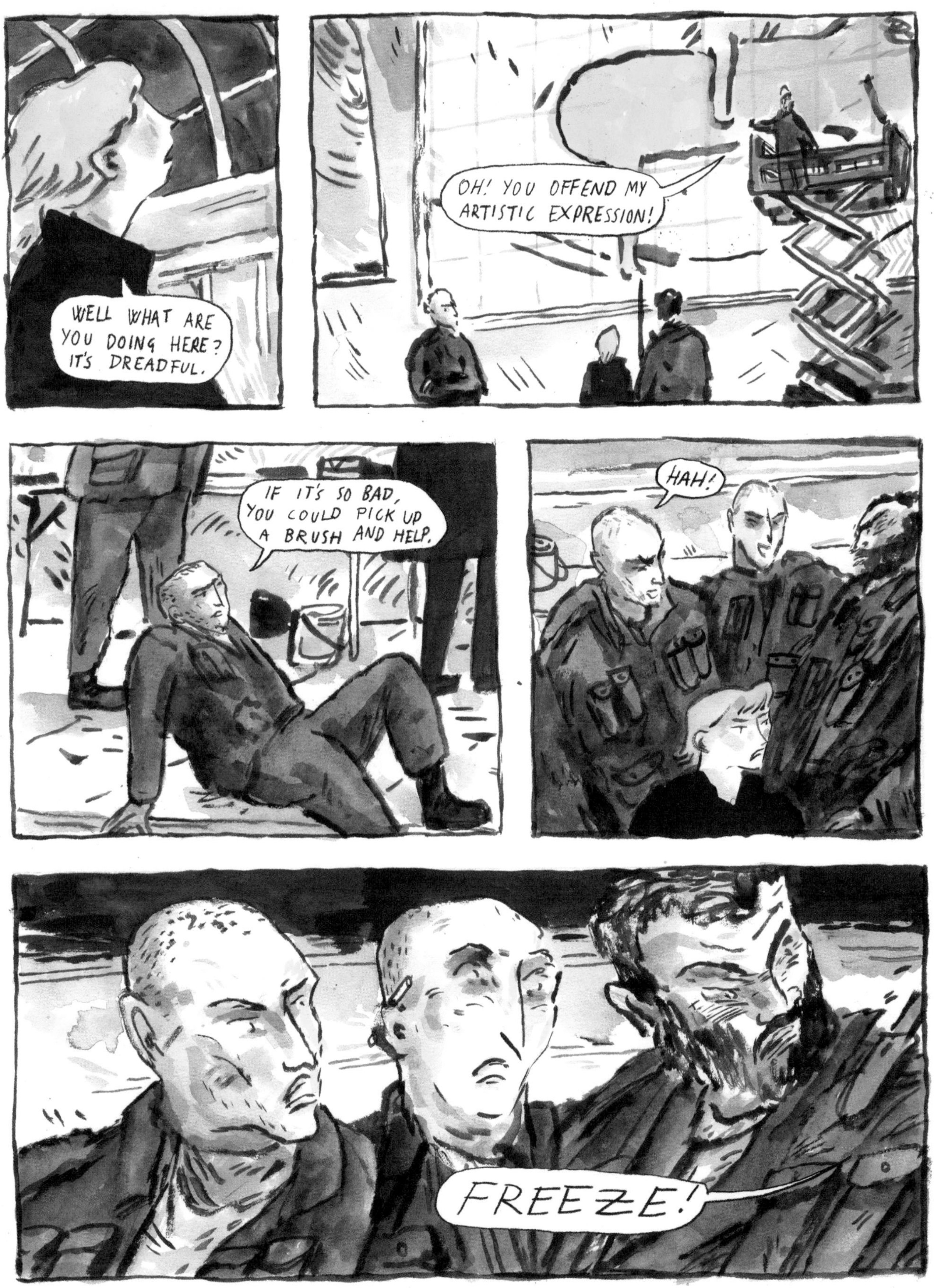
WELL WHAT ARE YOU DOING HERE? IT'S DREADFUL.
OH! YOU OFFEND MY ARTISTIC EXPRESSION!
IF IT'S SO BAD, YOU COULD PICK UP A BRUSH AND HELP.
HAH!
FREEZE!

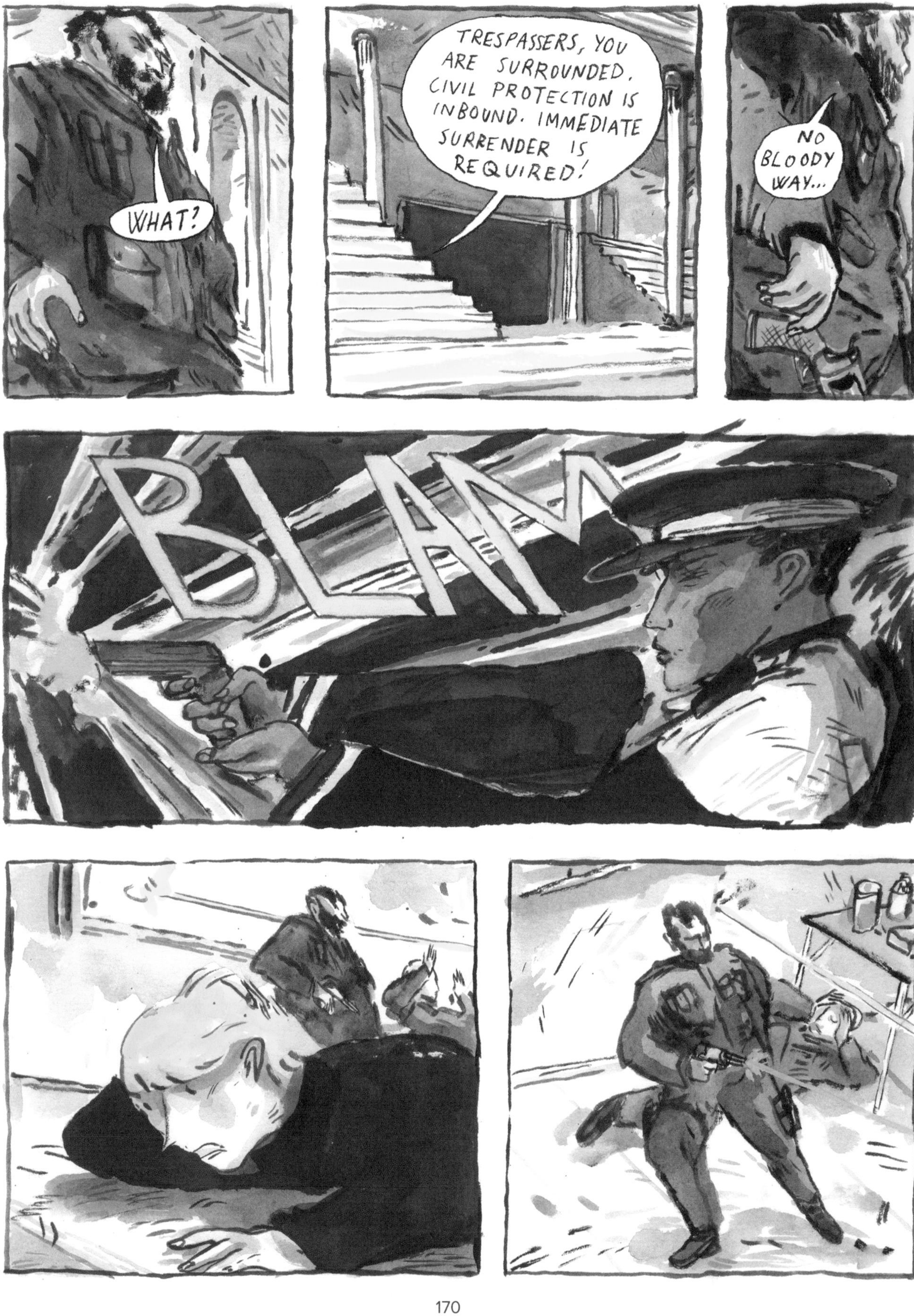
WHAT?
TRESPASSERS, YOU ARE SURROUNDED. CIVIL PROTECTION IS INBOUND. IMMEDIATE SURRENDER IS REQUIRED!
NO BLOODY WAY...
BLAM

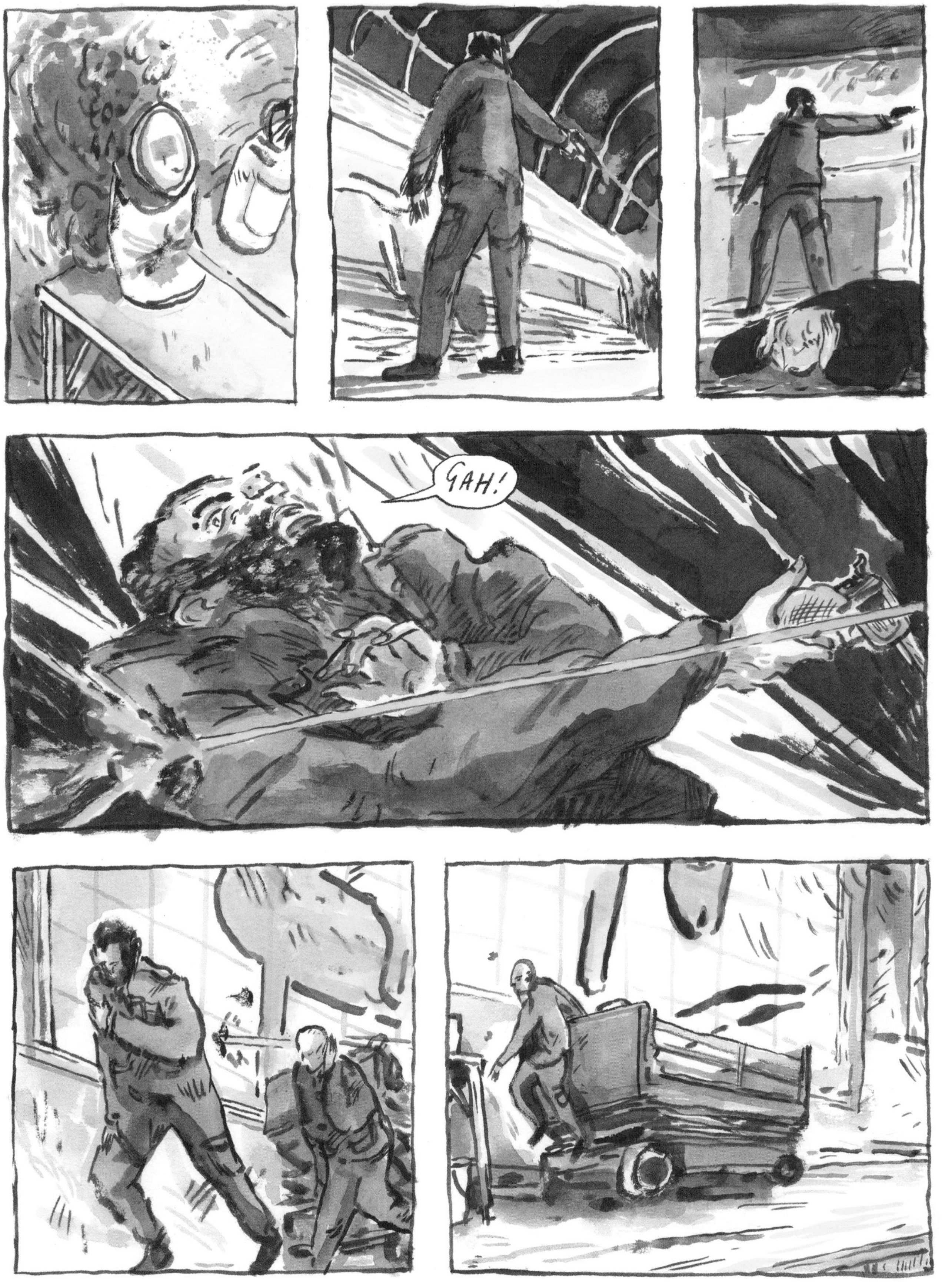
GAH!

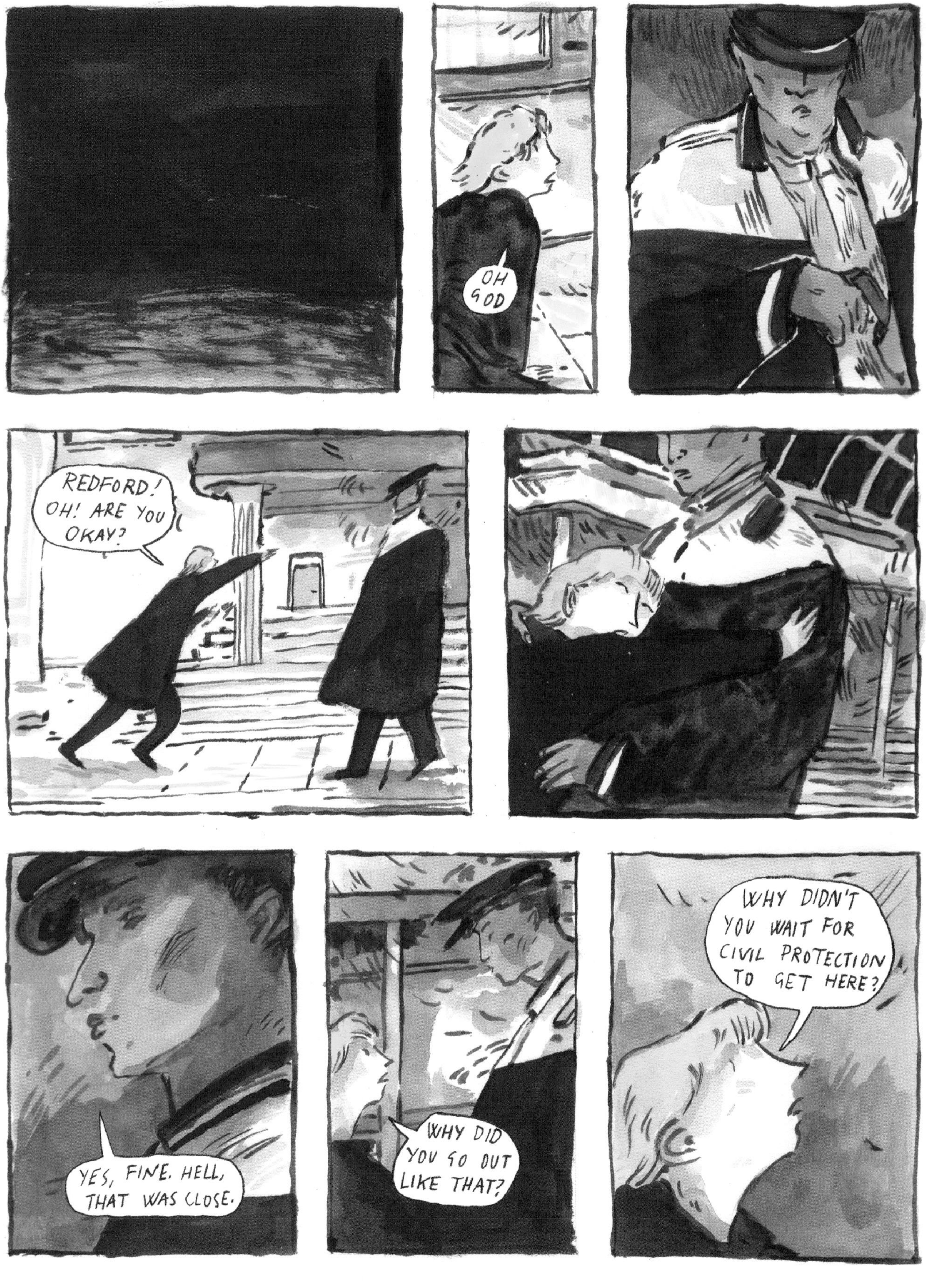
OH GOD
REDFORD! OH! ARE YOU OKAY?
YES, FINE. HELL, THAT WAS CLOSE.
WHY DID YOU GO OUT LIKE THAT?
WHY DIDN'T YOU WAIT FOR CIVIL PROTECTION TO GET HERE?

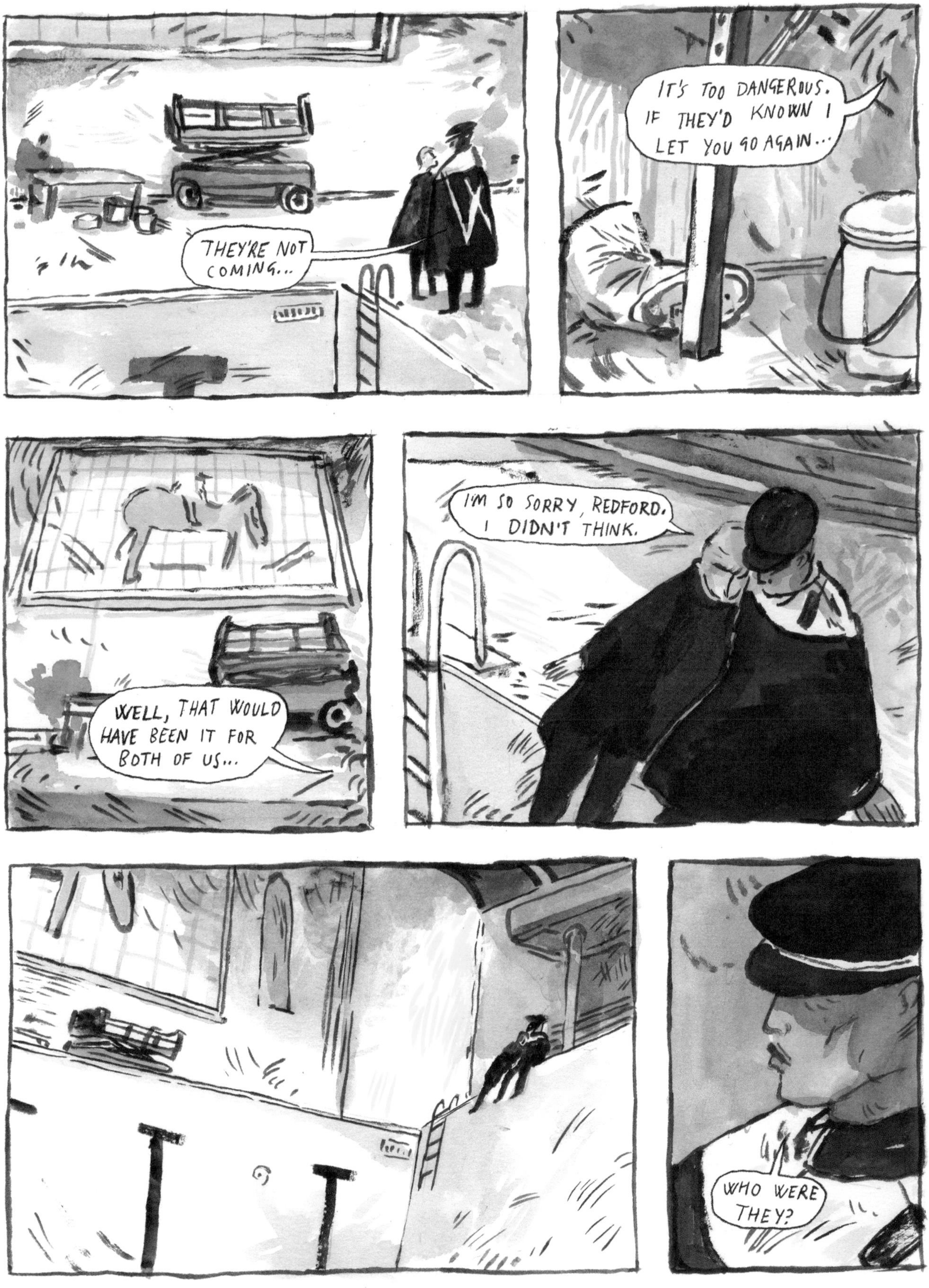
THEY'RE NOT COMING...
IT'S TOO DANGEROUS. IF THEY'D KNOWN I LET YOU GO AGAIN...
WELL, THAT WOULD HAVE BEEN IT FOR BOTH OF US...
I'M SO SORRY, REDFORD. I DIDN'T THINK.
WHO WERE THEY?

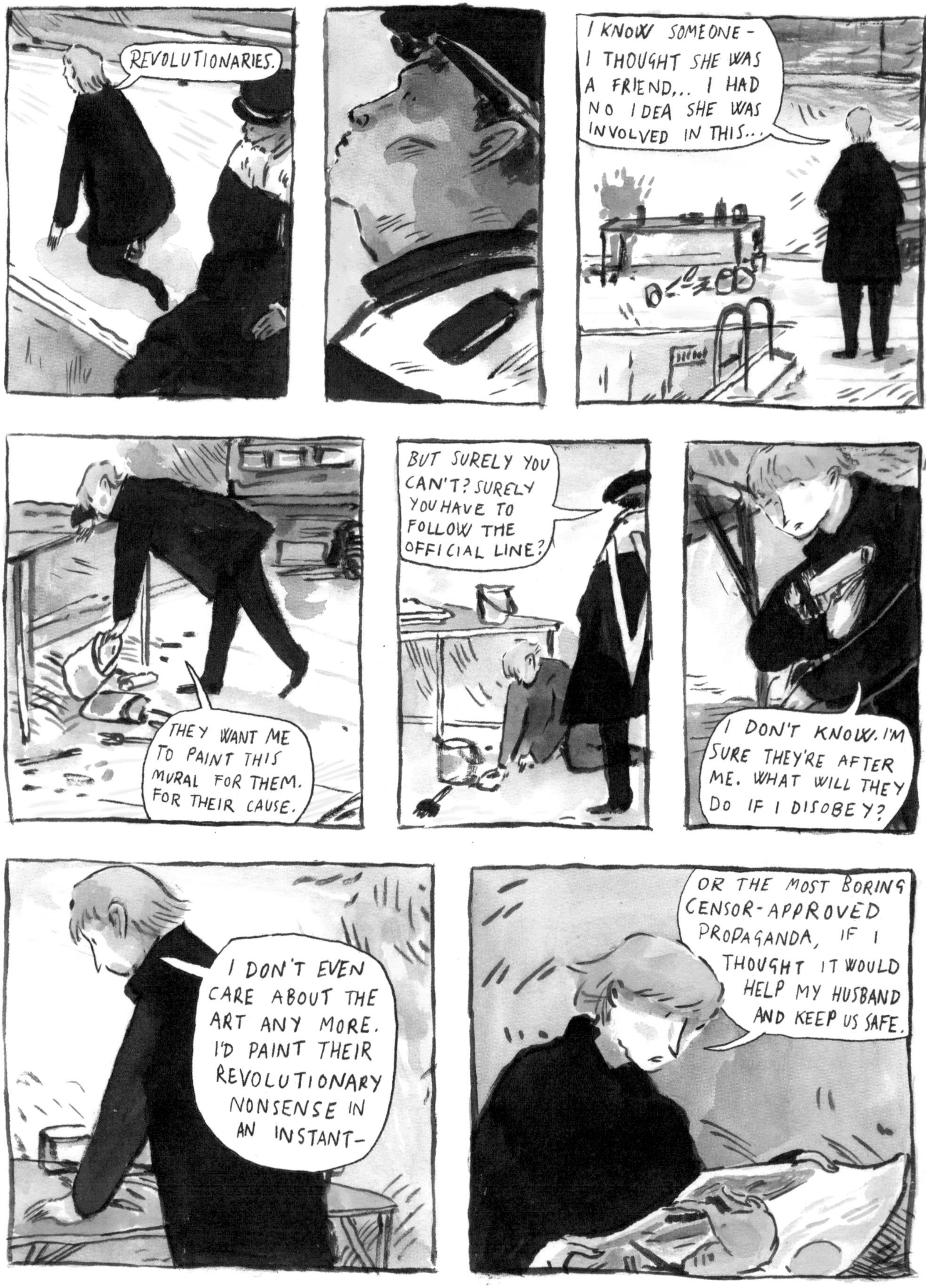
REVOLUTIONARIES.
I KNOW SOMEONE - I THOUGHT SHE WAS A FRIEND... I HAD NO IDEA SHE WAS INVOLVED IN THIS...
THEY WANT ME TO PAINT THIS MURAL FOR THEM. FOR THEIR CAUSE.
BUT SURELY YOU CAN'T? SURELY YOU HAVE TO FOLLOW THE OFFICIAL LINE?
I DON'T KNOW. I'M SURE THEY'RE AFTER ME. WHAT WILL THEY DO IF I DISOBEY?
I DON'T EVEN CARE ABOUT THE ART ANY MORE. I'D PAINT THEIR REVOLUTIONARY NONSENSE IN AN INSTANT-
OR THE MOST BORING CENSOR-APPROVED PROPAGANDA, IF I THOUGHT IT WOULD HELP MY HUSBAND AND KEEP US SAFE.

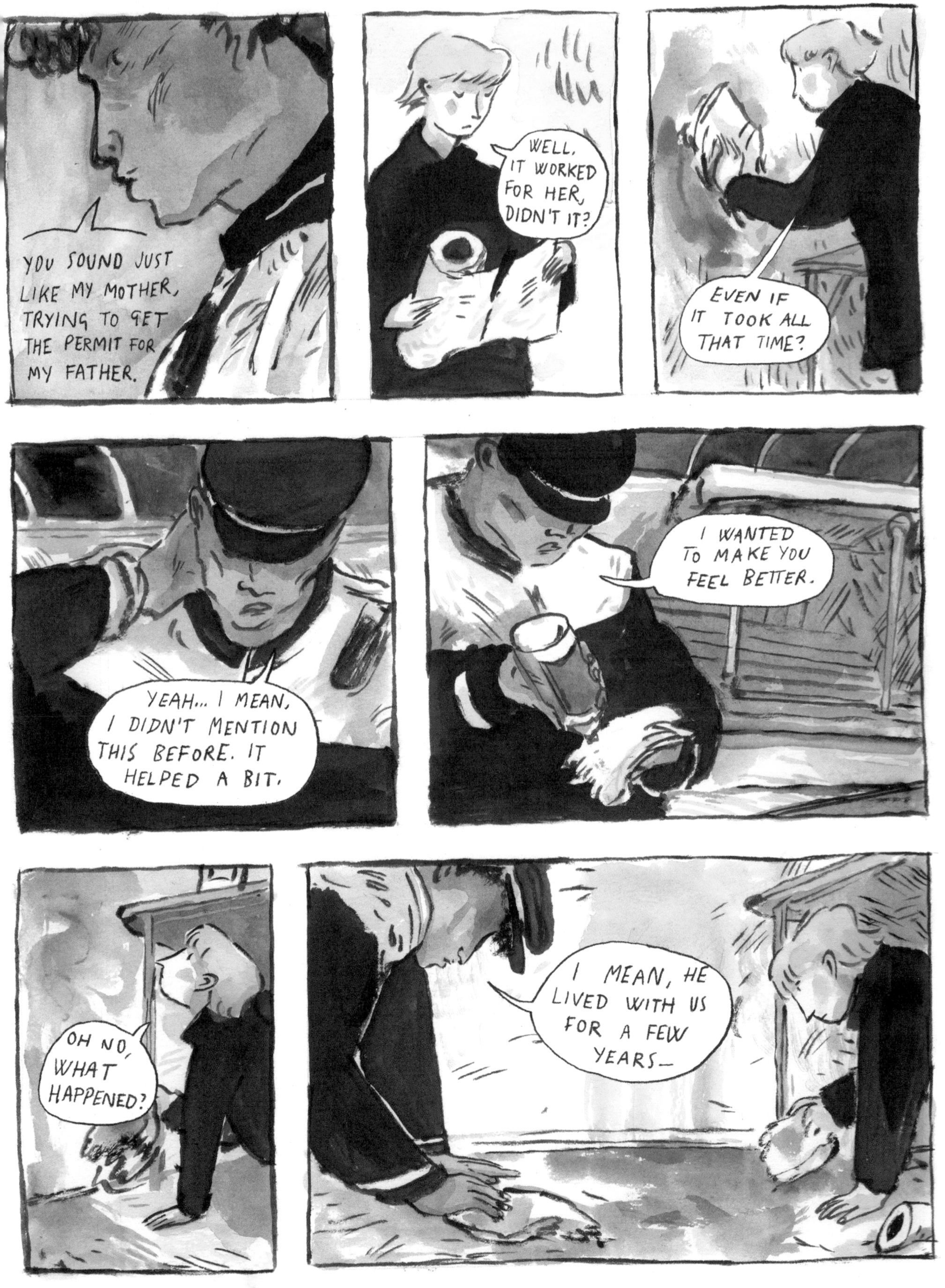
YOU SOUND JUST LIKE MY MOTHER, TRYING TO GET THE PERMIT FOR MY FATHER.
WELL, IT WORKED FOR HER, DIDN'T IT?
EVEN IF IT TOOK ALL THAT TIME?
YEAH... I MEAN, I DIDN'T MENTION THIS BEFORE. IT HELPED A BIT.
I WANTED TO MAKE YOU FEEL BETTER.
OH NO, WHAT HAPPENED?
I MEAN, HE LIVED WITH US FOR A FEW YEARS—

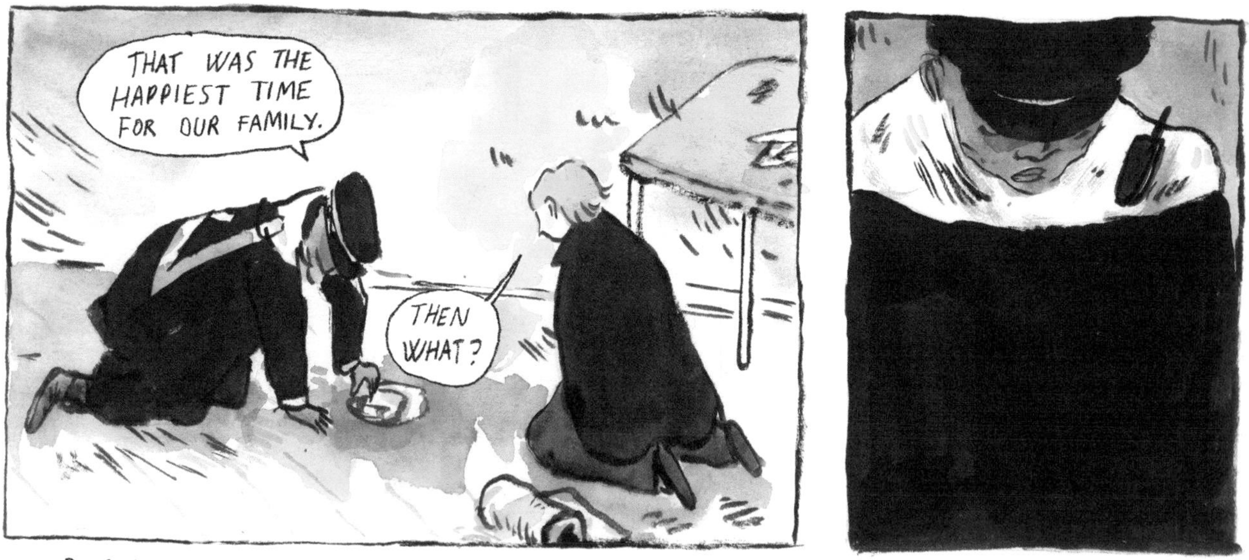
THAT WAS THE HAPPIEST TIME FOR OUR FAMILY.
THEN WHAT?

BEFORE HE CAME HERE, MY FATHER OWNED SEVERAL SHOPS IN OUR COUNTRY. SMALL GROCERY STORES, YOU KNOW. BUT HERE, THE REGIME BANNED HIM FROM OWNING A BUSINESS — IMMIGRANTS WERE LIMITED TO DOING MOSTLY MENIAL WORK. A LOT OF PEOPLE FORGED THEIR PAPERS TO GET ROUND THESE SORTS OF RESTRICTIONS.

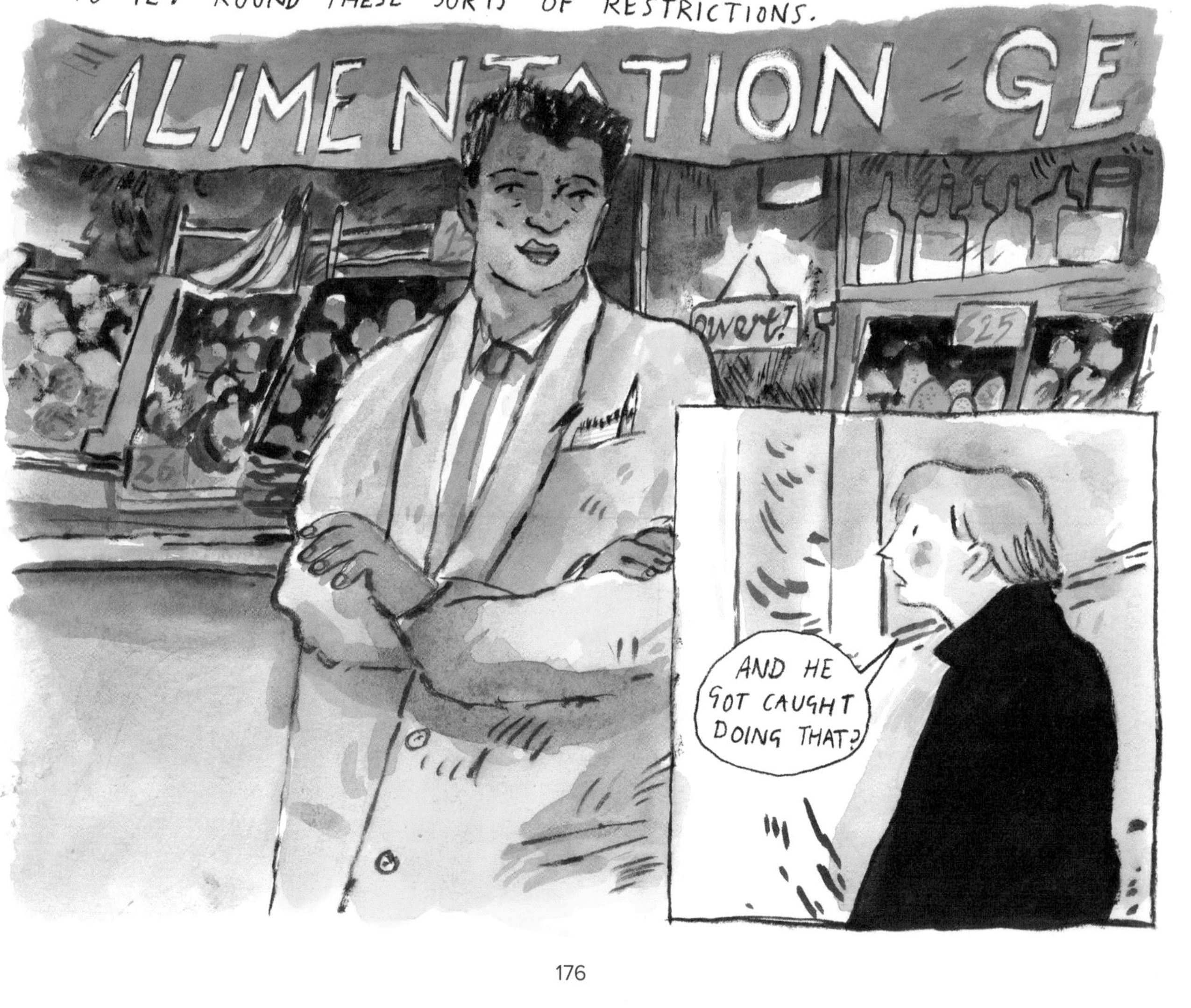
ALIMENTATION GE
AND HE GOT CAUGHT DOING THAT?

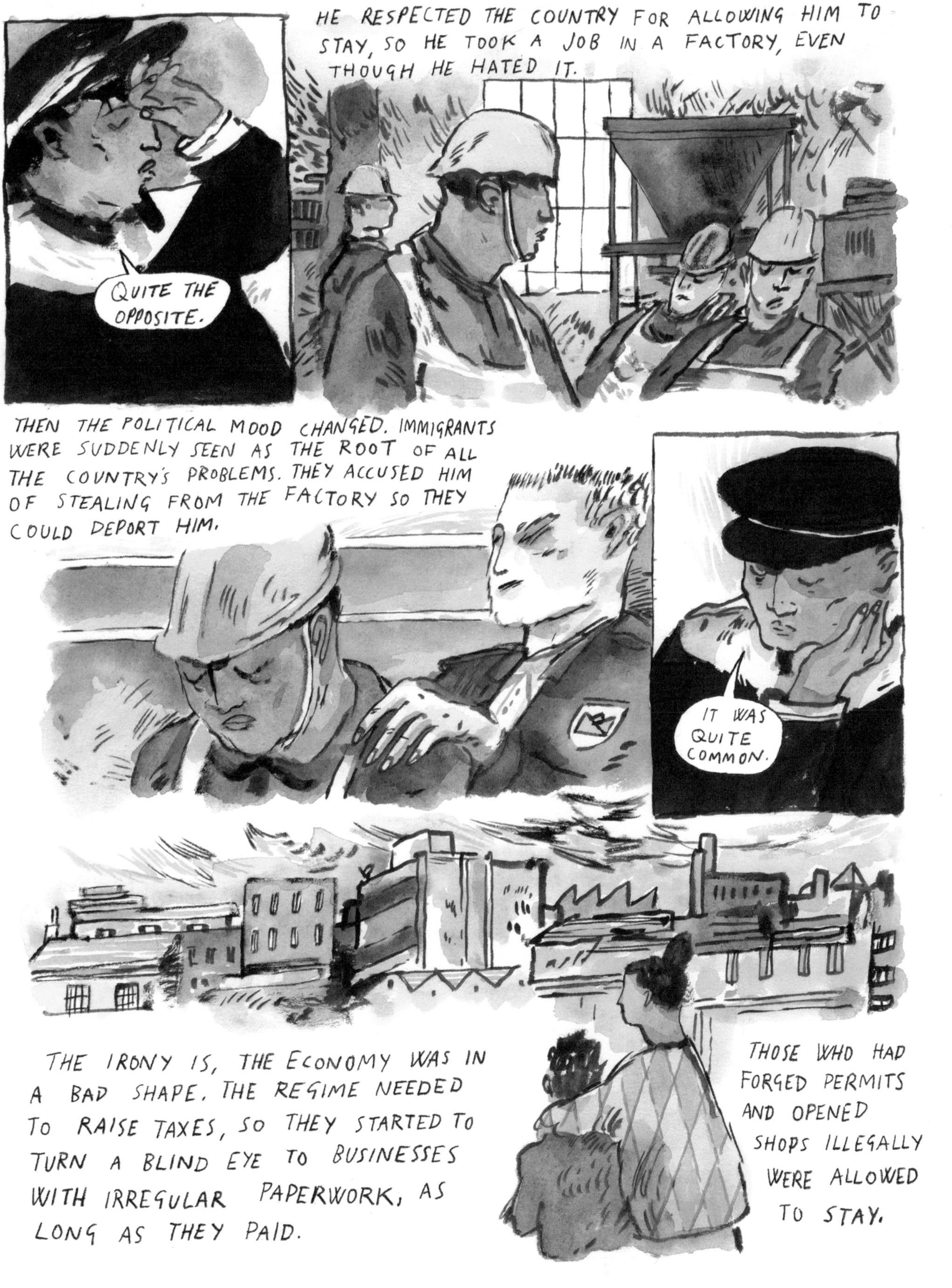
QUITE THE OPPOSITE.
HE RESPECTED THE COUNTRY FOR ALLOWING HIM TO STAY, SO HE TOOK A JOB IN A FACTORY, EVEN THOUGH HE HATED IT.
THEN THE POLITICAL MOOD CHANGED. IMMIGRANTS WERE SUDDENLY SEEN AS THE ROOT OF ALL THE COUNTRY'S PROBLEMS. THEY ACCUSED HIM OF STEALING FROM THE FACTORY SO THEY COULD DEPORT HIM.
IT WAS QUITE COMMON.
THE IRONY IS, THE ECONOMY WAS IN A BAD SHAPE. THE REGIME NEEDED TO RAISE TAXES, SO THEY STARTED TO TURN A BLIND EYE TO BUSINESSES WITH IRREGULAR PAPERWORK, AS LONG AS THEY PAID.
THOSE WHO HAD FORGED PERMITS AND OPENED SHOPS ILLEGALLY WERE ALLOWED TO STAY.

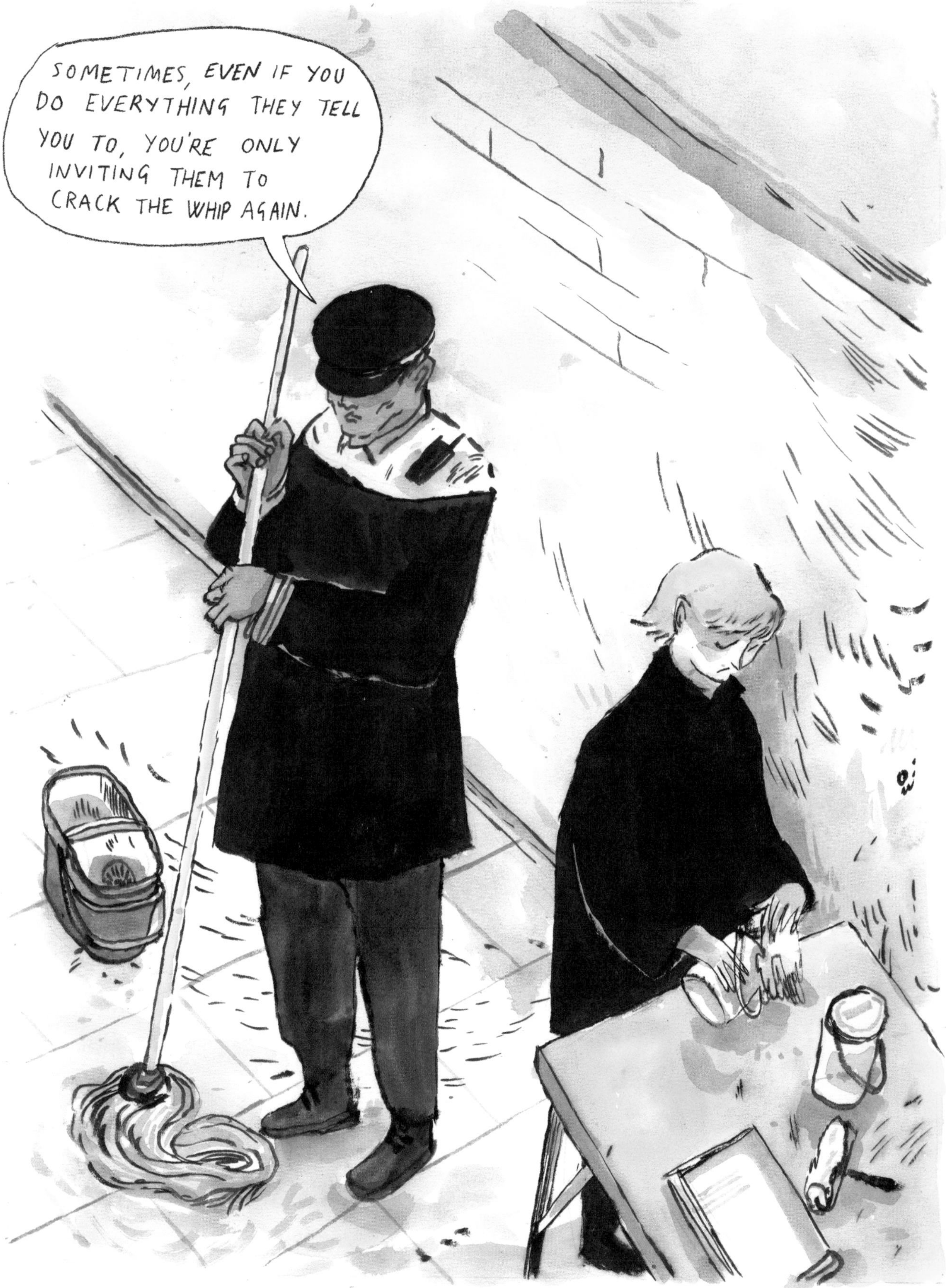
SOMETIMES, EVEN IF YOU DO EVERYTHING THEY TELL YOU TO, YOU'RE ONLY INVITING THEM TO CRACK THE WHIP AGAIN.

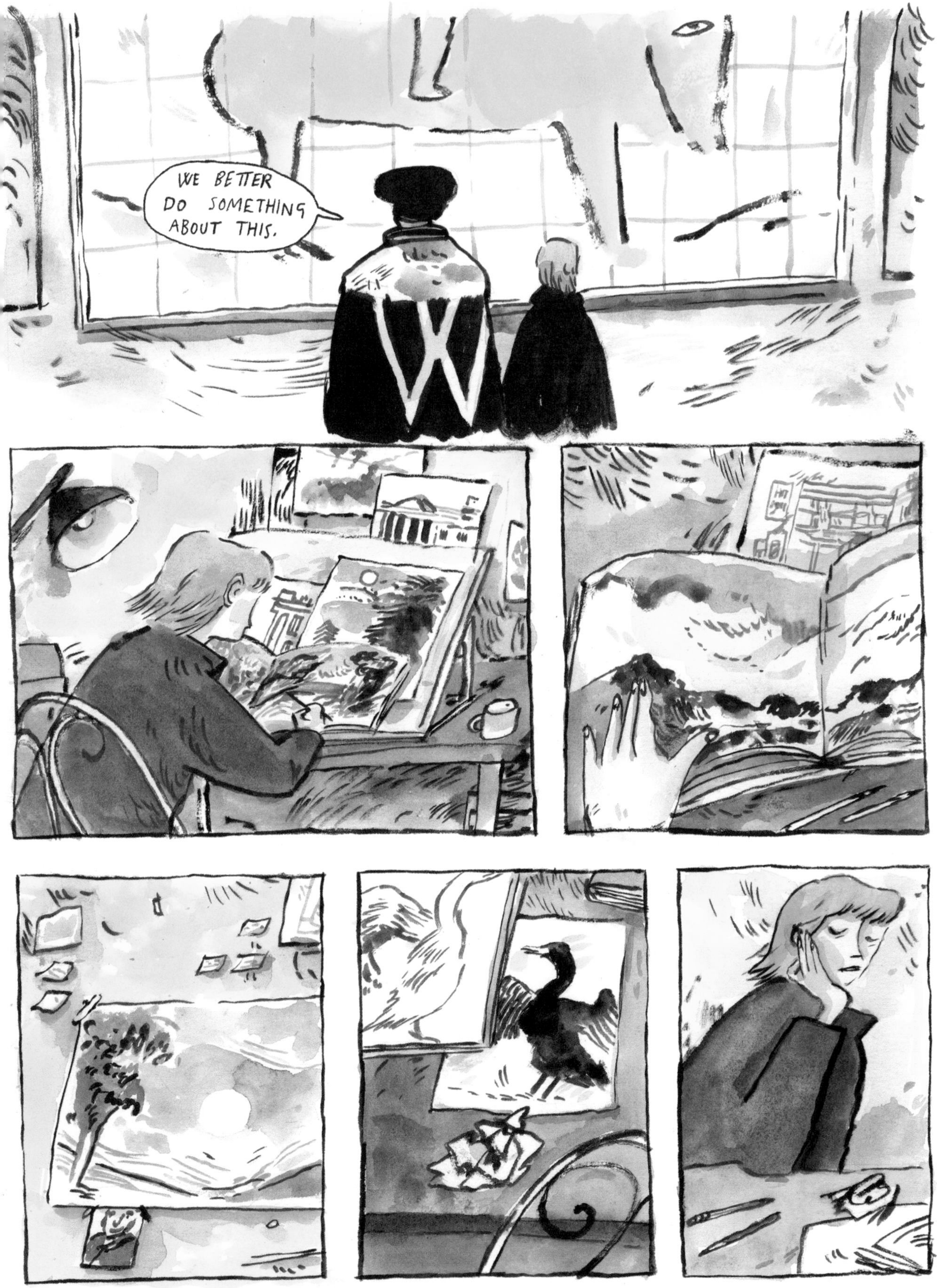
WE BETTER DO SOMETHING ABOUT THIS.

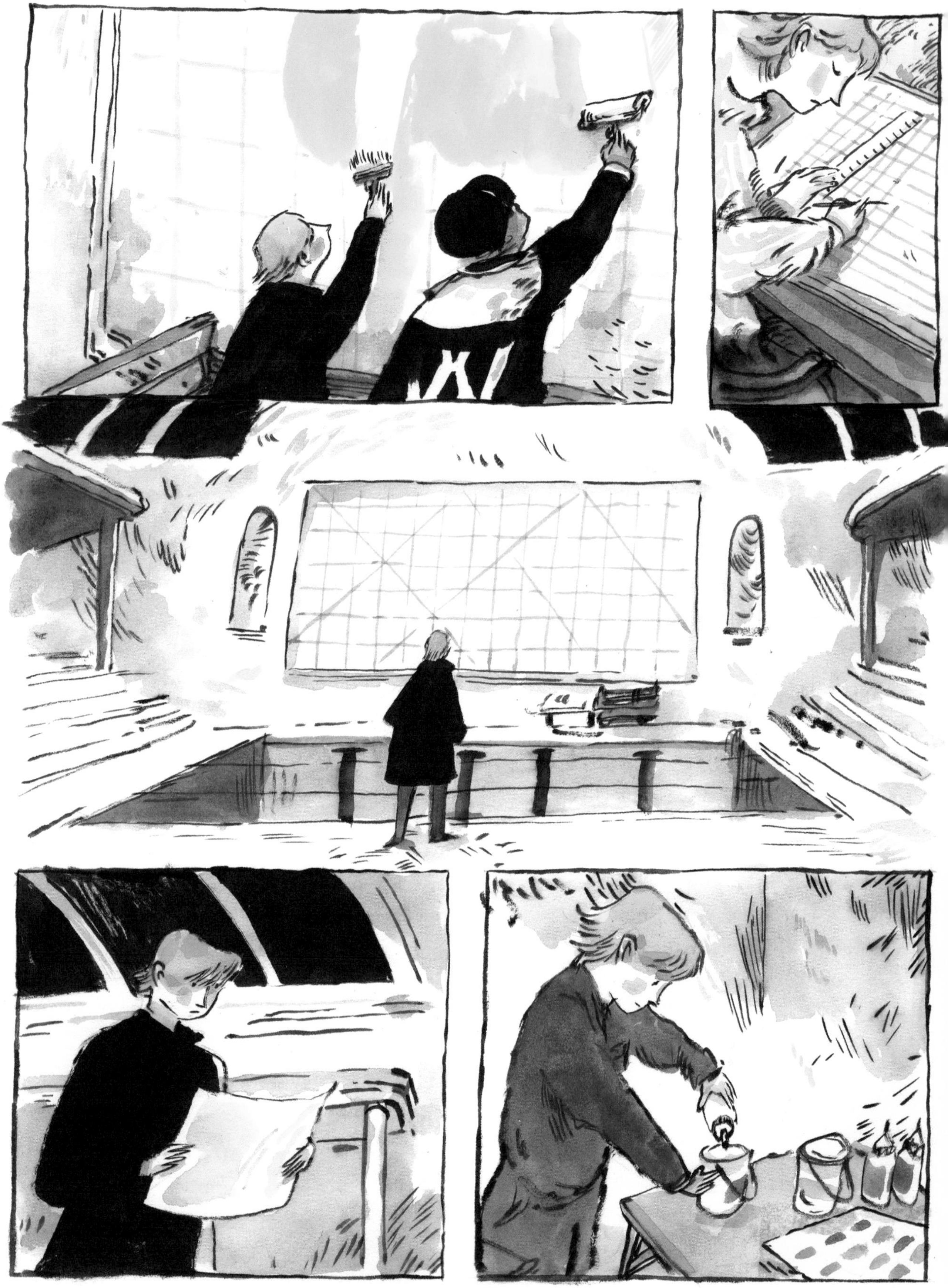

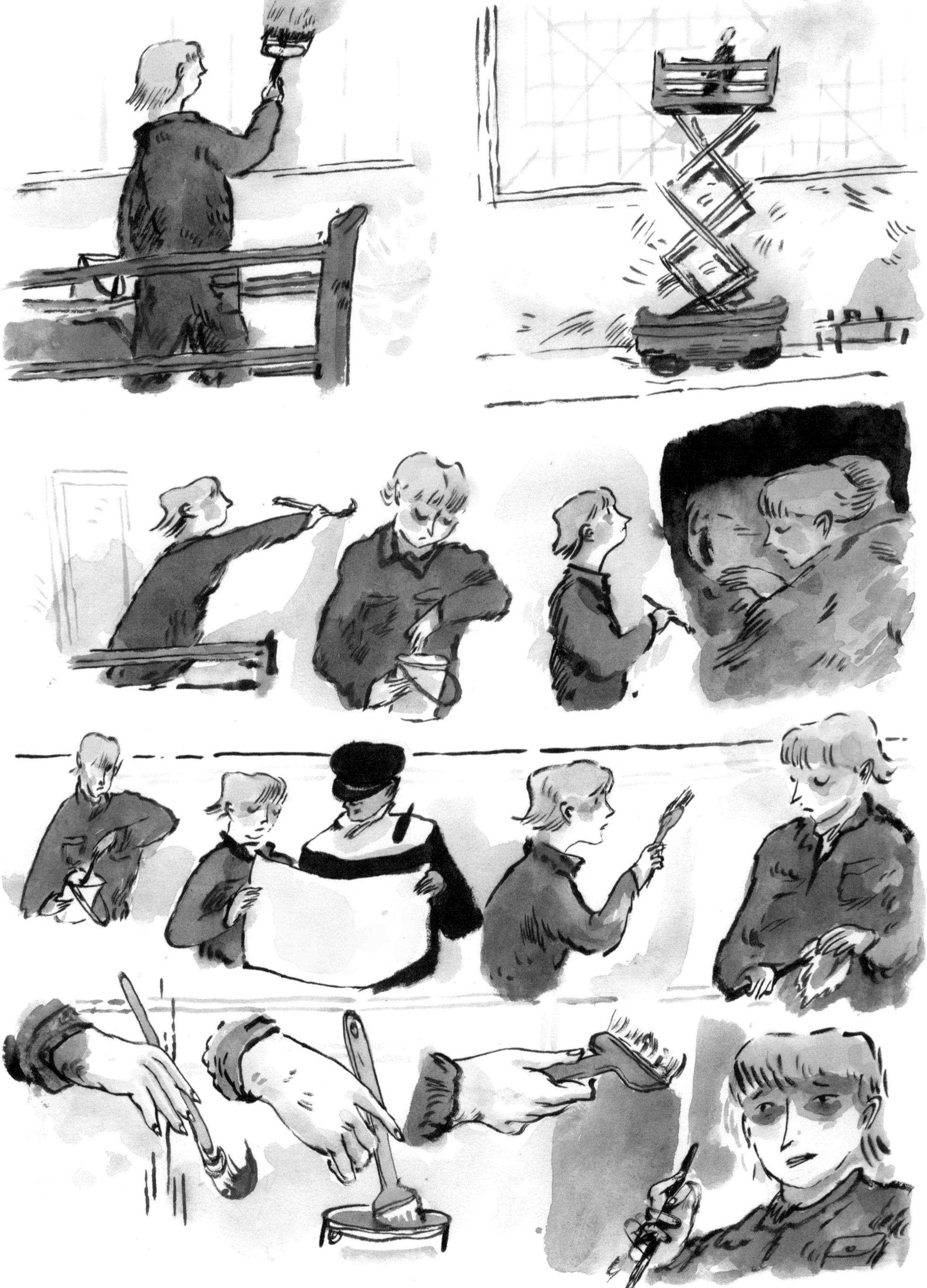

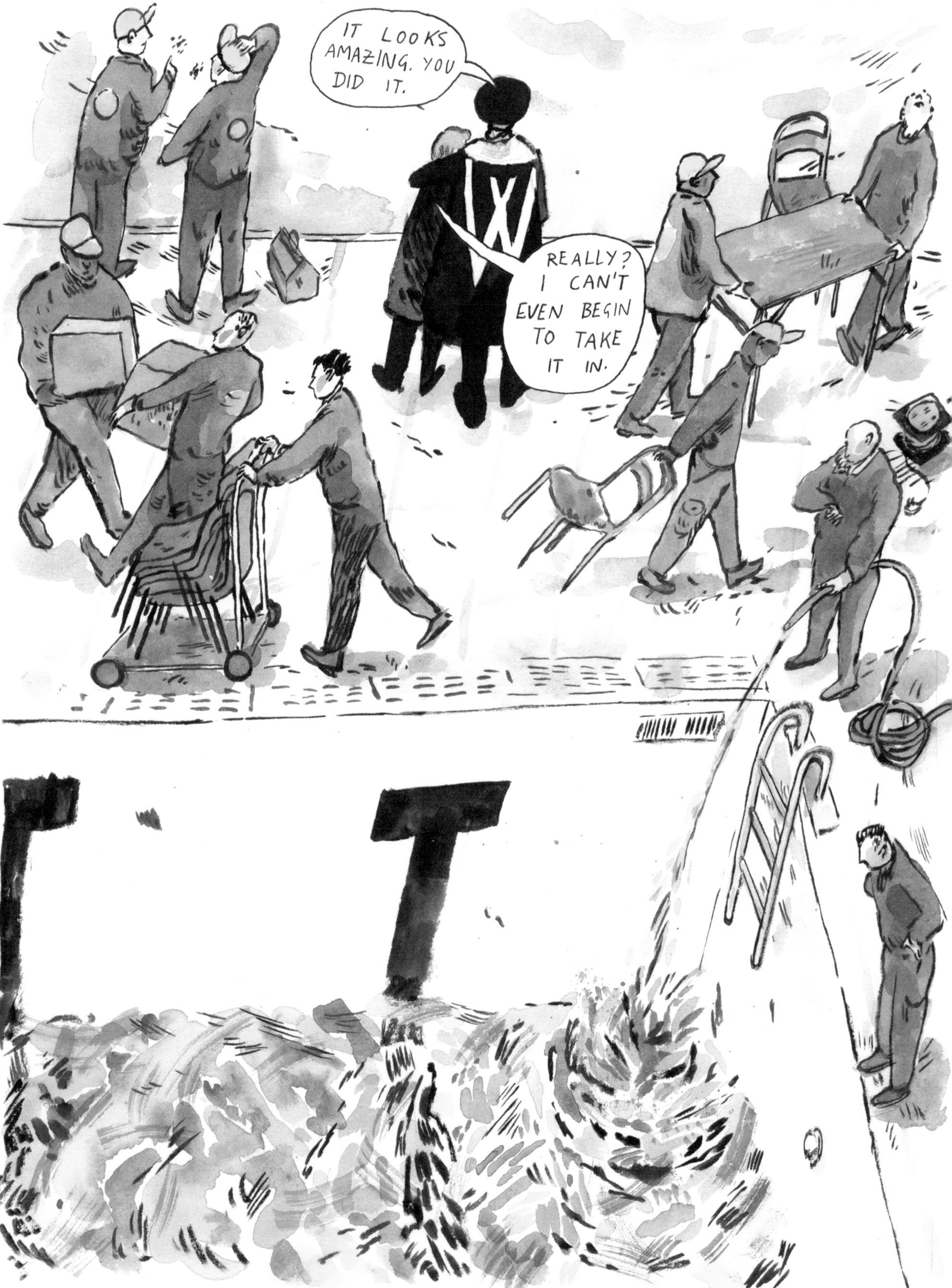
IT LOOKS AMAZING. YOU DID IT.
REALLY? I CAN'T EVEN BEGIN TO TAKE IT IN.

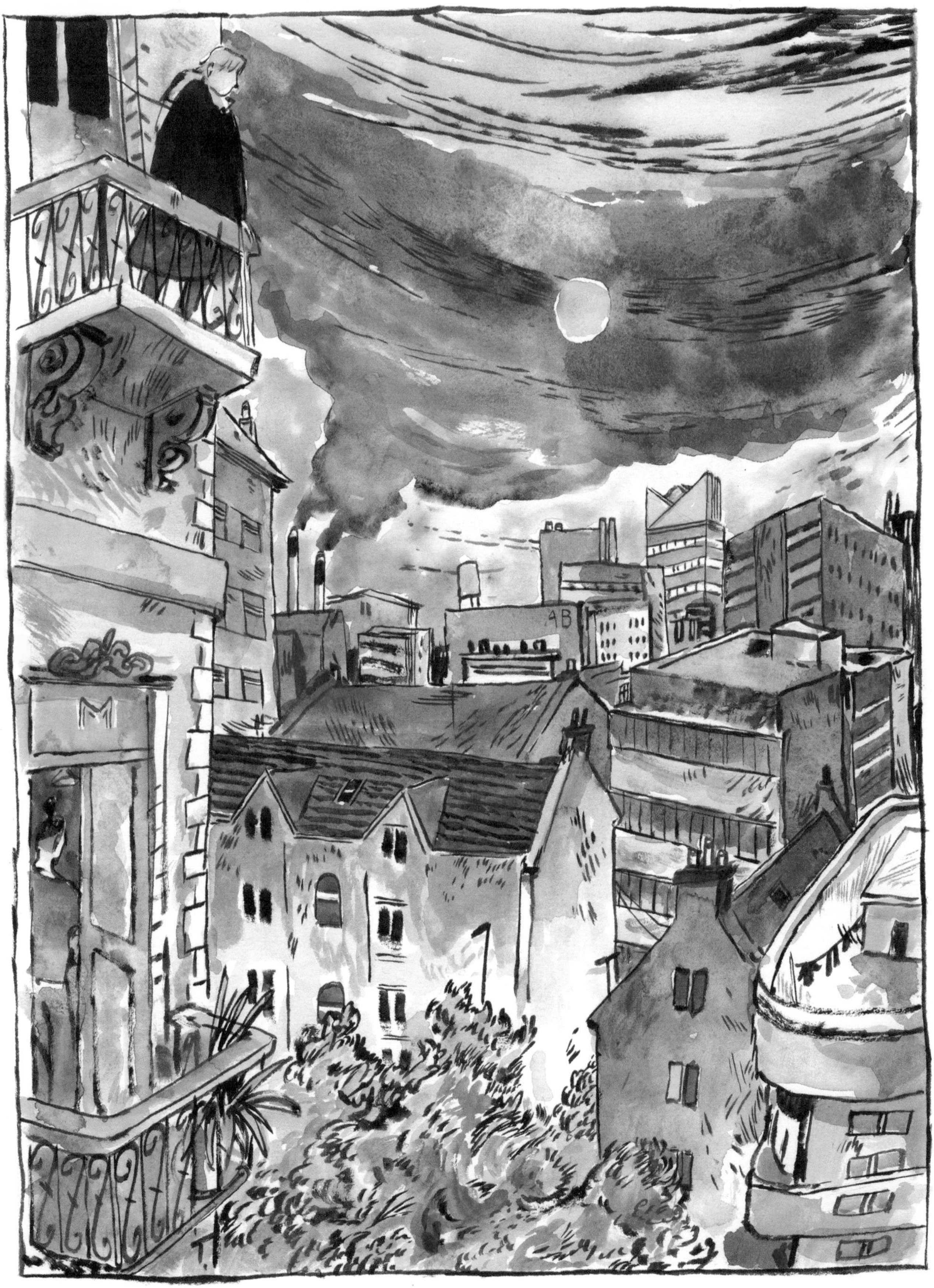
AB
M

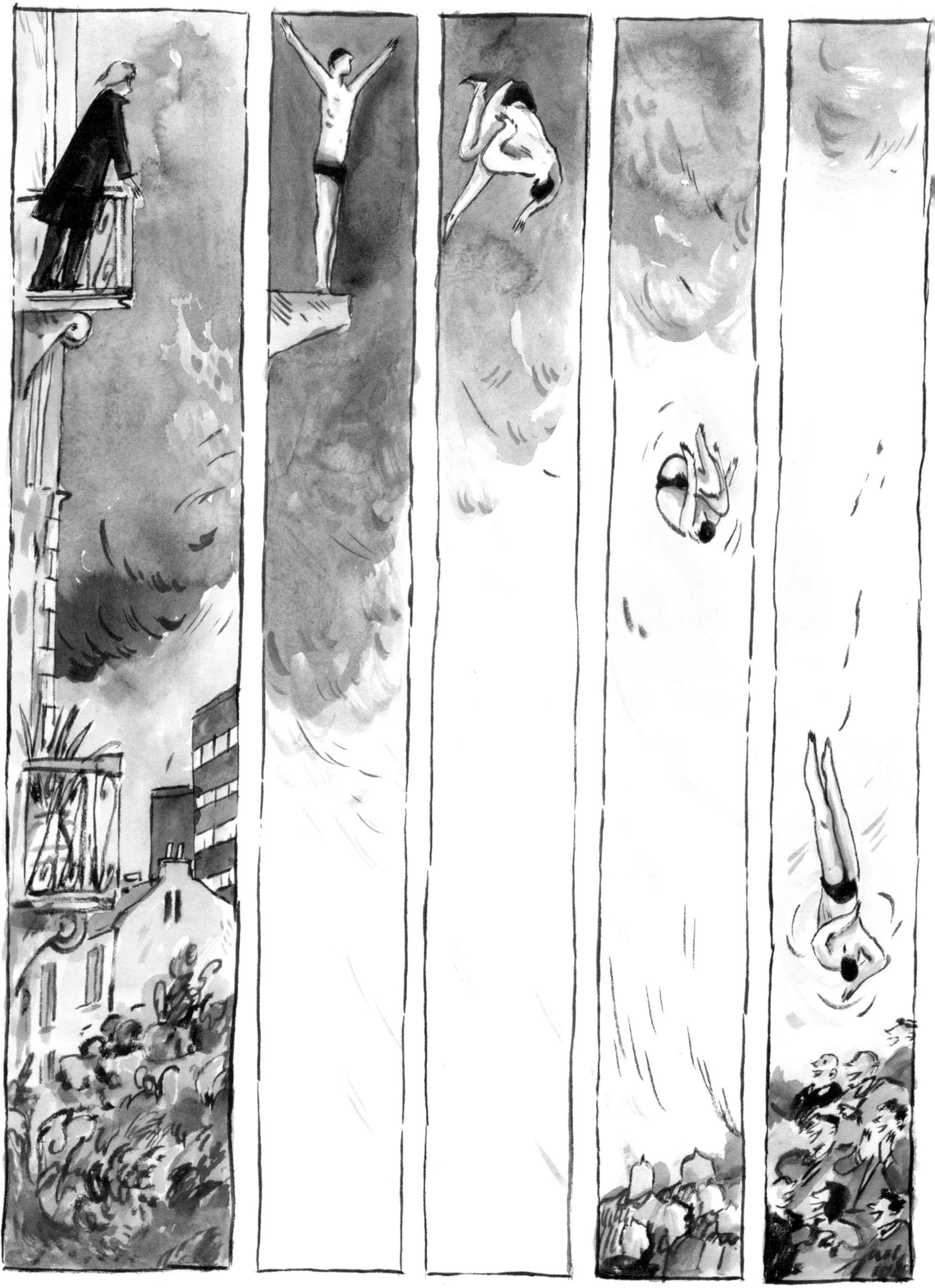

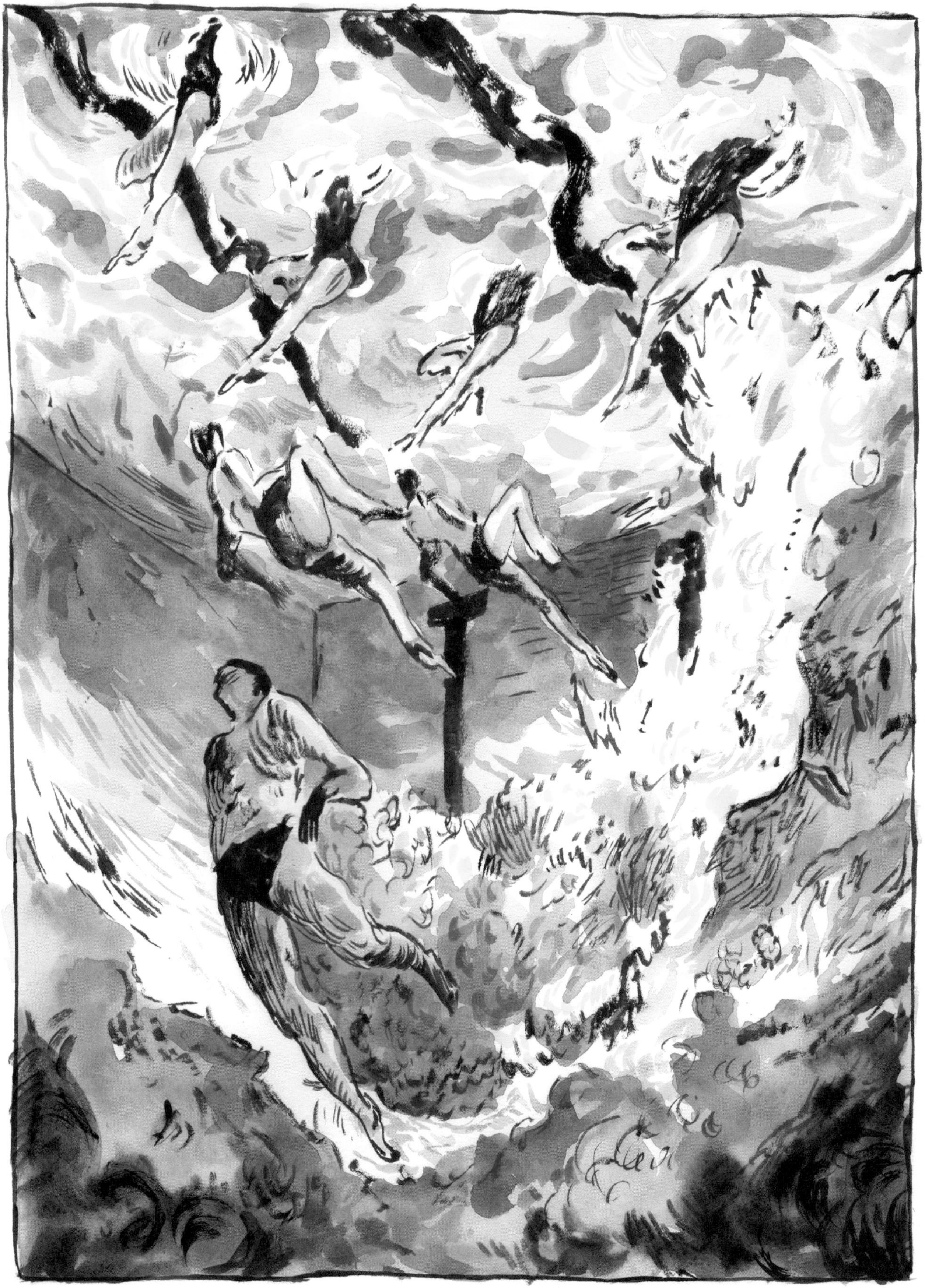

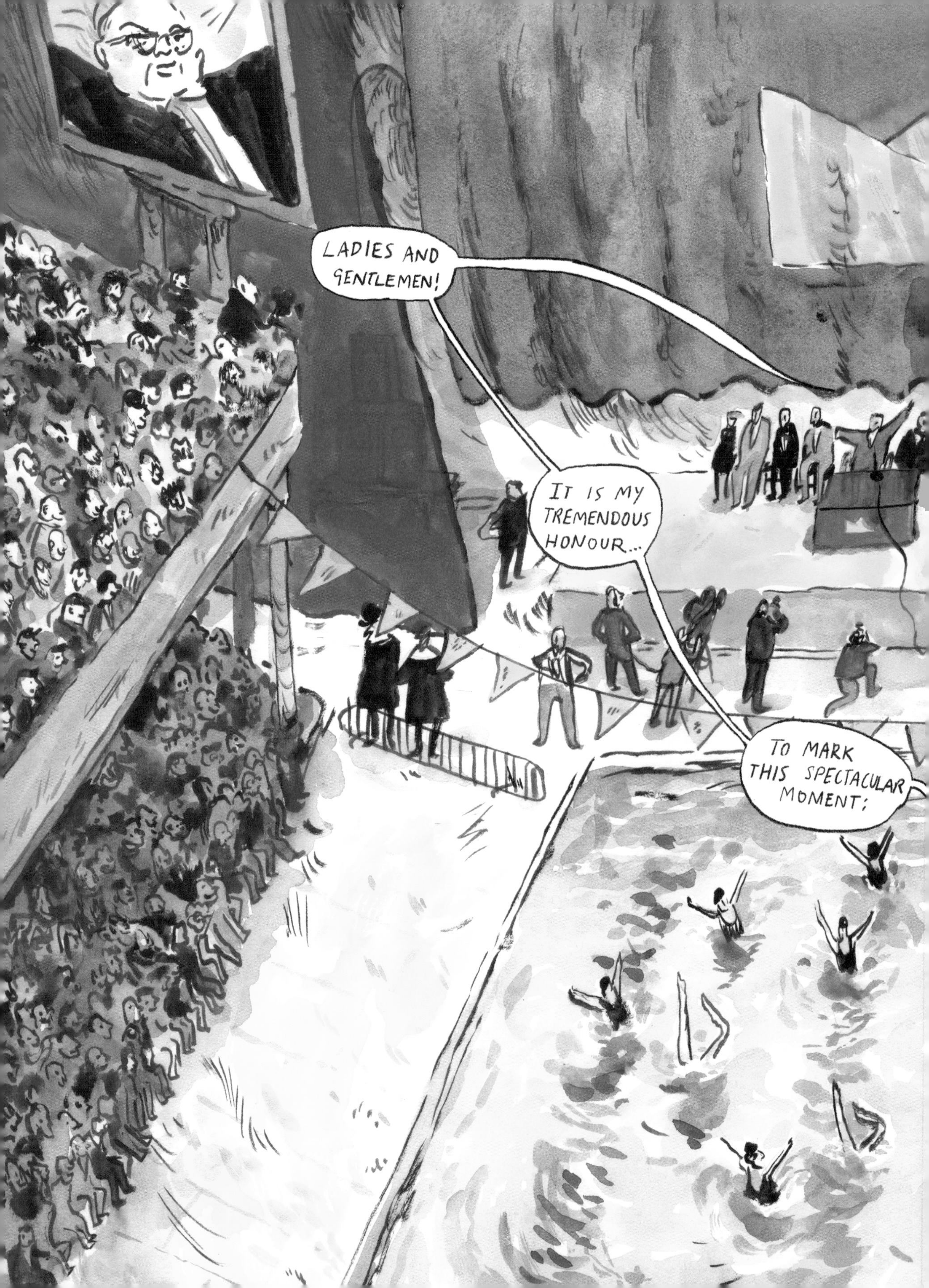
LADIES AND GENTLEMEN!
IT IS MY TREMENDOUS HONOUR...
TO MARK THIS SPECTACULAR MOMENT:

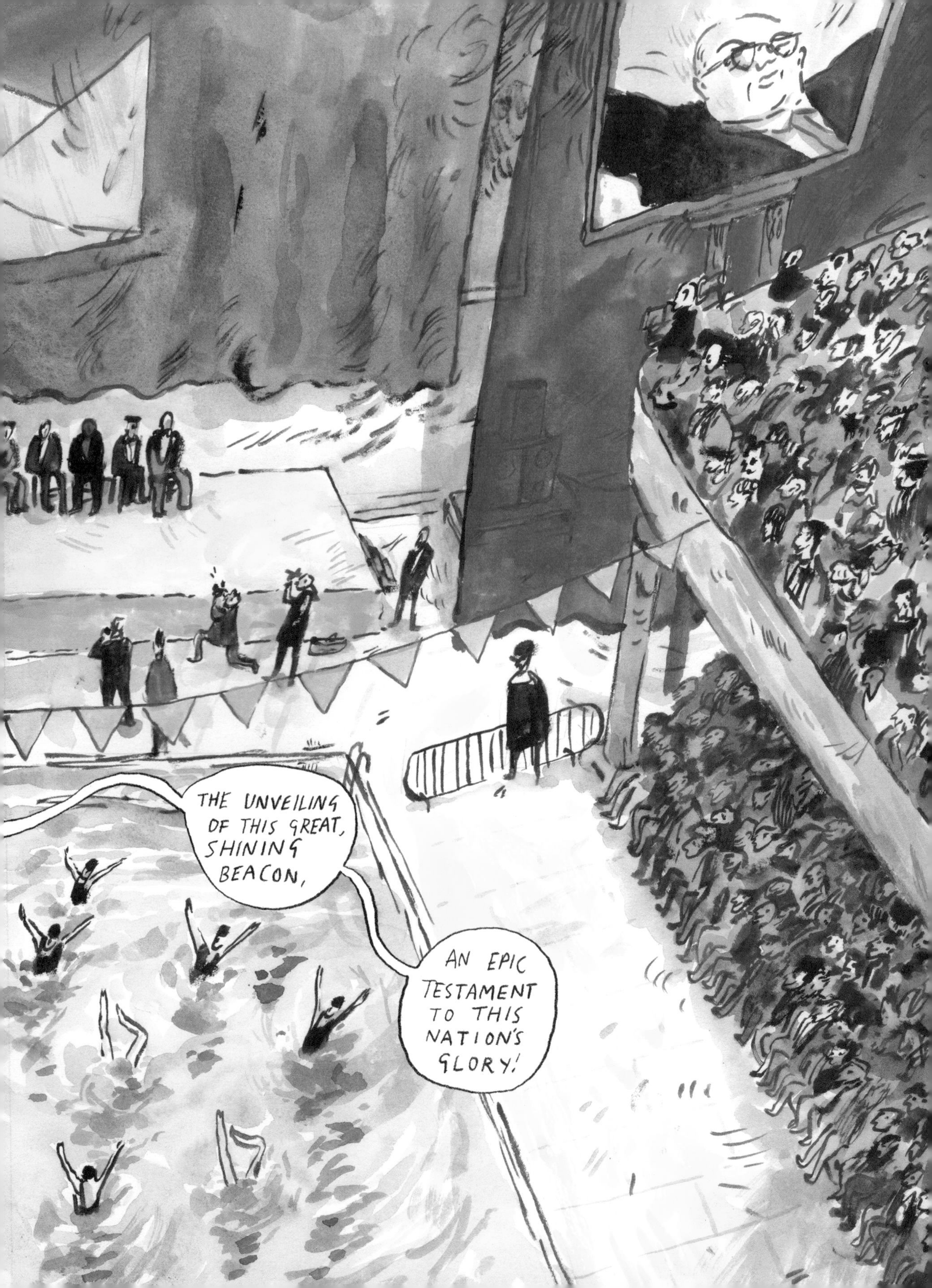
THE UNVEILING OF THIS GREAT, SHINING BEACON,
AN EPIC TESTAMENT TO THIS NATION'S GLORY!

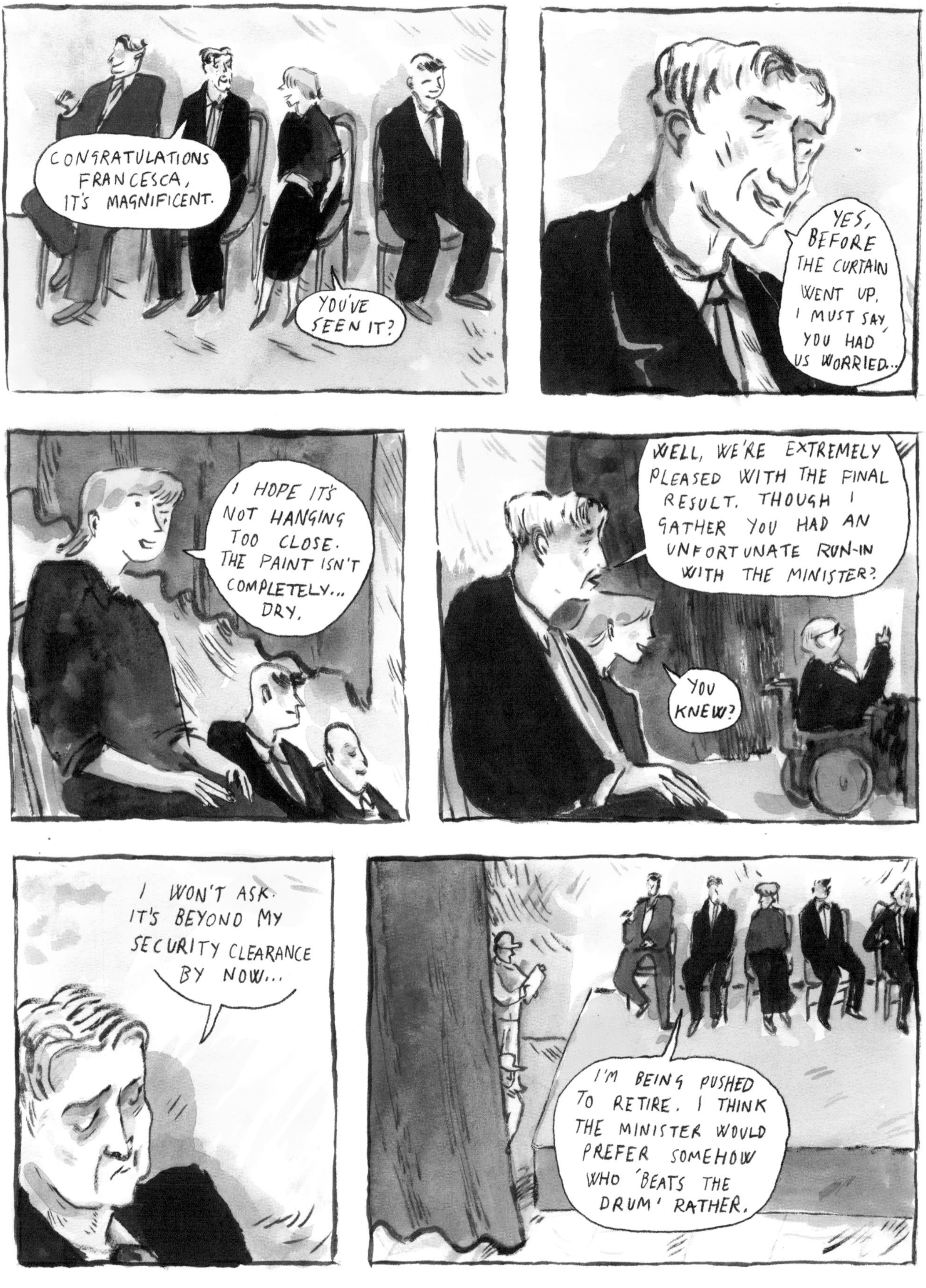
CONGRATULATIONS FRANCESCA, IT'S MAGNIFICENT.
YOU'VE SEEN IT?
YES, BEFORE THE CURTAIN WENT UP. I MUST SAY, YOU HAD US WORRIED...
I HOPE IT'S NOT HANGING TOO CLOSE. THE PAINT ISN'T COMPLETELY... DRY.
WELL, WE'RE EXTREMELY PLEASED WITH THE FINAL RESULT. THOUGH I GATHER YOU HAD AN UNFORTUNATE RUN-IN WITH THE MINISTER?
YOU KNEW?
I WON'T ASK. IT'S BEYOND MY SECURITY CLEARANCE BY NOW...
I'M BEING PUSHED TO RETIRE. I THINK THE MINISTER WOULD PREFER SOMEHOW WHO 'BEATS THE DRUM' RATHER.

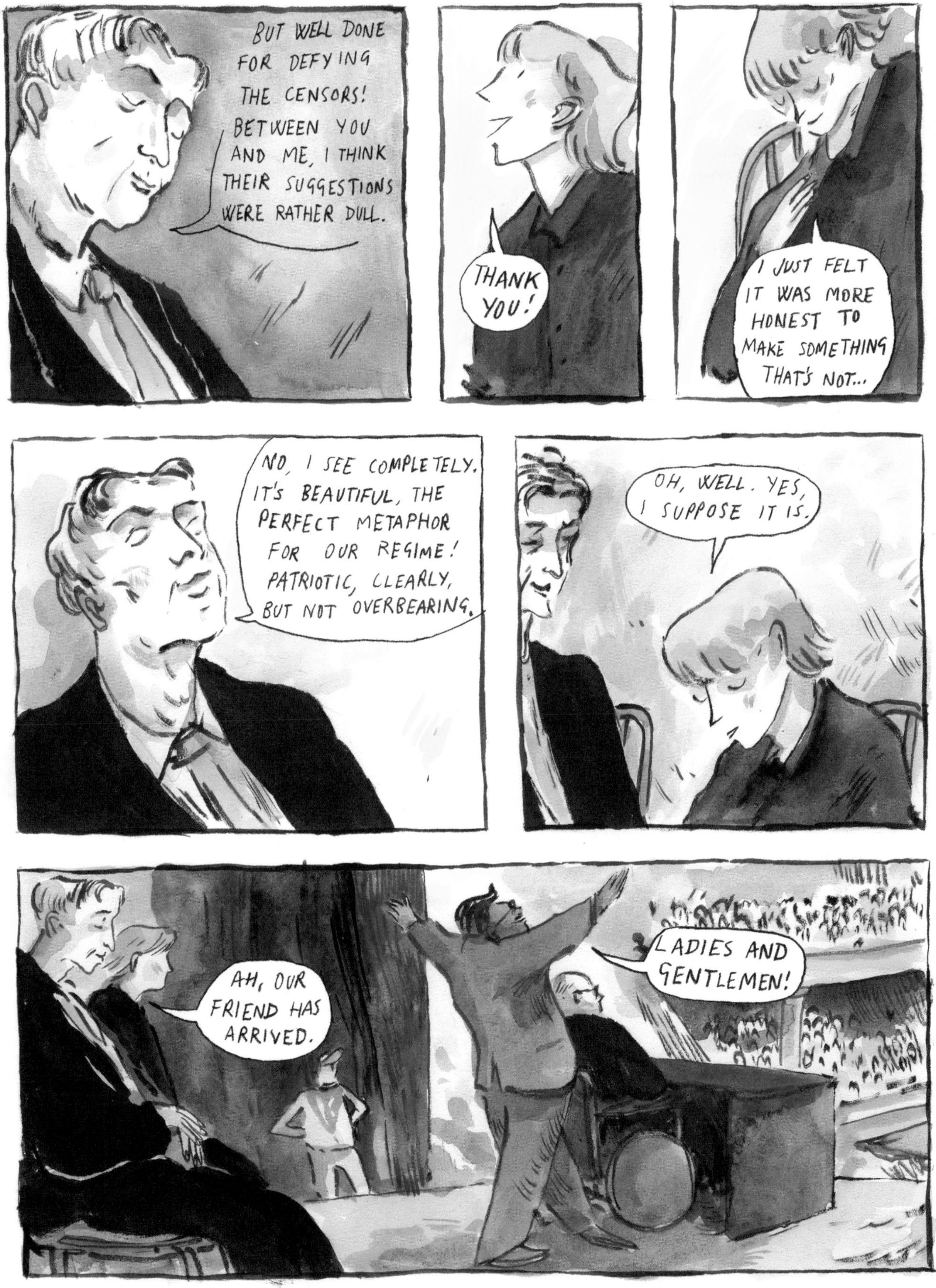
BUT WELL DONE FOR DEFYING THE CENSORS! BETWEEN YOU AND ME, I THINK THEIR SUGGESTIONS WERE RATHER DULL.
THANK YOU!
I JUST FELT IT WAS MORE HONEST TO MAKE SOMETHING THAT'S NOT...
NO, I SEE COMPLETELY. IT'S BEAUTIFUL, THE PERFECT METAPHOR FOR OUR REGIME! PATRIOTIC, CLEARLY, BUT NOT OVERBEARING.
OH, WELL. YES, I SUPPOSE IT IS.
AH, OUR FRIEND HAS ARRIVED.
LADIES AND GENTLEMEN!

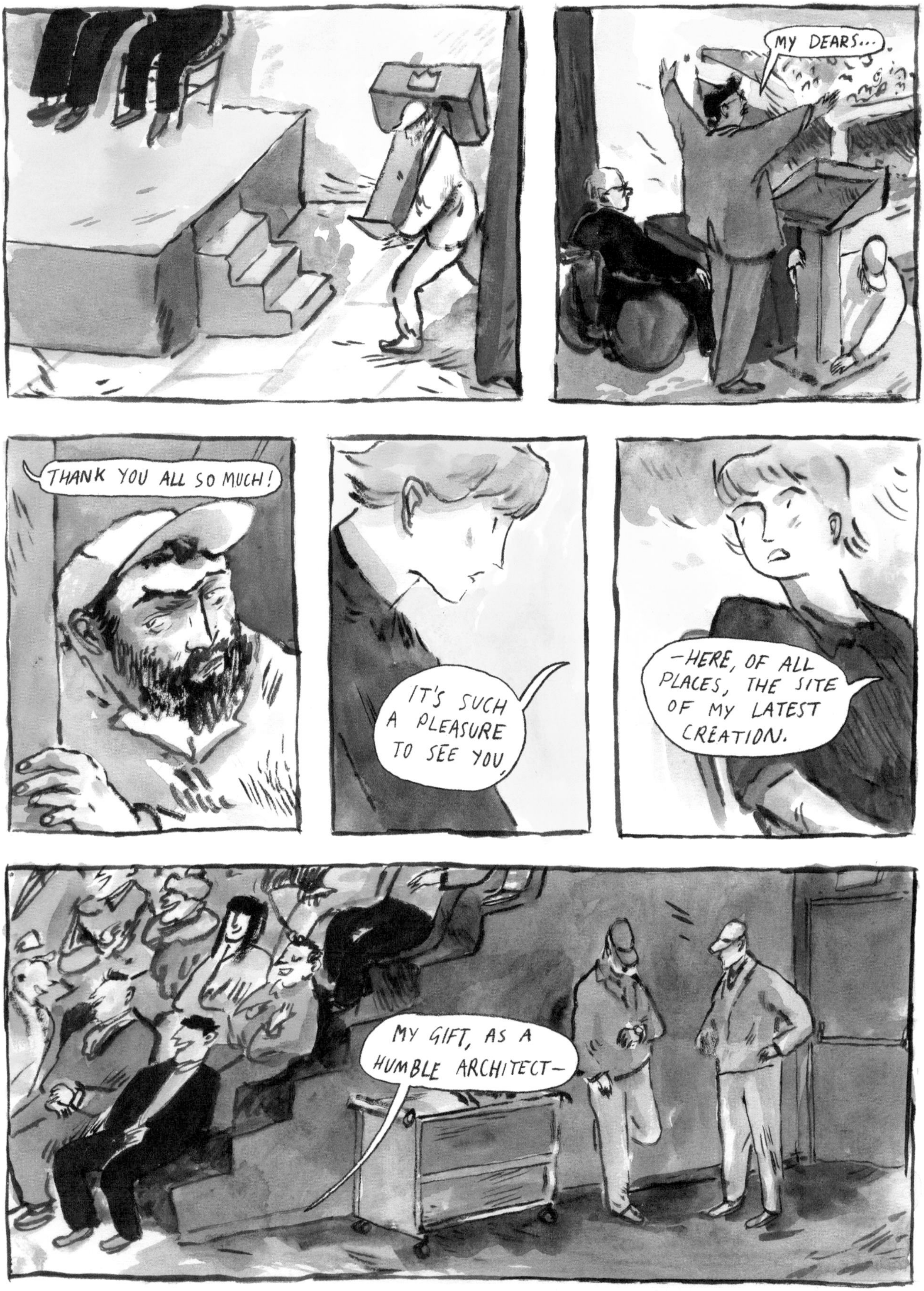
MY DEARS...
THANK YOU ALL SO MUCH!
IT'S SUCH A PLEASURE TO SEE YOU,
—HERE, OF ALL PLACES, THE SITE OF MY LATEST CREATION.
MY GIFT, AS A HUMBLE ARCHITECT—

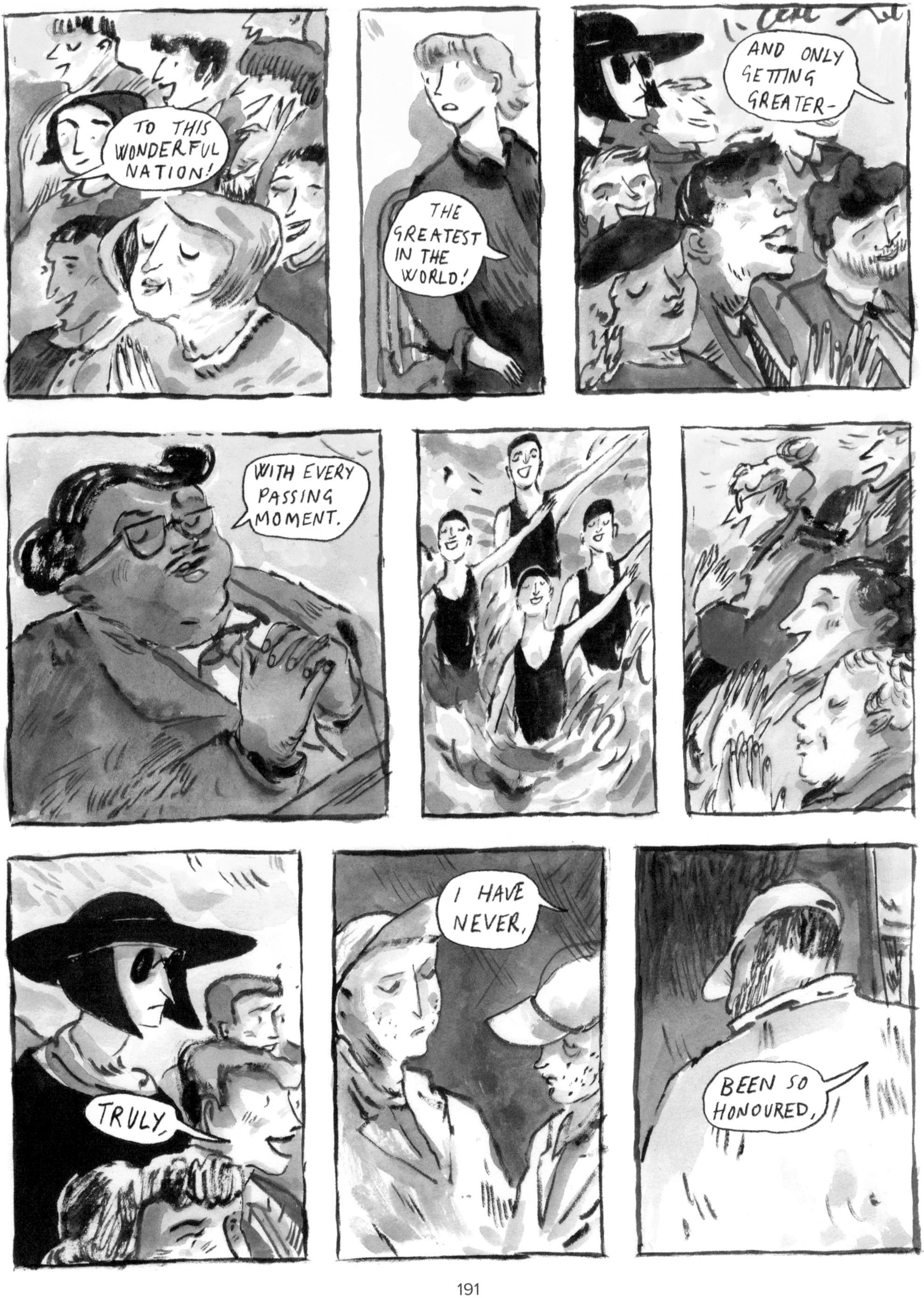
TO THIS WONDERFUL NATION!
THE GREATEST IN THE WORLD!
AND ONLY GETTING GREATER-
WITH EVERY PASSING MOMENT.
TRULY,
I HAVE NEVER,
BEEN SO HONOURED,

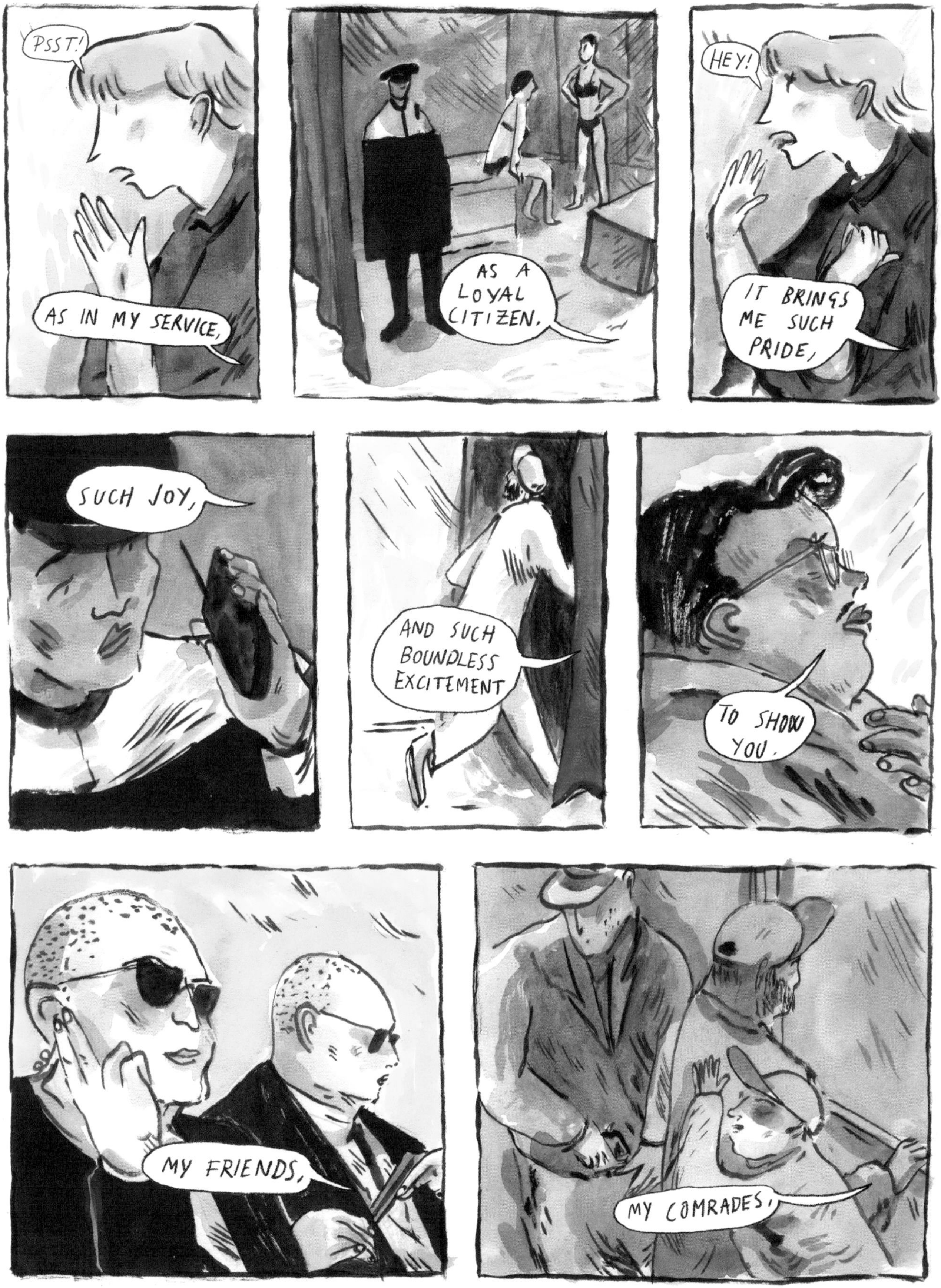
PSST!
AS IN MY SERVICE,
AS A LOYAL CITIZEN,
HEY!
IT BRINGS ME SUCH PRIDE,
SUCH JOY,
AND SUCH BOUNDLESS EXCITEMENT
TO SHOW YOU.
MY FRIENDS,
MY COMRADES,

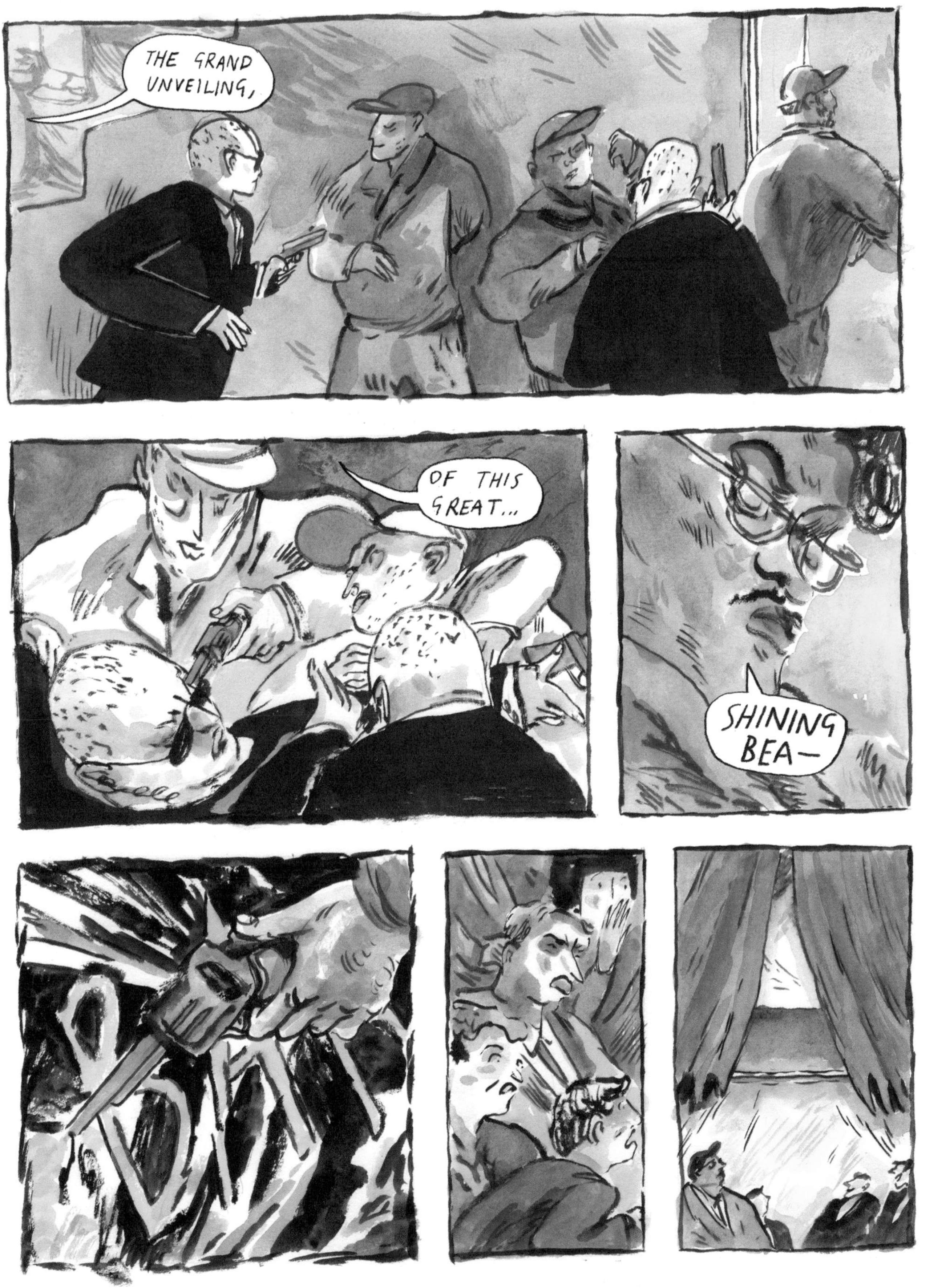
THE GRAND UNVEILING,
OF THIS GREAT...
SHINING BEA—

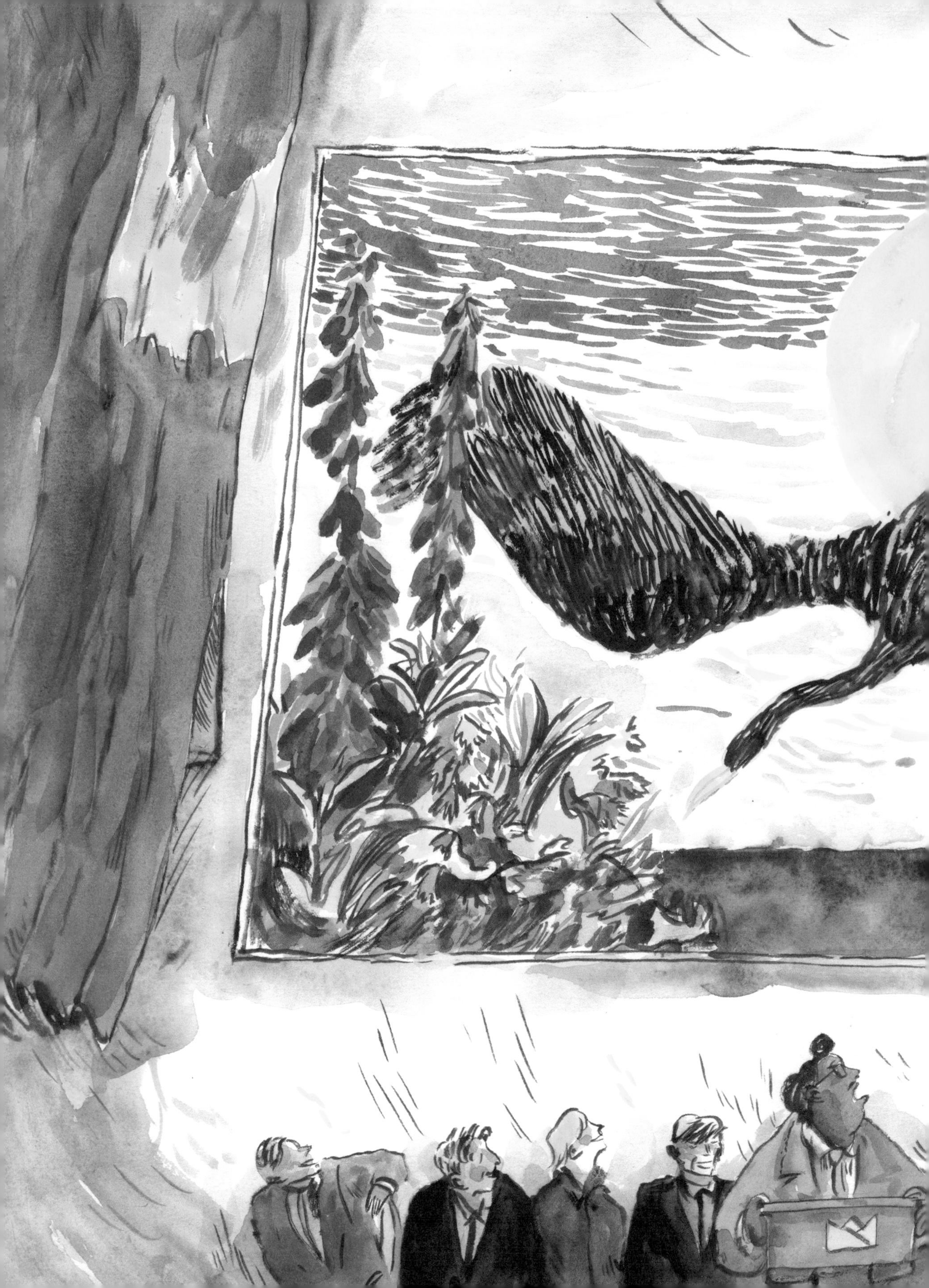

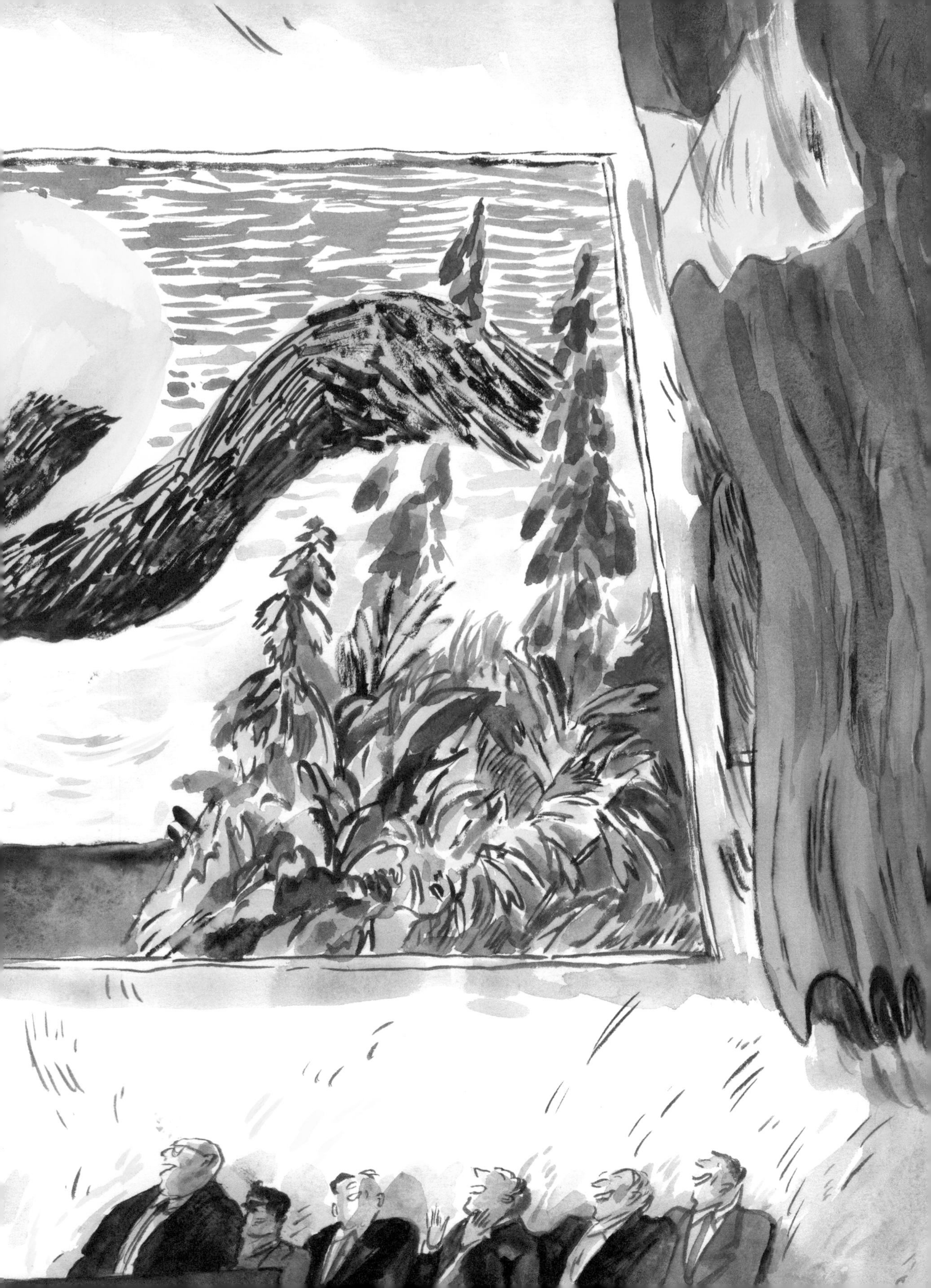

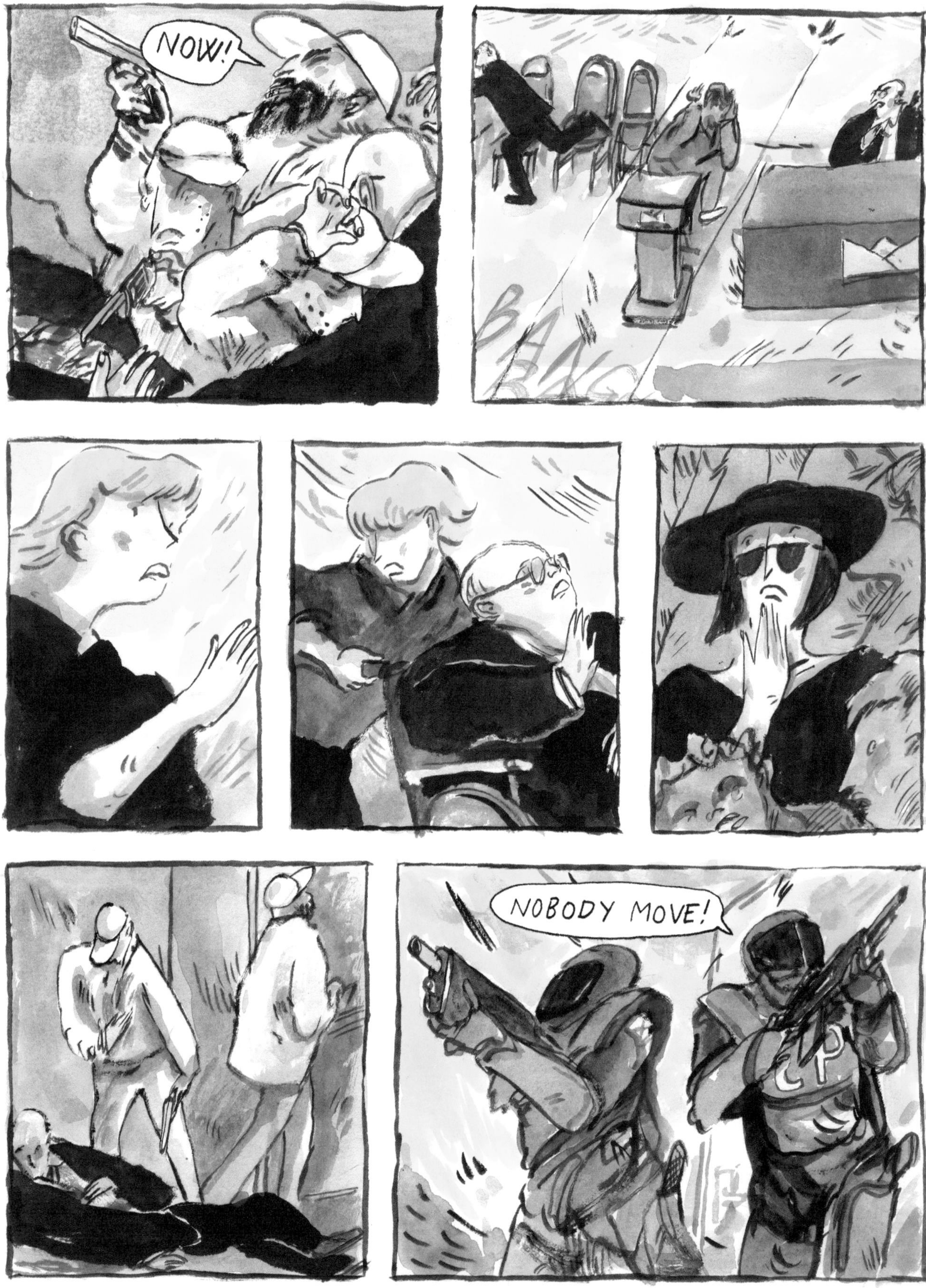
NOW!
NOBODY MOVE!

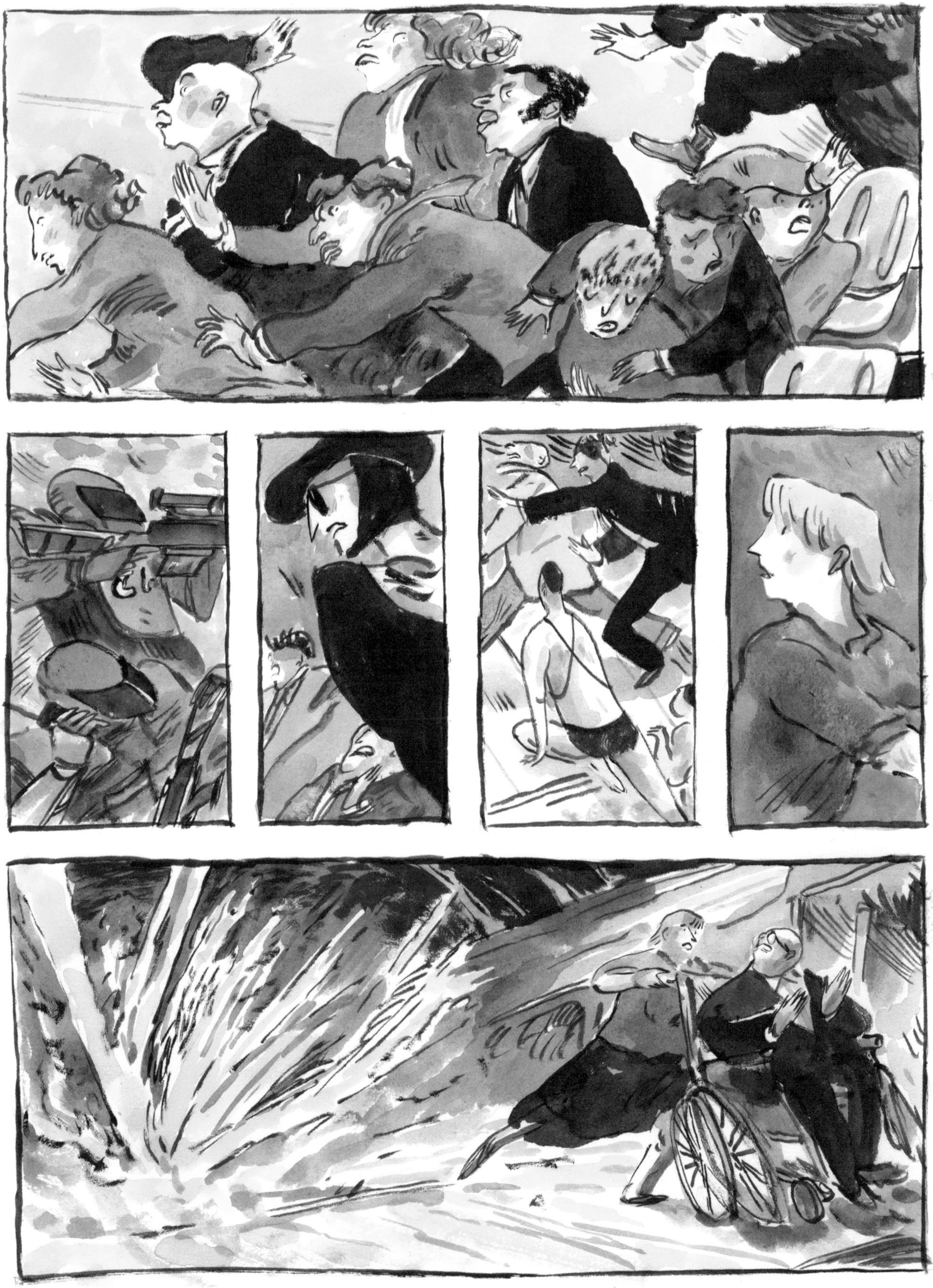

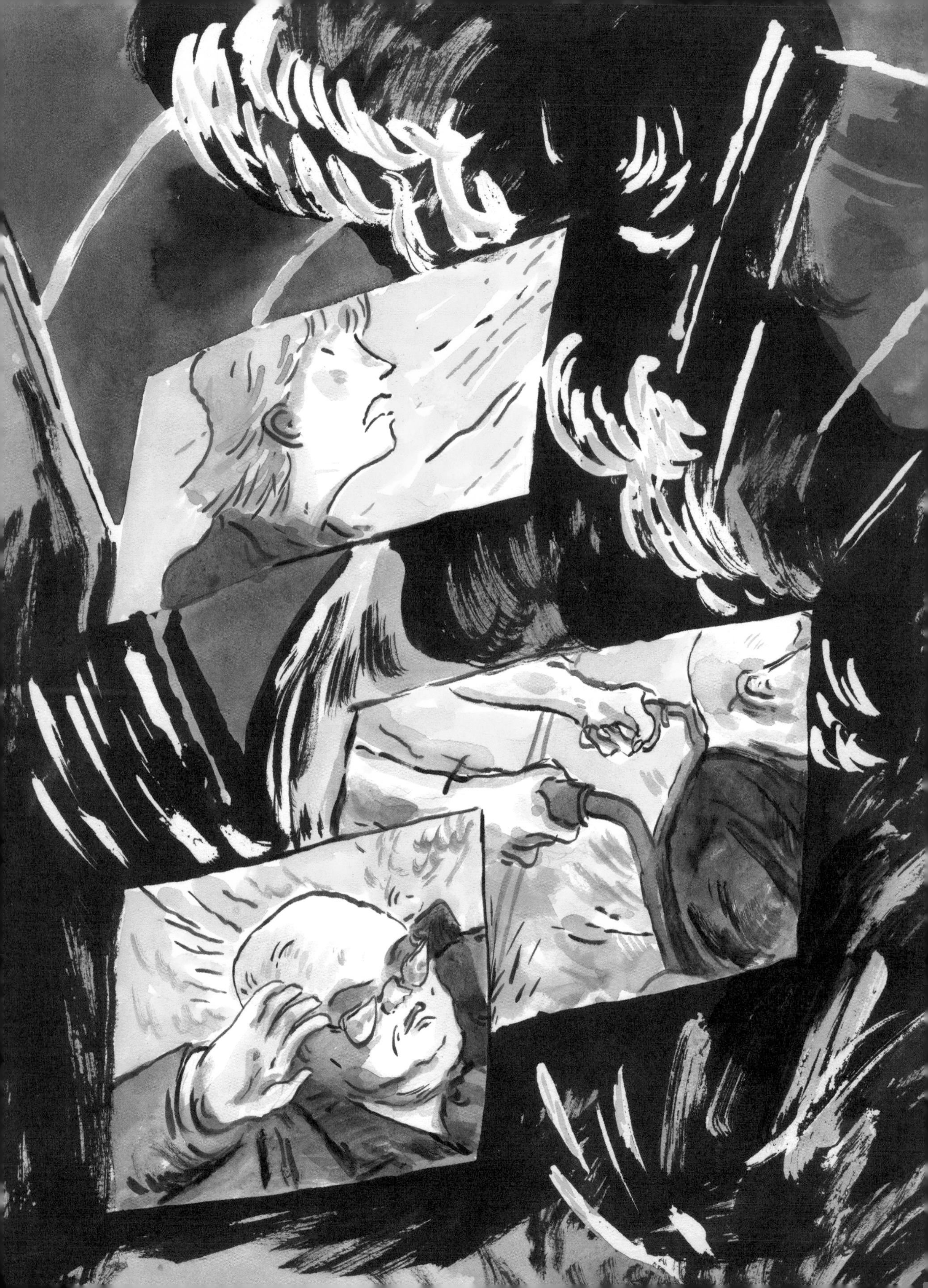

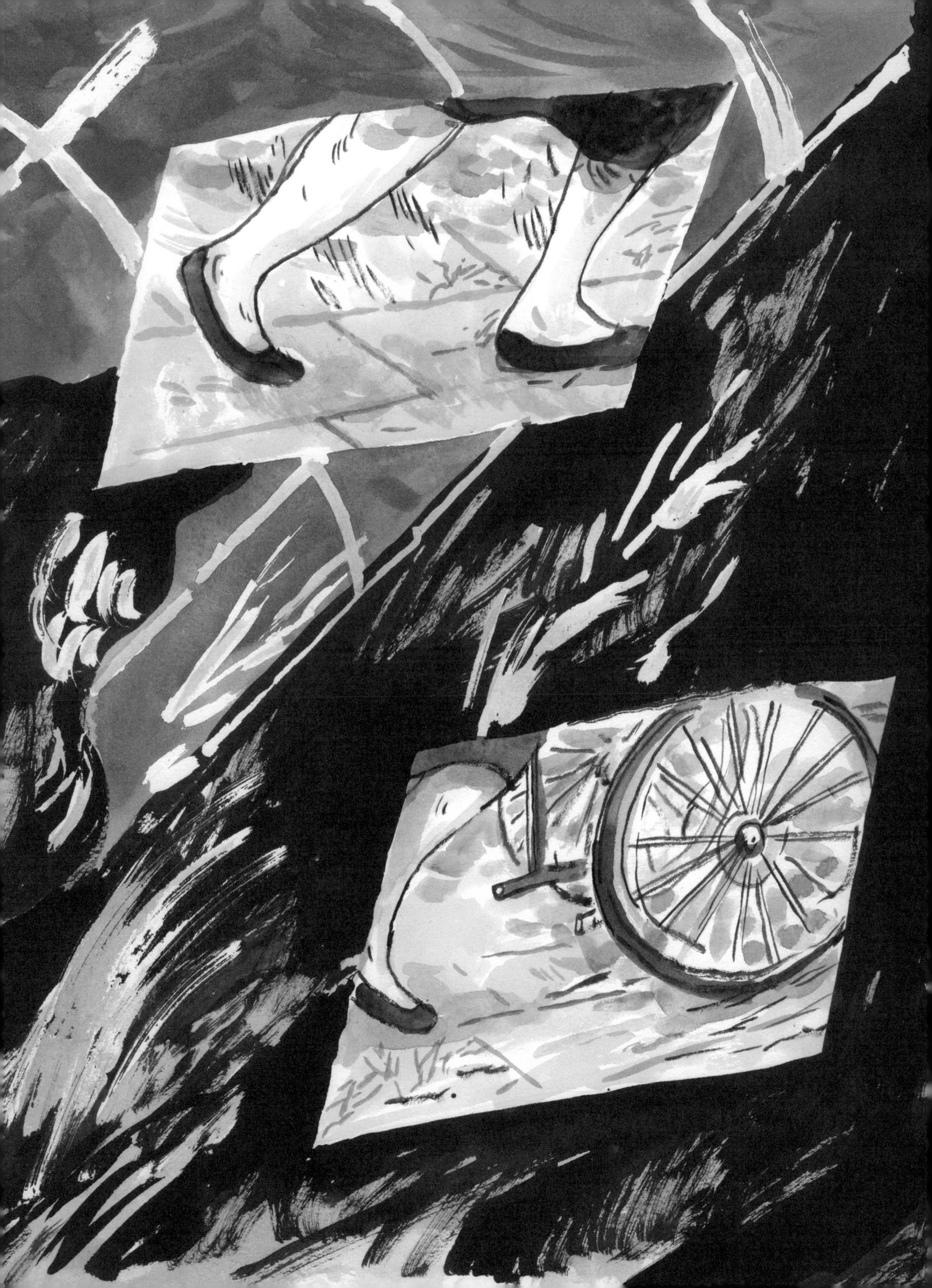

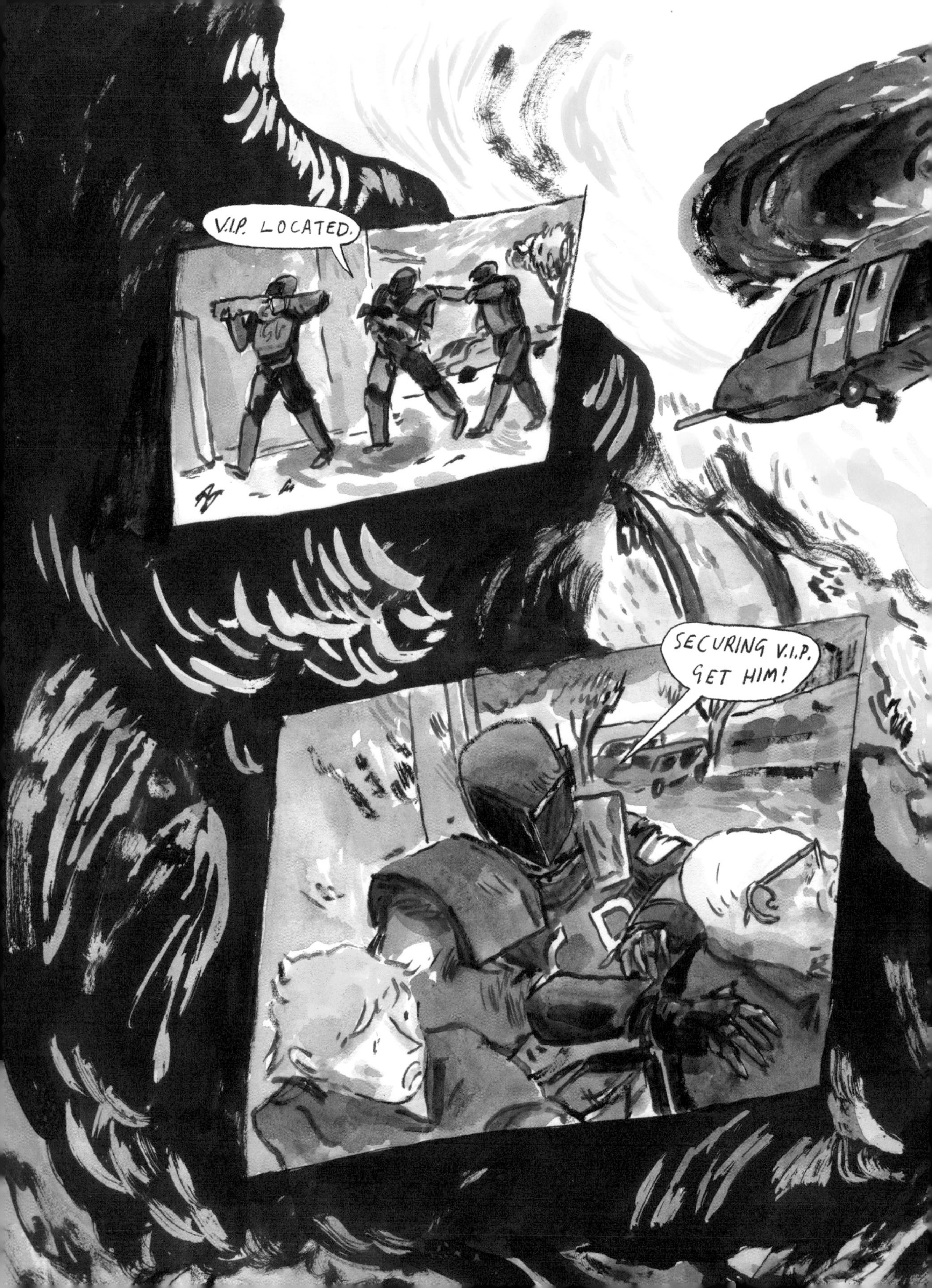
V.I.P. LOCATED.
SECURING V.I.P. GET HIM!

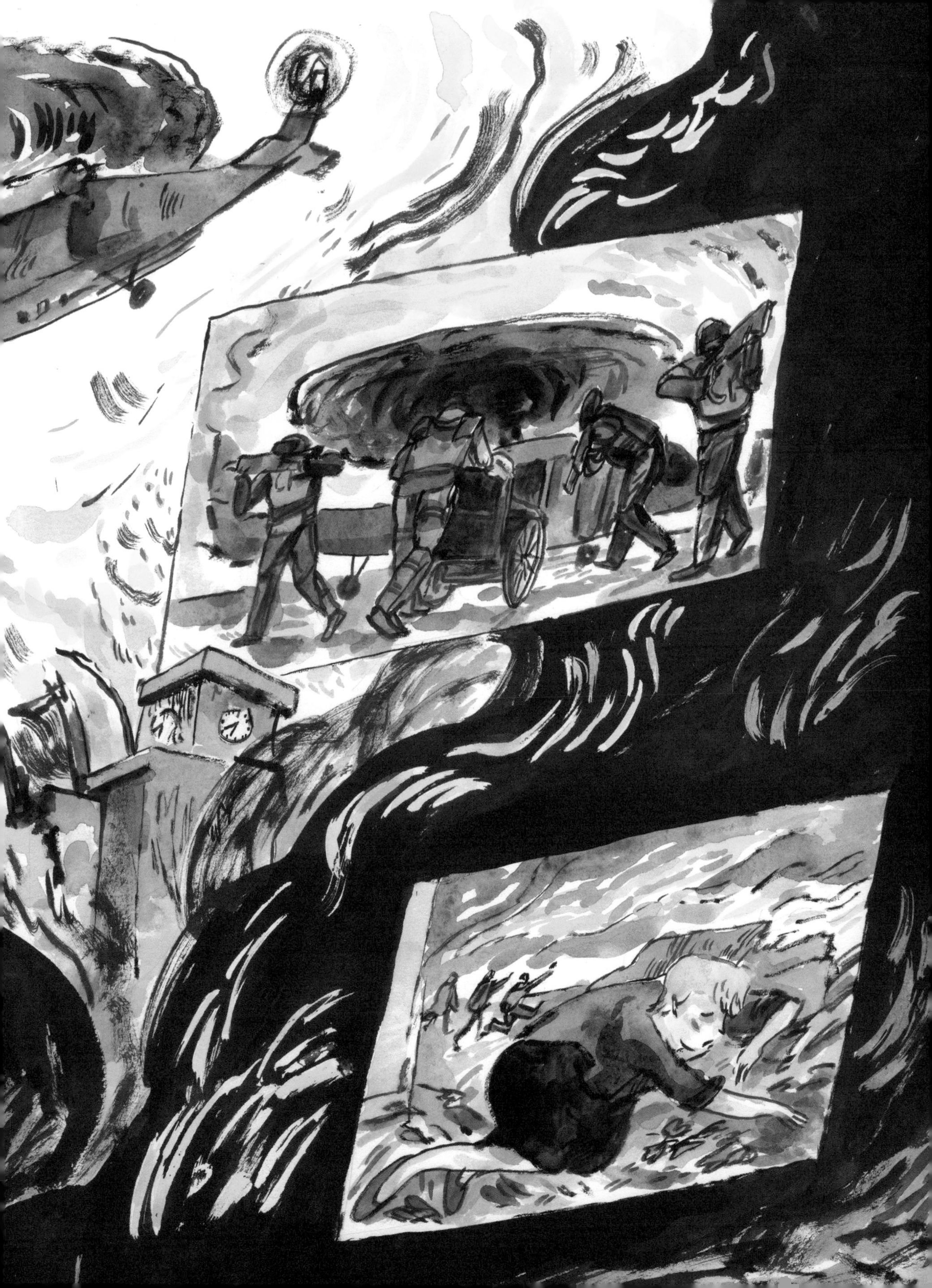

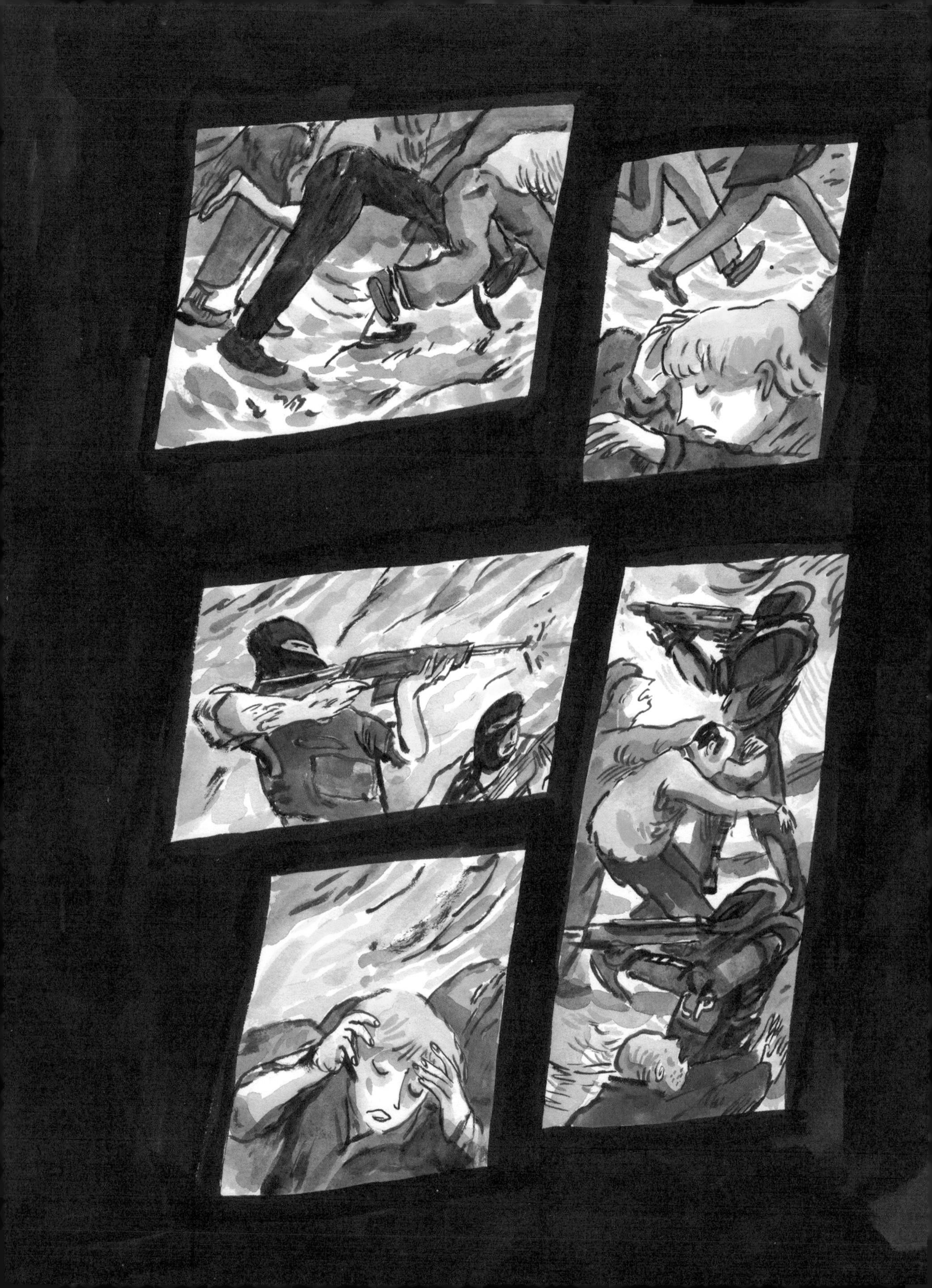

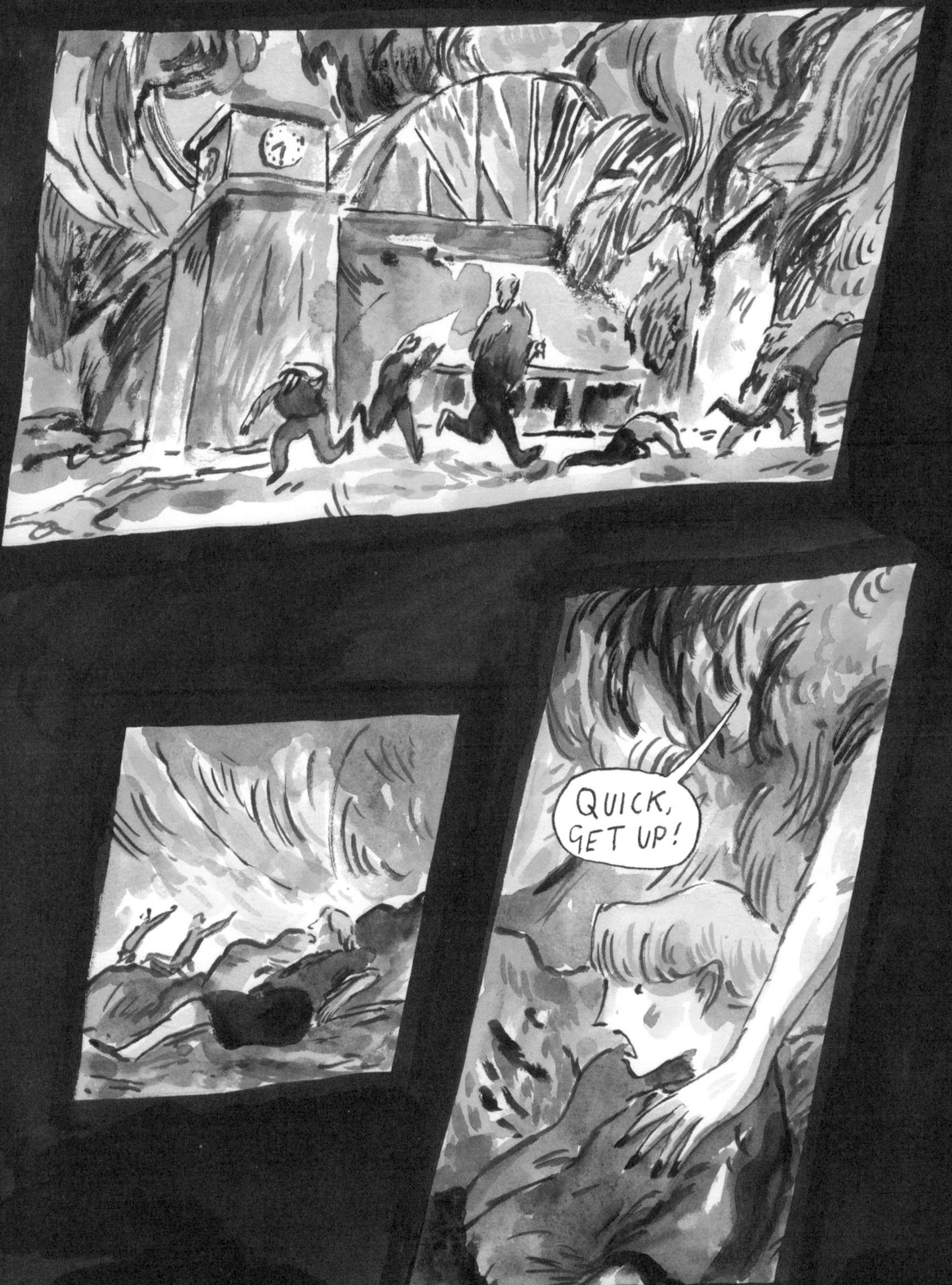
QUICK, GET UP!

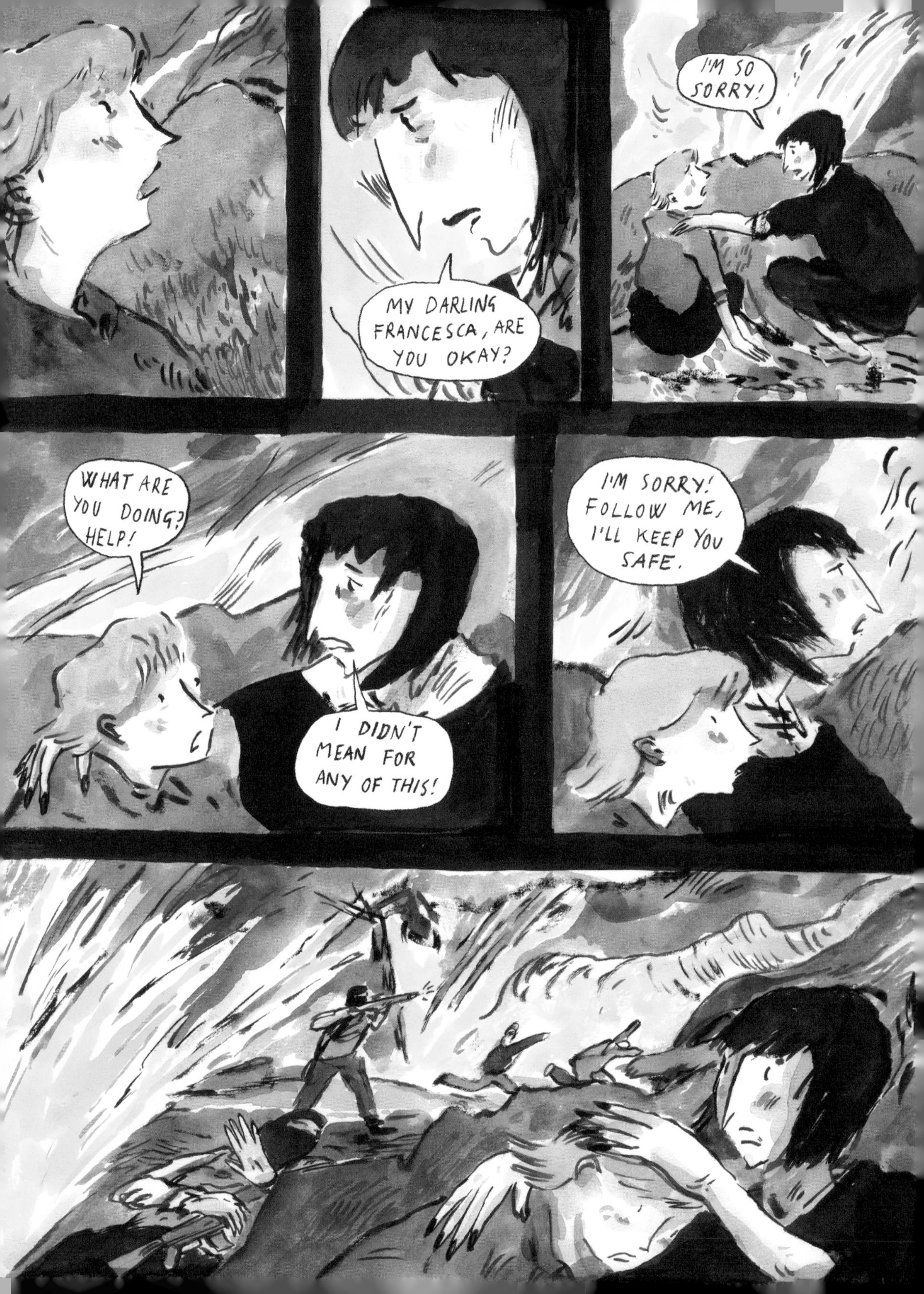
MY DARLING FRANCESCA, ARE YOU OKAY?
I'M SO SORRY!
WHAT ARE YOU DOING? HELP!
I DIDN'T MEAN FOR ANY OF THIS!
I'M SORRY! FOLLOW ME, I'LL KEEP YOU SAFE.

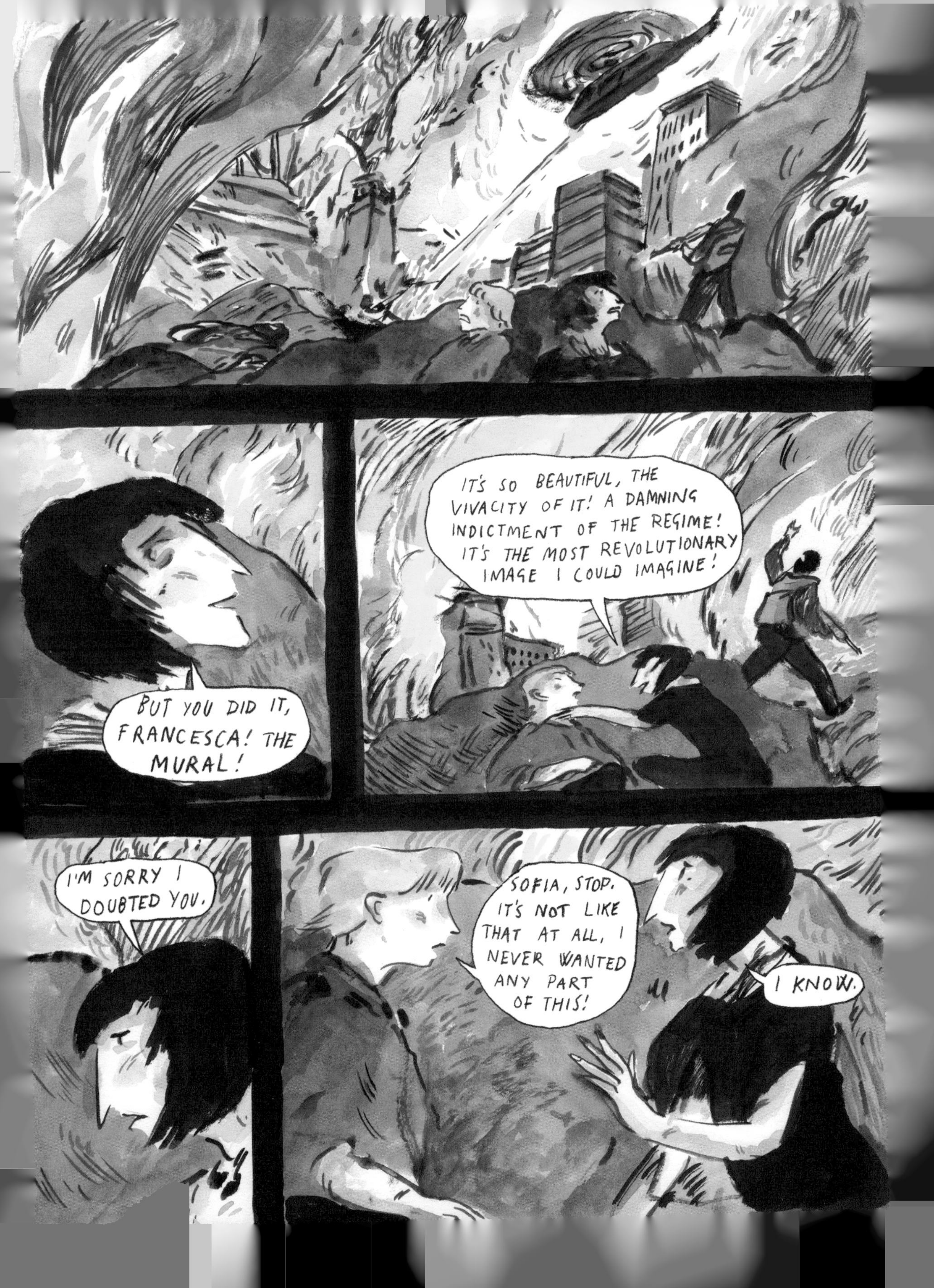
BUT YOU DID IT, FRANCESCA! THE MURAL!
IT'S SO BEAUTIFUL, THE VIVACITY OF IT! A DAMNING INDICTMENT OF THE REGIME! IT'S THE MOST REVOLUTIONARY IMAGE I COULD IMAGINE!
I'M SORRY I DOUBTED YOU.
SOFIA, STOP. IT'S NOT LIKE THAT AT ALL, I NEVER WANTED ANY PART OF THIS!
I KNOW.

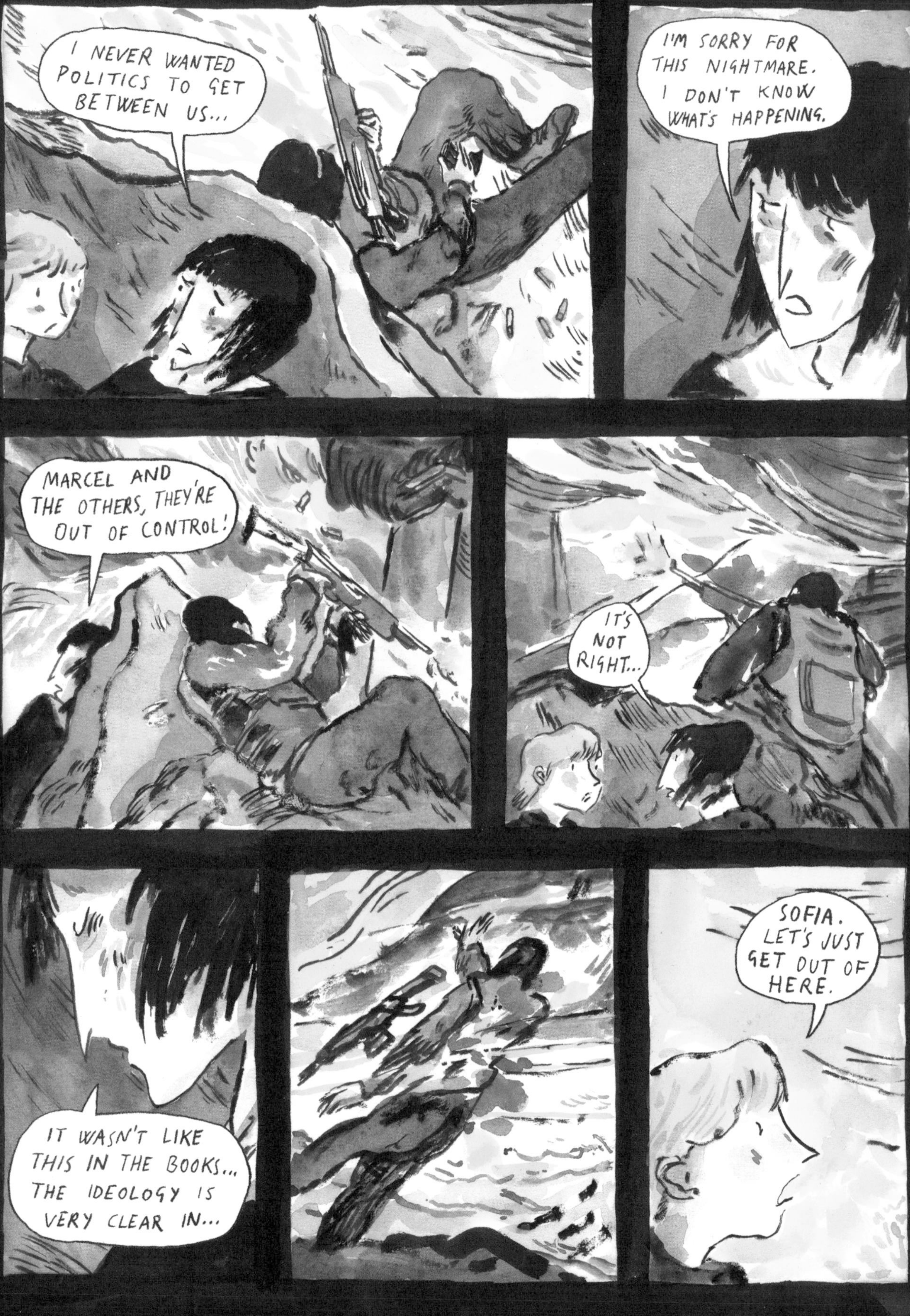
I NEVER WANTED POLITICS TO GET BETWEEN US...
I'M SORRY FOR THIS NIGHTMARE. I DON'T KNOW WHAT'S HAPPENING.
MARCEL AND THE OTHERS, THEY'RE OUT OF CONTROL!
IT'S NOT RIGHT...
IT WASN'T LIKE THIS IN THE BOOKS... THE IDEOLOGY IS VERY CLEAR IN...
SOFIA. LET'S JUST GET OUT OF HERE.

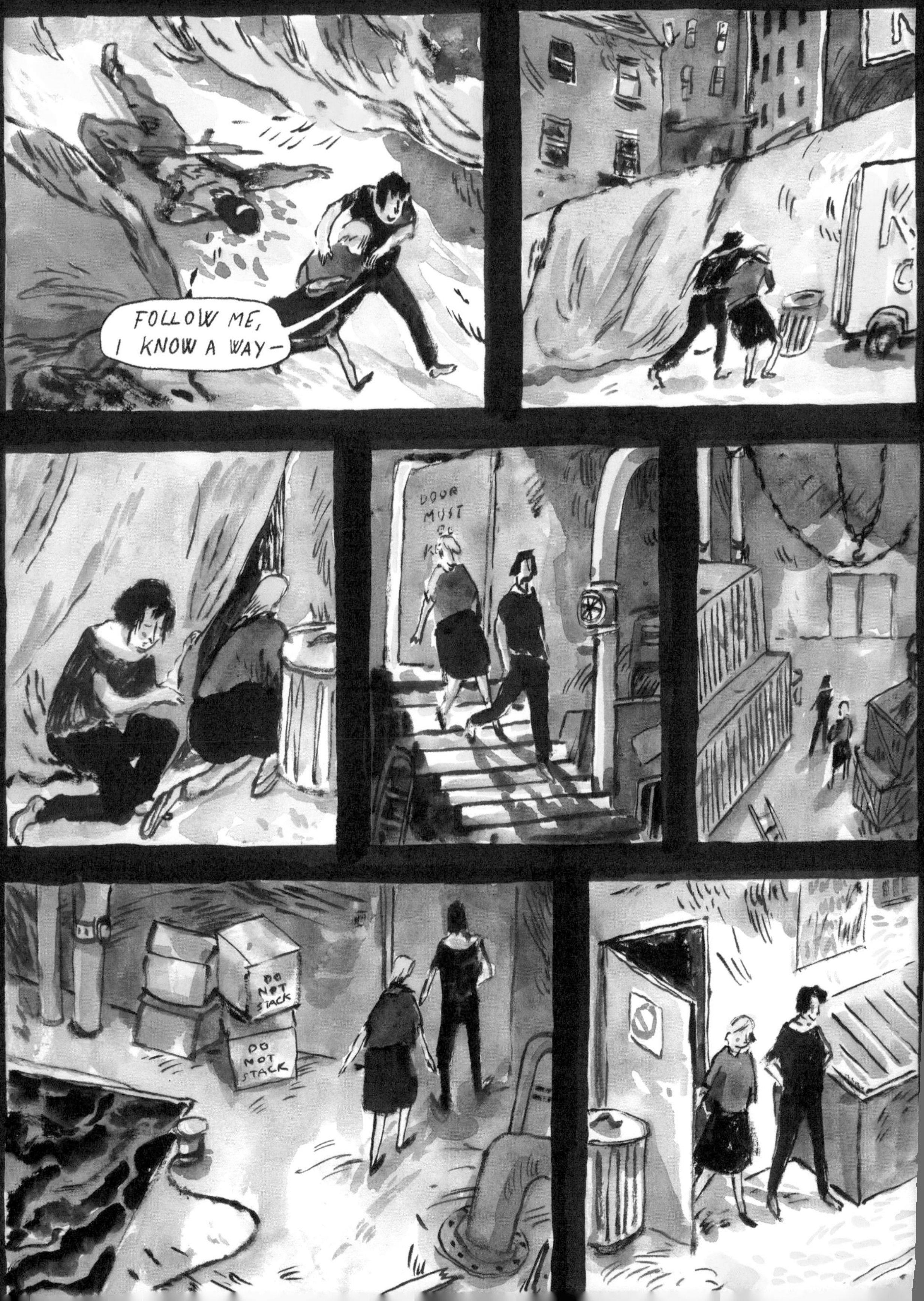
FOLLOW ME, I KNOW A WAY—
DOOR MUST
DO NOT STACK
DO NOT STACK

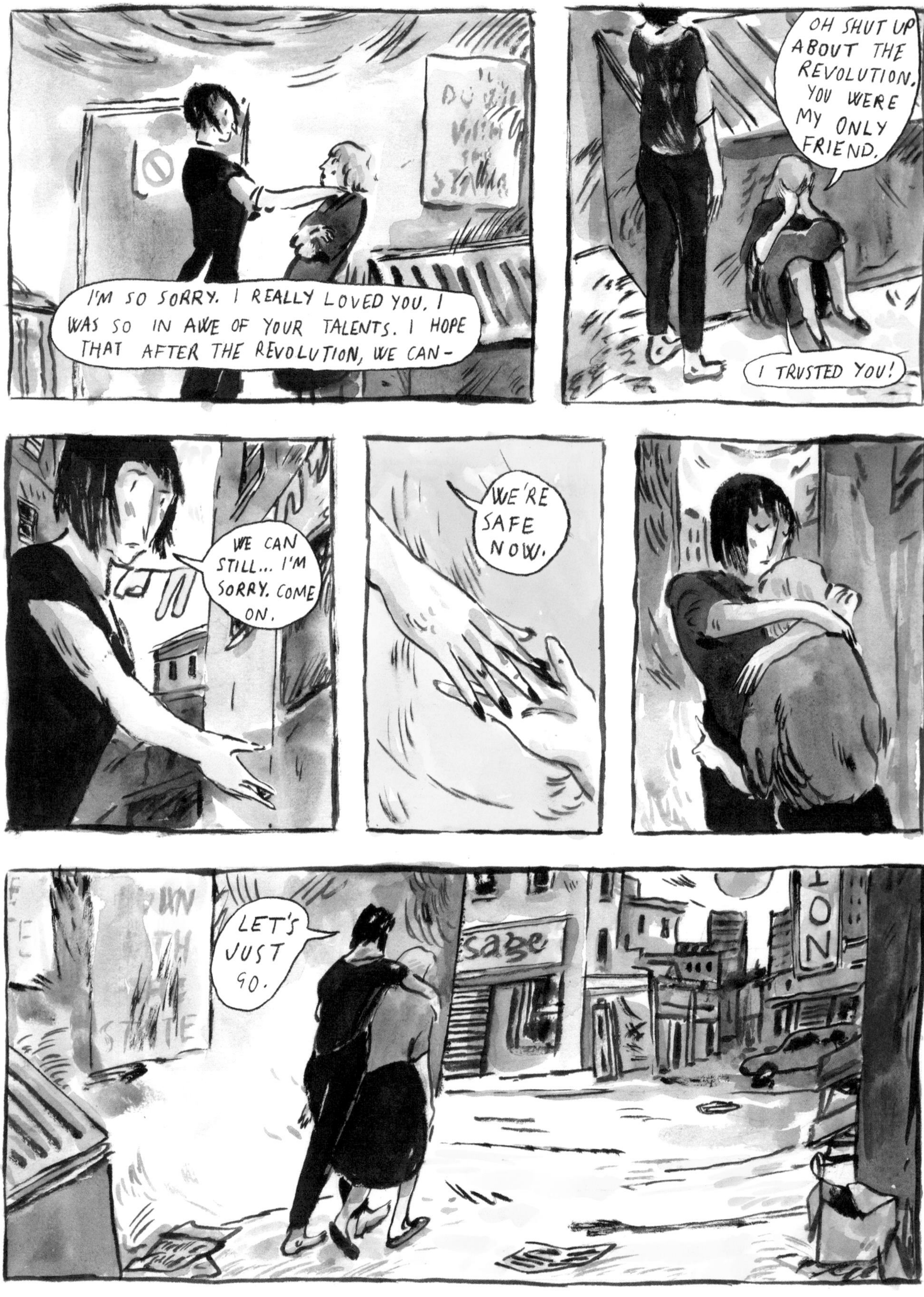
I'M SO SORRY. I REALLY LOVED YOU. I WAS SO IN AWE OF YOUR TALENTS. I HOPE THAT AFTER THE REVOLUTION, WE CAN-
OH SHUT UP ABOUT THE REVOLUTION. YOU WERE MY ONLY FRIEND.
I TRUSTED YOU!
WE CAN STILL... I'M SORRY. COME ON.
WE'RE SAFE NOW.
LET'S JUST GO.
sage

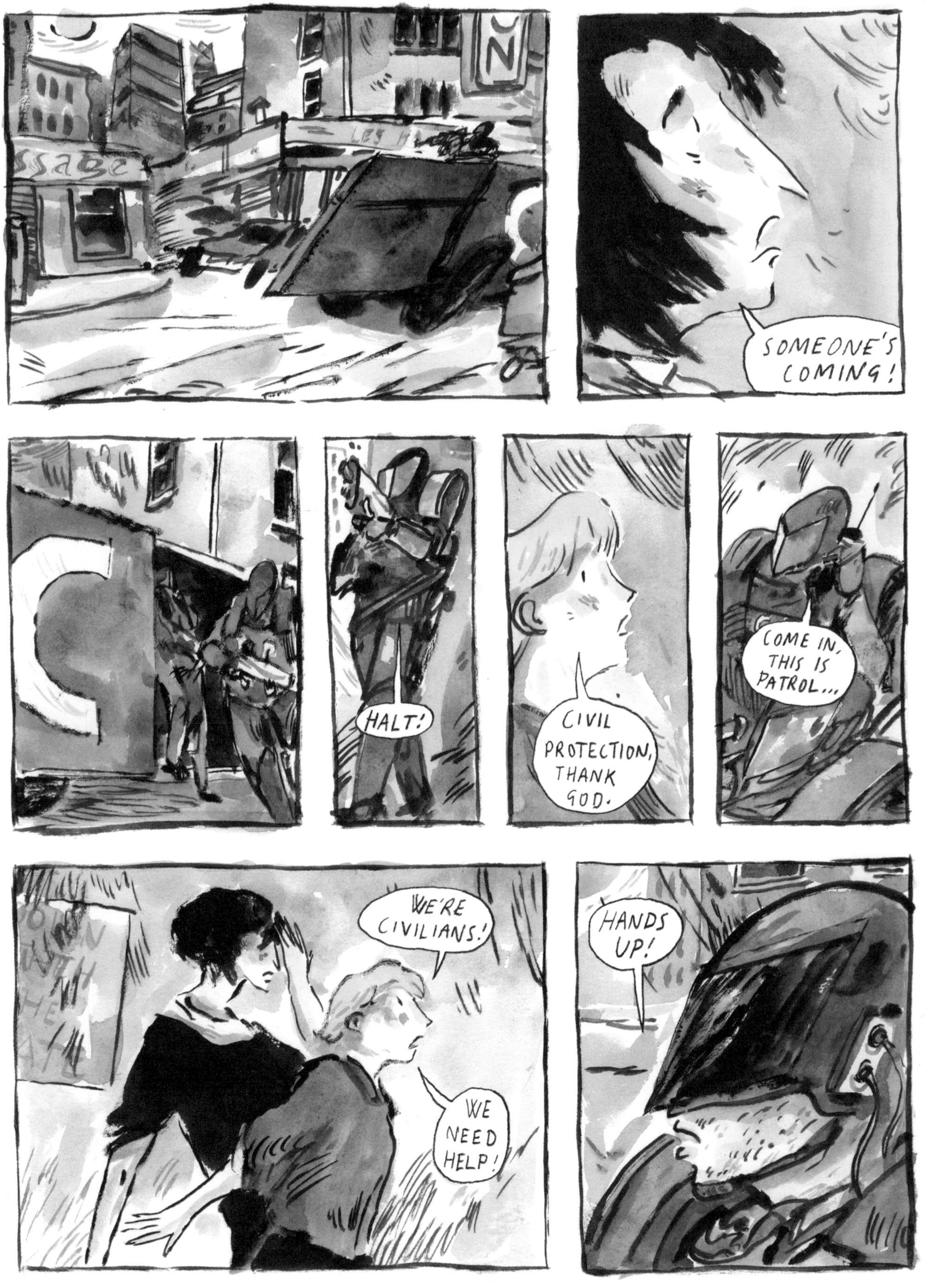
SOMEONE'S COMING!
HALT!
CIVIL PROTECTION, THANK GOD.
COME IN, THIS IS PATROL...
WE'RE CIVILIANS!
WE NEED HELP!
HANDS UP!

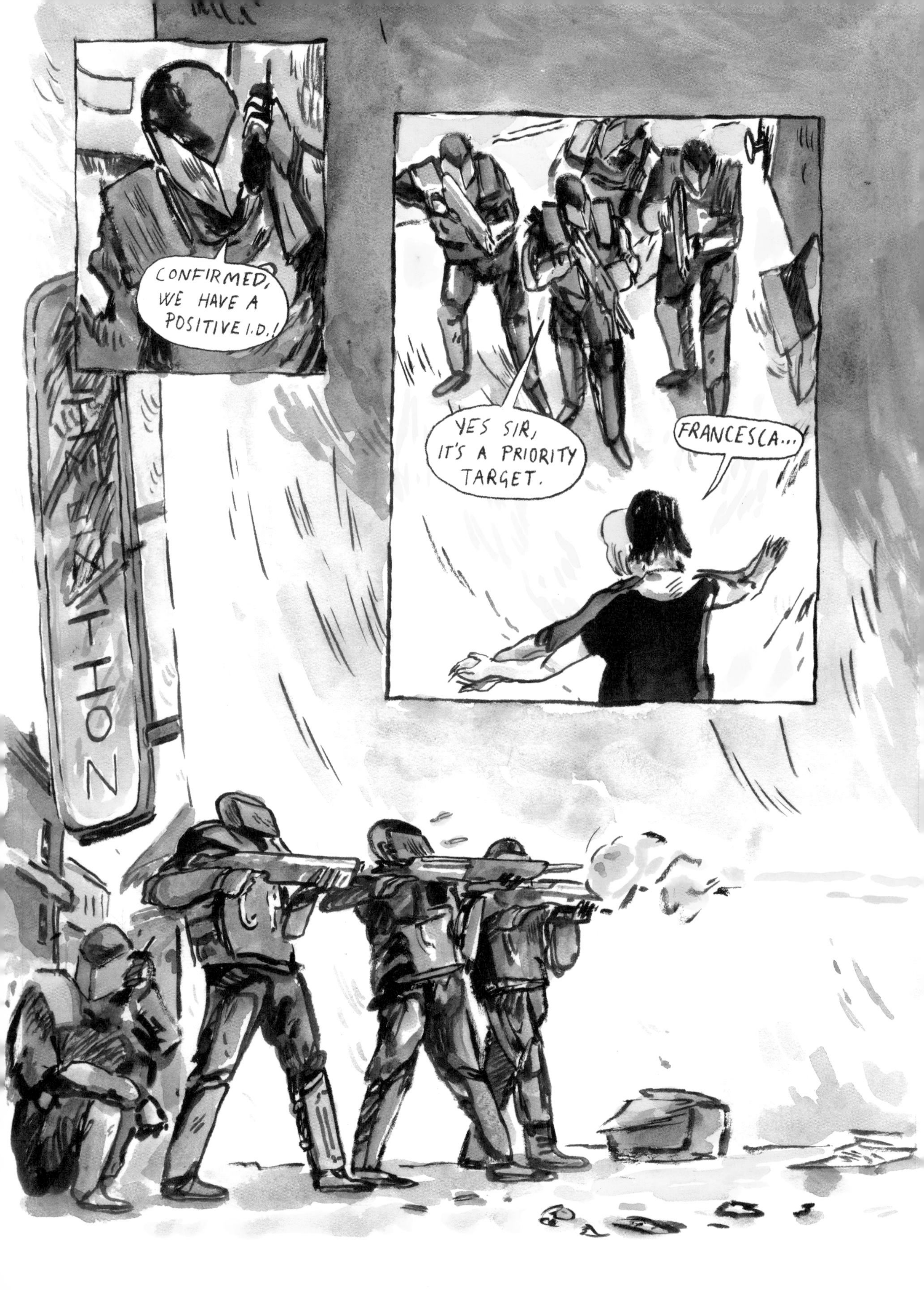
CONFIRMED, WE HAVE A POSITIVE I.D.!
YES SIR, IT'S A PRIORITY TARGET.
FRANCESCA...

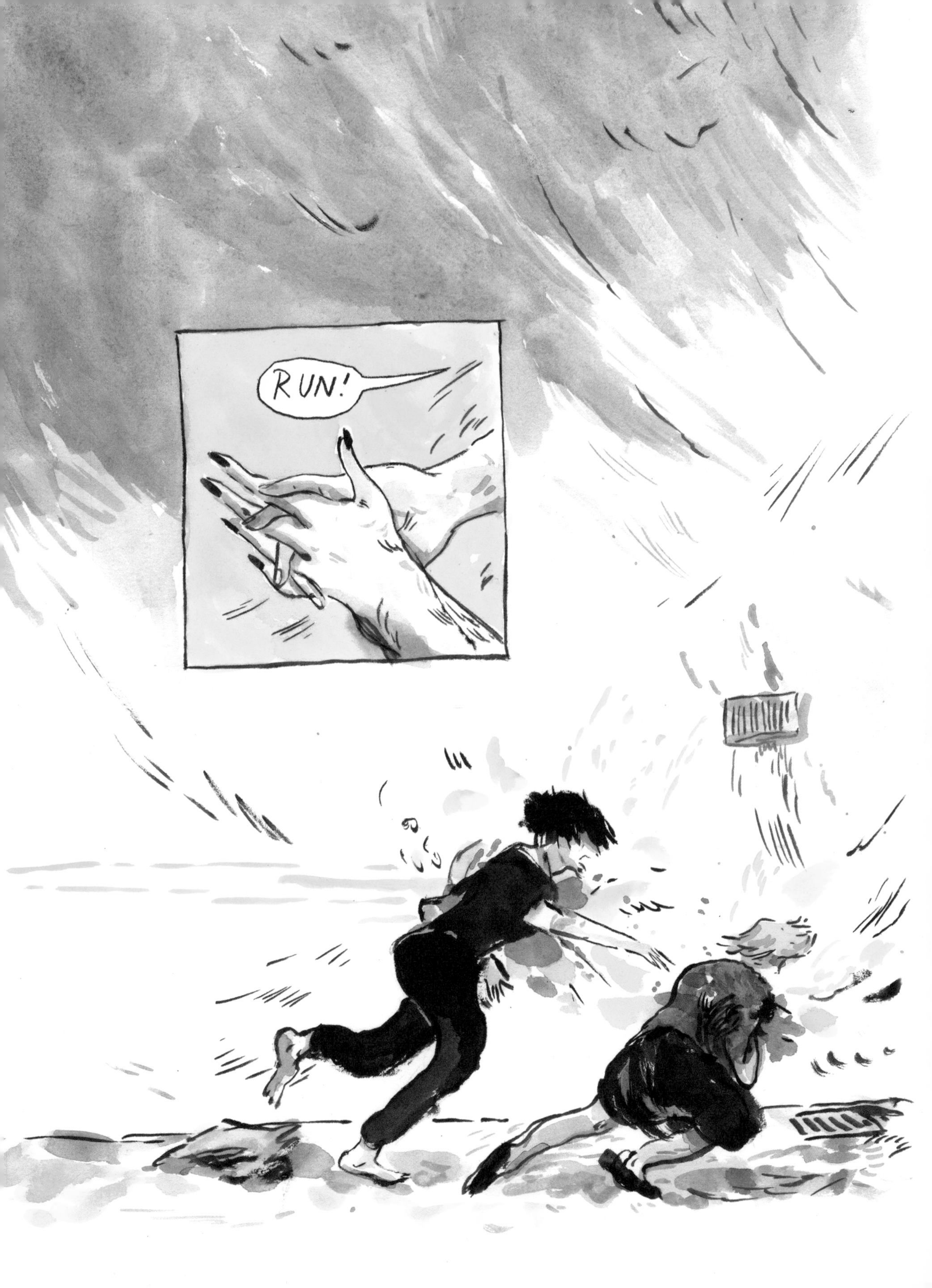
RUN!

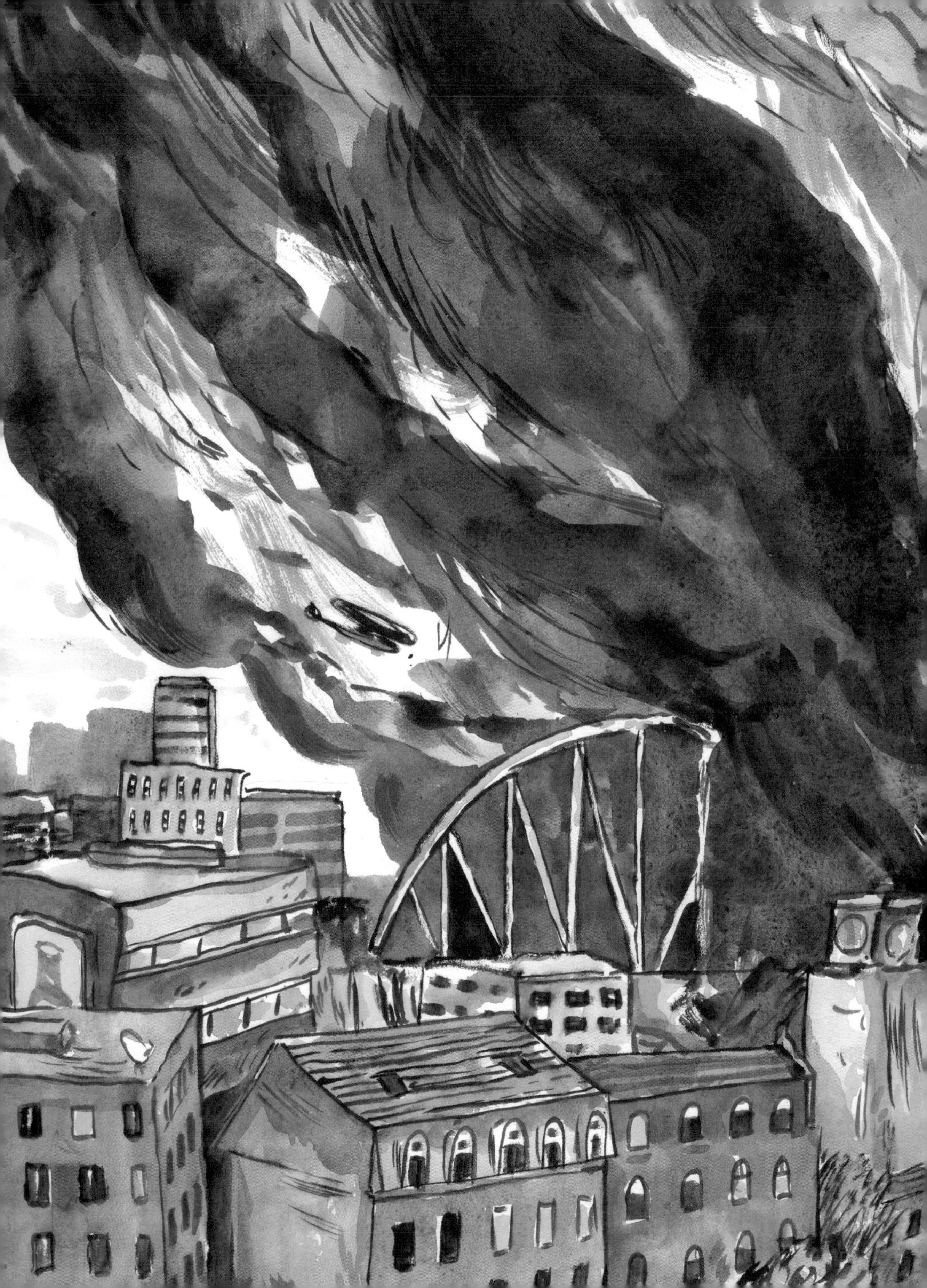

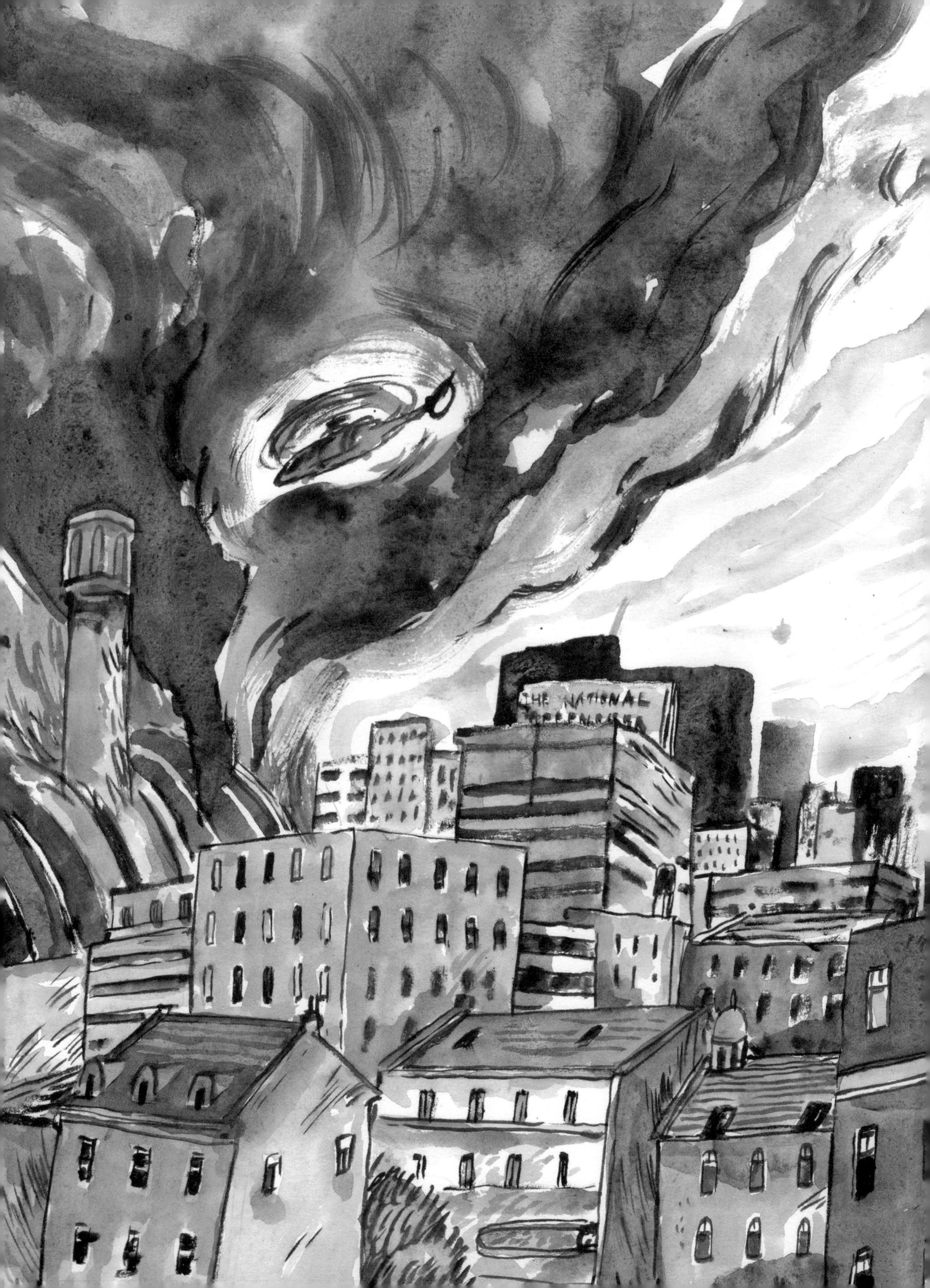
THE NATIONAL

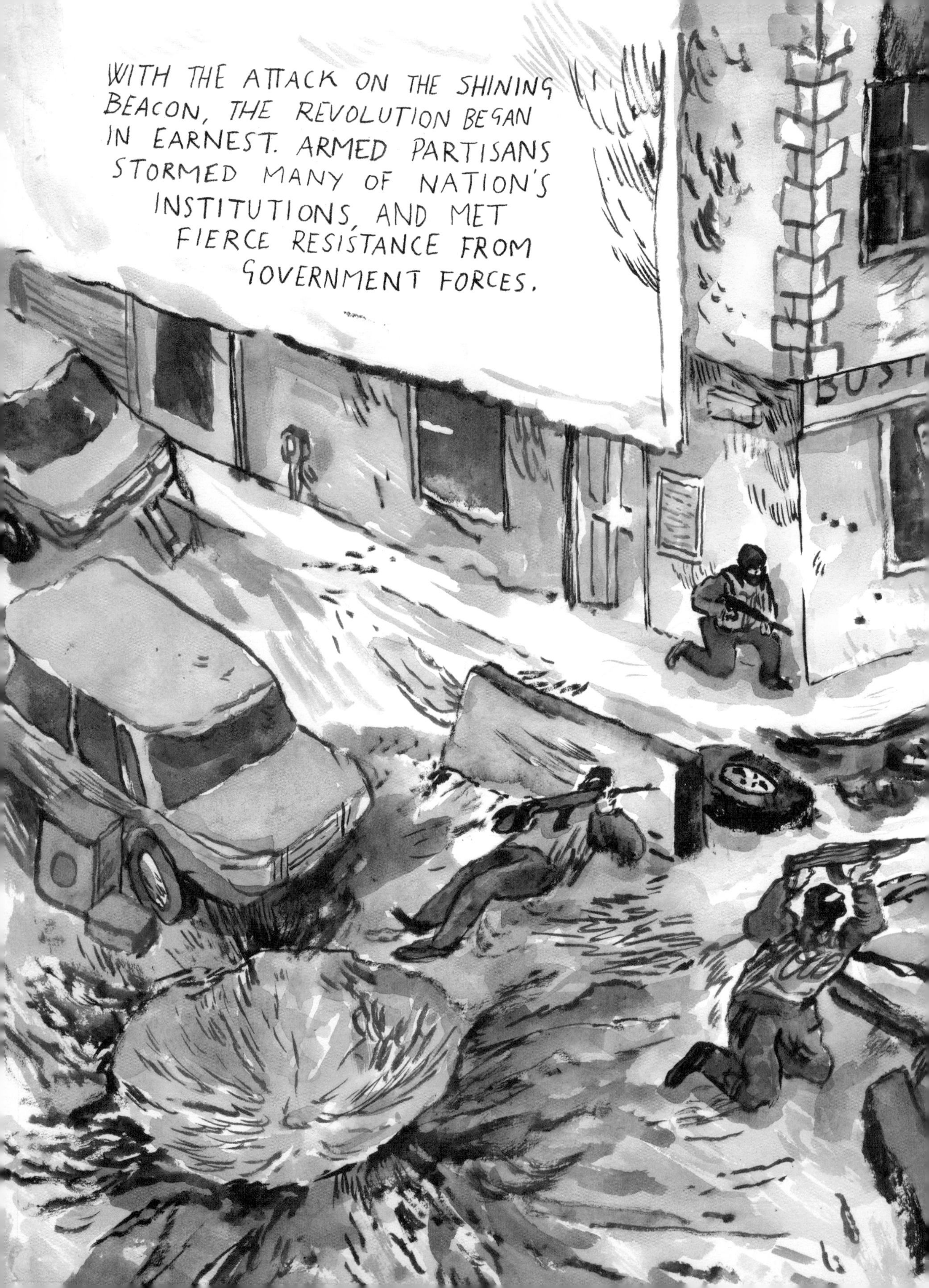
WITH THE ATTACK ON THE SHINING BEACON, THE REVOLUTION BEGAN IN EARNEST. ARMED PARTISANS STORMED MANY OF NATION'S INSTITUTIONS, AND MET FIERCE RESISTANCE FROM GOVERNMENT FORCES.

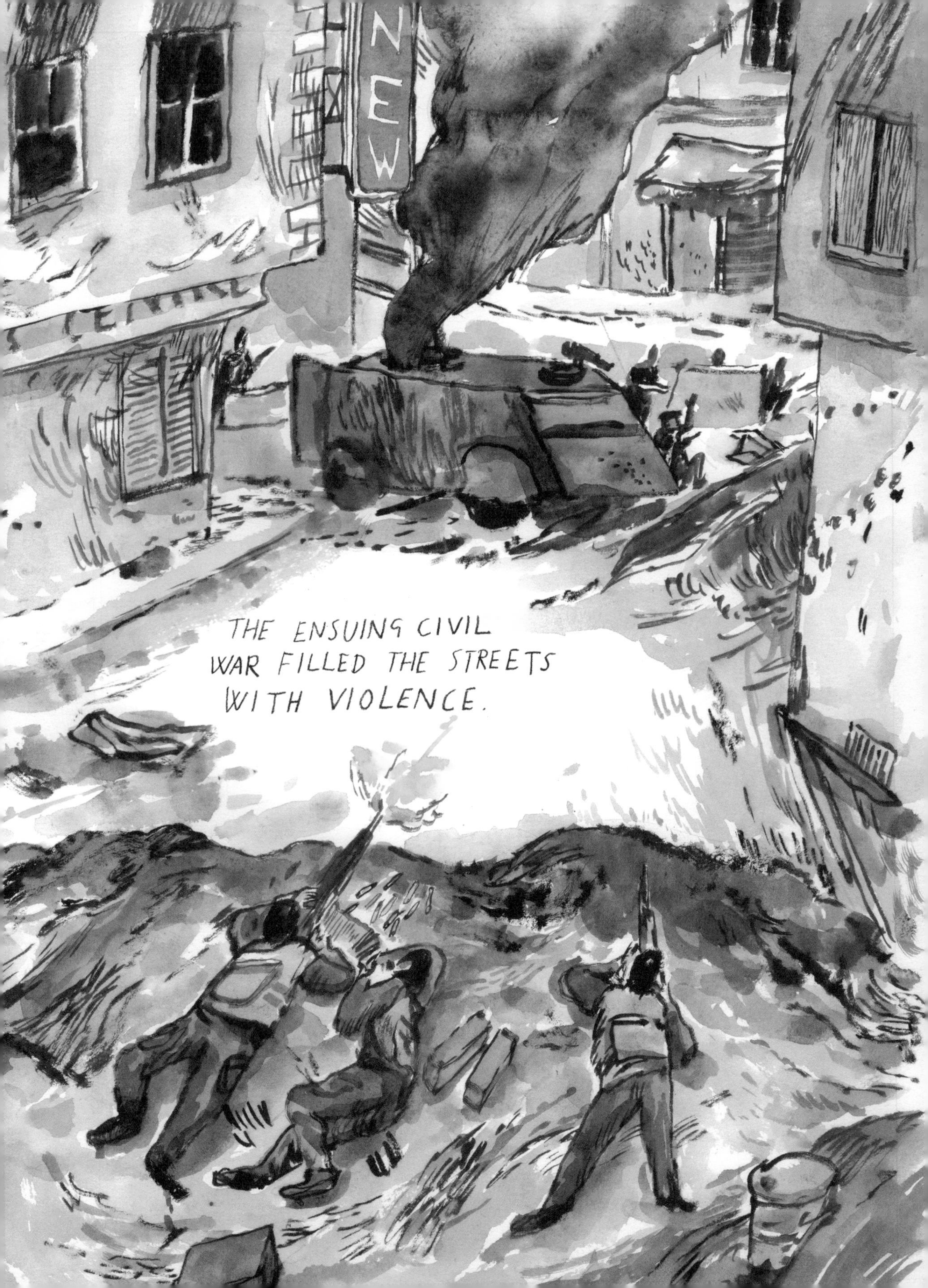
NEW
THE ENSUING CIVIL WAR FILLED THE STREETS WITH VIOLENCE.

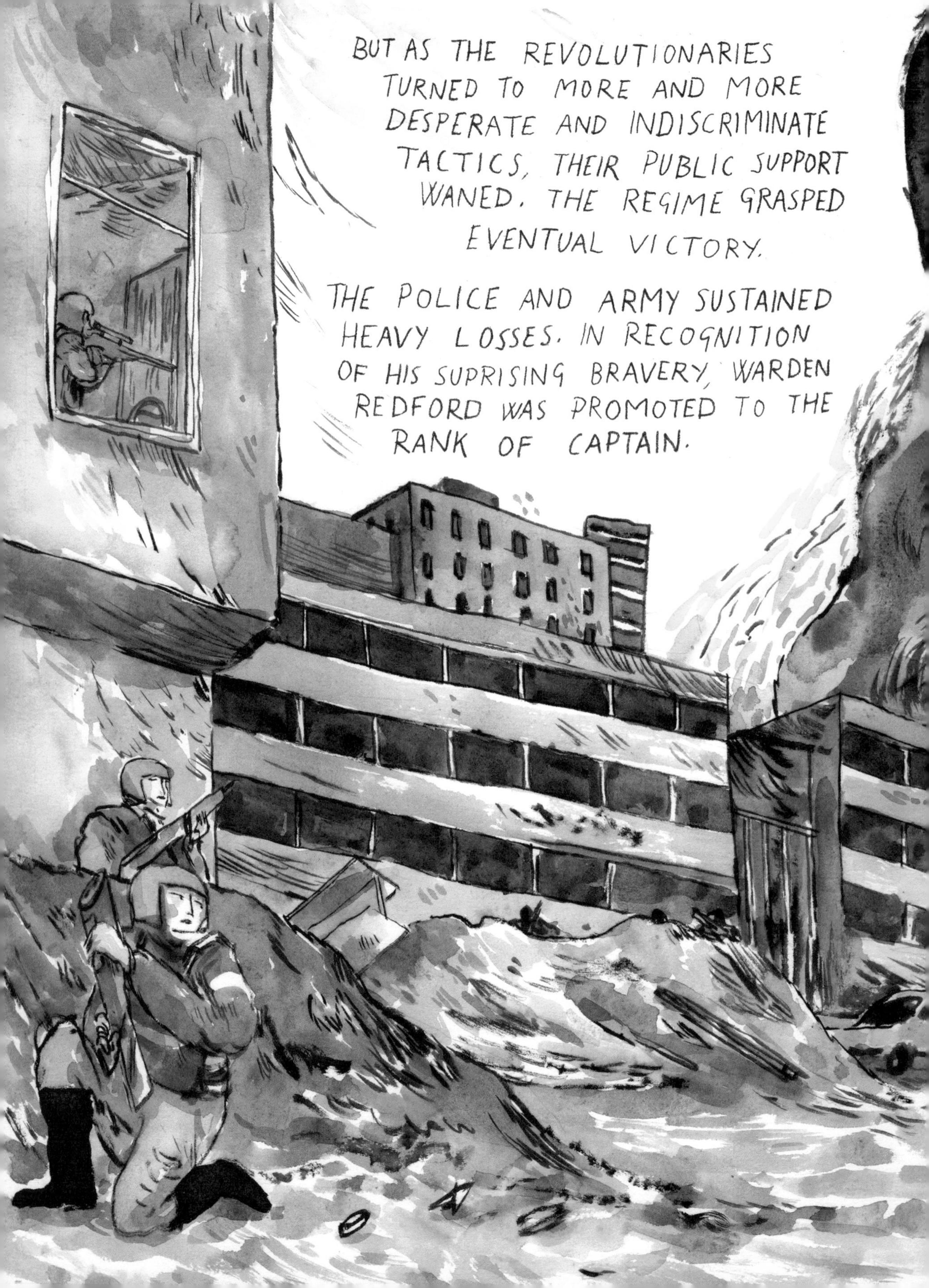
BUT AS THE REVOLUTIONARIES TURNED TO MORE AND MORE DESPERATE AND INDISCRIMINATE TACTICS, THEIR PUBLIC SUPPORT WANED. THE REGIME GRASPED EVENTUAL VICTORY.
THE POLICE AND ARMY SUSTAINED HEAVY LOSSES. IN RECOGNITION OF HIS SUPRISING BRAVERY, WARDEN REDFORD WAS PROMOTED TO THE RANK OF CAPTAIN.

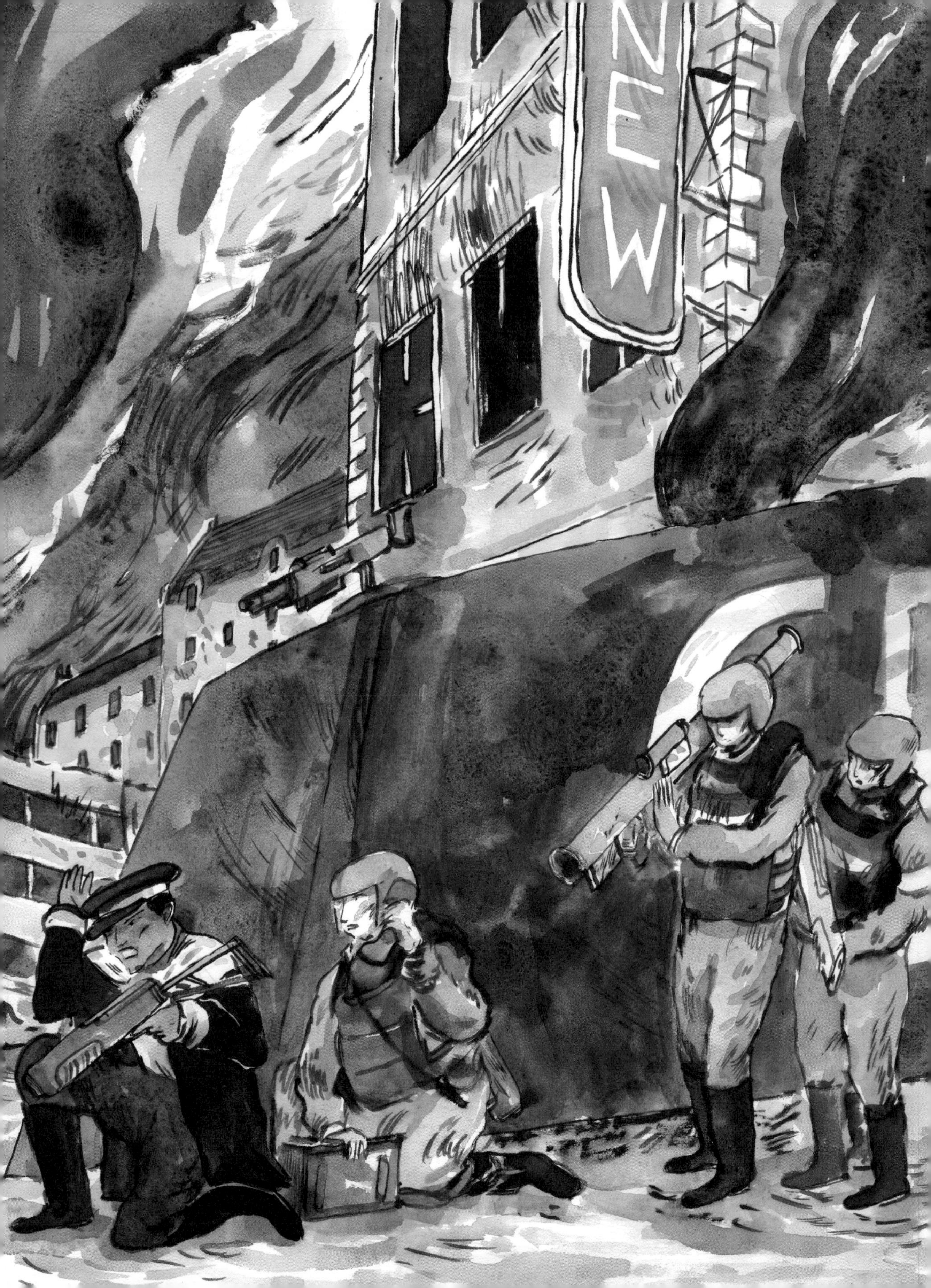
NEW

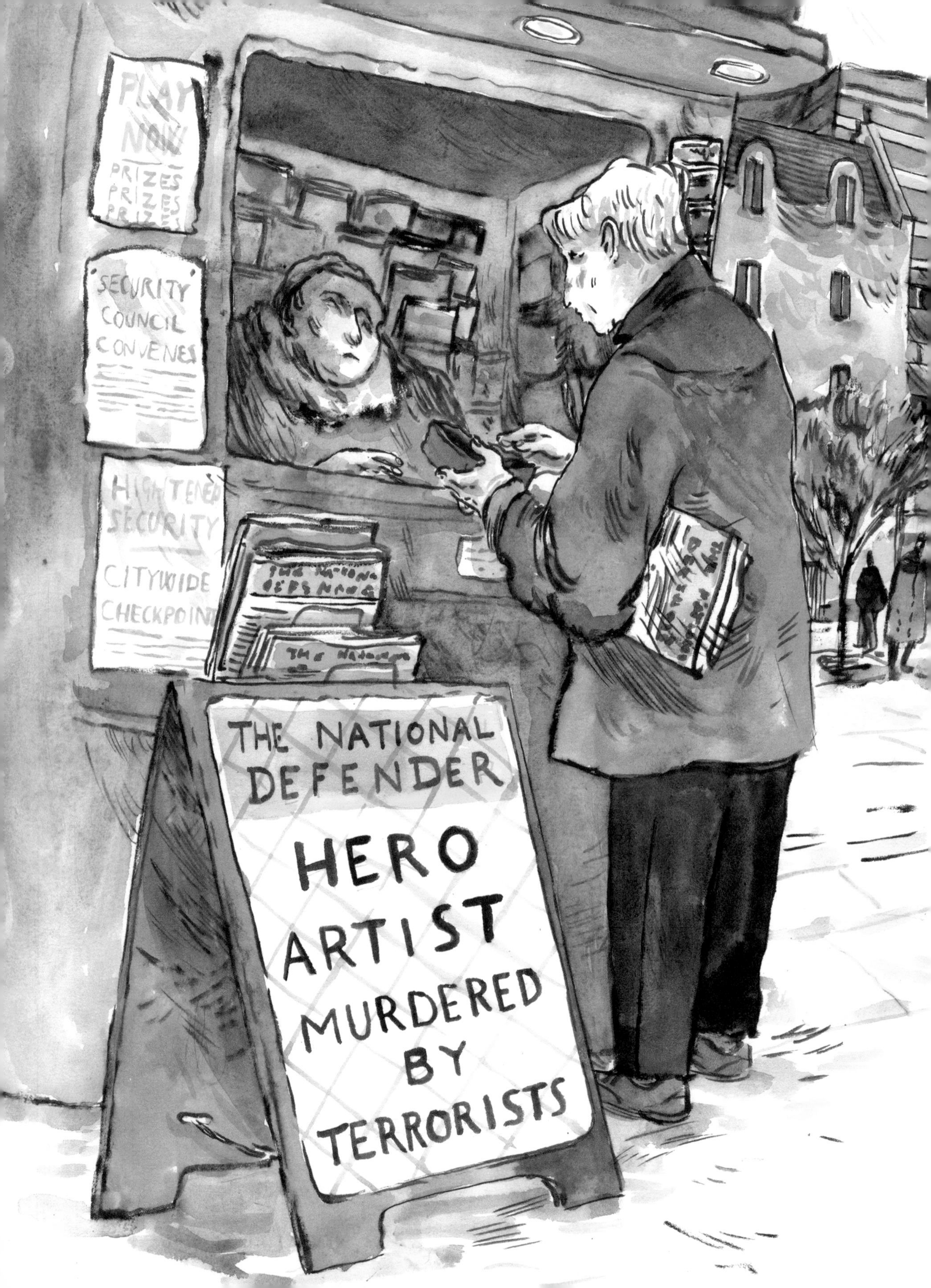
PLAY NOW
PRIZES
PRIZES
SECURITY COUNCIL CONVENES
HIGHTENED SECURITY
CITYWIDE CHECKPOINT
THE NATIONAL DEFENDER
HERO ARTIST MURDERED BY TERRORISTS

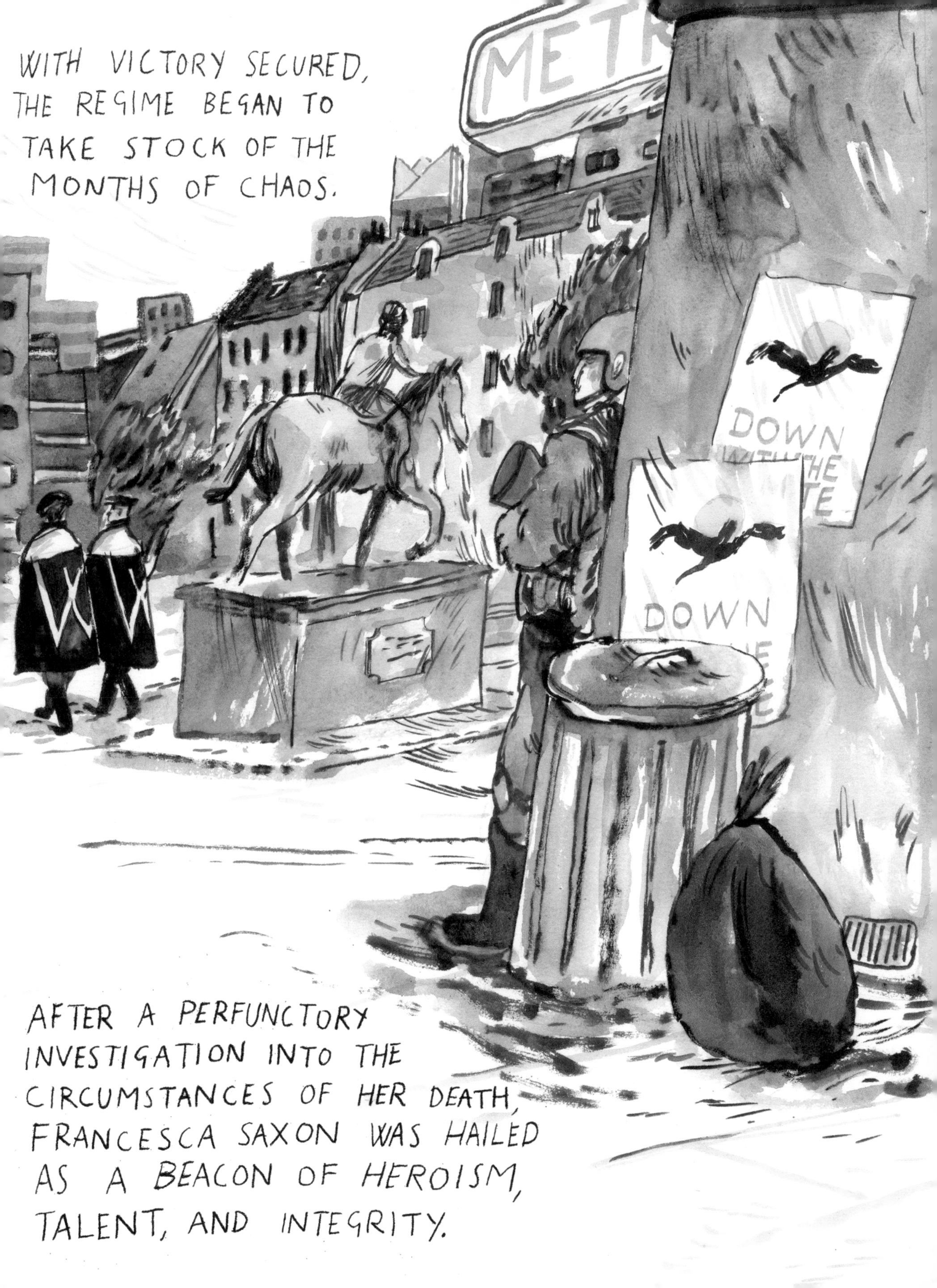
WITH VICTORY SECURED, THE REGIME BEGAN TO TAKE STOCK OF THE MONTHS OF CHAOS.
METR
DOWN
DOWN
AFTER A PERFUNCTORY INVESTIGATION INTO THE CIRCUMSTANCES OF HER DEATH, FRANCESCA SAXON WAS HAILED AS A BEACON OF HEROISM, TALENT, AND INTEGRITY.

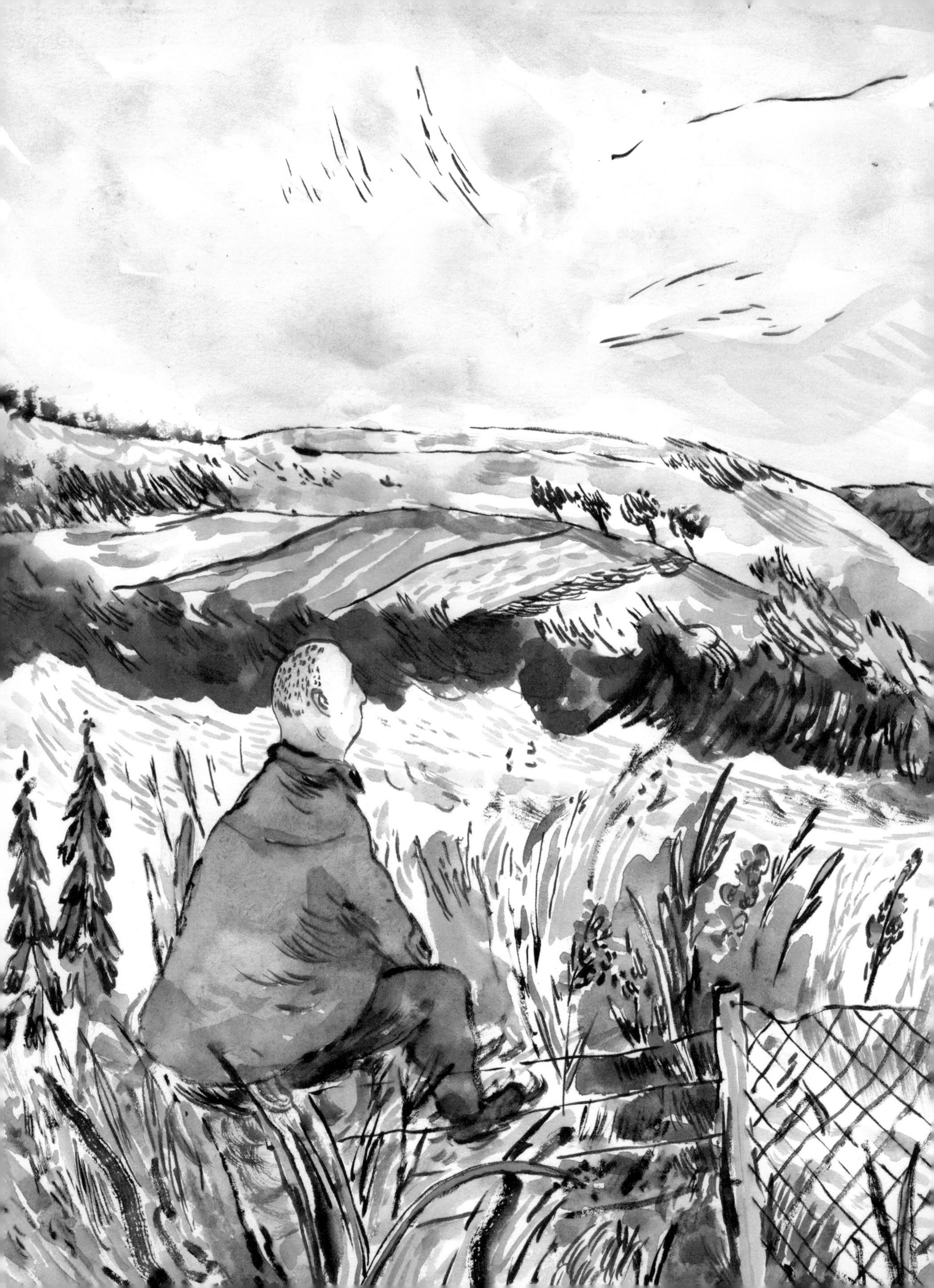

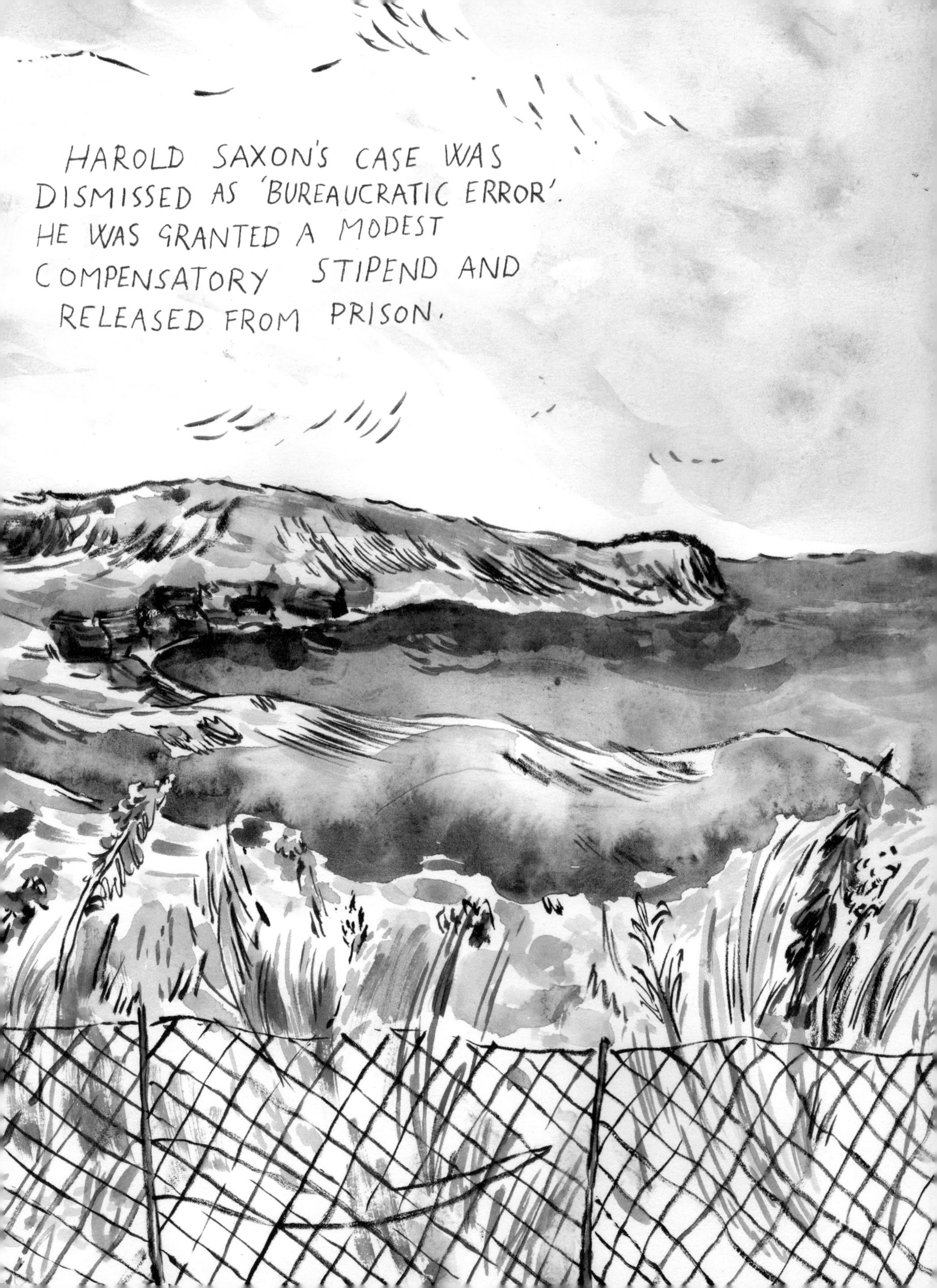
HAROLD SAXON'S CASE WAS DISMISSED AS 'BUREAUCRATIC ERROR'. HE WAS GRANTED A MODEST COMPENSATORY STIPEND AND RELEASED FROM PRISON.

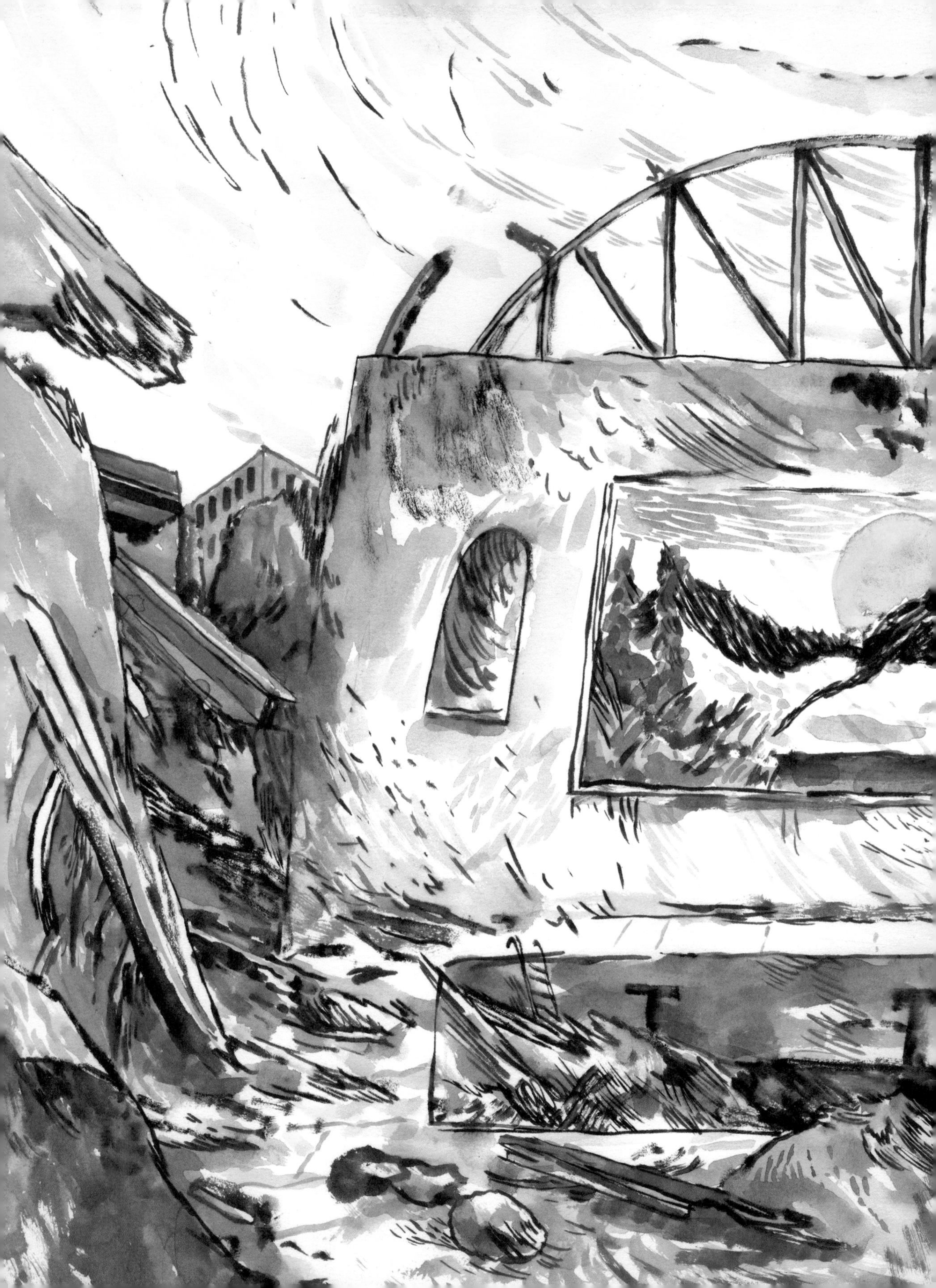

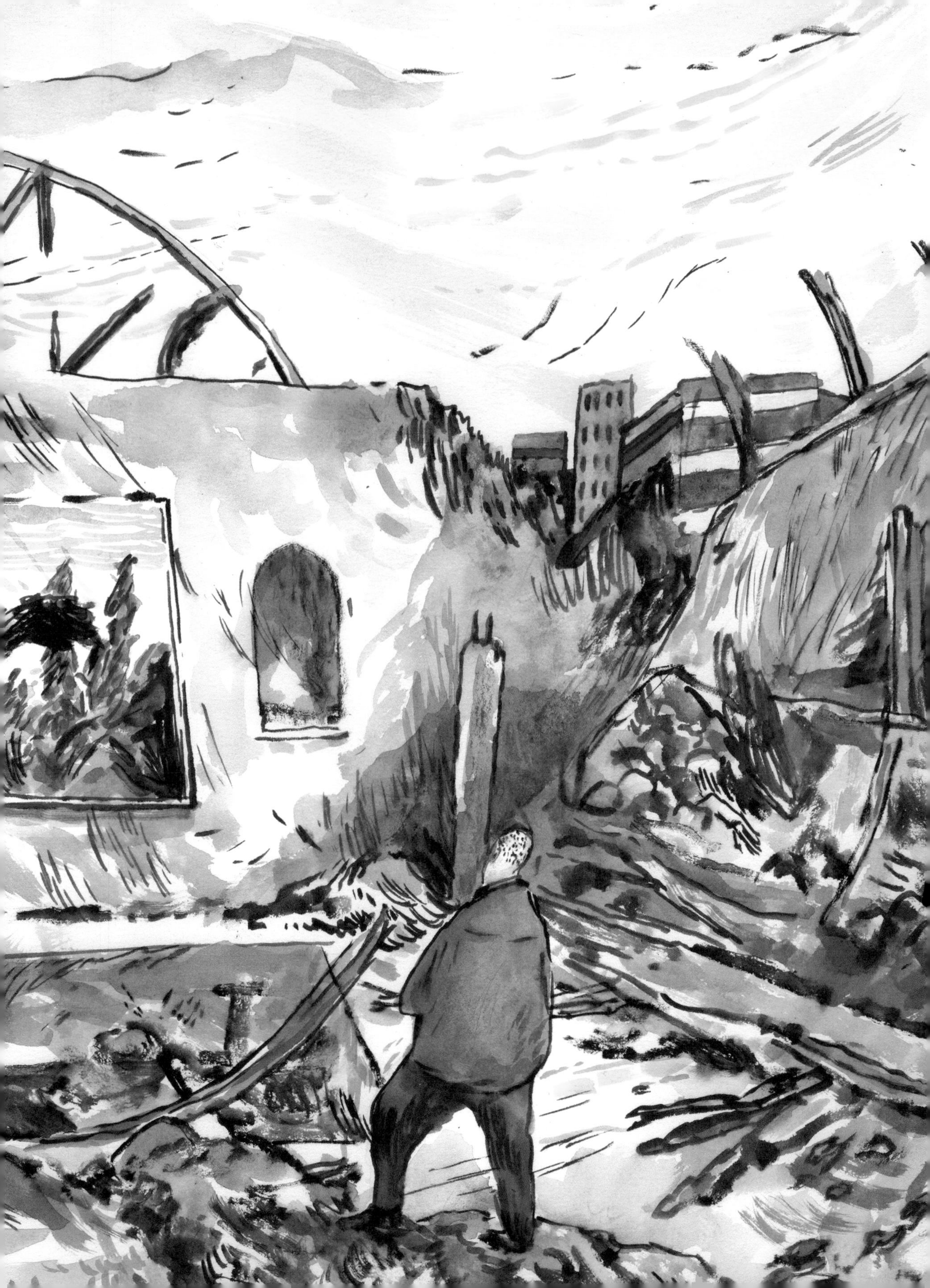

A SHINING BEACON © 2019 JAMES ALBON.
EDITOR-IN-CHIEF: CHRIS STAROS.
EDITED BY CHRIS STAROS.

DESIGNED BY JAMES ALBON.

PUBLISHED BY TOP SHELF PRODUCTIONS, P.O. BOX 1282, MARIETTA,
GA 30061-1282, USA. TOP SHELF PRODUCTIONS IS AN IMPRINT
OF IDW PUBLISHING, A DIVISION OF IDEA AND DESIGN WORKS, LLC.
OFFICES 2765 TRUXTUN ROAD, SAN DIEGO, CA 92106.
TOP SHELF PRODUCTIONS®, THE TOP SHELF LOGO, IDEA AND
DESIGN WORKS®, AND THE IDW LOGO ARE REGISTERED
TRADEMARKS OF IDEA AND DESIGN WORKS, LLC. ALL RIGHTS
RESERVED. WITH THE EXCEPTION OF SMALL EXCERPTS OF
ARTWORK USED FOR REVIEW PURPOSES, NONE OF THE
CONTENTS OF THIS PUBLICATION MAY BE REPRODUCED WITHOUT
THE PERMISSION OF IDW PUBLISHING. IDW PUBLISHING DOES NOT
READ OR ACCEPT UNSOLICITED SUBMISSIONS OF IDEAS,
STORIES, OR ARTWORK.

L'AUTEUR DE CET OUVRAGE A BÉNÉFICIÉ D'UNE
BOURSE D'ÉCRITURE DE LA RÉGION
AUVERGNE-RHÔNE-ALPES.

THIS BOOK WAS COMPLETED WITH THE SUPPORT
OF A WRITING GRANT FROM THE
AUVERGNE-RHÔNE-ALPES REGION.

VISIT OUR ONLINE CATALOGUE AT
WWW.TOPSHELFCOMIX.COM.

THE CONTENT OF THIS BOOK HAS BEEN
APPROVED BY THE MINISTERIAL CENSORSHIP
COMMITTEE. GLORY TO OUR GREAT NATION.

ISBN 978-1-60309-445-0 PRINTED IN KOREA. 23 22 21 20 19 1 2 3 4 5